Edward
Porter
Alexander

Edward P Alexander
Georgia

EDWARD
PORTER
ALEXANDER

Maury
Klein

University
of Georgia
Press
Athens

Library of Congress Catalog
Card Number: 71–90558
International Standard Book Number:
8203–0278–3

The University of Georgia Press, Athens 30601

Printed in the United States of America

To Joan and Stephanie,
with love and thanks

Acknowledgments

The writing of this book depended heavily upon the generous cooperation of many people, not all of whom can be listed here. I am particularly indebted to Professors Bell I. Wiley and J. Harvey Young for their unremitting aid and counsel during my work upon this project. The following colleagues and friends have provided me with valuable information or suggestions at one stage or another: Stephen P. Beven, R. Bingham Duncan, William Gard, Walter B. Posey, James Z. Rabun, Robert F. Smith, and Willard Wight. Mr. Ray Smith graciously furnished me with an index of references to Porter Alexander in the *Confederate Veteran.*

I cannot say enough about the unfailing kindness and help rendered me by the reference librarians and staffs of the following institutions: The Bureau of Railroad Economics, Columbia University, Duke University, Emory University, the National Archives, the University of Rhode Island, and especially James W. Patton and Carolyn Wallace in the Southern Historical Collection at the University of North Carolina, where the bulk of my research was done. A special note of thanks should be accorded Mr. Harmon Smith of the Georgia State Department of Archives and History, who provided me with several leads on important materials, facilitated my labors immensely and taught me a few sound lessons on what archives are all about.

The final manuscript would never have crossed the finish line but for the persistent labors of my typist, Mrs. Edith England, and my student assistants, Karen Gesmondi and Edith Mirman. A grant-in-aid from the University of Rhode Island enabled me to complete the typing of the manuscript.

Special mention should be made of a fine and gracious lady, without whose assistance this book could not have been written. Mrs. Elizabeth Hilton, a granddaughter of Alexander's, cheerfully furnished family papers, copies of family books, and the most enthusiastic encouragement of the whole project. In a very real sense the book belongs to her and her children.

Preface

Perhaps the most astonishing observation to be made about Edward Porter Alexander is that there exists no other biography of him. Historians assign him an important role in their military histories of the Civil War and rely heavily upon his memoirs as a source; moreover, there exist abundant manuscript and printed resources on his entire career. Still he remains a secondary and rather shadowy personality in most accounts. This is an unfortunate oversight, for of all the colorful and controversial figures that helped shape the history of the Confederacy, few have proved more versatile and paradoxical than Alexander.

A professional soldier and West Point graduate, Alexander tempered his stern sense of discipline with an impressive repertory of eccentricities. Trained as an engineer, he won his greatest fame as an artillery officer. Famous for his sober, scientific mind, he possessed a deep love for literature and sentimental verse. Often overbearing to the point of arrogance in his demands upon subordinates, he seldom advanced his own claims for promotion or favor. In his writing he was equally adept at turning out brilliantly analytical military history, treatises on weather patterns, local ecology, and other scientific observations, adventure stories for his children, and reams of somewhat maudlin poetry.

In many respects Alexander seemed to embody both the rich individualism of nineteenth century romanticism and the hard, calculating mentality of an emerging technological era. He was truly a transitional figure whose spirit hovered midway between Byron and Darwin. Even his physical appearance betrayed this charming incongruity. His erect bearing, gaunt features, and rigid jaw gave him an air of authority few men challenged. His dark eyes, set hard and unmoving, suggested a restless inner intensity; yet they were apt to explode suddenly into mischievous laughter. Without warning the austere soldier could become a puckish prankster willing to go to any lengths for a good joke. He was equally at home with hardbitten soldiers, shrewd financiers, dour businessmen, and small children in search of a game.

The most important key to Alexander's life is that it spans three distinct eras. Born in antebellum Georgia, his childhood took its structure from the values of southern civilization and his experience of plantation life. It was this deep loyalty to his heritage that prompted Alexander in 1861 to abandon a promising army career and cast his lot with the Confederacy. That decision closed the first phase of his life and sent his destiny in a much different direction than he had envisioned. Throughout the war, which can be considered the second era, Alexander participated in every major eastern campaign and won an enviable reputation as a soldier. But the South's defeat left him without an army and thus without a profession. Forced to begin anew, he eventually commenced a career in railroading that plunged him into the mainstream of American industrial development.

At no time in this study do I mean to imply that Alexander was a pivotal figure in history; destiny did not wait upon his pleasure for her cues. Nevertheless, his role in the war was an influential one, and a close account of it sheds much light on several major campaigns. In addition, his memoirs provide the most accurate and comprehensive account of the war written by any participant, and as a result they have done much to shape our modern concept of the campaigns. To understand the war's military history, therefore, we need to understand Alexander in both his roles of participant and scholar. Similarly, a study of Alexander as railroad executive provides insight into the complex dynamics of finance capitalism and the techniques of railway managements.

There are numerous other fruitful insights to be drawn from a study of Alexander's life. Consider, for example, the three eras through which he lived. Historians still argue over the extent to which these eras reflect continuity rather than disruption, and in their dialogue they must inevitably turn to individual experiences for part of their evidence. Alexander's case would seem to make the war a thoroughly disruptive force, and this becomes even more evident if patterns of thought, value, and interest are traced through three generations of the Alexander family. The world Alexander inherited from his parents bore little resemblance or relevance to the world he confronted after 1865. Curiously his basic instincts caused him to react to situations much as his father had done; yet both men derived their values from vastly different frames of reference. The process by which the father's devout Presbyterian tenets and the son's adherence to Darwinism led to equally fatalistic views of life is worth a separate study in itself.

Such examples could be given almost at will and constitute the working historian's primary interest in the biography as source material. But the purpose of this study is not just to furnish grist for the scholar's mill. It is rather to portray as fully and as accurately as possible the long life of a truly remarkable man. Throughout I have tried to keep Alexander at center stage instead of relegating him to the secondary role assigned him by standard histories. By this logic the war chapters become not another straight military history but the story of one man's war, though of course a certain amount of background detail is inevitable. Above all, however, I have tried to describe Alexander's uniqueness as a human being. His life furnishes a tremendous fund of richly rewarding human experience, and that in the end is what biography is all about.

Maury Klein

Kingston, R. I.
April 1971

Part One

A WORLD GOING BY

Chapter I

The world of Edward Porter Alexander was to a large extent already shaped for him before he came into it. Born on May 26, 1835, the sixth child of Adam and Sarah Alexander (they would produce ten children in all), his childhood took its structure from the devout, orderly lives of his parents and the rich if somewhat limited experiences of plantation life. His parents, though they had owned Fairfield plantation in Wilkes County, Georgia, for only about eleven years, boasted of an ancestry that had first taken root in Georgia before the American Revolution. His grandfather, Adam S. Alexander, was orphaned at an early age and was raised by two maiden aunts in Inverness, Scotland. After acquiring a medical degree from Edinburgh he migrated to Georgia in 1776 and promptly enlisted as surgeon's mate in the Second Georgia Infantry. He endured capture by the British and after the war accumulated a comfortable holding of land and slaves in Liberty County.[1]

Sarah Alexander traced her lineage to the prominent Hillhouse family of Connecticut and the Gilberts of Virginia. Members of both families had migrated to Washington in Wilkes County before 1800 and achieved success as merchants and planters. Adam Leopold Alexander met his wife while attending Yale; after their marriage in 1823 he took Sarah to his father's plantation in Liberty County where they planned to make their home. But when a quirk of fate brought the attractive Fairfield plantation into Sarah's hands, they took leave of Liberty to try their fortunes in Wilkes County.

Though beset like his peers by the financial vicissitudes of the early nineteenth century, Adam prospered as a planter and later as a banker. His investments were cautious and sound, his accumulation of land and slaves unspectacular but steady. Born into a modest sort of wealth, endowed with striking good looks, and blessed with an alert mind, he confronted life unhampered by doubt. A devout Presbyterian deeply imbued with the Christian notion of Duty, he feared only that he might somehow waste or dissipate those gifts assigned him by God. His fears proved unwarranted. By the time of his graduation from Yale he had thoroughly harnessed his talents to worthy goals. He epitomized the well-educated gentleman, at home with the Latin classics and sufficiently versed in Greek to read his New Testament daily in that language. Few of his peers could match his wit and none could rival the mellifluous ease of his conversation.[2]

If Adam Alexander seemed too perfect, none of his contemporaries recorded a contrary impression. Nearly every acquaintance, in fact, hastened to commend his unyielding integrity. Many years later a former classmate aptly characterized Adam's baffling lack of guile:

> At seventeen, as at seventy-seven, there was a peculiar transparency in his character—as if every thought and feeling might be read by the world; ready with words of cheerful kindness to all, though the most quick detector of falsehood and folly. . . . His greatest charm was in what he himself was: in his person, the admired of all; the absolute purity of his lips and life attesting the purity of heart.[3]

Charms such as these might well feed an insatiable ambition, yet Adam never entered public life. He argued, characteristically, that given the choice between devotion to his family or to politics, he should never hesitate to choose the former.

Trained as a lawyer, Adam never found occasion to practice the law. The unexpected acquisition of Fairfield and a surging boom in cotton thrust the role of planter upon him—a role not at all unwelcome. But planting alone could satisfy neither his financial needs nor his enormous energy. Eventually he ventured into banking and, later, that new fascination, railroads. Though abstaining personally from politics he followed their course closely. His views were conservative; like most of his fellow planters he pronounced himself a Whig and a hard money man. Sensing the realities of his age, he saw only too well the intimate relationship between finance and politics.

Even more than Adam did the pure vision of Christian Duty goad Sarah Alexander through the arduous demands of her responsibilities. Orphaned at an early age, she had been reared with loving but strict care by her grandmother, Sarah Porter Hillhouse. Educated in a carefully selected school in New Haven, Sarah passed her childhood in a world of adults. Driven by the exacting standards of her grandmother, she saw no choice but to embrace her responsibilities as a test of her worth in society and in the eyes of God. In her quest for self perfection the most trivial flaw magnified itself into some huge defect of character.[4] Fourteen years after her marriage she could lament to her husband:

> No one upon earth, without experiencing it, can ever know how the sense of my own unfitness and incapacity to discharge the duties of a mother, weighs upon my spirits. Nothing, my beloved, but your unwearying affection and kindness makes life desirable to me, for I can not feel that I am of any other use in life than to minister to your happiness . . . notwithstanding all my infirmities, physical and mental.[5]

But she need have no fear of complaint from any quarter. Though a tiny woman weighing scarcely a hundred pounds and nagged constantly by sickness and the physical drain of childbirth, Sarah mastered the complexities of a plantation household with a thoroughness that astounded her husband. Moreover, she felt it her duty to educate the slaves and to teach them the mysteries of religion. In Adam's absence she supervised the slaves and all field work as well.

Sarah differed from her husband not in lack of energy or ability but only in her mania for self perfection. She and Adam possessed, in fact, the rarest of relationships: an enduring love and devotion that time only strengthened. At no period of their marriage did their letters fail to exude a sincere ardor. Sarah made no pretense of worshipping her husband. "I am sure I shall be happier, my dear husband," she once wrote, "when you come back than I have ever been in my life, for I have only now fully found how necessary your presence is to my happiness, and how dependent I am upon you for all my enjoyments." [6] No less fervid was Adam's response:

> When I contrast myself to you . . . I am at a loss to know what you could have found in my poor self worthy of the Love & esteem and confidence *you* had to bestow. . . . How soon does a short absence convince me that my entire earthly happiness rests upon you. With you, is embarked my all—& without *you*, I am nothing. You must excuse me . . . for having said so much on the subject—after 8 years *possession* you must suffer me—for I see no prospect of my feelings ever moderating.[7]

No one sensed Adam and Sarah's deep devotion to one another more readily than the children, and of their number none was more perceptive than young Sarah. When once she asked her father how he could "write such long letters to Mother," he replied readily, "There is no end to words of love, when they come from a full heart." Sarah and the other children soon understood. One morning she said, "Father, I never saw a man love his wife as you love Mother." Adam smiled. "Because, my dear, you never saw so lovely a woman as your mother." [8]

Two such powerful personalities as Adam and Sarah could not help but leave indelible imprints upon their children. Love and affection they provided in abundance, but never beyond the pale of a strict and thorough training. No man to neglect his children's education, Adam scrutinized the progress of each child. He developed an intricate system to speed the process of learning along and discipline, swift and unerring, was its cornerstone. Formal schooling commenced as early as possible and required weekly records from the teacher for each offspring. No excuse for an unsatisfactory report could stay the sure hand of retribution. The slightest scholastic deficiency brought unexpected hours of leisure for extra study.[9]

Not that discipline sprang from a merciless or humorless heart. Adam resorted to every means in making his point. To the girls he might compose a few lines of highly didactic verse; for the boys he might deliver an apt Biblical quotation or more likely a few pertinent lines from Samuel Butler's *Hudibras*. None proved so intractable a rebel as Porter, whose early addiction to hunting and fishing bred in him a sturdy resistance to academic discipline.

Despite an occasional frustration Adam never relaxed the pressure upon his children. When the older girls required more specialized schooling he carefully selected a teacher in New England and brought her to Washington. As the girls matured and the boys grew older, Adam journeyed north once more, this time for a male teacher. He returned with Mr. Russell M. Wright, a recent graduate of Williams College. So popular and effective a teacher did Wright become that Adam, at the urging of his neighbors, agreed to let him teach a larger class at the Washington Academy.[10]

Of the four Alexander boys, Porter seemed the one most apt to go his own way. At age three he already revealed a consuming passion for hunting and fishing, and within a year he was scheming mightily for means to raise enough money to buy his father's pocket pistol. But he showed no taste for blood; shooting, not killing, intrigued him. "Mother, how *miserable* them poor birds is when the boys throws at them," he blurted out that same year. "I'm so glad I can't hit 'em when I throws at 'em." [11]

Though a frail, even delicate child he surrendered himself entirely to his two great loves. In these pursuits he found companions not among his peers but from the ranks of the aged. Elderly James Dyson never resisted a chance to go hunting with the boy, and old Frank Colley, though past seventy, still found the energy to rise at dawn, ride eight miles to Little River, and fish all day for suckers from the bank. In other free moments Porter concentrated with the loving devotion of a scholar upon the geography of rivers. When Adam hung some large maps in the sitting room Porter never ceased hustling the servants before them to lecture on the great rivers of the world. Though he amassed impressive statistics of length and depth, width and traffic, Sarah refused to be fooled. "I believe his especial interest in them," she noted wryly, "grows out of . . . their being depositories of fish." [12]

The slavish devotion to studies, the stern discipline, the perfection of manners, the careful preparation for the next life—all thwarted Porter's zest for the pleasures of this life. At nine he finally flew into open rebellion. Taking a single barrel shotgun and two biscuits purloined from the dinner table, he stole out of the house one morning before dawn and retreated deep into the plantation woods. There a man could build a wigwam and live the good life—keeping himself by trapping and shooting. But the biscuits disappeared with alarming haste, the traps remained unsprung, and no game presented itself before his eager sights. The hours dragged slowly into evening. At dusk he heard his name echoing through the trees. A defiant spirit stood unmoved by the distant servant's cry; an empty belly counseled surrender. The slender hope that joy over his return coupled with the earnestness of his protest might modify his punishment crashed into ruin. The only tears shed over his return came from his own eyes, and they were not tears of joy.[13]

Thwarted in rebellion, Porter soon plunged into his studies with a fervor that impressed everyone. A new passion now dominated him: he would go to West Point and become a soldier. Once he had made that decision everything seemed simple except for the fact that neither of his parents approved the idea. Adam had never considered soldiers to be of any worth, although the marriage of his daughter Sarah to Alexander Lawton, a West Point graduate, had moderated his feelings a bit. His wife feared only that Porter might be too frail for such a life. Once at age thirteen he had come home sick and faint from being cracked on the nose with a shinny stick. The alarmed Sarah called the doctor, who prescribed mustard baths. By the next day Porter had recovered, but Sarah was not convinced. In her mind he would never do for any life of hardship and exposure. "What a strange compound of roughness & sensitiveness he is!" she exclaimed in a letter to Adam.[14]

No amount of studying could curb Porter's many passions, and times were such as to give passions free rein. One day in 1848, while sitting on the bank of Little River, Mr. Colley explained to him what secession meant and why the southern states were talking about it. Porter shivered at the very idea; without quite knowing why, he affirmed that to prevent it he would sacrifice his dearest possession—his hunting rifle. Two years later, elections for delegates to a state convention pitted Washington unionists and secessionists against each other. Caught up in his passionate support for Robert Toombs as a union delegate, Porter ran afoul of two secessionist town boys, Tim Hester and Ben Cappell. Tempers flared as the argument raged; soon Porter heard that the two boys had armed themselves and were out to whip him. Quickly he borrowed a revolver from his father's overseer and loaded it. Scorning the usual "G.D." caps, he picked up six "Walker anticorrosive caps" for the nipples and marched out to face his tormentors.

He had no trouble finding Hester in town. The latter spied him, charged up and broke his shinny stick over Porter's head. Furiously Porter drew his pistol and fired, but the cap failed to ignite. Hester reached for his own pistol as Porter fired again. The second cap failed. Porter scowled;

would all of them fail? Hester stood motionless, the gun at his side, making no attempt to shoot. Porter hesitated; if he shot then Hester would, too, and Hester's cap might not fail. Suddenly other boys rushed between them and grabbed the pistols. "See if Porter's gun is loaded!" one cried. Another raised the pistol and pulled the trigger. A loud report jarred the quiet evening. Porter eyed the smoking barrel in astonishment.

Only a few days before Adam had warned Porter about staying out too late and missing supper. When he failed to appear in time his brother Charlie dashed off to find him. From the porch Charlie heard the distant bark of a pistol and hurried down the driveway. He met Porter coming home with a bleeding nose. When they reached the house Adam, towering above him on the porch, demanded an explanation. So shocked was he at the story that Porter escaped the usual severe punishment. Still, the sound of that exploding pistol haunted Porter's mind to the end of his life. Politics he now saw as a great breeder of passionate quarrels, and no man so reckless of consequences when excited as himself could safely afford to indulge in them. And so he never did.[15]

In the drift of studies and sports Porter pondered his future. Adam seemed no nearer to relenting on the question of West Point than he ever had— at least not until the summer of 1850. That June another West Point graduate, Jeremy Gilmer, wrote Adam to ask for the hand of his daughter Louisa. Adam decided upon a closer inspection and dispatched an invitation for Gilmer to visit the family.

The ranks closed tightly about Adam that summer. Gilmer arrived and proved to be genial, dignified, and eminently suitable material for a son-in-law. The Lawtons also descended for a visit at the same time. Two fine products of West Point could not help but sway Adam's prejudice against the officer class; nor was Porter slow to enlist their support. Conversation meandered gently onto West Point or a soldier's life or some equally relevant topic. The climax came one warm summer evening when after dinner Gilmer and Lawton joined Adam on the porch. Soon Porter was summoned and given the news: Adam would consent to his going to West Point if he would study hard and try for one of the coveted appointments in the engineer corps. In Adam's mind it was one thing to be a soldier and quite another to be an engineer. From that moment Porter bent his every energy to preparing himself for the Point. Informed of the decision, Mr. Wright contrived to strengthen Porter's program in those areas emphasized at the Academy. Occasionally during the summer Gilmer put him through the manual of arms.[16]

Adam had some arranging of his own to do. He called on neighbor and close friend Robert Toombs, then in Congress, and asked for the 1851 appointment from Georgia. Toombs agreed and made the attempt but found the place already filled. Not until February of 1853 did he gain Porter an appointment.[17] That winter Porter stayed with the Lawtons in Savannah, where he took lessons in French and drawing. Late in the spring he returned to Fairfield. In May, wrung dry with affectionate embraces, stuffed with food and advice, he boarded train for the long trip to New York. There he would have time for a visit with Cousin John Hillhouse (himself a West Pointer) in Troy and perhaps a day or two in the big city. But on Friday, June 10, he would sail for West Point, and from then on it would be all business.

Examinations for admission quickly huddled the plebes together. At the physical Porter measured in at 5′ 9½″ and 150 pounds. When Robert Anderson, a fellow Georgian and already a good friend, balked at being stripped by the surgeon, Porter reminded him that last year ten per cent of the plebes had been rejected. Already one homesick plebe had gone to the Superintendent, Colonel Robert E. Lee, and begged to go home. Porter snorted at the story: "Poor fellow, I expect he has some sisters." [18]

Soon afterwards the plebes went into summer encampment, where the tempo of activity stepped up. Porter had been stirred by the sight of cadets drilling when he first arrived; now he found the business less savory at firsthand. He had thought the other cadets helpful and friendly at first; now they seemed intent upon crushing him with their superior rank. Contempt for the plebes came most easily to the third class men, who had only recently vacated that lowly rank. Hazing and baiting soon became a weary ritual for the plebes or "animals." No small part of their disciplining derived from coping with sudden intrusions in the dead of night, the coarse insults, and occasional physical manhandling. The righteous rage of indignity flared up in Porter's eyes, but he curbed his tongue. Discipline he had come to know well; insult his temper had never suffered him to bear. Yet here he recognized these trivial outrages as a necessary part of the system and bore them with the patience of conviction. His brother Felix, visiting the encampment in July, marvelled at Porter's uncharacteristic restraint.[19]

The first summer encampment served as rugged introduction to life at the Point. Entrance examinations had already whittled the class down, and the rigors of camp life depleted the ranks even further.[20] The strain of inexorable discipline, the fumbling awkwardness of learning the drill, the fierce bellowing of the sergeants and lance corporals, and the inevitable dressing down after every mistake all took their toll on plebe ambitions.

Adjustment became a war of attrition. Porter felt himself winning the struggle; nearly half his mates would not be so fortunate. Only fifty-eight of ninety-nine plebes would survive even the first year. When September finally came tents were folded and packed away and the cadets returned to their barracks. Adam used the occasion to warn his son against straying from the path of righteousness: "We hope too my dear boy, that the change from Camp to Barracks will secure your greater privacy, & opportunity for religious reading & contemplation *daily*, & especially on the Sabbath." [21]

Academically Porter seemed fit for the long haul. It soon became apparent that his most serious problem involved not a lack of zeal but an excess of it. To meet the challenge of competition he resorted to studying after taps, a violation for which he could be punished if caught. Then he took to rising in the middle of the night to study for an hour. Informed of this new habit, Sarah was quick to deplore it. "You must not feel we expect so much from you," she argued, "that you must overtax yourself, & incur the risk of a broken constitution." Adam added a vigorous assent. "Don't impair your health on any account," he begged. No one would be crushed if Porter did not capture first place. "Should you my dear boy take position anywhere among the *first five,* you will meet every wish & expectation of your friends." [22]

Eventually the warnings made their point. Once settled into a more regular routine Porter thrived on the ritual of cadet life. By the end of his first term he had already impressed several of his teachers. Chaplain William T. Sprole took up his pen to give Sarah his opinion of Porter:

> His whole character is above reproach. All who know him, speak well of him. And we regard him, as one of the few about whose Christian character, there is no doubt. . . . This is not flattery. I take great pleasure in writing it, for I believe it to be strictly true.[23]

After completing his June examinations Porter found himself standing fourth in his class. Preparing for summer encampment, he learned that he had been promoted to corporal and assigned to Company B for the coming year. He learned, too, that his parents planned to come up to the Point that summer for a visit.

What began as a visit soon became a tragedy. Sarah had never enjoyed good health, and during the past few years she had deteriorated rapidly. In her agony she had grown dependent upon both opium and morphine to relieve her pain. Resolved to break her addiction, Adam took her north in the summer of 1854 to seek expert medical care. Under the guidance of a Philadelphia doctor Sarah had at last shaken free of the drugs, but the harrowing ordeal had seriously weakened her. Still she insisted upon making the arduous trip to West Point despite Adam's protests. Tormented by a cough, weighing only 79 pounds, she drove her body relentlessly towards the Academy only to collapse at the hotel there.[24]

For six weeks she remained in bed until the doctors permitted her to travel. Then home to Fairfield she went to linger for several painful months until her death in February. On the day she left West Point, Porter, ready to return to barracks, begged permission to say good-bye but Sarah refused to let him see her in so debilitated a state. For several months the entire episode darkened Porter's thoughts.

The second year proved a treacherous one for Porter. First term went smoothly enough but in the spring a cluster of demerits befell him. He acquired more demerits in the first ten days of March than he had accumulated during the past eight months. Several of the penalties outraged his sense of justice, and loud protests to the commandant got some of them erased. Discontent spilled over into the classroom, too, where Porter's French teacher seemed intent on deliberately giving him low marks. The climax came when, after a week of disappointingly average marks, Porter found that the professor's total average had put him at the bottom of the class. Immediately Porter swept into the professor's office and demanded some explanation. A mistake, the professor replied, a slip of the pencil that can happen to anyone. But Porter was not so sure. "It may have been accidental," he complained, "but it seems strange to me that a professor here can't multiply 1¼ by 4 without a mistake of 10." [25]

At the end of June examinations Porter had edged up a notch to third place in the class, trailing only John Palfrey of Massachusetts and Dick Meade of Virginia. The schedule granted third class graduates a summer furlough instead of camp, and Porter departed for Fairfield and a well-earned rest. It passed all too quickly, and in September he returned for a second class year that would prove even more distasteful than the previous term. The year's academics, especially natural philosophy and chemistry, promised a long and weary grind. His new position of orderly sergeant gave him a first and unsavory taste of the responsibilities of command. Barracks life itself came to be increasingly unsatisfying. Faced with such unpleasant obligations, Porter only threw himself into them with more vigor. He began once more to study during the odd hours, to cut his sleeping time, and to impose stiff demands upon his endurance. Adam, catching the drift of things by mail, responded sternly. It was not as necessary to maintain high class standing, he argued, as it was to maintain health. Duty may drive us only to the point of our abilities and endurance:

There are many things it would be our duty to do, *if we could*—but as we cannot, they are no part of our duty. Had your dear Mother learned sooner in life, she might have been with us still. But she was always attempting things confessedly beyond her strength—because *once,* when younger and stronger, she had been used to do them.[26]

No less energetically did Adam respond to his son's qualms over the obligations of his new rank: "Your office is one of *trust* & the trust *must be discharged.*" Some will no doubt resent such constancy to duty, but all who accept power incur this penalty. And after all, ill-will thus bred reflects more upon the culprit than upon his superior, for

No rogue who feels the halter draw
Has good opinions of the Law—[27]

To that same conclusion Porter speedily came, but it made his routine no more pleasant. An unfamiliar sense of loneliness and restlessness seized upon him; his chorus of complaints swelled steadily. Term examinations on January 2 brought no relief to Porter's distemper. In philosophy, for example, he had committed to memory some fifty demonstrations drawn from previous examinations. But at the recitation he was given one he had overlooked and wound up sixth in the overall standing. Discipline problems continued to plague his company. Stung by the recalcitrance of his command, Porter resolved to tolerate no flaunting of his authority. He meted out penalties impartially despite sullen glances and muttered threats of a later thrashing. He clashed head-on with the lackadaisical Fitzhugh Lee, a private in Porter's company, who used his popularity among his first classmates to evade work details. When Porter forced Lee to hew the line virtually the entire first class stopped speaking to him, but he refused to budge an inch. To be sure the entire second class and most of Porter's close friends gave him warm approval, but still he could not feel at ease. When a winter cold and toothache sent his spirits drooping, he endured the pain rather than risk the suspicious look of "wheatening" off duty.[28]

Spring brought some easing of tensions. Field drill had commenced with the advent of warm weather, and consisted for the second class of target practice with mortars and siege guns. Already Porter revealed a fondness for the artillery: "As there are three batteries drilling every afternoon at the same time the place is rather noisy," he wrote happily, "when the soft notes of the mortars are heard at the same time with the pleasant little voices of the field battery." Soon he would be surrendering his odious position as orderly sergeant for a new one. "It cannot be a *more* disagreeable one," he reasoned, "& there is only one office in the first class which can be near as disagreeable, that of First Captain." [29]

Even spring with its innate cheerfulness could not escape without a blemish, however, for below the surface pleasantries a deep-rooted antagonism lay smouldering. Early in May the quarrel exploded into the open as fights broke out between northern and southern cadets. The second class split along sectional lines, each group regarding the other in frozen silence. Porter stood firmly behind the southerners. During his first winter at the Point he often castigated his yankee acquaintances in his letters home. Stung by her son's vehemence, Sarah had roused herself from illness long enough to chastise him:

> These extreme prejudices are unworthy of liberal & enlightened minds, and are especially unbecoming one who has pledged himself to serve the country as a *whole,* & is therefore receiving an education from the government— You must bear in mind my dear son that there are many good people at the North, however they may be led to embrace mistaken views & opinions concerning the South & its affairs—& while the intermeddlers & agitators have given character to the whole, very many are quite opposed to them & their schemes. We have our errors & mistakes likewise. . . .[30]

Such words, though no doubt taken to heart by Porter at the time, proved but a straw in the wind. Only term examinations forced a closing of ranks in that spring of 1856. Porter hurdled his tests with predictable consistency. He had become a first classman. He received the post of captain for Company D. The future seemed finally to be looking up.

By early March of 1857 Porter could take stock of the situation. Ninety-four days remained in the final term. He still held third place behind Palfrey and Meade. If he could hold his position, chances for an engineering appointment looked good. But what if something went wrong? "I am willing to do anything possible for the place in the Engineer Corps which I covet so," he informed his father. One logical possibility would be an appeal to the influence of two close family friends, Alexander Stephens and Robert Toombs. Probably such an appeal would cinch the appointment, but Porter hedged at writing them: "I would have written," he explained, "but that I hate so much to ask a favor or to *seem* to desire what my merit would not procure for me, though I really think that if I am recommended on one side & applied for on the other it would not be unfair." [31]

As final examinations drew near, however, Porter's confidence swelled. He had the tailor make for him a handsome new engineer's uniform, and for the privilege of wearing it he endured his grueling schedule with grim determination. Not until spring did he relax his pace long enough to survey the available young ladies. At home Adam brooded over his son's flagrant readiness to pursue the opposite sex and tended to accept his naive eagerness at face value. Porter had shown no signs of backwardness in his dealings with the ladies, and rumor had already flown home that Porter was courting a minister's daughter. The story brought a prompt inquiry from Adam. Nothing to be concerned about, Porter replied blandly: a passing friendship only. A close friend, Tom Baylor, had recently broken his engagement, and Porter professed to have profited from Tom's experience. Adam lost no time in drawing the proper moral. "I hope that you speak truly," he wrote, "when you say that observation has made you a wiser man—for this has been a point, on which I think you had something still to learn—& tis best to grow wiser at others' expense." And why all the rush, he chided: "If you boys only knew your own worth, you would not be quick to sell yourselves to the first bidder." Lest Porter let the point slip, Adam repeated it again two weeks later:

> The increase [in pay] for the army is pretty respectable, & will now afford you a fine & liberal support, with means to lay up a little every year, unless you are foolish enough to throw yourself away in a marriage & fix your nose to a grindstone.

To these admonishments Porter made no reply. He had none except the obedient silence of a son unwilling to force an issue with his father in theory until it arose in actuality. But arise it would, in due time.[32]

May vanished quickly in the study grind and the vigorous new "Shanghai" drills taken up by the Academy that spring. In the barracks the coming ordeal of examination had already set nerves on edge, especially among the first classmen. No more chances to improve standing; in the hot race for top positions the next few days would count for everything. Examination of the first class began on June 2 and continued for six days. From 9 A.M. until 3 P.M. each cadet gave his recitation in engineering, ethics, mineralogy and geology, artillery, infantry, and cavalry tactics. Once the recitations ended each day the activities moved outdoors, and promptly at five drills in infantry, cavalry, and artillery were performed for the examiners. In each examination Porter carefully planned his effort, and final standings revealed no major surprises. Palfrey stood first, Meade second, and Porter third. The graduating class numbered but thirty-eight cadets.[33]

On the basis of these standings, Palfrey, Meade, Alexander, and Henry Robert received commissions in the engineer corps. His immediate reward would be a three month furlough. After that he would return to the Point, where he had been assigned as assistant instructor of practical military engineering. Now it would be his turn to "teach the young idea how to shoot." [34]

Chapter II

Lieutenant Alexander looked every bit the soldier in his new uniform. Home on furlough, he submitted himself willingly to the admiring inspection of his family and friends. Most of them marvelled at the transformation in his appearance. He had never seemed so dignified and erect in his bearing. A veil of solemnity now occasionally drew across his gaunt face with its high cheekbones, large, deep-set eyes and rigid jaw. A thick moustache roofed his heavy lips, and long straight hair struggled vainly to keep in place. Nothing both portrayed and betrayed his formidable military appearance so much as his intense eyes. Set hard and unmoving, they seemed to reflect relentless energy; yet they were apt at any moment to twinkle with mischievous laughter. Time had stamped upon his features the truth of his mother's remark: "What a strange compound of roughness and sensitiveness he is!" [1]

On September 30 Porter returned to the academy, received his assignment in Company A Engineers and commenced duty in the department of practical engineering. He attended drills, sometimes three or four daily, supervised his company, and took up extensive court-martial duties. Beyond these tasks he had only social obligations, calls to pay, teas to attend and, in the evenings, letters to write.

The rigors of teaching at the academy he endured obligingly but without enthusiasm. Always anxious for adventure, he missed no opportunity to volunteer for any special assignment that appeared. Early in January of 1858 a promising opportunity arose. During the previous summer the growing friction between the Mormons in Utah and the federal government had reached a tense climax. To a long accumulating list of grievances had been added recent clashes over Indian policy, jurisdictional disputes, and an acrimonious debate over mail delivery contracts. In June President Buchanan had appointed Alfred Cumming of Georgia to replace Brigham Young as territorial governor. He had also ordered a military expedition to accompany Cumming to Utah and insure the strict enforcement of federal law there. But the expeditionary force, plagued by indecisive leadership and effective Mormon harassment, had bogged down en route and gone into winter quarters at Fort Bridger. During the winter it was decided to reinforce the expedition with a second force of about three thousand men. Hearing that a detail for the force would be drawn from his own Company A of sappers and miners, Porter hastily applied for the trip and was accepted.[2]

Early in April sixty-four of the company's hundred men left West
Point for Fort Leavenworth, there to prepare for the expedition while elements from the 1st Cavalry, 6th and 7th Infantry, and 2nd Artillery
joined them. Not until May 7 did Company A, with Lieutenant James
Duane in command and Alexander as subaltern, take up the march with
the first column of infantry. Army headquarters in St. Louis had given
them two assignments: reinforce the Army of Utah and explore the value
of a new route of march for reaching Fort Bridger. The only currently travelled western route struck along the South Platte River via Fort Kearney,
crossed to the North Platte at Ash Hollow, and followed the south bank
to Fort Laramie. From there the trail edged along Sweetwater Creek up
into the south pass and then down to the southwest until it reached Fort
Bridger.[3]

An alternative route, shorter and more direct, had been hinted at by
Frémont after his 1842 expedition. The route involved taking the South
Platte to the mouth of Lodge Pole Creek and then following the creek to
its headwaters in the Black Hills, crossing the hills at that point and then
skirting the Medicine Bow Mountains to the headwaters of the North
Platte. Striking then for Sage Creek, the Rockies could be crossed at
Bridger's Pass; then down Bitter Creek Canyon to the Green River and
through Rabbit Hollow to meet the old trail from South pass just east of
Fort Bridger. Only Frémont had actually covered this entire route, and the
army wanted to know if it surpassed the older trail. The 6th Infantry
would blaze the trail and the engineers from Company A could open the
road.

Once as a cadet Porter had written, "I have always had an *intense*
desire to visit unknown & unexplored regions, & if I ever leave the army
it will be to gratify it."[4] Outfitted with a fine new horse, he spent much of
his time on the plains hunting antelope, wolves, wild ducks, grouse, sage
hens, and most spectacular of all, buffalo.[5] Once into mountain country,
however, the business of breaking a road absorbed most of his attention.
A constant scarcity of forage and fuel drove the column relentlessly forward from one grass patch to the next. At Bridger's pass the officers gathered in counsel. They were near the Continental Divide; ahead lay the
toughest and most unexplored region. It was decided to send the engineers ahead to open the road. They would take along a detachment of
infantry to serve as laborers, and the rest of the troops would follow in a
few days.[6]

Setting out on July 3, the advance party pushed forward at widely
fluctuating rates of progress. Occasionally they might make twenty miles,
while on other days they barely averaged half a dozen. Ever mindful
that they were wandering about uncharted regions with only limited sup-

plies, the party grew more tense with every passing day. Not until July 27 did they emerge from Rabbitt Hollow and reach the older emigrant trail. Five days later they stood before the shabby gates of Fort Bridger. The entire trip from Leavenworth had covered 978 miles in eighty-six days.

After surveying the records of the march the army concluded that the new trail offered more drawbacks than advantages. Moreover, the Mormon crisis had already come to a peaceful resolution while the column, cut off from all communication, had been working its way to Fort Bridger. A new crisis had blossomed in the Washington Territory, where the Spokane and Coeur d'Alene Indians had revolted and defeated an army expedition. That part of Company A still at West Point had already left for the Pacific coast, but Duane and Alexander received orders to take their men back to the Point.[7] The young officers eager for field service did not overlook the irony of the situation, but the trip had by no means been profitless. When he reached the Academy on October 13, Porter looked the picture of health. Brown and robust, he had thrived on the hardships and exposure of his adventure. What had once seemed to his parents to be physical frailty had become a wiry toughness. And he enjoyed one final buffalo hunt on the return march.[8]

After his service on the plains the academy seemed tame to Alexander, and almost immediately he looked about for some new special assignment. Post life offered a pleasant enough interlude and Gilmer, then stationed in California, advised him not to apply for relief from teaching duties but to wait instead for something to turn up.[9] He hoped that something would materialize that summer and it did, but it was not quite what he expected. Two Virginia belles, Bettie and Gussie Mason, arrived on the scene to spend a summer in the North. Porter took an immediate liking to Bettie. She was twenty-four and came from King George County. Her father, Alexander Mason, practiced medicine and pursued a wide range of other interests. The courtship bloomed into an engagement shortly before Bettie returned to Virginia.

Porter soon realized that new problems confronted him. His father would most probably disapprove of his action and would be doubly outraged because Porter had not consulted him first. No amount of tact could lessen the blow, and for several months an uneasy moodiness permeated the family correspondence. One of Porter's sisters, taking him to task for his unseemly haste, reminded him that not so long ago he had been just as desperately in love with "Mary L—." She was referring to Mary Lee, daughter of Robert E. Lee, who had firmly rejected Alexander's courtship, but Porter's mind had long since outrun that failure. Reading the letter to a friend, he paused in bewilderment at the reference and exclaimed, "Who in hell is Mary L—?"[10]

Adam responded with the virtuous indignation of a wounded lion. "My own mind has settled down into a feeling of utter hopelessness," he complained bitterly, "& I now care little when or whom he marries." What had hurt him most was Porter's slyness, "that he should so long have contemplated such a serious step . . . & yet kept *us* all in utter ignorance; till the thing was irretrievable, & then when for the first time announcing it, *done—hopelessly done,* to ask for my approval—*Approval* was out of the question . . . the most that can be done is to submit to the evil, that is irremediable." [11] Unable to disavow the match Adam sought to delay it, but Porter would not be budged. Not until the winter of 1860 did Adam finally relent. On March 1 he wrote Porter a letter of approval that spoke warmly of Bettie and congratulated both on the impending wedding. The ceremony took place April 3 at "Cleiveland," the King George County estate of Bettie's uncle, W. Roy Mason. [12]

While the wedding plans were hanging fire in the fall of 1859, Alexander unexpectedly received an intriguing new assignment. By chance he bumped into Albert Myer, an army surgeon with an interest in communications. One of Myer's first assignments was in New Mexico territory, where he became interested in the way Comanche Indians signalled to one another with their lances over great distances. The idea struck him that some such form of motion telegraphy could prove useful for military purposes. Intrigued, he began to devote his leisure hours to working out a suitable system of signals. [13]

Myer did not come a stranger to the subject of military signals. While training as an apprentice telegraph operator before going to Hobart College he had learned the Bain and Morse telegraphic alphabets. As a medical student he had shown keen interest in the problem of communications between deaf-mutes. His thesis, "A Sign Language for Deaf Mutes," contained some of the roots for the signal system he later devised. In 1851 he became interested in the general question of military signals. The art he found was an old and honorable one, feasible in theory but unsatisfactory in practice. A suitable signal system had to meet three basic requirements: it must be easily understood; the apparatus must be simple; and the apparatus must be light and mobile. Generous as these requirements might seem, they had never been adequately realized. Most devices proved to be too complex, inefficient, or cumbersome. In his own research Myer attempted to eliminate these drawbacks by combining his knowledge of the telegraph with the elements of visual communication he had explored in his study of deaf-mutes.

For simplicity nothing could equal a telegraphic code. The Bain alphabet used only two elements in forming its letters, dot and dash; the Morse utilized four—dot, short dash, long dash, and interval between dashes.[14] Myer devised a four-element code based upon the two-element concept of waving left for dot and right for dash. The difference between the two, small but crucial, rested in the fact that in the four element code numbers described not only motions *from* a vertical position but motions *to* it as well. The apparatus was equally simple. Any waveable object could be used, though colored flags on twelve-foot staffs worked best. The equipment could be transported easily, had no parts to break down, and could not be destroyed by the enemy. On a clear day the signals could carry as far as fifteen or twenty miles. At night torches or lanterns could be substituted for flags with only a slight loss of visibility range. Any attempt by the enemy to intercept the message could be thwarted simply by translating the signals into some prearranged cipher.

By 1856 Myer had worked his code out. He carefully took out patents on his system and then offered it to the War Department. Two years elapsed before a board was created to study the project, and now Myer was in the process of setting up his experiments. He had been authorized to enlist another officer in the project. Taking an immediate liking to Porter, he offered him the post. In October the two men set up headquarters at Fort Hamilton at the bottom of Long Island. Myer would remain there to transmit signals while Porter would cross lower New York bay to Sandy Hook, fifteen miles away, to receive them.[15] For nearly two months the experiments continued, with Porter travelling an endless triangle between Hamilton, Sandy Hook, and the city. For daytime testing Myer used only a sixteen-foot pole and a five-foot square flag; at night he resorted to mounting two copper torches doused with turpentine on the pole. Almost immediately the results bore out Myer's predictions. "No military signals have ever been sent over 8 miles before & they required machines," Porter wrote exultantly. Now the two of them conversed easily at a distance of more than fifteen miles, hampered only by dense fog or heavy rain. To test the code's versatility Myer dropped the flags and began to signal with plain cloth, bags, and other implements. Across the bay Porter picked up the messages easily.[16]

By late November Myer declared himself ready to demonstrate the system. They went to Washington to convince the board. On a clear, crisp day the observers gathered on the bank of the Potomac while Myer went across to Alexandria, some six miles distant. No longer range could be found. To Myer's delight the air proved even clearer than that over New York bay. He began to signal a message to the distant bank. Standing with the observers, Alexander read the code without even using a telescope. A buzz of astonishment swept through the visitors. Now Porter took out his pocket spy glass. Myer waved a signal with shirt sleeves alone; Porter repeated it effortlessly. Myer tacked a handkerchief to a walking cane and waved off a message with it. Again Porter received it flawlessly. The spectators were convinced. In his annual report, written a few days later, Secretary of War John B. Floyd gave the system his enthusiastic endorsement.[17]

But final approval had not yet materialized. The two men returned to Fort Hamilton for another three weeks of testing in bitter cold. By late December Myer was ready to write up the laborious reports and return to Washington to lobby for a suitable bill creating a signal corps based upon his system.[18] Washington was by no means a pleasant place to be in that winter of 1859–1860. No other city reflected the tensions of an uneasy nation more vividly than the capital, and no institution caged the furies of sectional animosity more strikingly than Congress. Wrangling over the volatile issue of John Brown's raid and deadlocked over the election of a House speaker, that august body seemed poor ground for lobbyists.

Politics. They were the bane of a soldier's life, and Alexander cared nothing at all for them. But they would not lie still that heated season. Despite his preoccupation with work Porter himself had uttered some strong words on the sectional conflict: "if it does come to war," he informed Adam, "you will have one son in it from the commencement, bearing a musket in the ranks if nothing else & if Seward is President, his first act shall be to sign my resignation." [19] But he reacted more from instinctive loyalty than from reflection, being far too engrossed in the delicious present to squander his energies on the murky future.

Despite the intense debate and latent current of hostility, Congress managed to get some work done. A bill calling for an appropriation to purchase signal equipment and provide for the creation of a signal officer was introduced, and the Senate Military Committee opened hearings on the question. Both Alexander and Myer appeared before the committee to testify. Meanwhile the War Department had launched a project to test the effectiveness of several different breech-loading rifles, and on February 1 Porter learned that he had been named to the testing board. He completed the assignment early in March and received orders to rejoin his company at West Point. Since the signal corps bill was about to become law, and since his wedding was scarcely a month away, he hastily applied for and was granted a three-month leave.[20]

Porter rounded up his available friends and took the steamboat for Virginia. The wedding on April 3 went smoothly and was followed by a trip to Georgia to visit the family. When all the Alexanders had met and approved the new bride, Porter and Bettie returned to Virginia for a round of visits with the Masons, all of whom showered the newlyweds with hospitality. Not until June 19 did they take leave of the Old Dominion, and within another week they had arrived at West Point. Still anxious for some new assignment, Porter had received no fresh orders. So far as he knew the future promised only an indefinite term at the Point, where quarters for married officers were virtually unobtainable and notoriously inadequate.[21] Overcrowded as usual, the post could provide them no accommodations. Only the kindness of Major Kendrick, professor of chemistry, who offered a wing of his house, enabled the Alexanders to set up housekeeping. The newlyweds purchased furniture and readied their two-room abode. Porter was willing to settle down at least for a time. Excused from visits and attendance upon the young ladies, he relished his new leisure. The Alexanders planned only a small housewarming to celebrate their first home.

But that very evening, before the guests arrived, an official caller handed Alexander new orders: he was to proceed at once to Washington Territory, there to relieve the lieutenant in command of the Company A detachment sent out during the Indian uprising in 1858. The ironic twist did not amuse Porter. "This is my first day in my new quarters where I have just gotten nicely fixed," he informed Adam, "& I open my writing desk in them, for the first time to tell you that we will have but one week to enjoy them." [22]

In fact, some kind of move had not been entirely unexpected. Major Myer, now the army's signal officer, was dickering with the War Department to let Porter join him in New Mexico, where a war against the Navajo Indians had broken out. The opportunity had tempted Alexander, but he hesitated. He willingly accepted orders no matter how perilous the assignment, but he balked uneasily at making any such decision himself. He hesitated, he explained to Adam, "because I did not like to assume any responsibility in *placing* myself in a situation where so much would be risked by & *upon* me." If the hand of Providence or the whim of capricious fate decreed his destiny that was all right, but he chafed at having to assume that burden himself. And now that Providence or fate had so decreed, there was no time to lose. Washington Territory was reputed to be a beautiful spectacle in the fall.

The long and tedious trip to Washington Territory consumed nearly a month and left Bettie weak from a severe fever she had caught in Panama.[23] When the Alexanders finally reached Fort Steilacoom, where Company A was stationed, they found it to be commanded by Lieutenant Colonel Silas Casey. A Rhode Islander, West Point class of 1826, the colonel had fought against the Creeks, the Seminoles, and the Mexicans.

He had been in Washington Territory since early 1856 and spent most of his free time working on a system of infantry tactics. Scholarly and reserved, Casey knew Adam Alexander and thought highly of the family. His son Tom, an old friend of Porter's, was in command of the Company A detachment. Both Casey families gave the Alexanders a hearty welcome and arranged quarters for them in one side of a cottage next to the colonel's quarters. By dint of much scraping and no little ingenuity the Alexanders scrounged furniture and other necessities, all of which were scarce in the remote territory. In less than a month they had settled into a new routine.[24]

It took Porter no time at all to fall in love with Steilacoom. With only company routine and light details to supervise, he basked in the luxury of leisure time for reading and playing chess. But most of his energies went to the outdoors, where a lingering autumn soaked the forest in brilliant colors. Every corner of the forest concealed some small lake or rushing stream, its water teeming with fish. Most of the lakes and streams lay within an hour's walk. Five miles to the southeast of the fort lay a large lake whose reedy marshes sheltered a favorite feeding ground for geese. Twice a week before daylight Porter would ride to the lake and hide himself on the far side to get some shots at the passing flocks. Once a week, too, he would ride at crack of dawn to the mouth of the Puyallup River (later the city of Tacoma would rise there) and hike upriver a couple of miles to an Indian village. There he could hire an Indian to paddle his "kynim" around the flats and creeks of the river, where Porter could alternately fish and hunt. Post social life provided an occasional picnic, riding or hiking excursion, and an infrequent hop.

But it was the country itself that Porter loved most of all. A paradise that would not wilt, where the temperature did not drop below twenty degrees all winter, where spring blossomed as early as February, and where nature seemed yet pristine and infinitely benign. Far, far away in some other world did the squally thunder of conflict seem to exist, and few of its jarring peals intruded upon the quiet forests. The face of Mount Rainier framed in a cluster of fir trees above the parade ground, shifting from one arcane expression to another, remained unimpressed by the rhetoric of sectional controversy. The soaring white cedars jabbed majestically at the sky as if they had never heard of politics. The dense primeval foliage, thick with berries, knew nothing of party loyalty. In the stillness of dusk only the cloak of darkness clouded the tranquil sky. High above the fort hidden birds chirped their isolated tunes. No man who loved the quiet of nature and who cherished the fresh excitement of the forest would willingly surrender his paradise, and Porter had no intention of doing so. To think that he might live out his life in just such a place, content and untormented by any higher ambition, pleased him as much as any thought he could conceive.

("As I look back at it now," he would write as an old man, "it seems to have been the last of my youth. Never to, or during that time, did I begin to realize what care & responsibility may mean. I had a position for life, & an assured support in the profession I loved; & I had only to get the most pleasure that I could out of my surroundings." [25])

Remote and secluded Washington might be, and distant from the tolling bells of the East, but not immune to their reverberations. News took three weeks to a month to reach California and wend its way north to Washington. But come sooner or later it must and would; there was no escape from it. Every southern officer on the coast marked time nervously. Helpless to effect the issue one way or the other, they could but sit and wait tensely for its resolution. What implications the presidential election held every man understood only too well; what results it might produce did not seem so clear, and the anxious mind could only speculate. ("I took little interest in politics," he claimed several decades later. "If the South seceded she would want an army & I would ... secure a place in it. If there was peace that was well & good; & if there was war I would see active service, which was even better. So I troubled my head not at all about what they did in the East.") But his detachment did not drive out the critical issue entirely. "Of course, we are all much exercised now to know the results of the election," he wrote to a sister on November 11. "We suppose from the latest news we have that Lincoln is elected, and if so I *hope* and *expect* to be called in to help secede. If he is once inaugurated, it will be too late to oppose him, as the purse and the sword will be in his hands. . . . If he is elected I believe the interests of humanity, civilization, and self-preservation call on the South to secede, and I'll go my arm, leg, or death on it." [26]

He could not know that even as he wrote the die had been cast: Lincoln had been elected, and already southern governors had opened a hurried correspondence over the question of secession. In Alexander's own state many people seemed stunned by Lincoln's victory. "The people here are taken greatly by surprise," Aleck Stephens reported from Crawfordsville. "They did not anticipate it and thought I was only indulging in unnecessary apprehension when I told them months ago how it would most probably be." [27]

In mid-February the dreaded news arrived: Georgia and the other southern states had seceded and formed a southern confederacy.

Porter concluded that the choice had been made for him. If Georgia had seceded he must resign and go with her, but secession did not necessarily mean war and he did not have to resign at once. The company would probably be ordered East again; he could wait until then to resign. ("I really never realized the gravity of the situation," the old man wrote. "As soon as the *right to secede* was denied by the North I strongly approved of its assertion & maintenance by force if necessary." [28])

He had called his shots well. On March 20 orders came for the detachment to return to West Point. No ship ran to Puget Sound on regular schedule, but the quartermaster arranged for a small warship to take the company to Port Townshend, where it could meet the regular steamer. Hurriedly the detachment packed up its gear. On April 9 a doleful retinue slowly wound its way down to the wharf, where the warship *Massachusetts* lay at anchor. There was a painful parting scene at the wharf as old friends made their farewell. As the detachment climbed aboard Porter heard his handsome pointer Ponto raise a mournful howl on the dock. It was late in the afternoon when the *Massachusetts* finally headed into the sound. ("Four years later, to an hour, I saw General Lee ride back to his lines from Appomattox." [29])

The plan called for Company A to catch the mid-month Panama steamer, but their incoming vessel passed that departing ship in San Francisco harbor. The next sailing would be May 1; that meant a ten-day layover. Coming down the gangplank Porter received a new surprise. A messenger standing on the wharf dashed up to him with special orders. Porter read the dispatch: he had been relieved from duty with Company A and was to report for duty to Lieutenant James B. McPherson on Alcatraz Island. Puzzled by the command, Porter went to see Gilmer, who was still stationed in San Francisco. Gilmer had a similar order for Porter, fresh off the telegraph, and at army headquarters General Albert Sidney Johnston had still a third copy. [30]

The new orders left Porter in a delicate position. He had planned to get back home by going with Company A. Now he could not return without first resigning and then paying his own fare. Home lay 6,000 miles away and connections in these times might well be uncertain. He left Bettie with the Gilmers and reported to McPherson as ordered. He told McPherson that he had no choice but to offer his resignation at once. Porter knew that his fate rested squarely in McPherson's hands. If he refused to forward the resignation or grant Alexander a leave of absence so that he might leave at once, the couple might be stuck in California for another two months.

But McPherson was no small or petty man. He listened sympathetically to the whole case and nodded in agreement. Then he stood up and offered his reply in an affectionate, almost fatherly tone. They were words that would haunt Porter to the end of his life: [31]

> Aleck, if you must go, I will give the leave of absence and do all in my power to facilitate your going. But don't go. These urgent orders to stop you here are meant to say that, if you are willing to keep out of the war on either side, you can do so. They mean that you will not be asked to go into the field against your own people, but that you will be kept on this coast, upon fortification duty, as long as the war lasts. Gen. Totten likes you and wants to keep you in the Corps. That is what these orders mean. This war is not going to be the ninety days affair that papers and politicians are predicting. Both sides are in deadly earnest, and it is going to be fought out to the bitter end. If you go, as an educated soldier, you will be put in the front rank. God only knows what may happen to you individually, but for your cause there can be but one result. *It must be lost.* Your whole population is only eight millions, while the North has twenty millions. Of your eight millions three millions are slaves who may become an element of danger. You have no army, no navy, no treasury, and practically none of the manufactures and machine shops necessary for the support of armies and for war on a large scale. You are but scattered agricultural communities, and you will be cut off from the rest of the world by blockade. Your cause must end in defeat, and individual risks to you must be great. On the other hand, if you stay out here, you will soon be left the ranking engineer on this whole coast. Every one of the older officers will soon be called East for active service, and there will be casualties and promotion, and probably increase of the Corps. Meanwhile you will have every chance to make a reputation for yourself as an engineer, and you will have charge of this big Lime Point reservation, about 10,000 acres, all covered with wild oats. Buy a flock of sheep and put them on it, hire a Mexican to herd them, and in four years you will be a rich man. The city of San Francisco, too, is filling in water lots, and the Engineer officers are consulted in fixing the harbor lines. This will give you information and opportunities in making good investments. Briefly, remaining here you have every opportunity for professional reputation, for promotion, and wealth. Going home you have every risk to run, and in a cause foredoomed to failure.

Porter sat stunned in his chair. McPherson had touched every vital nerve of the issue. That he was right could hardly be disputed. Perhaps Porter had approached the problem too mechanically, thought too little about the alternative of not resigning. But could he not resign? Could he sit idly on the sidelines while his people fought a bitter war? He tried to consider what should count most in his reasoning. Bettie? She would accept whatever decision he made, knowing that she could not be happy if he were not. Georgia, the South? They were his primal heritage; everything he had been taught to revere and value lay bound up in them. He had absorbed their values into his very marrow, and sentiment played a fine and compelling tune upon his tortured mind. Yet what were they after all but abstractions—ideals that his mind and heart fleshed out with more concrete images. Ah, but there was the rub, for what were those images but memory—memory of family, friends, places, events, a way of life? These were the central cords, the tangibles that mattered. Was it not, after all, a fight for survival? They were his people and his life; he could not escape or disavow them. If threatened they ought to be fought for even at the risk of death, for without them life had no meaning.

As for himself, he could not even feel involved in the decision. He understood none of the enormous complexities involved, so far did they transcend him ("I felt utterly helpless to avert or even to debate the question what I should do"). The decision seemed almost automatic, reflexive, but it could not be otherwise for there seemed no possible way to grasp the real problem (whatever it was) or come to terms with it. And perhaps there were other, less obvious factors at work: the fear that if he remained on the coast the army might order him to return later, thus forcing the decision again, and the ever present desire to see active service.

He had sat silent and pensive while a torrent of disconnected thoughts tossed about his head. Of all his reactions, however, that of loyalty fastened itself most firmly. He looked up and said quietly, "What you say is probably all true. But my situation is just this. My people are going to war. They are in deadly earnest, believing it to be for their liberty. If I don't come and bear my part, they will believe me to be a coward. And I shall not know whether I am or not. I have just *got* to go and stand my chances." McPherson smiled faintly, his face a deep shade of sadness. "In your place I would probably feel the same way about it," he said. "Go home, write out your resignation and bring it to me. I'll have orders drawn up granting your leave."

Porter had crossed a momentous chasm. In writing out his resignation he was irrevocably altering the course of his life. In a nearby chair Bettie sat crying softly the whole time. She said nothing; the dialogue had already passed between them and had no need to be spoken: Do you know what you are giving up? Yes. Does it have to be done? Yes. Then there could be no regret, and her tears were those of sorrow not bitterness. They need only wait for the steamer *Golden Age* to arrive on May 1.

Then, suddenly, a Pony Express rider brought startling news: the Confederates had attacked Fort Sumter. Up to that very moment many people still believed or at least hoped that war might be averted. The city plunged into turmoil and confusion. Fights broke out between partisans on both sides, and mass meetings seemed on the verge of exploding into violence at any moment. The position of any southerner in the city became very awkward, for San Francisco claimed a large majority of unionists.[32]

At last the first of May rolled around, and the *Golden Age* docked on schedule. The quartermaster department had persuaded the steamship company to give the Alexanders half-fare rates, and now McPherson walked down to the gangplank with them. Tom Casey and his family also climbed aboard, as did the rest of Company A. The ship hauled up its lines, and within a short time San Francisco harbor had become a fuzzy speck on the distant horizon.[33]

The Alexanders reached New York early on the 24th. Ignorant of events since his departure from California, Porter now learned that Lincoln had called for 75,000 militia after the fall of Sumter, that Virginia, Tennessee, Arkansas, and North Carolina had seceded rather than provide troops. Kentucky was still struggling to remain neutral; they could go to Louisville and from there to Chattanooga and Washington, Georgia. Disturbed by the news, the Alexanders decided to start south at once.

The train clattered monotonously across the countryside. In each town Porter could see makeshift camps thrown up to drill volunteers. Whole regiments and even brigades massed in loose formations on village greens. And they knew their business, or at least had some sense of discipline. Most of them seemed to be carrying good rifled muskets, and the camps reflected decent equipment.[34] The train reached Cincinnati at sunrise on Sunday the 26th. Here they learned that no trains ran to Louisville until that evening. The Alexanders spent an impatient day of waiting; Porter grew increasingly uneasy about the imposing "u. s. ARMY" stamped on his baggage.

In Louisville Porter hunted up an old West Point friend, Simon Buckner, to learn about the situation in Kentucky. Leaving Louisville that same night at eleven, they awoke to have breakfast at Chattanooga. At the hotel Porter happened to meet Leroy P. Walker, the newly-appointed Confederate Secretary of War. Walker informed Porter that a commission as captain of engineers awaited him in Richmond.[35] Porter accepted the commission and promised to report after he had deposited Bettie in Washington.

As they travelled to Atlanta Porter scanned the Tennessee and Georgia countryside. He could not help but compare it to the North. Camps had sprung up here, too, but where regiments and brigades gathered in Ohio only one or two companies assembled in each village here. They carried not rifled muskets but a motley assortment of smooth bores, hunting rifles, squirrel guns, shotguns, and anything else they could find. They formed lackadaisically and seemed indifferent to drill or discipline.

On Thursday, May 30, the Alexanders were met at the Washington depot by Adam, Porter's brother James, and two of his sisters. As they drove back to Fairfield, Porter told his father that he could stay but one night before going on to Richmond. And a short night it proved to be. There seemed barely time to greet the servants, walk over the grounds, get Bettie settled, and bid the family good-bye.

Bettie was the hardest of all to leave. They had never been separated since their marriage and now seemed to be an especially cruel time, for she was expecting a baby in late autumn. But it would not be for long, he promised. Let him get settled in Richmond, ascertain the state of things there, and find out where his orders would take him. Then he would send for her—at once, without delay. And early the next morning he was aboard the cars for Richmond.

Part Two

THE CHASM CROSSED

Chapter III

Turmoil and confusion engulfed Richmond that June. The infant Confederate government had barely begun to organize itself, and everywhere new departments moved hastily into new quarters or opened temporary offices to conduct business. Government officials from the President down to lowly clerks scrambled for rooms at overcrowded hotels, and the sudden influx of humanity into the city overwhelmed the limits of Virginia hospitality. Troops poured into the depot as fast as overtaxed railroads could transport them, and uniformed men thronged through streets in which women were conspicuously absent. Already the government had denied telegraph dispatches to newspapers and asked them not to notice troop movements. Delegations of all types called upon the new cabinet, including a group of Creek and Choctaw Indians who offered to raise twenty-five thousand troops for the Confederate cause.

On Monday June 3 Davis handed Porter his commission but had no immediate orders for him. They would be forthcoming, he promised, as soon as the War Department could sort itself out but Porter's impatience would not be soothed. "My commanders have their hands full & cant look after me closely enough to keep me employed," he complained to Bettie, "& if I go & ask for anything to do their manner only says 'just now leave me & go do any thing so that you dont bother me.' " [1]

But he did not have long to wait. Davis, who had formerly served on the Senate Military Committee, remembered Porter's part in the demonstration of Myer's signal system and soon ordered him to start a small factory for signal apparatus. The army also needed engineers badly, and Josiah Gorgas suggested that Porter be assigned to duty in that field. Within a few days General Robert Garnett asked that Porter be added to his staff, and Toombs proposed that Porter become an officer in a battalion being organized in Wilkes County. Both these requests Davis denied, insisting that the Confederacy badly needed Porter's signal experience. Then, on June 11, Beauregard also tendered an application for Porter's services. He got no immediate reply. [2]

The factory took little time and Porter's impatience soon revived, but Davis remained silent on his future. He began to suspect that the president was saving him for something, "for I've taken good care that he shant *forget* or *overlook* me." His suspicion seemed justified when on June 28 he received orders to take charge of five artillery batteries then in bivouac at the Baptist College. The batteries lacked even basic equipment and had no experience in drill; nevertheless Porter pushed through requisitions for supplies and organized classes of instruction for the officers. Already he had in mind the rough idea of shaping his batteries into a cohesive battalion in order to mass their fire and facilitate smooth movement. Heretofore the prevailing practice had been to attach single batteries to individual infantry brigades, making them part of the brigadier's own command. This had two grave defects: it fragmented the artillery's firepower and it hampered the formation of an artillery corps as such, since the batteries remained under the control of infantry officers.[3]

To what extent Porter's ideas on the subject had already developed remained a mystery, for on the very next day he received new orders to join Beauregard at Manassas Junction as signal officer. The abrupt shift in orders annoyed Porter. He had already grown enthusiastic over his artillery batteries, and he had just written Bettie to come on to Richmond. Now she would arrive and he would be gone. Still he found consolation: he would be going, after all, to the largest army in the most prominent place under the man he considered to be the most important general, and so he begged Bettie to come ahead as planned. "I'll pay those yankees for separating us if ever I get a chance," he promised.[4]

On his way to the post office Porter met General Lee, who admitted he had planned to send Porter to Wilmington on assignment only to be thwarted by Beauregard. Lee promised that he might still get Porter away from Manassas after the signal system had been installed there, and Porter was not inclined to doubt his word.[5]

Porter reached Manassas on July 2 and reported immediately to Beauregard. He knew no one on the general's staff except Sam Ferguson, a classmate from West Point, but all bade him welcome and gave him a room and a place at the general's mess. The Creole's grave courtesy and confidence deeply impressed Porter and strengthened his belief in the general's ability. Beauregard wished him to install the signal system at once; a major clash might occur at any moment and the rambling countryside about Manassas made communication awkward and time consuming. Only part of the necessary equipment had arrived with Porter, but he immediately detailed ten or twelve privates and put them on a course of instruction. When not drilling his recruits he rode about the countryside making a careful survey of the topography. Soon he possessed a knowledge of the terrain that was a military rarity at the time, and he used it to locate his four signal towers. The central tower stood upon a high rocky point near Wilcoxen's farm about a mile east of Manassas and provided a clear view of the open ground to the north and west. A second tower went up on a small bluff to the northwest near the Van Pelt house, a third near the Mc-Lean house some two miles north of the central tower, and the fourth near Confederate headquarters in Centreville. From these strategically-placed towers observers could scan virtually the entire area and relay information by signal to each other.[6]

The going proved slow for Porter. He complained that his privates were "so stupid that I have to knock them down & jump on them & stamp & pound them before I can get an idea into their heads." He had to do everything for them, including the provision of rations, and his signal equipment arrived piecemeal from Richmond. On July 18 Federal troops advanced into Centreville and eliminated the observation tower there. But gradually his fledgling signal corps took shape, and by the 21st his men could effectively relay signals between the towers. At the tower nearest headquarters couriers stood ready to carry the messages to officers in the field, and even though he had lost a tower Porter considered the ground well covered. He put his men to relentless practice with flags by day and torches by night, and detailed a guard to protect the towers.[7]

While Porter trained his men Beauregard grappled with the problem of organizing his army and preparing attack plans. He had already projected several elaborate strategical gambits only to have the government reject them. By mid-July it had been decided that he and General Joseph E. Johnston would collaborate in an offensive, and Johnston's troops were slowly arriving by train from the Valley. But Beauregard could scarcely organize his own force into cohesive battle units. Federal troops had reached Centreville and an attack could be expected at any moment, but no fortifications had been constructed and no final battle plans adopted. Moreover Beauregard feared that he might lose command of the field to Johnston, who outranked him, but the latter arrived on the 20th and deferred gracefully to him.

On the night of the 20th Porter decided to camp by the tower near the Van Pelt house. Shortly before six the next morning he was roused by artillery fire from across the stone bridge. One shell ripped through his tent but inflicted no casualties. Quickly everyone scrambled to his post. Hoping to get into the fight, Porter remained with Beauregard until about eight, when the general ordered him to go to the central tower and report any enemy troop movements. He obeyed with obvious reluctance, seeing little hope for action atop a tower. Some of his best men had been on the platform for three hours looking for enemy troops and had seen nothing. Porter relieved them, took out his powerful glass, and settled down to watch.[8]

Half an hour passed uneventfully. Then, about 8:45, turning to check the Van Pelt tower, Porter noted a faint glimmer in the distance. The sun was low in the sky behind; could the glimmer be sunlight reflecting off some metallic object? He followed it carefully and discovered it to be a brass cannon and some muskets with fixed bayonets moving behind the drab backdrop of a fence. Porter had discovered the key to Federal tactics for the day: a large column of troops swinging northwest to turn the Confederate left. At that moment the head of the column had reached Sudley Springs, eight miles from Porter's tower and less than two miles from the Confederate position commanded by Colonel Nathan Evans.[9]

Realizing the danger, Porter immediately signalled the Van Pelt tower: "Look out on your left; you are turned." From there a courier took the message to Evans, who received similar news from a picket about the same time. While Evans hurriedly deployed his meager forces to meet the threat, Porter sent a dispatch to Beauregard, "framed after my idea of what the reports of reconnoitering officers should be—i.e., the exact mathematical truth, the whole truth, and nothing but the truth":

> I see a body of troops crossing Bull Run about two miles above the Stone Bridge. The head of the column is in the woods on this side. The rear of the column is in the woods on the other side. About a half mile of its length is visible in the open ground between. I can see both infantry and artillery.[10]

The message caused a change in Confederate plans. Originally Beauregard had planned to turn the Union left; now the report that his own left was threatened caused him to hesitate. The troops of Bee, Jackson, and Hampton were hurried to reinforce Evans, and Johnston urged Beauregard to abandon his plan and shift most of his troops to the left. While the generals debated their course the Confederates on the left bought valuable time with their plucky resistance and more of Johnston's men continued to arrive from the Valley. Then came a new message from Porter's tower.

The day was unpleasantly hot and dry. About 10:30 Porter noticed an immense dust cloud about ten miles distant on the northwest horizon. He puzzled over the sight; obviously it meant the approach of a large train, but whose train was it? In slipping away from the Valley Johnston had counted on eluding Federal General Robert Patterson, whose eighteen thousand men were supposed to keep him occupied. What if Patterson had uncovered the deception and come on in pursuit of Johnston? Seeing a perfect opportunity to get nearer the scene of battle, Porter took the message in person to Johnston and Beauregard whom he found on a hill near Mitchell's Ford. Fear that Patterson might be approaching clinched Johnston's argument that the proper field of battle lay to the left, but Beauregard still hesitated to abandon his plan. Finally a fresh storm of artillery on the left about 11:30 ended the debate. "The battle is there! I am going," Johnston cried and rode off to the left. Beauregard paused only long enough to order Alexander back to his post on the central tower.[11]

From the platform Porter watched the changing course of battle, judging its progress by the smoke and changing lines of musket fire. At 1:15 he relayed his last message, reporting a new position for the dust cloud and noting the arrival of another Union brigade at Sudley Springs. By 3 P.M. he realized that the crucial fighting about the Henry House had turned in favor of the Rebels. Convinced that his services as observer were no longer needed, he rode for the left to rejoin Beauregard. The field about him swarmed with stragglers, and both armies had been thrown into confusion. The Federal troops were fleeing in disorder; the disarrayed Confederates were slow to organize any effective pursuit. Only Joseph Kershaw, with two regiments, had been ordered after the routed enemy, and now Beauregard had second thoughts about him. Having won his plum the general was in no mood to let it slip from his fingers. He ordered Porter to tell Kershaw not to follow the Federals too fast or attack them.[12]

Surprised by the lack of pursuit, Porter ventured the suggestion that the order be amended, but Beauregard only replied, "Kemper's battery has been ordered to join him. Let him wait for it to come up. Then he can pursue, but cautiously, and he must not attack unless he has a decided advantage." That offered little promise, but Porter rode out obediently. After delivering the order to Kershaw, Porter started back. At the stone bridge he met Sam Ferguson looking very disgusted. "I'm going to bring everything back to our side of the river," he told Porter. "Some fool has sent some rumor about yankees south of Bull Run way down about Union mills and everything is ordered to come back."

Upon rejoining Beauregard Porter learned that scarcely anyone except the generals believed the rumor, but the recall order had been issued and the hour had grown too late for any organized pursuit. He remained with Beauregard until ordered to accompany Johnston back to Manassas Junction. The Confederates could claim a glorious victory, but they had little more than a treacherous self-confidence to show for it. Porter could claim more for himself. His signal system had done vital service for the Confederate cause, and he had put in an impressive day of service. In his report Beauregard praised both Porter and his signal system.[13]

Only one spectacle marred his pleasure. Later he had occasion to visit the Henry House, scene of some of the battle's bitterest fighting, and there he saw the body of old Mrs. Henry. A bedridden invalid, she had been struck by a cannonball and at least three musket balls.[14]

On the day after Bull Run Porter became chief of ordnance and artillery for Beauregard's command. He also remained in charge of the signal service, largely for the purpose of training and dispatching signal officers to other areas of the Confederacy. When the Confederacy finally established a separate Signals Department in the fall Porter was offered a promotion to take charge of it but declined. Burning with energy and ambition, he could not have been content to sit out the war in a Richmond office. He preferred field service because it suited his demand for constant, vigorous activity and because his constitution thrived on outdoor life. "My health under canvas," he observed, "has never been equalled elsewhere." [15]

Porter's brilliant array of talents made him a general's dream, and Beauregard became the first to fully appreciate and utilize them. In appointing Alexander chief of ordnance he hoped to make full use of his genius for organization. The government had by no means developed anything resembling an efficient wartime organization, and nowhere was this more true than in the fields of ordnance and supply. Porter faced the immediate task of creating a system for supplying arms and ammunition to every branch of the corps. Unshaken by the size of his task, he first issued blanks to every unit in the army to report what arms it had and what it needed. From these reports he would learn the kinds and amounts of ammunition needed by each command as well. He organized a storehouse for general supplies at the railroad depot and saw to it that each organization of the army had its own wagon train to carry enough ammunition and equipment for at least one battle. He demanded weekly returns from every regiment, battery, and wagon train to keep his eye on shifts in need and usage.[16]

Soon Porter found it necessary to create a travelling repair shop as well. He put old Major Duffy, an Alexandria jeweler, in charge of it. Duffy proved to be a superb mechanic. Starting with two or three wagons of tools and arms needing repair, he eventually captained a train of over sixty wagons (including reserve ammunition) and became an institution in the Army of Northern Virginia.

The new supply system, however effective, could not solve the even greater problem of acquiring materials. Despite the heroic efforts of Josiah Gorgas, countless problems in arming the troops plagued the Ordnance Department. The weapons on hand were few in number and often obsolete. Muskets varied greatly in caliber, thus complicating the provision of ammunition. Field pieces were scarce, uneven in quality, and varying in caliber. Ammunition was limited and poor in quality. Material for the manufacture of all ordnance supplies was exceedingly scarce and only one plant, the Tredegar Iron Works in Richmond, could cast heavy cannon.

But the war could not wait for the government to establish itself, and so Porter improvised as best he could. He found one primary source of supply in the harvest of ordnance abandoned by fleeing Federal troops and reaped a large haul after Bull Run.[17] He opened a correspondence to convert sporting weapons into military arms and worked diligently to improve existing weapons. He experimented with new weapons that could be produced easily and in quantity, ranging from rockets to flaming spears. At one point Beauregard authorized him to create a rocket battery, but Porter found the missiles too uncertain and reluctantly abandoned the project.[18]

On July 31 Colonel William N. Pendleton became temporary chief of ordnance for the entire Army of the Potomac and soon went to Richmond to scrounge for ordnance equipment. Porter assumed Pendleton's post as chief of artillery during his absence, and worked relentlessly at drilling the batteries. Confronted by complaints about the artillery fuzes, he improved them to the gunner's satisfaction. Again he toyed with the problem of creating a more effective artillery organization, but he held his post for too short a time to make any lasting changes. In October Pendleton returned and both men resumed their original offices, and by that time Johnston had extended Porter's duties to include his corps as well as Beauregard's.[19]

In addition to ordnance, signals, engineering, reconnoitering, and other odd jobs, Alexander gradually became the army's chief of secret service. Throughout the summer and fall of 1861 he hatched one scheme after another for obtaining information on Federal troop movements. When Johnston advanced the Confederate army to within five miles of Washington in August, Porter devised a plan to smuggle a spy into the city. The agent would take a room in one of the homes visible from the hills within the Confederate lines. Once located he would indicate his house by inserting an advertisement in one of the Washington papers received by the Confederates. Porter would then train a powerful telescope upon the house, and the agent would put a coffeepot in his window to identify the correct room. He could then use the window blinds to signal information to Porter.[20]

Elated over the plan, Porter procured a powerful telescope from Charleston and recruited a volunteer agent from among his signal trainees. The agent, E. Pliny Bryan, was a Maryland secessionist who had joined a Virginia infantry regiment until he became fascinated by the wig-wag system. Disguised and packed with instructions, Bryan made his way into Washington but to no avail. While he was en route, Johnston decided it unwise to maintain his lines so close to the growing Union army and on

September 20 withdrew to the vicinity of Centreville. No longer in possession of the key observation posts on Munson and Mason hills, Porter
had to abandon his plan and the luckless Bryan had to grope his way back
to the Rebel camp.[21]

Undismayed, Porter produced a new scheme. Bryan would establish
himself in a new position across the Potomac about fifteen miles below
Alexandria. His communication line would run north into Washington
and south into Manassas. A lady friend of Bryan's would be the key
agent in Washington, and Bryan would relay information either by the
wig-wag system or by messengers in small boats. The principal activity
would be to keep Porter supplied with various northern newpsapers,
which he had already come to appreciate as the most reliable source on
northern troop movements. In a letter to Davis, Porter outlined his scheme
and asked compensation for Bryan and his female cohort. His request was
granted and the operation worked well until the following spring, when
Bryan and several other agents fell into Federal hands. Even so, Porter
managed to draw up a roster of the Union army complete with commanding officers down to the regimental level from the information he garnered.[22]

Porter also worked diligently at both composing complex cipher codes
for Confederate use and deciphering enemy coded dispatches that fell into
Rebel hands. He prepared a fake letter to be delivered into Federal lines
as bait for bagging Federal spies, only to be thwarted by the diligence of
his own people. A first letter he had a picket give to a Negro woman to
take into the Union camp, but an alert citizen saw the picket conversing
with the woman. Smelling a traitor, he pounced upon the unsuspecting
servant, seized the letter and presented it to Confederate headquarters with
excited demands that the author be caught and hanged. Patiently Porter
sent off another letter but this one fell into the hands of a Rebel picket
who had not been let in on the plot. In the long run he proved more
successful at unravelling enemy codes than in carrying out his own
schemes. "I am managing a good deal of the secret service," he informed
Adam in November, "& find that to do it well, I have to be utterly un-
scrupulous myself in words & deeds & can only hope that the end will
justify the means." [23]

The drift of events that autumn left much to be desired for Porter. Overworked and lonely, he longed to see Bettie but could not get away. The
baby was expected in early November, and Porter would be absent for the
occasion. The burden of duties thrust upon him threatened to overwhelm

even his enthusiasm, and his brother James complained privately that Porter ought to be relieved of all but his ordnance duties and given an assistant as well. In dark moments it seemed to him as if all his valuable suggestions had either been shelved or given insufficient consideration. His attempts to organize the artillery batteries had been ignored; his plan to create rocket batteries had been countermanded; the secret service ventures had not received the support he thought they should have had; and in the fall he tried vainly to stir the War Department into more positive action on expanding usage of the signal system.[24]

In October Porter had written Davis about the glaring need for more effective signal service and offered to send trained men to key locations. He argued that they could be effectively used at coastal forts, cities and harbor lookouts threatened by the Federal blockade, and cited Fort Pulaski near Savannah as a striking example. Both Davis and Secretary of War Benjamin expressed a lively interest in Porter's proposals. The President gave it a favorable endorsement and noted that the system might be useful for trans-Mississippi communications, while Benjamin pointed to Pensacola, Charleston, and Columbus, Kentucky, as likely prospects. The correspondence did help speed the creation of a signal department that fall, but admonitions on establishing coastal communications went unheeded. Federal gunboats soon demonstrated the folly of that oversight by cutting off Pulaski from Savannah that winter, and the government declined Porter's repeated offers to try and restore communications.[25]

To make matters worse, Porter's position was complicated by an ambiguity in the relationship between Beauregard and Johnston. Though a member of Beauregard's staff Porter did service for both generals, but throughout the summer and fall the Creole had fallen into a steadily deepening rift with Davis. Finally, on January 26, Beauregard accepted a command in the west and offered to take Porter with him as chief of ordnance. The choice left Porter in a quandary. He esteemed both generals highly and deeply regretted Beauregard's departure, but he could not bring himself to go west. Personality did not affect his decision; he remained in Virginia, he said, "to complete all the plans I now have, & because I think it the most important & prominent place. I lament Beauregard's going *very much,* on account of the moral effect of his presence both on the enemy & our own men, but I have fully as much confidence in Johnston's strategy & ability." [26]

Very soon Porter's own situation improved. He found a place just north of Gainesville for Bettie and the baby to stay, and every Saturday afternoon he would ride over to stay the weekend. More than one comrade envied him the convenience. "I wish my wife was as near as yours," John-

ston himself noted sadly, "I'd ride with you." And one cold snowy January
night, at the Gainesville station, Porter viewed his daughter Bess for the
first time, unwinding her from beneath a "wonderful bundle of shawls &
blankets." He carried her all the way to the house—with Bettie warning
him sternly not to slip.[27]

During the winter of 1862 it became painfully evident that the military
situation had worsened for the Confederacy. In the west Forts Henry and
Donelson had fallen, and Albert Sidney Johnston was retreating from
Nashville. In the east it seemed certain that General George McClellan
would move his huge army against Richmond. Fearful of Johnston's exposed position at Manassas, the government ordered him to move his army
to the more fortified lines behind the Rapidan River.

The order confronted Porter with logistic problems of staggering pro-
portions, and for over a week he worked furiously at shipping supplies to
the rear. But mud-clogged roads also plagued the Confederates, and an
overzealous accumulation of stores at Manassas made it impossible to save
everything. By March 8 Alexander had salvaged all he could and the remainder, about a million and a half pounds of various goods, was put to
the torch. All depots were thrown open to the public, and citizens and
servants alike gathered up armloads of clothing and other items. Inevitably much criticism descended upon Johnston for the stores and equipment lost, but Porter insisted that everything of value had been saved. "Of
course the Generals now on detached duty as newspaper editors & critics,
will have a great deal to say about this important movement when it is
known," he noted acidly, "but if there was *ever* a plainer or more necessary one, history has failed to record it." He praised Johnston for his
handling of the situation, and confided that his "great confidence in, &
admiration of Gen. Johnston is now more firmly rooted and grounded than
ever."[28]

On the march to the Rapidan Alexander formally joined Johnston's
mess and staff, taking with him little more than his servant Charley, a
fifteen-year-old Negro boy he had hired from his master at Manassas
shortly before the retreat.[29] Once in position along the Rapidan he resumed his ordnance duties in earnest. The scarcity of arms compelled
him to plead in the Richmond papers for the return of all arms taken
from the Manassas battlefield as souvenirs. Despite the constant shortages
and thorny problems he found himself growing fonder of ordnance work,
and in early April admitted to Bettie that he might go into the field permanently. A few days later he applied for a major's commission in the
provisional army's artillery corps with an eye toward permanent assignment
in the regular army's ordnance division. Gorgas gave the application a

glowing endorsement, and on April 18, 1862, Porter received the commission.[30]

Despite Alexander's warm approval of the Rapidan line, the army did not occupy it for very long. McClellan had elected not to move upon Richmond but to take his army instead to Fort Monroe and come up the peninsula. By April 5 he had gathered his army outside Yorktown. Johnston hurried his army down to confront McClellan, and for two weeks the Confederates sat idle beneath an unceasing torrent of rain. During this interlude Porter had been sent back to the vicinity of Richmond to help select a battle line on the east side of the Chickahominy River. Upon his return he learned that McClellan had commenced a siege of Yorktown, and Johnston ordered a general retreat up the peninsula. In the confusion and delay of the withdrawal Alexander saw Johnston lose his temper and swear. Never again did he ever hear that general utter an oath.[31]

Johnston's strenuous efforts, aided by McClellan's slowness, got him safely out of the Federal trap, but the loss of Norfolk and an attack upon Drewry's Bluff caused him to concentrate his army nearer Richmond by May 17. McClellan followed close behind and slowly massed his forces while Johnston pondered his decision. He could ill afford to sit idly by and watch the enemy accumulate troops until they were ready to attack; the only alternative was to seize the initiative. By the end of May he was ready to attack.[32]

Porter knew little about these plans. In mid-May he had succumbed to the measles and remained in bed for nearly two weeks. On May 30 he learned that Johnston planned to attack the next day. Though still weak he left his bed and rode through a drenching thunderstorm to reach the Confederate camp. But the ride wore him down; once there he tumbled right into bed and fell asleep. When he awoke next morning he learned that Johnston had already launched the attack. Quickly he joined Johnston on the field and remained with him throughout the battle.[33]

Seven Pines proved an abortive effort for the Confederates. What had looked to be a sound plan on paper failed utterly of execution because orders went askew, because troops went askew, and because the orders had not been clearly drawn by Johnston in the first place. By day's end the Rebels had thoroughly bungled their chances, and in the failing twilight Johnston himself fell with two severe wounds that left his staff pessimistic over his chances for survival. Porter had been with the General throughout the day and remained at his side after he fell. For a day General G. W. Smith assumed command, but he fell victim to a mysterious malady that he could only describe as "paralysis."

For a few dismal hours the army stood leaderless. On June 1 Davis responded to the crisis by naming General Robert E. Lee to command. Porter could not know it, but the accession of his former academy superintendent would profoundly influence his military career, to say nothing of the future course of the war.

Chapter IV

The accession of Lee to command produced mixed reactions. Most of the rank and file did not know him, and those who did might be inclined to distrust a man whose reputation had been made in engineering. In very little time, however, Lee established himself as a sound leader with no entangling political liabilities and a great gift for diplomatic tact. Only one question remained unanswered: could he fight? The threat of McClellan's army outside Richmond lingered, and as Lee prepared his army he gave no indication of his plans. Naturally the officers speculated over his intentions. In confiding to Alexander his views on Lee, Colonel Joseph Ives proved to be remarkably prophetic:

> Alexander, if there is one man in either army . . . head and shoulders above every other in *audacity* it is Gen. Lee! His name might be audacity. He will take more desperate chances and take them quicker than any other general in the country, North or South; and you will live to see it, too.[1]

In only a few days Lee confirmed Ives's prediction by launching his Seven Days campaign, an offensive marked by boldness and simplicity of design but utter failure of execution. For a solid week the army marched and fought at a furious pace, suffering enormous casualties. Throughout the campaign Porter tended to his ordnance trains and saw to it that unbroken supplies of ammunition reached the troops. In its first extended test his system functioned smoothly. He emerged from the bloody campaign without a scratch, but Bettie endured constant anxiety. Still housed temporarily in Richmond, she and little Bess could hear the distant storm of musketry and artillery, and every night they witnessed the long trains of ambulances returning with their cargoes of moaning wounded.[2]

In addition to ordnance duties Lee tendered Porter one novel assignment during the campaign. Captain Langdon Cheves had succeeded in making an observation balloon for military use by garnering silk dresses from the ladies of Charleston and Savannah and then having them sewed together. When the balloon arrived in Richmond on June 23 Lee entrusted it to Porter and ordered him to ascend and observe the enemy lines. Since the only available gas supply was in Richmond, Porter contrived to have it inflated there and then run down the York River Railroad on a flat car. No doubt the sight of a brilliantly colored patchwork orb floating through the countryside on a railroad car kept the neighboring farmers in good yarns for some time.[3]

On the morning of June 27 Alexander went aloft to watch the battle of Gaines' Mill. He could not rise above 600 feet, and at that altitude the heavy timber obscured Federal troops below him. But dust clouds indicated every moment and the distant slope of the Chickahominy valley, where most of the fighting took place, could be seen clearly. That afternoon, during his second ascension, he watched most of the battle and signalled the movement of Slocum's division across the Chickahominy River. On the 29th he took the balloon down to Drewry's Bluff on a steamer and made another flight. After refilling he went up again the next morning but spent the rest of the day posting his ordnance trains and carrying orders for Lee. For the next few days Porter alternated between ground duty and air patrol. When the action moved to the area about Malvern Hill he went aboard the steamer, sailed down the river and made several more flights from the ship deck.

Lee apparently expressed pleasure at the results of Porter's observations and Porter himself grew enthusiastic over the balloon's potential, but it all ended abruptly on July 4. Early that morning, with the balloon emptied and folded on deck, Porter's steamer came under fire from Union troops along the bank. As the pilot maneuvered closer to shore to return the fire he ran aground on a mud bank. Desperately he tried to shake free, but the tide was ebbing and they could do nothing but sit helplessly and wait. Porter went ashore to collect some arms for defense, but when he returned that afternoon he saw an enemy gunboat bearing down on his steamer. The ships exchanged fire briefly before the Confederates abandoned ship and floundered ashore into the woods. Porter managed to escape by borrowing a horse from a rebel picket, but the Federals captured the balloon and Lee would never get another one. Though Porter never made another flight, he retained a healthy respect for aerial reconnaissance.

However varied and unobtrusive Porter's duties had been during the campaign, they did not go unnoticed. The performance of his ordnance system had pleased everyone, the balloon reconnaissances had done good service while they lasted, and in addition he had undertaken several other assignments for Lee. Already the general considered him one of the brightest and most promising young officers in the army, and on July 17 a promotion to lieutenant-colonel was forthcoming.[4]

After the campaign Porter continued to function in a number of capacities. Knowing that Lee might soon attempt a northward movement, he overhauled the ammunition supply for the entire army and enlarged Major

Duffy's reserve train. He also performed cheerfully as engineer, signal officer, and reconnaissance officer. Concluding that he could manage his business more efficiently if he had his own wagon, he fixed one up with tent, cook, camp equipage, travelling desk, and driver. Charley served as cook and for driver Porter hired an older Negro named Abram, who would remain with him until the end of the war. Whenever possible Porter parked his wagon near Lee so as to be available for any service required of him.[5]

After Seven Days another important task fell to Porter: the training of artillery batteries. As chief of artillery Pendleton had sorely disappointed Lee (and many other officers) by his performance during the campaign. A graduate of West Point and classmate of Lee, Pendleton had resigned, entered the ministry in 1837, and accepted a small Episcopal parish in Lexington, Virginia. He became captain of a local battery in 1860, performed well at Manassas, and quickly rose to ranking artillery officer in the Army of Northern Virginia. But at 53 he lacked the stamina and quickness of judgment for field duty, and his handling of the artillery had been notoriously poor. The soul of tact, his real talent lay in smoothing over personality clashes and coping with administrative problems.[6]

Although much of the complaint levied against Pendleton remained tactful and implicit, Lee knew of it and shared the sentiment. But he did not have another artillery officer experienced enough to handle large numbers of guns. He might charitably dismiss Pendleton's performance as one of bungled opportunities, but even his legendary patience could eventually wear thin.[7] On July 5 Porter received a note from the general's headquarters:

> General Lee directs me to say that Genl. Pendleton is absent, and he does not know who is in charge of the Reserve Artillery; he therefore desires that you will go at once and . . . have it all put in condition to move to 'Malvern Hill' tomorrow morning. . . . If the Artillery is ordered down the Genl desires that you go with it.[8]

In August Lee commenced a northern move that culminated in his brilliant and decisive defeat of General Pope's army at Manassas. Scarcely had his troops savored that victory when he led them on a full-fledged invasion of the North. Such a risky venture could not help but tax his supply lines. The battle of Second Manassas had taken Porter's ordnance trains some distance from their depots, but they had functioned smoothly and efficiently. Now the new movement would extend them across still greater distances and leave them vulnerable both to internal breakdowns and to attack by marauding Federal cavalry.[9]

Throughout August Porter had been hard at work maintaining his trains and improving the quality of Confederate artillery. When the army began its northern movement it left the reserve trains behind, and Porter did not catch up until the troops had passed Chantilly. There he filled all trains and cases, and the army entered Maryland with a full supply of ammunition. He then set up a main depot at Staunton to supply by shuttle all advanced stations established on the march. During all the bloody fighting that ensued, Porter's system functioned smoothly, enabling him to boast proudly that "there never was a breath of complaint anywhere of our men ever being short of ammunition—either for small arms or artillery." To insure constant supply he arranged for extra trains to be near each engagement and took pains to coordinate his movements with Lee.[10]

Keeping up with Lee proved no easy task. After crossing the Potomac September 4–7 the general daringly divided his army, sending Stonewall Jackson to capture Harper's Ferry, D. H. Hill's division to occupy Turner's Gap and Boonsboro, and the rest of the army toward Hagerstown. By a rare stroke of luck a copy of Lee's marching orders fell into McClellan's hands on September 13 and presented him with a golden opportunity to crush the Rebels before their army could unite. But McClellan again dawdled, and a counter-stroke of luck brought Lee the news that his adversary knew of the Confederate plans. Hurriedly he moved to reunite his army. Porter's reserve train, some eighty wagons strong, had accompanied Lee to Hagerstown; now they joined in the rapid march toward Boonsboro. There D. H. Hill struggled mightily to hold South Mountain against heavy Union attacks early on the 14th.[11]

Lee ordered Alexander to take his train across the Potomac at Williamsport, leave it in Shepherdstown and return to Sharpsburg, where the General planned to concentrate his forces. Darkness had already fallen but the moon was full. Porter started at once and pushed the train along all night. For the first time he experienced an extended bout with sleepiness, dozing on his horse until he nearly pitched to the ground. Eventually he took to walking for a short time but he nearly went to sleep on his feet. At dawn he reached the ford unaware that he had narrowly missed being struck by a brigade of Union cavalry. He left the train at Shepherdstown about noon on the 16th and crossed the river to rejoin Lee.[12]

Tired and saddlesore, he got little rest. Lee ordered him to take every empty wagon he could find to Harper's Ferry to collect the ordnance supplies Jackson had captured there. He left soon afterward and camped that night near the Ferry. The next day he gathered in a rich harvest of captured ordnance. Some seventy-three guns and a large supply of ammunition unsuited for Confederate calibers he dispatched back to Winchester; other ordnance equipment he had to gather directly from the enemy intrenchments on Bolivar Heights. From there he could see the smoke and bursting shells of battle in the distance. A great battle was taking place at

Sharpsburg, but he would not be there to see it. To his chagrin he had missed the bloodiest single day of the war.[13]

When he had finished his work next morning he rode to Boteler's Ford, where he received orders to await the army. That night Lee took his battered men back across the Potomac and put them into camp near Stevenson's Depot, about five miles north of Winchester. Exhausted by the battle and badly in need of refitting, reorganization, and rest, the army spent a pleasant month in replenishing its supplies and refilling its ranks. Porter used the time to improve his supply line, which still extended over a hundred miles from Staunton.

McClellan obligingly gave Lee the time he needed to restore his army; not until October 26 did the Federals resume the offensive. Slowly the two armies maneuvered down opposite sides of the Blue Ridge Mountains. Porter took his trains first to Ninevah, then across the Shenandoah River to Gaines' Cross-Roads. On November 4 he reached Culpeper and went into camp. A stiff log of ordnance work confronted him at every step, but it would not long detain him. He was, in fact, about to exchange it for a new assignment that promised some of the active fighting he had so vainly sought.[14]

On the night of November 7 a severe snowstorm blanketed the camp. Hard at work on some routine office matters, Porter looked up to see Captains Moody, Jordan, and Woolfolk of Stephen D. Lee's artillery battalion entering his tent. They had come on more than a social call: Steve Lee had just been promoted brigadier of infantry and ordered to Vicksburg. He had recommended to General Lee that Porter replace him as colonel of the battalion, and the captains had come to express their approval of the choice. Alexander thanked them and admitted that the job appealed to him, but he would wait for General Lee's decision. The captains promptly left to visit Lee, and on their heels came Steve Lee himself to persuade Porter.

There was no doubt that Alexander wanted the post. It meant both promotion and prestige, but most of all it meant field action. Still he did not jump at it, nor was he playing coy. The old reluctance to ordain his own fate once again stayed his eager hand. If Lee wanted him he would accept gratefully but he would not go to Lee on his own. Later he tried to explain his reasoning:

> The fact was that I was perhaps a little too good a presbyterian, & disposed to let happen what would. . . . So during the whole war I . . . simply obeyed all orders. And I valued Gen Lee's approval & good opinion far more than

general reputation or even high rank in our volunteer army. For my highest ambition was directed towards position in our regular engineer Corps, after we had conquered. . . . Perhaps my passive acceptance of whatever orders came was illogical, but it had its advantages. . . . I had the whole four years . . . entirely free from any anxiety, or care where I was to be sent, or how employed, & I had . . . delightfully independent positions, congenial duties, & pleasantest possible associations.[15]

That very same evening Lee called Porter in and gave him the command. Only one matter troubled the general: who would he find to replace Alexander as chief of ordnance. Porter suggested a man in the Richmond Arsenal whom he had never met but with whom he had corresponded almost daily. Lee summoned the officer from Richmond and found him fully equal to Porter's recommendation. On December 4, 1862, Briscoe Baldwin became the new chief of ordnance; until that date Porter retained the post in addition to his new command.[16]

It took Porter little time to discover that he had inherited a battalion worthy of his talents. Composed of six batteries, it combined with the famous Washington Artillery to form the reserve artillery for Longstreet's Corps. When Steve Lee wrote later in the month that he would "find all the Captains staunch & reliable men, some of the Batteries in fact you may say need dulling," he was not telling Porter anything new: [17]

> George Moody, the senior captain, commanded the Madison, Louisiana, battery. Well over six feet in height and weighing about 200 pounds, a large, strong face softened by deep blue eyes, he was straight and muscular and prided himself on a carriage and fastidiousness of dress not unlike that of Lee. He had proved himself a good soldier and superb disciplinarian, but then his men consisted largely of former stevedores and ship hands from the Mississippi River docks and required a strong hand to restrain them. Known as the "Tips" because of their habit of carrying large butcher knives for impaling any edible game within reach, they were prone to drinking, brawling, and carousing, but they fought well. A hard man to get along with, Moody constantly got embroiled in altercations with his fellow captains, but Porter always managed to remain on excellent terms with him. He was 42 years old.

> Pichegru Woolfolk, commanding the Ashland battery, equalled Moody in height and handsomeness but not in bulk. Jolly, sociable, hospitable, and somewhat careless, his dark eyes were always ready to explode into laughter. Two of his brothers served in the battery with him.

> Tyler Jordan, commanding the Bedford battery, had been strongly recommended for promotion by Lee just before the latter's departure. Medium sized with brunette hair and eyes, pleasant features and manners, he had been a lawyer before the war. He had proven himself a superior

officer. His command boasted a high degree of literacy and included Lieutenant John Donnell Smith, a tall, refined, bespectacled intellectual who devoted his leisure hours to the study of botany.

J. L. Eubank commanded the Bath battery until his later election to Congress, where he remained until the war ended. A stout, stolid farmer looking man, he was the oldest of the captains and very popular at home. When he departed for Congress his first lieutenant, Osmond B. Taylor, succeeded him. An intense, energetic officer, Taylor would perform efficiently until his tragic death on the retreat toward Appomattox.

A. B. Rhett, commanding the Brooks battery, also left his position soon after the year's end. Two of his lieutenants were eminently qualified to replace him but neither wanted the job. Finally S. C. Gilbert, the senior, assumed command and held it until Gettysburg, when he managed to pass it to his friend William Fickling. A lanky youth of about 6-4, Fickling commanded the battery for the duration of the war with Gilbert as his lieutenant, and both performed with consistent efficiency.

No captain appealed more to Porter than William Parker, who commanded the Richmond battery. A kindly, congenial man, Parker had been a physician and his battery consisted largely of boys taken from the families of his patients. Because of their youth they became known as the "Boy Battery," but they fought hard and well under their captain. Parker was eminently qualified to father his charges, for he impressed everyone with the depth of his Christian convictions. He believed in a religion of action rather than dogma, and at the heart of his belief lay the simple principle that if he died he would go at once to heaven. As a result he displayed an utter disregard for danger in battle, and his boys responded quickly to his example. Nothing better illustrated his character than a remark he made to his lieutenant in the thick of a hot fight: "Mr Saville, I dont see sir how you *dare* to expose your life as you do, knowing that you have not made your peace with your maker." [18]

The battalion had wanted Porter for its commander even though he was known to be a stern taskmaster. They soon adapted to his ways and found that, for all his West Point background, he had his own peculiar style. In taking up the march he did not issue a formal order to begin; instead he simply ran his personal wagon to the head of the column and yelled loudly, "Drive on, Abram!" And though he insisted upon strict obedience to orders, he paid little attention to dress or appearance or any of the other amenities of rank.

Porter for his part came early to appreciate and love his men. Near the end of his life he would write, "Of all my earthly ties the dearest in its memories and its ties, outside of those of family, are the memories & ties of the old Battalion." [19]

On the same day Porter assumed his new command Ambrose Burnside replaced McClellan as Federal commander. Under strong pressure from

Washington and uneasy in his new post, Burnside tried to take the offensive. His plans hinged upon a rapid crossing of the Rappahannock at Fredericksburg, but in this he was undone. His leading Grand Division under Sumner reached the river on November 17 and wanted to cross at once by fording. Burnside refused to allow it, however, fearing that Sumner might be trapped on the opposite shore by a rising river and attacked by Lee. He elected to wait instead for pontoons, but these arrived over a week late. Having lost momentum, Burnside sat down to wait, and once again Lee profited from his adversary's inaction.

Porter learned of the army's move toward Fredericksburg on November 18. He had to prepare both his battalion and the ordnance trains to march; he also had to serve as Longstreet's chief of artillery until Colonel J. B. Walton returned from sick leave early in December. On the 22nd he encamped behind Fredericksburg and confronted an uncertain situation. Burnside was massing his troops on the opposite shore but no one knew his intentions. Jackson's troops were just leaving Winchester to join Lee. Since Burnside had rimmed Stafford Heights behind the river with artillery, the Confederates hastened to locate emplacements on the heights behind Fredericksburg. To Porter fell most of the responsibility in selecting these gun positions.[20]

Lee used his time to construct a powerful line. No one seriously believed the Federals would charge the powerful left, based as it was on the commanding heights behind the town; consequently Lee wanted the guns placed so they could duel effectively with the Union cannon on Stafford Heights. That meant digging the pits on the reverse slope of each hill. Porter agreed that the left would not be assaulted, and in fact believed the attack would fall on the far left flank of the line. Since he played the dominant role in arranging the positions he could have placed his own guns anywhere on the line, and he elected to hold most of them in reserve behind the left. Still he disputed Lee's logic. The inferior Rebel ordnance could not possibly duel effectively with the distant enemy guns; therefore they might as well be placed to sweep the ground directly below the heights in case an attack should occur. After a lengthy discussion he persuaded Sam Johnston, Lee's chief engineer, to modify the General's order by locating the guns on the *brow* of each hill instead of on the reverse slopes.[21]

Johnston agreed with obvious reluctance. After the pits had been completed he informed Alexander that Lee was inspecting the line and had blamed him for not positioning the guns further back on the hills. "You made me put them there," he snapped, "now you come along & help me take the cussin." When they joined Lee the general said, "Oh Col Alexander just see what a mistake Captain Johnston has made here...

putting them forward at the brow of the hill!" Porter admitted that he had persuaded Johnston to do it so that the guns "could see all this canister & short range ground this side of town. Back on the hill they can see nothing this side of the river." Lee countered that the guns as placed would lose valuable range behind the town, but Porter dismissed that as a "refinement wh wd cut no figure in comparison with the increased view." As always Lee had the last word. He pressed his earnest subordinate into obedient silence but left the gun pits unchanged. By December 1 the guns were moving into position.[22]

Throughout early December the Confederates worked furiously at improving their position. Bitter cold (the temperature hovered near zero) and lack of tools made digging painfully slow, but Burnside obligingly gave them plenty of time. When the line was finished, the Confederates occupied a virtual cul-de-sac. The key point, Maryes Heights, overlooked the sunken Telegraph Road. A low stone wall protected the road for some distance, and dirt from a shallow trench behind the wall had increased that cover. The left flank ran down the heights through a boggy lowland and rested on Taylor's Hill near the river. The right was the weakest point, running across a string of heavily wooded hills into a marshy thicket dense with underbrush. The extreme right flank was secured by Stuart's cavalry with the horse artillery.

The beauty of the artillery position in the center lay not only in its thorough sweep of the ground below but also in its functional simplicity. The guns were well concealed, the men protected, and the lines of communication simple and immediate. Porter had confronted and neatly solved the key problems of effective fortification and ease of ammunition supply. Later, when Longstreet inspected the line and noticed an idle cannon, Porter replied proudly, "General, we cover that ground now so well that we will comb it as with a fine-tooth comb. A chicken could not live on that field when we open on it." [23]

On December 1 Longstreet ordered Porter to put a gun in every redoubt, drawing on brigade batteries to supplement the corps reserve if necessary. On the left Lane's battery of six guns occupied Taylor's Hill; from there to the Plank Road were lined the batteries of Huger, Grandy, and Lewis. On Maryes Hill Maurin's battery went to the left and the Washington Artillery to the right of the Plank Road, while Mosely's guns stayed in reserve behind them. Twenty-one guns covered the ground from Lee's Hill to the right with seventeen smoothbores behind them in reserve. Parker's battery occupied Stansbury Hill and Rhett enfiladed the Plank Road from a rise to the rear of Maryes Hill. The other batteries, Moody, Woolfolk, and Jordan, Porter put into reserve behind Stansbury Hill.[24]

On December 10 the unhappy Burnside finally committed himself to a general plan of attack. Having failed to cross the river behind the Rebel right at Skinner's Neck, he decided to build his main bridges in front of Fredericksburg and deliver his attack there. That night Longstreet warned Porter of an impending attack; when the Federals commenced laying their bridge at 4:30 A.M. the Confederate gunners raced to their posts. While Porter readjusted his line Jordan and Woolfolk carved eight more pits out of their frozen plateau. A heavy mist enshrouded the heights as Burnside tried to push his bridges along, but in Fredericksburg Barksdale's sharpshooters held up progress. Citizens of the town began to stream back behind the heights with their possessions to take shelter until the battle had ended.[25]

Harassed by the delays, Burnside ordered his guns on Stafford to bombard the town, and as the mist lifted Porter witnessed a spectacle of overwhelming magnitude. The 147 guns threw a furious blanket of fire through the fog, leaving dense pillars of smoke hovering above the still atmosphere. The Federal army had broken camp and stood in huge squares waiting to cross the river: one hundred thousand men neatly formed into compact units. Behind them on the distant slopes, parked in orderly rows, stood immense columns of white-topped wagons and ambulances interspaced with the darker squares of artillery batteries. Far above the whole glittering spectacle floated two enormous balloons. It looked for all the world to Porter like a gigantic oil painting, still and brilliant in its composition.[26]

Burnside was in no mood to enjoy the scenery. His devastating bombardment had gutted the town but caused few casualties among the sharpshooters, who had taken refuge in cellars. Once more his engineers ventured onto the bridges only to take a severe peppering from Barksdale's men, and not until that night did the Federals begin to cross the river. The Confederates slept on their arms and a ban on fires that cold night caused great suffering, but Burnside consumed yet another day in getting all of his army except Hooker's Grand Division across the river. Already it had become apparent that he had blundered seriously in his choice of battlefield: he simply could not find enough room for his huge army, to say nothing of his artillery.[27]

Atop the heights Porter harassed the enemy by throwing shells down the streets leading to the pontoon bridges and drew a healthy return fire for his efforts. That night he checked his lines again. Parker suggested moving an unused howitzer directly behind the Stansbury house, since it stood some five hundred yards in front of the line and overlooked the canal in front of the town. Mahone already had some infantry about the house; they could protect the piece. After dark the gun was run up and the horses hidden in the basement. That night everyone again slept at his post.[28]

Fog still covered the town next morning. Before it lifted at about 10 A.M. Porter put three of Moody's guns opposite Rhett on the south side of the Plank Road. Still assuming that Burnside would never dare attack the left, he tossed some more shells toward the bridges. Burnside launched the expected attack against the right. When the pressure there began to mount about noon, Longstreet ordered Alexander to throw a diversionary fire into Fredericksburg. The devastating fire provoked a fierce shelling from the opposite heights, but the Confederate pits neutralized the worst effects. So effective was Porter's bombardment that it drew a note of congratulations from Longstreet.[29]

Then, to everyone's amazement, Union troops began to spread across the open ground below Maryes Heights. Porter readied his guns and watched the enemy infantry (French's division) form for the assault. Federal artillery continued to pound the heights and Moody for one began to suffer from it, but no one considered returning the fire. Scarcely had the Federals deployed when a gruesome salvo from Walton's guns atop the heights and the infantry behind the stone wall swept away the lead ranks, leaving only the planted colors. Derisively the Rebels yelled, "Set 'em up again." [30]

They did. French's shattered ranks took refuge in a ditch at the foot of the heights, and after a brief lull Hancock's division poured onto the field only to meet the same bloody repulse. Howard's division then tried its luck. Of his three brigades only one actually got into the assault and was broken; the other two were diverted and did not suffer heavily. Nearly every brigade broke and ran at about the hundred yard mark, where the infantry fire began to have its full effect; none got any closer to the Rebel line. Sturgis and Griffin coaxed their divisions onto the field but to no avail. Sturgis had his formation wrecked trying to support French while Griffin took a severe pounding trying to reinforce Sturgis. Getty's division, only partially engaged, got off much more easily. The piecemeal attacks had virtually wrecked the Second and Ninth Corps. Moreover, Union artillery support had slackened because some shells had been falling short and hitting friendly troops. Still Burnside refused to budge. He ordered Hooker to take his fresh Fifth Corps across the bridges and renew the assault.[31]

The Federals had undertaken an impossible task: a charge across 400 yards of open ground broken only by a few houses and garden fences, under the direct fire of fourteen guns and a sizable body of infantry. Porter's guns had inflicted heavy casualties with practically no loss to them-

selves. At one point Porter even allowed himself to be distracted by a
covey of partridges stunned by the uproar and flying aimlessly. Amidst the
shelling he calmly drew his pistol and shot down a few choice birds for
his mess. Not that he was safe from enemy fire. One shell fragment cut
Dixie's tail and another landed right beneath her feet but failed to explode—saving them, Porter quipped later, from "another balloon ascension." [32]

By 2:30 Hooker had put his men in motion to renew the attack. Again
the Federal artillery opened in force to cover Hooker's deployment. He
brought up the divisions of Sykes and Humphreys and even managed to
sneak two batteries across the canal, where they could fire at close range.
The shattered remnants of the earlier assault units huddled behind the
canal ditch and waited for Hooker to form. He was almost ready by
3:30. [33]

At 3:40 Porter received a note from Walton, commanding the guns
atop Maryes: "You will send to the pits now occupied by my guns nine (9)
guns from yr. Batt. to relieve them. I am nearly out of ammunition. . . ." [34]
Since there was a lull in the firing, Porter rode to Stansbury to gather his
reserve batteries. He called up Woolfolk's four guns and two of Jordan's;
on the way back he could summon three of Moody's Napoleons. To reach
the pits the caravan would have to dash across Maryes Heights along a
narrow road open to enemy fire. As they rattled down the Plank Road Porter suddenly noticed an enemy shell coming his way. His aide, Joe Haskell,
had gone ahead to silence Rhett's guns while they passed; he too saw the
shell and expected to see horse and rider cut down. There was no time to
dodge. Porter could only watch it richochet about a hundred yards in front
and tumble towards him, wondering where it would hit. The shell went
directly beneath Dixie's stomach and landed behind him, and the caravan
struck out beneath the heaviest fire Porter had ever seen.

Now the noise became deafening. The column dashed madly across
the heights to pick up Moody's three guns south of the Plank Road.
Horses fell dead and wounded men tumbled off the lurching caissons
while the survivors clung desperately to their weaving perches. Beneath
the din of artillery the drivers swore violently at their teams to keep them
moving. In the distance Walton saw them coming and commenced with-
drawing his guns. Hooker's deploying columns, seeing Walton's guns departing, mistook the move for a general withdrawal. With a mighty cheer
they surged toward the heights. Lee too noticed the guns leaving and
wondered what it meant. But soon he could see Porter's guns lurching
down the road behind the pits.

It had in fact become a race between the artillery and the Federal infantry. Suddenly Porter's lead driver swerved to avoid the bodies of two

dead men in the road and plunged into a deep ditch. His wagon blocked the narrow road entirely, and the cannoneers fumbled desperately to extricate the piece. At last it was free, and Porter brought his guns to the pits and swiftly deployed them. The charging Federal line had approached within three hundred yards of Porter's position despite a galling infantry fire. The nine fresh guns were loaded with canister and fired into the oncoming line while Parker added a devastating enfilade fire from the Stansbury house. The blue line reeled and faltered; the two batteries sent across by Hooker took a severe pounding as well. Hooker, seeing the columns stagger back to cover, tried vainly to dissuade Burnside from ordering another assault. Reluctantly Hooker prepared Humphreys's two brigades for another assault. It was dark by the time he had finished.[35]

Porter used the brief interlude to strengthen his position. He brought up Jordan's two remaining guns and tried to replenish his dwindling ammunition supply, but the next Federal wave came on too fast. Humphreys's well-planned assault broke apart quickly. His first brigade, Allenbach's, joined the fragments of other units and lay down to fire instead of charging. The second, Tyler's, bellowed a loud cheer and started up the hill only to be met with one-second canister and case shot. By this time the darkness had forced Porter's men to fire at gun flashes and cheers, but the effect was no less devastating. Humphreys himself had two horses shot from under him as the attack became no less a bloody rout than the others. Then the firing slowly died, and silence drifted over the field.[36]

The Federals had no taste for renewing the battle. Burnside's senior officers finally discouraged him from further attempts, and by the morning of the 16th the Union army had safely retreated back across the river. The artillery had played a decisive role in inflicting a crushing defeat upon Burnside's army, and every Confederate report gave Porter his just praises.[37] Yet once again personal sorrow dampened his happiness. On the frozen battlefield lay the body of Dempsey Colley, Porter's boyhood friend. Dempsey had never cared in the least for politics, and in Porter's mind "war ought to have left him alone." [38]

The onset of winter left the Federals reluctant to do more than settle down into winter quarters. The Confederates followed suit, but acute shortages of supplies (especially forage) forced Lee to disperse his artillery about the country. Porter took his battalion down to the North Anna, and eventually encamped in some woods near Mt. Carmel Church about five miles north of Hanover Junction. There the cannoneers built their crude log cabins while Porter tried to beg a leave of absence to see Bettie. It was not easy since, as Gilmer noted, "poor fellow *he* is too useful to be spared." Finally he got a three-day leave at year's end and hurried to meet

Bettie in Richmond. In short order he found quarters for his family at the Wortham house, less than a mile from his camp. Their presence made all the difference to Porter. In later years he would describe the next three months as "one of the happiest periods of all my life." [39]

He had good reason to be satisfied. Lee had already recommended his promotion to full colonel and had expressed deep pleasure at his performance during the battle. Nor did Porter allow the general to forget the crucial debate over the proper location of the pits. A few days after the battle Porter happened to be with Sam Johnston outside Lee's headquarters. When the General came within earshot Porter brayed loudly to Johnston, "Sam, it was a mighty good thing those guns about Maryes were located on the brows of the hills when the yankees charged them!"

If Lee overheard Porter's gibe he gave no sign of it. But Porter noticed that henceforth he was frequently called upon by Lee to select battle lines, and only once did Lee ever scold him again. [40]

Chapter V

Winter life could be trying on occasion. Late in January Burnside commenced an abortive move that soon bogged down in the mucky terrain, but Porter had to bring his battalion towards Fredericksburg to meet the threat. Nothing came of the venture except that Moody's boys managed to turn up roaring drunk. Porter provided a stiff punishment detail to sober them up, but they remained incorrigible all winter. On one occasion a squad of the "Tips" located a pair of illegal whiskey merchants following the camp and promptly began to drink on credit, promising that one of the men would fetch their money. A private did in fact return to camp, but instead of getting money he informed Alexander of what was taking place. Porter hastened to arrest the illicit merchants, the remaining whiskey went to the surgeons, and the "Tips" ambled back to camp satisfied and without paying their bill. Nor did they overlook the local livestock. On one occasion they blandly impersonated Porter and other officers and embezzled a hog from an old farmer. Shortly afterwards Porter was astonished to hear the old man scurrying through the camp yelling that Colonel Alexander had stolen his pig.[1]

In a more regular vein a series of court-martial hearings absorbed Porter's time, but they could not last forever. For relaxation he got in some hunting and fishing, and on mild days he and Bettie could stroll about the Wortham's plantation. The Worthams proved genial and gracious hosts, and during the winter of short rations their pantry remained generous. Gradually his battalion duties lessened and Porter spent most of his time at the Worthams. In April Pendleton paid a visit to baptize little Bess. The ceremony went well notwithstanding the curious mixture of an Episcopal minister, Presbyterian parents, and Baptist witnesses.[2]

By far the most important piece of business transacted that winter was a long awaited reorganization of the artillery, and in the recasting Porter played a prominent role. The artillery had been making slow but sure progress in establishing itself as a separate arm. After Manassas the army had continued to assign individual batteries to brigades. Before long each battery grew accustomed to serving with a particular brigade, which meant that gunners and brigade alike resented any attempt to send the battery elsewhere, regardless of how badly it might be needed. Pendleton had formed a general army reserve under his command to provide fresh batteries for relief and for massing firepower at the crucial points of battle. But such a reserve required vigorous handling, and during the Peninsular campaign Pendleton had failed conspicuously to provide it.[3]

The scattering of the batteries throughout the army also created uncertain lines of authority between infantry and artillery officers. Spurred by Lee to correct this shortcoming, Pendleton drew up a new set of systematic regulations for the artillery in June of 1862. The new orders created a chief of artillery for each division to take charge of all its batteries. He might also form a divisional reserve to supplement the general reserve—an important step toward making the guns more flexible and mobile. Still the divisional chief surrendered control of a battery once it reported to the brigade commander.[4]

The division reserves never achieved formal organization. In August Lee divided his army into two wings under Jackson and Longstreet. A loosely organized reserve of ten batteries accompanied Longstreet to Second Manassas, but Jackson received no formal reserve. The old system of attaching batteries to brigades gave way to the practice of pooling several batteries for the use of the entire division. This provided a more flexible artillery arrangement within the division, but these batteries continued to assume a permanent relationship to their division. If guns had to be massed in large numbers on a division's front, they were expected to be furnished by the reserve even if the guns of a nearby division were standing idle.[5]

Such a flagrantly parochial system tended to subordinate ease of handling to questions of unit pride. The spectacular success of the Confederate guns at Second Manassas helped spread the conviction that some more flexible arrangement was needed. Before the Maryland invasion a new plan of organization was devised to form the batteries into loose battalions and assign one battalion to every division. There would also be a reserve for each of the corps as well as the general army reserve. Unfortunately this new plan did not go into use during the Sharpsburg campaign. Longstreet received two reserve battalions for his corps but Jackson got none. In November Lee formally divided his army into two corps under Longstreet and Jackson. To streamline the artillery in his charge Pendleton eliminated unfit or reduced batteries and eventually pared the number of units down from seventy-three to fifty-four.[6]

The reduced number of batteries in itself facilitated handling of the artillery. Now Longstreet kept his corps reserve, composed of Alexander's battalion and the Washington Artillery, and Jackson also received a reserve battalion. Pendleton had long since organized the general reserve into battalions, but the label was misleading: it represented mere groups of batteries rather than tactically cohesive units. And the regular division batteries remained unorganized.[7]

The new plan, drawn up by Pendleton, Alexander, and Stapleton Crutchfield, tried to eliminate the last vestiges of the old concept of artillery. It abolished brigade and divisional batteries and formed all artillery into battalions of four batteries each, with larger reserve battalions. Each regular battalion would be assigned to a division and made responsible to its commander, although Lee or the corps commanders could recall the battalion in any emergency. In addition the corps reserves would remain intact, two battalions for each corps, and the army reserve of two batteries with six guns each would also continue. Guns would be redistributed to equalize the armament of each battery as much as possible. Each battalion would have two field officers, a surgeon, an ordnance officer, and either a bonded supply officer or both a quartermaster and commissary officer.[8]

Since the new plan created a need for more officers, Pendleton dutifully submitted a full list of recommendations. Ever the faithful administrator, he never failed to record the progress and ability of his officers. Of Porter he said simply, "Lieutenant-Colonel Alexander, of Georgia, is really entitled to the full rank of colonel at the head of this battalion. We have no more accomplished officer." [9]

The new plan appealed to Lee. On February 15, 1863, he authorized the reorganization with only minor changes in the recommendations concerning officers. He forwarded the plan to Davis on March 2 but did not get authorization for all the promotions until April 14. Two days later a special order confirmed the new arrangement and announced the new promotions.[10]

The artillery had taken a giant stride forward. It had gained a new flexibility that would pay handsome dividends immediately, but more important it had achieved recognition as an independent arm requiring its own officers with specialized training. Alexander's imprint clearly permeated the reorganization plan, and its acceptance meant recognition at last for the battalion system he had long advocated. The era of modern artillery usage had dawned, and no man did more than Alexander in creating the innovations that produced it. As he proudly noted in later years, the Army of Northern Virginia was the first army to implement the battalion system. Eventually the Union artillery, under its guiding genius, Henry J. Hunt, would follow suit, as would most of the armies of Europe.[11]

At the moment Porter's thoughts were anything but cosmic. His long-delayed promotion finally reached him by March 11, soon followed by another disturbing offer. Jackson let it be known that he wanted Alexander as a brigadier to command Lawton's brigade. The rank and prestige flattered Porter, but he had no desire to quit his artillery command. He considered his battalion to be as "independent & as conspicuous as a Division of Infantry." Pendleton also raised immediate objection and wrote Lee a careful letter noting how difficult it would be to replace a man of Porter's talents. Whatever the deciding factor, Porter stayed with his battalion.[12]

The winter routine passed with no easing of Porter's duties. Court-martial duty dragged on until late April, and the gunners continued their depredations unabated. In February Pendleton asked Porter to supervise construction of a large bridge over the North Anna, and in April he was appointed to an ordnance board to report on the condition of Confederate ammunition. But it was not all work. He still found time to hunt and fish, and he had also managed to obtain Frank Huger, an old friend and fellow West Pointer, as his subordinate field officer in the battalion. Most of all he had Bettie and little Bess, and he spent every spare moment with them. "Bessie & I are still together," he wrote his father, "& enjoying each others society as if each day were the last." [13]

Well it might be. The Federal army had roused from its hibernation. Shortly after the Mud March "Fighting Joe" Hooker had replaced Burnside. In short order he reorganized his army, whipped it into superb shape, and looked eagerly for some way to seize the initiative. By contrast Lee had his problems. He had sent Longstreet with two of his divisions down to Suffolk to repel a threatened invasion and incidentally to ease the critical rations problem. Short of men and supplies, uncertain of Hooker's intentions, Lee could only wait upon his adversary's pleasure. It would be a long hot summer.

Hooker was determined to strike Lee a fatal blow and was confident of his ability to do so. His army of nearly 130,000 men stood opposed by only 62,500. His bold and simple plan called for a turning column to cross the Rappahannock and come in on Lee's left flank while a holding force diverted Confederate attention on the right. He knew the Confederate line had to be stretched thin; he hoped to crush it before it could contract.

On April 27 the Fifth, Eleventh, and Twelfth Corps struck out along the Rappahannock. They crossed the river at Kelly's Ford on the 29th and converged the next day on Chancellorsville, where they were joined by the Second Corps minus Gibbon's division. The Third Corps remained in reserve but moved toward United States Ford. Early on the 29th the First and Sixth Corps under Sedgwick crossed the Rappahannock below Fredericksburg and opened their demonstration. By the 30th Hooker had

54,000 men posted on Lee's left flank. All had gone smoothly, and he boasted openly of the coming Confederate disaster.[14]

It would be a pleasant diversion, Porter thought, to spend the night of April 28 with his former comrades on Lee's staff in Fredericksburg. There he was when word arrived next morning that the enemy was throwing a pontoon bridge across the river. While Lee pondered Hooker's intentions Porter telegraphed his winter camp to order all the artillery forward. Huger quickly sent Charley to tell Bettie the news and fetch Porter's two horses, but Bettie refused to surrender the animals unless Porter claimed them in person and gave her a decent farewell. Not until an adjutant convinced her that holding the horses would not bring Porter did she surrender them. That afternoon the battalion started for Fredericksburg.[15]

Lee remained baffled by Hooker's movements until telegrams from Stuart on the afternoon of the 29th disclosed a Federal column crossing at Kelly's Ford. Events and reports of the 30th confirmed his suspicion, and he promptly began pulling his scattered forces together. At 8 A.M. that morning Porter began positioning a battery near the intersection of the Plank and Mine roads. Two hours later Huger reached the intersection with the battalion. A heavy downpour had mired the roads but he had pushed the teams hard all night. Porter hurriedly sent Woolfolk's battery forward and held the other guns in reserve, but no further orders reached him that day.[16]

May Day dawned clear and beautiful. Hooker reconnoitered the Rebel position and ordered his army to advance. He had lost his swift momentum of the past few days, however, and delays beset his every movement. Success depended upon getting his army clear of the entangling Wilderness, but Hooker seemed not to appreciate this decisive fact. He sent most of his troops down the Plank and Turnpike roads while the Fifth Corps minus one division moved via the River Road. If he could skirt the Confederate line before him he would be in excellent position to squeeze Lee's army between his two wings.

But Lee had no intention of standing still. Knowing Hooker's army to be divided, he clearly had to attack one of the wings. Sedgwick's position appeared impregnable; therefore he elected to hold Fredericksburg with a skeleton force and take the rest of his army to strike Hooker's flanking force. It was a desperate chance but one well calculated. If Hooker knew Lee's army to be divided he could overrun Fredericksburg and crush the Confederates piecemeal with his superior force.

But he did not know. Swiftly Jackson brought the bulk of the army to the Tabernacle Church. Richard Anderson had entrenched his division across the Plank Road, directly in front of the Federal advance. Instead of merely waiting for the Federals, however, Jackson prepared to go after them down both roads. Porter sent Jordan's battery to accompany the brigades of Wilcox and Mahone down the Turnpike while he followed Jackson and three brigades on the Plank Road. By 11 A.M. the two armies were swinging down both of the crucial Turnpike arteries toward one another.[17]

The Turnpike column, under McLaws, ran into action first, and by 1 P.M. a hot fight was raging on both roads.[18] Half an hour later, however, Hooker ordered his troops to break contact and withdraw to the ground about Chancellorsville. Having elected to fight a defensive battle, he spent the night throwing up fortifications. Baffled by the sudden retreat and suspicious of a trap, the Confederates pursued slowly and the day closed with only minor skirmishing. During the fight Jackson had supervised Porter's guns, and the battalion got a taste of the general's fierce spirit. One of Woolfolk's sergeants, while taking a gun through the woods, passed a row of abandoned Yankee knapsacks and helped himself to a rubber overcoat. Porter happened to be behind him at the time and chose to overlook the incident. But when Porter reported to Jackson shortly afterward, the hawk-eyed general spotted the bright new coat. "Where did that man get that coat?" he demanded. Sheepishly Porter told him of the knapsacks. "Put him immediately under close arrest for stopping to plunder on the battlefield," Jackson snapped. Porter did so but felt equally guilty. Next day, before an expected fight, he took the responsibility of returning the man to Woolfolk for duty. ("All of this was very unmilitary," Porter mused later, "& I have often wondered . . . what would have happened to me had Jackson lived." [19])

The Confederate position remained desperate. No one knew how long Sedgwick could be stalled by the puny Rebel force at Fredericksburg. The scattered Confederate army still posed an inviting target for an energetic opponent. Long after midnight Lee and Jackson huddled about a small fire deep in conference. Reports filtering in during the moonlit night made it clear that only the left offered any hope of successful attack. On this premise Lee made his most audacious decision: he would hold the present position with a small force while Jackson took most of the army through the Wilderness to fall upon Hooker's right flank. He would split the already divided army again.[20]

Jackson wanted to commence his march at 4 A.M. but delays foiled his good intentions. Beneath a full moon fifteen brigades, all of Jackson's artillery, Porter's battalion, and some ambulances and ammunition wagons formed into a ten-mile column. It was past seven when Jackson exchanged a few last words with Lee near Decker and rode forward. Though not driving his men to the limit of their endurance, Jackson kept them stepping along with few rest periods. The day was hot and the water scarce. Shortcuts were missed, but the column swept on past the Catherine Furnace and up the Brock Road.[21]

The Confederates did not go unnoticed. From Hazel Grove General Birney's scouts spotted the column and turned some artillery on it, and about noon General Sickles threw out some troops to harass the unknown force. Jackson scarcely paused in leaving detachments to cover his rear, however, and the Federals remained baffled over the meaning of the Rebel movement. Hooker knew about the column but incomprehensibly judged it as a general Confederate retreat toward Fredericksburg. Though he did bolster his position somewhat, he lacked sufficient knowledge of his right to deal with it adequately.[22]

On the column trudged in high spirits. As it approached the intersection of the Brock and Plank roads Fitzhugh Lee galloped up breathlessly to tell Jackson of a golden opportunity for attack down the Turnpike. Off Jackson rode to reconnoiter. He saw for himself the unprotected Federal right flank and the men lolling about with stacked arms. Eagerly he ordered the column to march for the Turnpike. Having found his attack he burned with impatience to open it. But the march had taken its toll. It was 4 P.M. when the column began to form battle lines, and the rear units still had to come up; that left little daylight. Porter would have no chance. His guns would be held in reserve until a place could be found for them on the crowded road. Parker and Moody took their batteries along with Fitz Lee's cavalry and Paxton's brigade to guard the Plank Road, which merged with the Turnpike near the Wilderness Church at a point behind the Federal line.[23]

Unopposed and unobserved, the Rebels hurried into position in a small clearing across the Turnpike. The enemy line lay well over a mile away. Shortly before 6 P.M. Jackson unleashed his ragged host. They pressed forward and soon drove an army of terrified wildlife before them. The bewildered menagerie scampered through the startled Union camp. It was their first warning, and it came too late. No embargo on noise now, and the fierce Confederate yell echoed through the patches of woods about Chancellorsville. Desperately the Federals tried to form a line on the rear edge of the open ground, but the Confederates pushed right through them without even pausing to reform their lines. Crutchfield ran up the advance batteries and reaped a fearful harvest with them, but Porter, further back in the column, did not arrive until Jackson's men had swept across the entire two miles of open ground. At that point thick underbrush and oncoming darkness halted the advance, and by dusk the Federals had finally thrown up a line about the Chancellor house.[24]

The Confederates had made stunning gains but the army still lay dangerously divided. Beneath a brilliant full moon Hooker worked feverishly to patch up his lines. He had night, numbers, and the tangled terrain on his side. The element of surprise no longer existed.

Darkness brought disaster for the Confederates. A. P. Hill's men were deploying on the Plank Road to continue the attack. In supporting their movement Crutchfield unwisely brought up three guns and opened on the powerful enemy artillery stronghold at Fairview Cemetery. A blistering counterfire threw Hill's men into confusion and raked Crutchfield's position until he silenced his guns. When the shooting ended Jackson rode out to reconnoiter the front. About 9 P.M. the 18th North Carolina, tense and uneasy, mistook Jackson's party for Union cavalry and fired a nervous volley. Despite pleas to cease fire they unloosed a second volley, and Jackson fell wounded.[25]

A distraught Hill rushed to Jackson's side and then left to push his attack down the Plank Road. Enemy pickets spotted his column and promptly opened two signal guns at it. Immediately the artillery nest at Fairview unleashed a new cannonade, a blind bombardment that cost the Confederates dearly. The wounded Jackson was dumped painfully on the ground when his anxious litter bearer tripped. Hill himself received a painful foot wound and limped reluctantly off the field. His chief of artillery, Crutchfield, also fell with a shattered leg.[26]

At 9:30 P.M. the army stood leaderless. With both Hill and Jackson incapacitated, it lacked an officer who had ever commanded so much as a division. In desperation Jackson dispatched a courier to summon Jeb Stuart as the new commanding officer. The debonair cavalry officer arrived between 10 and 11 P.M. and hurriedly surveyed the chaotic state of affairs. Finding that he had no artillery officer, he sent for Porter to replace Crutchfield. Confident and cheerful, Stuart did much to lift the pall of gloom about the Rebel headquarters. He knew nothing of the situation before him, but obviously the attack had to be pressed, the army reunited, and all necessary arrangements made before dawn. When Porter arrived Stuart ordered him to reconnoiter the entire line and find some place for his guns.[27]

Taking a courier to hold his horse, Porter threaded a delicate path through the underbrush. He covered the entire Confederate line, tried to get views or ideas of the Federal position, and looked for roads by which his guns could be moved. All along the line he could hear enemy axes strengthening the line, and occasionally his movements provoked a false alarm. A few shots or a full volley would be sent his way, and he would dive behind a tree to wait for things to quiet down. It took nearly four hours to survey the entire line, and the results did not unduly excite him.[28]

The whole Federal line bristled with abatis and breastworks, and Porter noted but two openings through which artillery might be advanced to shell the enemy line. The first and most obvious was the Plank Road, which Porter discarded for two reasons: both Federal infantry and artillery could enfilade the road at a range of four hundred yards; and the attacking columns would be utilizing the road, thus leaving room for only a few guns at best. He would post two four-gun batteries on the Plank Road but no more.[29]

The second and more promising route Porter called a "vista," a straight clearing some two hundred yards long and twenty-five yards wide. There would be ample room for the guns to move up, and a small hill at the end of the clearing dominated the open plateau in front of it. The powerful Federal artillery nest at Fairview lay some four hundred yards across this plateau. Since the hill faced Fairview from the south, Confederate guns placed there could enfilade the enemy artillery farther down the Plank Road and could also pour a strong oblique fire on Fairview. Two rough roads branched off from the Plank Road behind the Rebel line and ran into the clearing, which gave Porter's guns easy access to the hill. Possession of the clearing would also dominate the Dowdall Tavern—Catherine Furnace road, a route that could quickly reunite the Confederate army.

This clearing and its hill, known as Hazel Grove, held the key to Confederate success, but at the moment Porter knew neither its name nor all its potential. He did know that Stuart would have to launch his main attack down the Plank Road—there was no room to mass troops elsewhere—and he realized that the vista offered the only chance of delivering effective artillery support for the attack. Unfortunately Federal troops occupied the vista at the moment, but Porter thought they could be dislodged. Drunk with sleep, he could barely keep in his saddle while riding back to get the necessary guns. He had left most of the batteries massed in open fields, the horses still in harness, and the men asleep on the ground. Groggily he hunted up Lindsay Walker, told him what batteries he wanted, and fell into Walker's warm blanket.[30]

Walker returned in ten minutes and Porter awoke at once, feeling wonderfully refreshed. In less than an hour he had his batteries posted with full instructions and loaded guns. Six rifles and two Napoleons went onto the Plank Road with instructions to fire only solid shot lest the fuzes burst prematurely and hit friendly troops. He put three Napoleons into the woods on the first road leading to the Grove, about three hundred yards south of the Plank Road. Captain Page, their officer, was to shell the enemy line when the attack began and then roll down the road to the clearing when the Union line broke. Two more Napoleons went into the woods at the very head of the lane to support the infantry attacking Hazel Grove. Major Willie Pegram would position four Napoleons on the second road, some four hundred yards from the lane, to fire over the trees at enemy smoke and then move to the clearing. The remaining guns, Alexander's, Carter's, Jones's, McIntosh's, and the rest of Walker's battalions, would be held in reserve where they could quickly reach either the Grove or the Plank Road.[31]

As dawn began to break Stuart finished arranging his line, and Porter had readied his guns. Three lines of infantry stood waiting for their orders. On the far right the brigades of Archer and McGowan, trying to straighten their line, confused their orders and opened the attack. A rare punctuality for commencing a dawn attack, it came purely by accident. Unruffled by the chance engagement, Stuart promptly sent the whole line forward and Archer led his brigade towards the Grove. There, to his surprise, he found not stiff opposition but the rearguard of a retreat. During the night Hooker had decided to smooth out his line by pulling Sickles back from the Grove. It was as subtle a blunder as it was fatal: Hooker saw the Grove as a vulnerable salient; he did not see that it protected the entire Federal position.[32]

Had the attack opened on schedule Archer would have found the Grove deserted. As it was he bumped into the rearguard and swiftly captured four guns and a hundred prisoners. Pausing only long enough to reform his line, he plunged into the woods after the enemy, but now the Federal line stiffened behind its breastworks and a fierce battle began. Still no one entirely appreciated the significance of the Grove. A filmy mist partly obscured the high ground, but the morning sun was beginning to penetrate it. Stuart's first line, Hill's troops, broke the first Federal position only to watch the enemy regroup behind an even more powerful set of works. Again Hill's eager veterans attacked but were repulsed in a savage exchange of fire. Both Rebel flanks were soon overlapped, forcing the battered first line to fall back into the entrenchments they had won. The Federal guns on Fairview were hurting Stuart; calmly he called up his second and third lines.[33]

At this critical moment Stuart happened to be near the Grove. Seeing the hill cleared, he ordered it crowned with thirty guns. Porter went one step further and crowded nearly fifty guns onto the hill, forty of them firing constantly while the others replenished their ammunition. Now

Porter fully understood the Grove. From the hill he could scan the entire Chancellorsville plain and could even see the Chancellor house, some two thousand yards distant. Fairview stood some fifteen hundred yards away, and Porter opened a devastating fire on it. The startled Union guns quickly turned their attention to the new Rebel position, and an incoming shell almost ended Porter's career.[34]

The Grove possessed other excellent benefits. The bushy, depressed front of the hill neatly shielded Confederate guns while the Fairview guns were badly exposed. For over an hour the Rebel guns raked Fairview despite the exasperating failure of many of their fuzes to explode. Stuart sent his last two lines against the second Federal line only to be stopped by Union reinforcements. But no longer did the Fairview guns hurt so badly; they had been forced to divert their fire to the Grove in self-defense, and they were getting much the worse of it. Federal infantry along the Plank Road also took a severe pounding from the Grove. The Rebel gunners reveled in the accuracy of their barrage. Young Willie Pegram, his bright eyes dancing behind drab wire spectacles, yelled gleefully to Porter above the din, "A glorious day, Colonel, a glorious day!" [35]

The Wilderness trembled in the fury of the fighting. Then, about 9 A.M., the Fairview guns began to slacken. For once the Federals suffered the rare embarrassment of having exhausted their ammunition. The impotent batteries stood the punishment briefly and then limbered to the rear. About the same time Anderson's division had linked up with Stuart on the right, and the reunited army surged forward in a fresh assault. This time they caught the Federals with their guns departing to form a new line about the Chancellor house.[36]

Stuart's attack broke the Union line and sent it reeling toward the house. Immediately his infantry scrambled into the abandoned works while the artillery limbered up and rattled across the plateau to Fairview. Porter rode with Stuart down the Plank Road, and together they decided to take some guns straight down the road into the open. Porter sent ten guns after Stuart and followed his batteries across the plateau. Some twenty-five guns unlimbered on Fairview and poured a blistering fire into the mass of fugitives, artillery, wagons, and horses swarming about the Chancellor house. The guns run up with Stuart enfiladed the Plank Road all the way down to the river. Unprotected by earthworks, the Federals found themselves raked by fire from every direction. One shell struck a pillar of the house and hit Hooker in the head with a piece of brick, knocking him senseless for several hours. It was, Porter noted, "the part of artillery service that may be denominated 'pie.'" [37]

The new Federal line could not long stand this scorching fire. In short order they bolted to another set of intrenchments toward United States

Ford. Protected by the Fairview guns, cheering Rebel infantry surged into Chancellorsville about 10 A.M. Lee rode up to the burning house to meet Stuart, and the dirty, exhausted veterans greeted him with a burst of cheers. For a few golden moments, in the brilliant sunshine, the war seemed very near its end.[38]

But Hooker's beleaguered host staggered back in some order to its new line and began feverishly to strengthen it. Lee wanted only to strike them again before they could reorganize, but his army was spent. The troops brought up ammunition, rested and watered the horses, and cooked a hasty meal. Porter rejoined his battalion for a huge meal, but he could scarcely remain awake long enough to eat it. There would be no rest for the weary, though, as Lee pressed his men to renew the attack. Before he could issue the orders to advance, an unhappy dispatch arrived: Sedgwick had finally broken through the flimsy Rebel line behind Fredericksburg and was moving down the Plank Road in force.[39]

Once again Lee saw victory snatched from his hands. He could not very well attack Hooker's strong position while Sedgwick menaced his rear, and his army faced grave danger if the Federals could coordinate their movements. But Lee sensed that Hooker's men were demoralized and in no mood to fight; he would hold them at bay while a large force went after Sedgwick. He would have only thirty-five thousand men to contain Hooker's seventy-five thousand, but he correctly assumed that attack was the furthest thing from Hooker's mind. McLaws could take three of his own brigades and one of Anderson's to surprise Sedgwick. Belatedly he decided to send Porter's battalion along to support them. Hastily Porter drove his command toward Salem Church but failed to get there in time to take part in the fight.[40]

For three more days Lee tried to administer a fatal blow to Hooker's army, but the disheartened Federals managed to slip across the river during the night of May 5. The campaign was over. It had been one of mixed superlatives. The Confederates had won a striking victory but had nothing to show for it. Hooker had escaped destruction and the irreplaceable Jackson lay dying. Only the artillery had emerged in a bright light. The new battalion system had performed brilliantly in its first important test, and few reports denied that the gunners at Hazel Grove had turned the tide of battle. For his own part Porter had enhanced his already envious reputation. Throughout the fighting he had handled his guns superbly. On the night of May 4 he shelled a retreating Federal force by using firing directions he had marked out earlier in the day—one of the rare uses of indirect firing during the war.

In the future Alexander's superiors would look to him for even more crucial responsibilities. For the present he quickly sent Bettie a telegram indicating that he had survived the long fight. Three days later he rode to see her in person. She could go on to Milford now, he promised, and stay with Mrs. Woolfolk. She was pregnant again and more loath than ever to let Porter leave her, but at Milford she would have the horses once more under her eye.[41]

Chancellorsville had utterly exhausted and disrupted the army, and Lee well knew it. The campaign had wreaked a frightful loss of key officers. They could not be replaced; the only solution was to reorganize the army to fit the material on hand. Again the Confederates had thwarted a Federal offensive, and again they lacked the resources to pursue their victory immediately. As a result the usual time-out ensued, allowing both sides to heal their wounds and gather their strength. This time it would be a brief respite, for plenty of good campaign weather still remained.

The most crippling loss had been Jackson, and his absence alone required a revision of the army's existing structure. The two corps system had proved unwieldly in requiring each corps commander to handle about thirty thousand men. A Jackson or a Longstreet could manage such a task, but now Jackson was gone and Lee faced an uncomfortable dilemma: he could either retain the existing system and thrust an inexperienced officer into the job of directing so vast a body of troops, or he could break the army into three corps. The latter course would lessen the number of troops in each corps but would require two new corps commanders, and it would also complicate overall coordination of the army by placing an even heavier burden upon Lee's undersized and overworked staff.[1]

Lacking a really good choice, Lee selected the three-corps alternative as the most practicable. The new organization went into effect on May 30. Longstreet continued to command the First Corps with the divisions of Hood, Pickett, and McLaws. Ewell became commander of the Second Corps comprised of Early's, Johnson's, and Rodes's divisions. The newly-created Third Corps, composed of Pender's, Heth's, and Anderson's divisions, was given to A. P. Hill. Naturally enough the reorganization involved numerous changes on the lower levels of command. Lee was not without talented officers, but most of his new appointees lacked experience in commanding the number of troops now entrusted to their direction. That boded ill for the coming campaign.[2]

Reorganization of the infantry meant realignment of the artillery, but this was a welcome event. Pendleton continued to lose status. If he had done nothing wrong during the campaign he certainly had done nothing right: the general reserve had again proved of little use, Pendleton had gotten entangled in a controversy over his handling of the guns atop Maryes Heights, and no report gave him the smallest morsel of credit. A

man of considerable self-pity, Pendleton faltered unless bolstered by frequent commendation. It was not ego but lack of self-confidence that
spurred his appetite for approval. He was an aging man among a host of
brilliant officers, and no one seemed to appreciate him that spring.[3]

The restructuring of the artillery provided a happy solution to most of
the existing problems. Each corps received three regular battalions and two
reserve battalions. That would require fifteen battalions but only fourteen
existed, so a new one was created by drawing upon the batteries of the
general reserve. The new organization, created June 2, assigned four batteries to each divisional battalion but left the reserve battalions uneven
in battery strength. The guns needed for this plan wiped out the general
reserve and therefore left Pendleton without a palpable command. Retaining his ambiguous title of chief of artillery, he could now devote
himself to administrative work and leave the field action to younger and
more alert officers. The new arrangement pleased everyone. It satisfied
most personal desires and it further increased the flexibility of the artillery.
Porter's hand in shaping the plan was apparent, and to him went the
credit for its success.[4]

The reorganization brought in two new artillery chiefs, Lindsay
Walker for the Third Corps, and J. Thompson Brown to replace the
wounded Stapleton Crutchfield. Ironically it was the First Corps, whose
artillery organization had remained intact, that provided the thorniest
problem. Colonel Walton remained chief of artillery, but his case paralleled that of Pendleton. He had long embodied the spirit and tradition of
the distinguished Washington Artillery, but he too was no longer young
or alert to his opportunities in the field. Longstreet wanted Porter for his
artillery chief, but neither he nor Lee wished to slur Walton by promoting
Alexander over his head. Tactfully Longstreet tried to have him assigned
as commander of an infantry brigade but the proud Walton declined the
offer.[5]

As a result the situation remained muddled. More than once Porter
had been recommended for brigadier, but to promote him into Walton's
position without first finding a suitable place for the latter would be a
grievous breach of military etiquette. No one suggested that Walton be
promoted; that would only compound the difficulties. The only solution
lay in finding him a command elsewhere, but that would require some
time. Meanwhile, determined to have Alexander directing his guns but
unwilling to offend Walton, Longstreet would resort to an impromptu
compromise: Walton would retain his title as chief of artillery but Porter
would perform most of the duties.

It proved an unwise arrangement. As the next campaign would painfully reveal, any attempt to assign actual command to Porter could not

help but offend Walton, and his smouldering resentment would make him all the more reluctant to surrender his position. What had begun as a question of physical fitness for field duty soon became a matter of personal pride. The arrangement also left a dangerous anomaly of command within Longstreet's artillery, and it allowed Porter ample room to brood over the unjust thwarting of his ambitions. A more sensitive soul (and they were all too plentiful in the Confederate army) might harbor his resentment for the duration of the war. Porter well understood the reasons for his deferred promotion and was quick to denounce them as unjust, but he had no time for bitterness. "If I had any political friends in Richmond I should fell tempted to try their aid," he wrote his father, "but not having these I will try the next fight instead & then if I dont get it—I shall always think I ought to have." [6]

Most of the battalions dispersed about the countryside in search of good pasture. Porter took his batteries to a rich meadowland below Bowling Green where his horses fattened, his men indulged in the novelty of a little leisure, and he worked to refit his battered command. As always the greatest need was horses, and when the quartermaster procured some 396 animals in late May Porter received 55 of them. Shortly afterward a fresh supply of Napoleons arrived from Richmond and were promptly distributed. By the end of May Porter's battalion had eleven rifles, nine Napoleons, and three 24-pounder howitzers.[7]

While the army recuperated Lee pondered his next move. He had again repulsed a Federal invasion of Virginia, but this had little practical value other than preserving the government. He lacked the resources to follow up his victories with a killing blow, and after each battle the enemy had limped back to the Potomac to lick its wounds and refill its ranks. If Lee stood idle the result would only be another invasion by an even larger force, and he could ill afford a war of attrition. Moreover, Lee's success in the East was not being duplicated in the West. Confederate setbacks there plus the growing efficiency of the naval blockade made it perfectly obvious that stalemate in the East could bear no real fruit. Only an offensive could prove decisive, and Lee renewed his plans for an invasion.

The question was where to strike the blow. The South possessed the interior lines and could shift troops from one theatre to another much faster than the Federals. Should Lee therefore utilize this advantage by temporizing in the East while he sent the bulk of his forces west? Longstreet thought so and strongly urged sending troops to relieve the pressure against Vicksburg. It was an intriguing possibility but Lee demurred. He loathed the thought of dividing his army or abandoning the defense of his beloved Virginia, and he badly wanted another crack at invading Maryland and Pennsylvania. Such a move might draw Union troops away from threatening points along the southern coast, obtain provisions for his hungry army, and perhaps even precipitate the decisive battle of the war. If nothing else it would at least carry the fighting away from war-ravaged northern Virginia. After a day or two of deliberation he declined Longstreet's suggestion and resolved to carry out his original plan.[8] The East it would be.

Rumors of an impending invasion had been floating through camp all spring but no one had any tangible notions on the subject. On June 3 Lee commenced his movement by sending Longstreet's Corps to Culpeper, Porter's battalion and the Washington Artillery following close behind. Reaching Culpeper on the 5th, the two battalions promptly encamped until the 15th. Lee succeeded in keeping his ultimate intentions closely guarded. "No one," Porter noted on the 14th, "appears to have the faintest idea what we are going to do here." Some kind of invasion seemed clearly in the wind. On the 6th Porter helped prepare Rodgers Ford for John B. Hood's division to cross. Hood mentioned the possibility of an invasion and admitted concern about all the chances Lee seemed to be taking. Porter conceded the dangers but refused to worry; all would be secure as long as Lee was in command.[9]

Still the army speculated over Lee's plans. On the 10th Ewell's Corps had left Culpeper for the Valley. Five days later Longstreet marched his command toward Winchester, leaving only Hill in front of Hooker. Now it seemed obvious that Lee was trying to maneuver Hooker out of position, and the reason could only be another invasion. Still Porter remained uncertain, and his reactions were mixed. On one hand he admitted that the bold and hazardous movement could be attempted because "the enemy are so demoralized." On the other: "I only hope for us that we wont cross the Potomac for I dont believe we can ever successfully invade." [10]

The next few days unmasked Lee's intentions. On the 17th Porter's battalion crossed the Shenandoah and reached Millwood the next day. Longstreet's infantry fanned out to protect the line of march at Ashby and Snicker gaps, and Porter hurried forward to help select a line of battle, but the Union troops turned back after reaching Upperville. For six days the battalion lolled in the sun at Millwood and enjoyed the beautiful scenery. Ewell had already gone well into Pennsylvania, and on the 23rd Lee ordered his other two corps to follow. Next day Longstreet took up the march again. At 5 P.M. on the 25th the First Corps reached Williamsport and crossed the Potomac. Next day they reached Hagerstown and pushed on for Greencastle. On the 27th they plodded into Chambersburg and bivouacked a mile beyond the town. Now they were deep within enemy territory but still ignorant of their future dispositions.

The march burdened Porter with no end of problems, the most serious of which concerned a growing tension between his battalion and the Washington Artillery. Normally on a long march it was customary for commands to alternate the lead, since the advance battalion had no dust to swallow and could select the choicest camp site. But Walton, who as ranking officer determined the order of march, had ignored the custom and put his battalion in the lead every day. Porter's officers burned with rage at the affront, and at Millwood demanded that he protest formally to Walton. The hot-tempered Moody offered to challenge one of Walton's captains, but Porter soothed ruffled tempers and persuaded them not to protest. Despite all the dormant difficulties beneath their relationship Porter had always remained on good terms with Walton, and he argued that the colonel had been neglectful rather than spiteful. Let them have the lead, he assured the captains; the Alexander battalion would get in front once the fighting began. With manifest reluctance the officers agreed to drop the issue, but their resentment smouldered for years after the war.[11]

Charley added his share to Porter's troubles by stealing some apple-jack from the medical stores and getting tight. When he had sobered up Porter rewarded him with a good thrashing. And Bettie knew now of the invasion, and in her letters insecurity swept away every pretense of bravery:

> I have since seen by the papers that Longstreet's Corps has passed into Maryland, & am afraid it will be a long time before I hear again from you. I dreamed last night of your coming home & of our being so happy together —but I reckon there is no such good luck in store for us, at present at any rate. If you are only preserved thro' this summer's campaign, I will try & bear your absence without murmuring—but Oh! Ed—I want to see you *so* much that I sometimes think I will go crazy . . . If this war ends in my life time I don't think anything in the world could induce me to leave you for even a day.[12]

Lee was moving blindly. He did not have Stuart, who had departed on a raid of questionable merit, to inform him of the enemy's movements. His plan on the 27th was to move the army toward Harrisburg, but the following night a spy informed him that the Federal army under its new commander, George C. Meade, had crossed the Potomac and was moving northward. With the enemy approaching his rear Lee could not afford to leave his army scattered; he decided to unite his army east of the mountains. He searched his map for a convenient point of concentration and chose the small town of Gettysburg.[13]

The First Corps, after two days of rest, stirred into action on the 30th. Pickett's division remained at Chambersburg as rear guard while the other two divisions marched toward Greenwood with the artillery. The Corps reached Greenwood at 2 P.M. and made camp. That same afternoon Porter rode over to Lee's camp and enjoyed a long visit with his friends on the staff. No one had any premonition of an impending battle; the conversation in fact rang unusually careless and jolly. But next day Longstreet put Hood and McLaws in motion toward Gettysburg. They promptly got ensnarled with Johnson's division coming in off the Shippenburg Road and were badly delayed. McLaws reached Marsh Creek near Gettysburg shortly after dark, but Hood did not get there until midnight.[14]

Benjamin Eshleman, Walton's second in command, had taken active command of the Washington Artillery while Walton acted in his capacity as chief of artillery. He and Porter remained with their battalions in Greenwood all day on the 1st. They knew nothing of the battle raging that day in Gettysburg until shortly after dark, when orders came to march for Gettysburg at 2:30 A.M. The night was hot and dry, the moon bright, and the road fairly clear when the two battalions finished their breakfast and corn coffee and took up the march.[15]

Shortly after 7 A.M. Porter pulled his lead guns into a grassy grove about a mile west of Seminary Ridge to feed and water while Walton rode forward to report to Longstreet. He returned in less than an hour and tersely informed Porter that Longstreet wished him to report in person. Now the anomaly in their relationship bobbed to the surface, and Porter sensed at once what had happened: in this critical hour Longstreet would not defer to Walton's feelings. He wanted Porter to command the guns and left Walton to exercise a vague general supervision. In actuality the Washington Artillery would bivouac in reserve all day and Walton would share their idleness. Porter squirmed uneasily at the dilemma. "I could not but feel sorry for Walton," he admitted later, "who evidently felt himself over slaughed [sic]." Walton dismounted and went to his battalion, and Porter saw him no more that day.[16]

It was not the only anomaly ripening on the field. Between those inseparable commanders, Lee and Longstreet, there had grown a corrosive difference of opinion over what course of action should be followed. Longstreet had acquiesced in Lee's choice of an eastern invasion on the assumption that Lee planned to fight a defensive campaign in which he would force the enemy to attack him in a superior position. That was

Longstreet's kind of battle, and when the two opposing armies accidentally collided on the fields about Gettysburg he assumed Lee would follow this course. To his chagrin he learned on the 1st that Lee had never committed himself to such a tactical policy, and that he was in fact looking for a good attack. In a long conference that afternoon Longstreet renewed his arguments and begged Lee to get between Meade and Washington and force the Federal army out of position. He got nowhere. For a number of reasons Lee chose an immediate battle as the wisest course. Unaware of the depth of Longstreet's feelings on the subject, he did little to soften or explain his decision. The interview plunged Longstreet into gloom. Certain that Lee would now attack on the 2nd, he would use every means to dissuade him from it. That could mean trouble, for if he failed then how willingly or energetically would he carry out the repugnant assault orders given him by Lee? Would his troubled spirit impair his performance? [17]

Into this welter of conflicting emotions Porter rode in cheerful ignorance. He found Longstreet conferring with Lee on Seminary Ridge. "Old Pete" did not appear to be in the best of humor; he informed Porter that an attack would probably be made against the Union left. Porter would take charge of all the corps artillery and reconnoiter the right to find positions for his guns. Pendleton had just returned from surveying the ground; he could show Porter the results of his search. There was a Federal signal tower on Little Round Top, Longstreet warned, and it must not be allowed to see the guns when they moved up. Ten short minutes the conference had lasted. Porter galloped off with Pendleton and Longstreet returned to his earnest discussion with Lee. [18]

The reconnaissance took more time than Alexander hoped, as enemy sharpshooters hampered his movements. A burst of gunfire on the left attracted Pendleton's attention and he rode off to investigate. Shortly before 11 A.M. Porter completed his reconnaissance and went to bring up his guns. Meanwhile Lee, over Longstreet's dogged objections, had finally issued definite orders for an attack upon the Union left. The attack orders had been issued shortly after 9 A.M. but Longstreet wisely decided to wait for Law's brigade of Hood's division to join his column. Law had been left at New Guilford on picket duty and moved forward at 3 A.M. A splendid march in arid heat brought him behind Hood's waiting veterans on the Chambersburg Pike shortly before noon, whereupon Longstreet ordered the column forward. He still lacked Pickett's division, which had not yet caught up with the army. [19]

While Longstreet formed his column Porter mobilized his guns. Placing Huger in command of the battalion, he left the Washington Artillery in reserve and took his own batteries to the right. The guns rumbled down the Chambersburg Road and turned off into the fields until they picked up Marsh Creek, where they followed the wandering stream until it reached a small hill less than two hundred yards south of the Black Horse Tavern. If Porter crossed the hill his column would be spotted by the Federal tower on Little Round Top.[20]

But there was a way. Porter eased his guns further down the bank of Marsh Creek to a point where it meandered sharply, just north of the Curran's farm. Here the battalion cut across the meadow south of the hill and northeast of the Curran's farm until it safely eluded the eyes on Little Round Top. After a few hundred yards the guns cut back to the road and galloped past the Plank farm to the bank of Willoughby Run. Along the run the gunners marched now, and crossed it at a point above the school-house. Then into a shallow gully near the schoolhouse between the run and a wooded area opposite the Emmitsburg Road where Huger would halt and await orders. Alexander rode back to fetch the battalions march-ing with Longstreet's divisions. It was nearing midday.[21]

Unlike Porter's crisp movements, Longstreet's march bogged down in a maze of confusion. When the order to form was given, his two divisions stretched all the way from Herr Ridge to the McPherson house. Kershaw's brigade of McLaws's division was resting behind the ridge only five hun-dred yards up a lane from Black Horse Tavern. Between noon and 1 P.M. Kershaw received his orders and dutifully hiked his men back to the Chambersburg Pike, where they formed the van of McLaws's division. Hood's division, assembling in the area between McPherson and Herr ridges on the road, would follow McLaws.[22]

However opposed to the undertaking, Longstreet determined to keep his movement secret from the Federals. Lee had left Sam Johnston to ac-company the column. Since Johnston had made a thorough reconnais-sance of the right, Longstreet assumed that he would act as guide and hence the General rode in the middle of the column while Johnston rode with McLaws at the head. Unfortunately Johnston did not understand that he was supposed to guide the movement. In fact he had reconnoitered only the position to which the column was moving, not the ground en route. As a result the column plodded along a route unfamiliar to every-one, including the supposed guide.[23]

For a time the column did well. It turned off the road and followed the same route along Marsh Creek taken by Alexander's guns. As the column curled around the creek Porter rode up to detach the two artillery battalions and lead them back down the route he had used with his own battalion. With all of his guns parked and nicely concealed near the schoolhouse, Porter had only to wait for the infantry he thought to be right behind him.[24]

But the infantry was in trouble. Before long the column trudged past Black Horse Tavern—a sight distinctly familiar to Kershaw—and confronted the hill visible from Little Round Top. After halting the column McLaws and Johnston rode ahead to the hill, where they realized the awful truth. In vain the two men scoured the area for a route around the obstacle. When Longstreet rode forward to inquire about the delay McLaws took him to the hill and pointed out the distant Federal tower. By now the last reserve of Longstreet's humor had vanished. McLaws suggested a countermarch and Longstreet agreed. Unhappily Hood's division had not received orders to halt. His lead units piled into McLaws's rear and entangled the ranks. When McLaws insisted upon continuing in the lead, more time was lost while ranks were reformed and McLaws filed past Hood. Again Porter rode up to find out what had happened to the infantry. Before he could persuade anyone to follow his route around the hill the countermarch began and no one on the spot had the authority to stop it. Disgustedly Porter rode back to his guns.[25]

In passive bewilderment the infantry marched obediently back past the Black Horse Tavern, turned up a road near the Forney farm, and struck out across the countryside. To save time Longstreet doubled his rear division on the front, which sent Hood swinging wide to the left of McLaws. The wandering divisions soon passed the point where Kershaw had started out the morning, then turned down an old road until they reached Willoughby Run. Now they plodded down another crude road along the bank.[26]

Here Pendleton, returning from the left, encountered Longstreet's overdue column and offered to help with the artillery. Unaware that the guns had already crossed the run, Pendleton dispatched his staff to hurry them along. His message probably provided Porter with his first information on the whereabouts of the infantry. Riding forward a short distance with the guns, Porter discovered the column waiting impatiently for him.[27]

About 3 P.M. Longstreet sent McLaws into the woods to the right of Anderson's division. Kershaw filed his men down the lane below the schoolhouse and along the stone wall stretching between the Snyder and Flaharty farms. While McLaws jockeyed into position the Confederates made a startling discovery: the Federal line, thought to run down Cemetery Ridge across the round tops, now jutted out in a sharp salient with the point anchored in a peach orchard just across the Emmitsburg Road. Studying the new Union line bristling with well-planted guns, Longstreet found himself confronting a far stronger position than he had expected.[28]

What should be done? Hood thought he found an opening and asked to be allowed to circle behind the Federal left, but Longstreet refused. Lee had ordered an attack across the Emmitsburg Road and Lee would get just that. Hood's men took up position on the extreme right, and Porter sent Henry to post his battalion behind them near the Emmitsburg Road. Cabell's battalion he sent up to the Warfield house, a scant six hundred yards from the peach orchard. His own battalion would remain in reserve for the moment.[29]

The Federals did not stand idle. About 3:30 P.M. Union gunners spotted Hood's movements and opened on his column. Henry replied with two of his batteries, and Cabell joined in support. More Federal guns jumped into the fight, and for half an hour the duel raged. Cabell's exposed position took a beating from the superior Federal metal. He needed support, Porter concluded, and swiftly ordered up Moody, Gilbert, Parker, and Taylor, eighteen guns in all. Hood did not yet have his lines formed; Porter would have to buy time with his cannonade.

By 4 P.M. Hood was ready, and his eager veterans leaped toward the left side of the salient. While his troops grappled fiercely with the Federal Third Corps, Porter's gunners waged their bloodiest fight. With fifty-four guns blazing he hoped to crush enemy resistance quickly, but his expectations got a rude jolt. The Federals not only developed a host of guns but they stuck doggedly at them. Horses and men from Porter's battalion dropped at the fastest rate in its history. Gilbert lost forty men and two guns in half an hour; the other batteries suffered almost as badly. Within forty minutes the battalion suffered losses equal to those of Antietam, and Steve Lee had called that "artillery hell!" [30]

Grimly Porter clung to his position. He galloped back and forth between his own and Cabell's guns scanning the Federal line with his field glass. So exposed was his position that couriers were reluctant to approach him. A piece of shell gashed Alexander's horse in the thigh, and a spent ball ripped through both pants and drawers before bouncing harmlessly off Porter's leg. Moody's big 24-pounder howitzers, planted on a rocky slope, were wearing down even the rugged Tips. When the captain asked for more men to help roll the guns back into position after the recoil, Porter rode to Barksdale's brigade sheltered behind him and asked for help. The Mississippian provided eight volunteers for the heavy guns, but in short order two of them were killed and three fell wounded.[31]

Longstreet had not yet sent McLaws to Hood's aid, and the latter's brigadiers fidgeted impatiently while Hood fought his battle alone. Finally Evander Law, who assumed command when Hood fell wounded, appealed to McLaws for help, whereupon Longstreet gave the word to advance. It was well past 5 P.M. when McLaws hurled his men into the peach orchard *en echelon*. First Kershaw and then Semmes threw their brigades across the field only to falter in confusion before a blistering fire. Then the impetuous Barksdale swept into the Union line and broke it, with Wofford's brigade following up Barksdale's successful stroke.[32]

Meanwhile Porter, feeling his position deteriorate, ordered up his eight reserve guns for a last effort. Major James Dearing then galloped up to tell Porter that his battalion was coming up but had not yet reached the field. As they talked and waited for Jordan and Woolfolk to appear with the remaining guns, McLaws's men came pouring out of the woods. Their advance briefly masked Alexander's guns just as Jordan and Woolfolk arrived. Instantly Porter put Dearing in command of the fresh guns and prepared to charge. Huger got the same order for his guns.[33]

Porter could not know it but he had badly cuffed the enemy artillery, and the Union line was in no condition to withstand another savage charge. Barksdale stunned the line, then Wofford came in on his right to be followed eventually by some of Anderson's brigades on his left, again *en echelon*. A wave of excitement swept through the exhausted gunners. Parker, seeing Wofford's hairless dome glinting in the sun, shouted "Hurrah for you of the bald head!" Other gunners took up the cheer as the salient crumbled and Rebel infantry streamed through the peach orchard.[34]

This was the moment, and another might never come. There was no rarer sight than a formal artillery charge, and Porter vowed to make the most of it. Relentlessly he rode along the line urging his men to hurry their limbering up, telling them that they could "finish the whole war this afternoon." The gunners cheered and strained every nerve to cut dead horses from their traces and wheel the batteries into line. Behind them galloped Dearing with the fresh guns. At last they were formed and ready.[35]

Alexander gave the signal and twenty-four guns lurched forward at breakneck speed toward the peach orchard. For six hundred yards they rattled across the field in perfect order while most of the gunners ran breathlessly alongside. Dearing, seeing a rail fence in his path, barked "Move those rails!" to a group of passing Federal prisoners and the fence disappeared as if by magic. A corporal in Taylor's battery fell with both legs crushed by an enemy shell. When his mates stopped to aid him he cried "You can do me no good, I am killed—follow your pieces." At the peach orchard the guns wheeled magnificently into battery and opened a devastating fire on the confused Federal ranks. On the right Henry moved forward to support Hood's advance and captured three enemy guns.[36]

But the war would not be ended that afternoon. The Union line had not been permanently ruptured, and fleeing remnants formed behind fresh reinforcements to fight again. Another artillery duel ensued as a Federal counterattack drove the Rebels back down Little Round Top. All sense of order had been thrown to the wind now; disjointed units fought separate battles all over the field while Porter's guns rushed back and forth to give support wherever possible. With chaotic fury the battle raged into the settling dusk.

The Union counterattack by Crawford's division drove the Confederates back into the wheat field just north of Devil's Den but there ran into Porter's fire and fell back again. Not until 9 P.M. did the firing slacken and finally die away. A glowing moon lit up the field, and an uneasy silence drifted across the ravaged field. Thick clouds of smoke clogged the hot summer air.[37]

When the fighting had ended Charley wandered onto the field in search of Porter, bringing with him food and a fresh horse to replace the wounded Dixie. For a few short minutes Porter sat down to rest and eat. He watched servants poking through the groaning ruins of the field in search of their masters, living or dead. The moans were chilling and the stench unbearable. Porter left to survey his guns. They had exchanged blows with the superior Union cannon at ranges of five hundred to a thousand yards for nearly four hours, and they looked it. At those scant ranges every gun, rifle or smoothbore, had been deadly, and if Porter complained about the damage to his command so did his Federal counterpart.

Mindful of the work still to be done, he went to find Longstreet, who told him of the day's fruitless struggle on the left. The army had suffered terribly from its new organization, its green commanders, and the tragic difference of opinion between Lee and Longstreet. Disjointed, uncoordinated assaults had brought appalling casualties but no important results. No one, not even Lee, seemed up to his task, though the troops had fought magnificently. But tomorrow was not far off, and something would have to be done. Sick at heart from the day's performance, Longstreet had shaken off his sullen bitterness but not his depression. He told Porter to make preparations for renewing the attack as soon as Pickett's fresh troops arrived.

Innocent of any knowledge about the cleavages in higher circles, Porter wearily readied his command for another fight. The batteries pulled back about half a mile to water and feed the surviving horses. Dead and disabled beasts were cut loose and replaced by wagon teams. Ammunition had to be brought forward to replace the day's huge expenditure and the ground had to be checked to relocate the guns. The gunners tended to their wounded as best they could, but groans drifted on the air throughout the night.[38]

Work proceeded rapidly beneath the brilliant moon, and by 1 A.M. Porter was ready for a short nap. The trampled peach orchard did not appeal to him; he threw together a bed of fence rails. It had been a full day.

Chapter VII

Longstreet still loathed the thought of maintaining the offensive. Reports from his scouts indicated that Round Top could be taken in reverse which, if done, would give the Confederates a chance to slide around Meade's army and force him out of position. This was much more to "Old Pete's" liking. As he commenced to draft orders Lee rode up—the first time he had seen Longstreet since the previous afternoon. Eagerly Longstreet told the General of his plan and proposed to slide the First Corps around the Federal left while Ewell struck the right. He seemed certain that Lee would accept his prognosis; after all, had not events of the previous day confirmed his judgment that the army should fight a defensive battle? [1]

To his bitter astonishment Lee declined the suggestion. He had already decided that the Federal center must be broken. The Confederates had not been defeated on the 2nd; rather they had suffered from lack of coordination. The day's fighting had gained good positions for the artillery, and with proper support the army could carry Cemetery Ridge. The entire First Corps must attempt the attack—about fifteen thousand men. Not enough, Longstreet replied but to no avail. When he insisted that Hood and McLaws could not be withdrawn without undermining the right, Lee substituted all of Heth's and half of Pender's division. Stubbornly Longstreet argued that the assault would cover fourteen hundred yards, too great to be covered by artillery, and that the Federal artillery on Round Top could enfilade the column. Colonel A. L. Long, an artillerist of some distinction, commented that the enemy guns could be silenced, whereupon Longstreet reluctantly dropped the discussion and the necessary orders were drawn up. [2]

Long had made a rash and obviously unsound statement, and the wonder is that neither general took exception to it. Under the best of circumstances Confederate guns could barely match the Federal rate of fire, much less silence their guns. The Union ordnance was far superior, and it possessed much the stronger position. But Lee wanted the attack and was not inclined to challenge Long. Why Longstreet failed to use the colonel's remark as a springboard for his objections remains a mystery. Perhaps he had grown disgusted from the futile wrangling. With misgivings he readied his orders for the coming assault.

At 3 A.M. Alexander learned that Longstreet had ordered all batteries to report to him for assignment. Hastily he scanned his front for good positions and found little to suit him. The smoke and confusion of the previous afternoon had kept him from pinpointing the exact location of the enemy line. It was still dark and the peach orchard offered a wretched choice of ground anyway, since it all sloped toward the Union line. The entire position—guns, horses, limbers, and caissons—would be exposed to enemy fire, and Porter could find no effective way to conceal his guns.[3]

Eshleman brought the Washington Artillery up from reserve, and Porter added it to his line. There was no friction; Eshleman himself was not very popular with his command but he fought well and was not inclined to quibble over protocol. Dearing's guns would soon arrive, and before dawn Porter had drawn his line. Henry left eight guns to guard the extreme right flank and moved the rest of his command near the Emmitsburg Road southeast of the wheat field. Alexander's own battalion stretched across the Emmitsburg Road on the fringe of the peach orchard. On its left was the Washington Artillery with five of Cabell's rifles stationed between their two left companies. The rest of Cabell's command occupied the ground directly opposite the cemetery, leaving a gap between it and the Washington Artillery. Dearing's guns would fill that gap when they appeared.[4]

About 4 A.M. Parker heard some skirmishers in his front and opened on them. As the first rays of dawn broke Eshleman came trotting up to Porter: his position looked exposed. Would Porter have a look at it? Riding over, Porter discovered to his horror that the whole left of his line could be enfiladed by the Federal guns on Cemetery Hill. They would have to be shifted quickly before the enemy noticed the movement and opened on it. It was still too dim to observe movement clearly and Porter pulled the guns back quietly, losing a few men to random Union firing.[5]

As Porter rearranged his guns Lee rode up to inform him that the plan of battle had been changed: the army would strike the Union center instead of the left. That meant Porter would have to shuffle his line again to concentrate his fire upon the attack area. He asked to be shown the point of assault; someone pointed out a clump of trees and referred to it incorrectly as the town cemetery. Lee was tense with expectation. As he rode along the front with Porter he remarked gravely, "Col. Alexander we must drive the enemy from his stronghold to day if you have to charge his position with your artillery."[6]

Now the sun was rising, and movement would be detected and punished by enemy guns. Nevertheless Porter shifted his guns as unobtrusively as possible and drew only a few shells. There would be no response, he ordered sternly; ammunition was running short and must be conserved for the assault. Shortly afterwards Dearing's battalion arrived and went into position. By 10 A.M. he had his guns ready for the attack. Pendleton rode up to inspect the line, complimented Porter on his disposition, and left it intact. Porter wanted more information on the exact point of attack. Pendleton provided it and offered Porter the use of nine 12-pounder howitzers from the Second Corps reserve.[7]

The howitzers lacked sufficient range to be useful in the bombardment, but they could be used to follow the infantry at close range. Porter left them in charge of Major Charles Richardson and took him to a wooded hollow behind the forming infantry columns with orders to remain there until sent for. His preparations done, Porter gave his line a final check. He had utilized every one of the First Corps' eighty-three guns. From Henry's eight guns on the far right, the remaining seventy-five cannon stretched thirteen hundred yards in an irregular line from the wheat field to the edge of Spangler wood.

To the left and rear of these guns Lindsay Walker posted sixty guns along Seminary Ridge and put two fine Whitworth guns on a rise of ground opposite the Hoffman and Forney houses on the Mummasburg Road. Between the Whitworth guns and cannon on Seminary Ridge Colonel Tom Carter of the Second Corps located twenty rifles. Four more rifles of this corps were posted about a mile and a half northeast of Cemetery Hill. But fifty-six guns of the Second Corps stood idle, and only Pendleton could shoulder the blame for that oversight. He alone had toured the entire line and as chief of artillery could adjust it where necessary. The flaw was glaring but he did nothing.

The infantry formed slowly. Shortly after 11 A.M. the Third Corps artillery got provoked into a foolish artillery duel. Porter held his fire and raged inwardly over the waste of ammunition. After about half an hour the uproar subsided and an eerie silence settled over the field. Some infantry began to come up. Wilcox's brigade arrived to support Alexander's guns. As noon approached Porter received his final instructions from Longstreet. The signal to open the cannonade would be the firing of two guns from the Washington Artillery. Porter was to find a position where he could best observe the firing. From there he would notify Pickett of the most favorable time to advance.[8]

Taking one of Pickett's couriers with him, Porter galloped to the extreme left of the line. He found a good observation post on the edge of some woods in front of Pickett's forming columns. There, behind a tree, he settled down with his eyeglass to watch the Union line. General A. R. "Rans" Wright, a Georgian commanding a brigade in Hill's Corps, soon

joined him. As they discussed the impending attack Porter tried to calcu-
late how long he would wait before giving Pickett the word to go. He
figured between twenty and thirty minutes. It should not be sooner because the enemy line must take as much punishment as the guns could
inflict, and it should not be longer because the column had a lot of ground
to cover and he did not want to consume all his ammunition before the
decision had been reached. It seemed a plausible solution, and he gave it
no more thought.[9]

The bombardment would commence at one; it was approaching half
past twelve. Suddenly a courier approached Porter with a new note from
Longstreet:

> Colonel: If the artillery fire does not have the effect to drive off the enemy
> or greatly demoralize him so as to make our efforts pretty certain I would
> prefer that you should not advise Gen. Pickett to make the charge. I shall
> rely a great deal upon your judgment, and shall expect you to let Gen.
> Pickett know when the moment offers.[10]

Porter blinked in astonishment. What was this? Originally Longstreet had
ordered him to decide *when* Pickett should charge; now it seemed as if
he were asking Porter to decide *whether* Pickett should charge.

Lacking any knowledge of the simmering conflict between Longstreet
and Lee, Porter was at a loss to interpret the note. He could not know that
Longstreet was grasping at a last desperate straw. It seemed obvious that
he was trying to avoid the distasteful responsibility of ordering a charge
he strongly disapproved, but it is not obvious, as some of his critics later
charged, that he was deliberately trying to saddle Porter with the whole
responsibility. More likely Longstreet hoped to suggest to Porter that sound
reasons existed for not making the charge, and that if Porter would offer
some encouragement he would call off the attack.[11]

Fate had cruelly thrown the soldier and the man into conflict. Longstreet believed, with considerable justification, that his concept of the situation was sounder than Lee's, but he was trapped by the soldier's worst
dilemma: the necessity of obeying orders and the realization that the orders are bad and possibly fatal. Longstreet wanted no part of what he
thought would be a futile slaughter, but he was too much the soldier to
disobey his superior flagrantly. Enmeshed as he was in this dilemma, he
could only cast about desperately for a way out. The note represented his
last hope.

Porter puzzled in consternation over the note. During his busy morning the thought of failure or hesitation had never occurred to him.
Strong as the enemy position was, his own indomitable confidence and his
abiding faith in Lee's judgment left him with no doubts that the Con-

federates would carry it. "But here was a proposition that *I* should decide the question," he noted later. "Overwhelming reasons against the assault at once seemed to stare me in the face." One central implication glared at him: that there was a possible alternative to the attack. But hadn't Lee issued definite orders for the attack? If so, where did the possibility of an alternative arise, and by what absurd chain of reasoning should such a decision be thrust upon a mere colonel of artillery? He did not distrust Longstreet but rather the situation itself, and in his bewilderment he turned to Wright for advice. The Georgian suggested that he send his own views back to Longstreet, and Porter promptly drafted a hasty note:

> General: I will only be able to judge of the effect of our fire on the enemy by his return fire as his infantry is but little exposed to view, and the smoke will obscure the field. If, as I infer from your note, there is any alternative to this attack it should be carefully considered before opening our fire, for it will take all the Arty ammunition we have to test this one thoroughly & if the result is unfavorable we will have none left for another effort & even if this is entirely successful it can only be so at a very bloody cost.[12]

The note must have greatly saddened Longstreet. Porter left no doubt that he thought any question of an alternative should not be taken lightly. In proper but blunt terms he had suggested that the decision of whether or not to attack should not be his to make, and he emphasized the fact that paucity of ammunition required the decision to be made *before* the guns opened. Again Longstreet's response seems strangely dull and unperceptive. Porter had in fact given him a potential out: the dangerously low supply of ammunition. But somehow the point escaped Longstreet. In his depression he saw in the note only a demand to know whether or not an alternative existed, and if not how Porter should determine when to let Pickett go.

Time was running out on Longstreet. He could not bring himself to disobey Lee overtly; instead he dispatched another note to Porter:

> Colonel: The intention is to advance the Inf if the Arty has the desired effect of driving the enemy off, or having other effect such as to warrant us in making the attack. When that moment arrives advise Gen. P. and of course advance such artillery as you can use in aiding the attack.

The note hinted at an alternative to the attack. It did not say what to do if the artillery did *not* have the desired effect or the moment did *not* arrive. It did imply that the artillery would definitely open. The question left unanswered was, would the infantry have an option of advancing or not once the guns had opened? Glancing at the note, Wright smiled and noted sympathetically, "He has put the responsibility back on you."

Porter nodded. He asked Wright for his frank opinion of the attack, and the general replied candidly:

> The trouble is not in getting there. I went there with my brigade yesterday. There is a place where you can get breath and re-form. The trouble is to stay there after you get there, for the whole yankee army is there in a bunch.

The full implication of Wright's words did not strike Porter, but he got the gist of them. It was a question of support; if the assaulting column was properly supported by the rest of the army, then the attack should succeed. Porter knew nothing of Lee's overall plan but the general had never failed to make the necessary arrangements. At any rate that was his job and not Alexander's, and a rumor floating about camp that morning had Lee ready to put the entire army in to support Pickett.[13]

Inexorably his chain of reasoning tumbled into place. He had already decided that his observation of the cannonade would give him nothing to go on; the question of whether to attack or not had to be decided before the bombardment began. He had tried to avoid responsibility for the decision but in vain. Lee had planned the attack and half the day had been spent preparing for it. He had never doubted Lee's judgment; why should he presume to do so now? The question of support belonged to the General and not to him. He could ill afford to cause a loss of time by his own indecision.[14]

Time was passing and Longstreet required an answer. Hastily Porter rode back to visit Pickett himself. He found the Virginian in good spirits and pleased at his coming opportunity. That settled the issue. On the way back to his observation post Porter realized that "if the artillery opened Pickett must charge." He would send Longstreet a note announcing his intention of putting Pickett in. It could not have been more terse: "General: When our Arty fire is at its best I shall advise Pickett to advance."[15]

They had come full circle now, and Longstreet remained in his original quandary. Shortly before 1 P.M. he reluctantly sent Walton a note to fire the signal guns. Porter meanwhile anxiously sent for his nine reserve howitzers so that he could run them up ahead of the infantry instead of behind them. The courier returned and announced that they were not in the hollow. Impatiently Porter gave him more explicit directions and sent him off again.[16]

It was one o'clock by Porter's watch when the signal guns fired. A single shot shattered the quiet; the friction primer had failed on the second gun. It was replaced and the cannon fired, and on its report the whole Confederate line opened its barrage. To most of those present the sudden harsh intrusion of deafening bombardment upon the still afternoon was a jarring, profane experience. To Porter the uproar broke the silence "almost as suddenly as the full notes of an organ would fill a church." [17]

Soon the Federal guns took up the challenge, and the ground trembled from the awesome duel. Beneath the shrieking shells Porter revised his calculations on when to send Pickett word. Better too soon than too late, he reasoned—twenty minutes at most and fifteen if the situation looked good then. The Confederate gunners had picked their targets and were firing by battery to conserve their limited ammunition. But the Union line looked to Porter like an erupting volcano ablaze from Cemetery Hill to Round Top. Numerous guns now developed that he had not seen. It would be madness to send troops into that holocaust. He would have to wait longer than his fifteen minutes, but how long would the ammunition hold out? His courier returned and insisted that the nine howitzers were gone and no one knew who had taken them.[18]

Every minute seemed an hour as Porter waited for some break in the Federal sheath of fire. Gladly would he have waited another hour for the storm to weaken, but the ammunition supply would not stand it. Once he had dispatched the note to Pickett, it would take probably half an hour for the infantry to come up. That meant Pickett would have to be sent for now. At exactly 1:25 he informed Pickett of the situation:

> General: If you are to advance at all, you must come at once or we will not be able to support you as we ought, but the enemy's fire has not slackened materially and there are still 18 guns firing from the cemetery.

Five minutes later the eighteen guns mysteriously withdrew. Porter stiffened. What could that mean? He waited another five minutes to see if others would take their place, but none did and a gap of some four hundred yards remained in the Union line. That was it. At 1:35 he hurried a second note to Pickett, and there was no mistaking its tone:

> The 18 guns have been driven off. For God's sake come on quick or we cannot support you. Ammunition nearly out.[19]

To reinforce the message Porter also dispatched two men from the nearest gun to deliver it verbally. But ten minutes passed and the infantry did not appear. More bad news arrived: the caissons sent back earlier to replenish their ammunition supply had not returned because they could not find the ordnance trains. Pendleton, fearing the wagons would be hit by the bombardment, had moved them safely out of range. Unfortunately he neglected to tell anyone where he put them.[20]

Pickett took Alexander's note and handed it to Longstreet. Should he advance? "Old Pete" could not utter the words; he dropped his head on his collar. Pickett saluted and said, "I shall lead my men forward, sir." That galvanized Longstreet into action. He rode forward to Porter's post and scanned the enemy line with his glasses. Where was Pickett, Porter asked impatiently. His guns were nearly out of ammunition and there would be no decent support unless the infantry hurried. The words exploded in Longstreet's ear. "Go and stop Pickett where he is," he said sharply, "and replenish your ammunition."[21]

"We can't do that, sir. The train has but little. It would take an hour to distribute it, and meanwhile the enemy would improve the time."

Longstreet did not look down from his field glasses. "I do not want to make this charge," he rasped haltingly. "I do not see how it can succeed. I would not make it now but that Gen. Lee has ordered it and is expecting it."

He paused again. Was he expecting a reply? Did he wish Porter to agree, to offer encouragement, perhaps even to suggest that the attack be halted? If so he waited in vain. Porter said nothing. He suspected that Longstreet wanted encouragement to stop the charge, but

> that very feeling kept me from saying a word. . . . I had almost a morbid fear of personally causing a loss of time.

In every battle Porter had displayed an impressive maturity of judgment. Now the weight of his youth and inexperience pressed onerously upon him. Who was he to offer an opinion unless directly asked? Awkwardly he stood by while Longstreet fought the battle within himself.

Then Pickett's troops began to emerge from the woods and masked Porter's line of guns. The matter had passed out of Longstreet's hands, and pride for his men submerged his misgivings. He walked to a fence and perched on it to watch the attack. Porter did not join him; he was already galloping down the line to find guns with enough ammunition to support the assault. Most of them had only five to fifteen rounds remaining, but they were needed. On the right John Haskell took five guns from Henry's battalion to the left of the peach orchard and Eshleman sent up four from the Washington Artillery. Porter rode back to the center of the line and led Carlton's battery and a few individual guns forward to a slight rise just west of the Emmitsburg Road.[22]

Already the magnificent sea of infantry, stretching as far as the eye could see, had broken into a run toward the Federal line, leaving in its wake a heavy toll of mangled casualties. As the guns wheeled into battery Pickett's troops buckled beneath intolerable pressure. The withdrawn Federal guns had returned and were pouring a murderous fire into the column. Union infantry staggered the Rebel line with one withering volley after another. In vain did the Confederate artillery open once the infantry had passed; the Federals simply concentrated their fire upon the faltering infantry. But the gunners took their lickings too. Hugh Garden tried to move his battery *en echelon* across the plain to support the infantry, but only one section got away and a devastating salvo from Round Top dropped every horse and man. Desperately Garden unhitched fresh horses and called for volunteers. After two dangerous attempts he succeeded in getting his guns and survivors out.[23]

The rest of the line fared no better. On the left Carlton kept his guns working feverishly in the face of a heavy fire until he fell with a shell wound. Near the peach orchard Haskell saw a swarm of Federal infantry deploying on Pickett's right flank. Porter saw them too and both men turned their guns on the column. The Yankee infantry scattered, but their departure unmasked the guns behind them. Horses and men dropped rapidly beneath the scathing fire, and in no time most of Haskell's guns had been knocked out. Only another daring rescue saved the survivors and remaining pieces.[24]

But another Federal column swarmed into Pickett's left, and during the hand-to-hand fighting Porter had to silence his guns. Within twenty minutes the attack stalled and survivors began straggling to the rear. Then Wilcox's brigade moved past Porter's guns. They had been sent to reinforce Pickett and could do nothing now, but no one had authority to recall them. When a galling fire hit the ranks the men halted and returned a few desultory shots before their exasperated commander ordered them back under his own responsibility.[25]

The assault had been shattered, and now waves of survivors fled back past the artillery. Suddenly Lee rode up to join Porter at his forward guns. A short time later Colonel Arthur Fremantle of the Coldstream Guards, a spectator of the charge, also rode forward. When Lee did not bother to introduce the Englishman, Porter suspected it might be "on account of my disreputable pants with my naked knee showing; & I was moreover in my grey shirt sleeves without coat or mark of rank." Still the colonel eagerly plied Porter with questions, and for over an hour Porter patiently answered them. In the back of his mind he wondered why Lee had come forward by himself. He could only have done so by his own design, and Porter reasoned that the general feared an enemy counterattack. For the entire hour Lee exerted the magnetic effect of his personality in rallying the dazed stragglers to reform their ranks and hold together, his unruffled bearing disguising the anxieties that tormented him.[26]

When Lee and Fremantle departed Porter rode down his line. The situation had become critical; with the infantry streaming to the rear only the artillery remained in position to repel an enemy advance, and they had little ammunition. Dearing's batteries and some of Moody's guns had completely emptied their chests but held their position under heavy fire until Dearing reluctantly ordered them off the field. Longstreet promptly rode to the right and ordered those guns still having ammunition to shift into Dearing's vacant position. Cabell had ceased firing while moving to cover the retreat, and Taylor's battery had withdrawn to take up the new position. Eshleman withdrew his forward guns and sent them to the gap, and Porter also dispatched Parker's battery and Moody's remaining guns. Union sharpshooters began to scatter across the field and the guns blasted away at them. One of Parker's guns worked so furiously that water had to be used to cool it.[27]

The Federals did not attempt pursuit but sharpshooting persisted all afternoon. Just before dusk a column of Union skirmishers ventured out. Parker and Thompson Brown threw everything they had at the enemy, Brown firing until he had but two rounds of canister left. Parker recruited drivers from his caissons to man the guns and could find no rifle ammunition. Only some timely aid from a section of the Richmond Howitzers enabled him to hold his position. Darkness brought an end to the firing and the guns, still lacking infantry support, slowly withdrew a few at a time to their original position of the day before. Not until 10 P.M. did the last battery leave the field.[28]

Of the units under Alexander's direction his own battalion had suffered worst, losing 139 men and 116 horses. Woolfolk had been severely wounded in the charge on the 2nd, and the five infantry volunteers killed and wounded that same day increased the toll. Cabell lost 42 men and 80 horses, Henry 27 men, Dearing 17 men and 37 horses, and the Washington Artillery 45 men and 37 horses. Together the First Corps artillery lost 270 men. By contrast the Second Corps artillery had lost 145 men and the Third Corps 164. The army itself had lost roughly one-third of its effective force.[29]

The campaign left a grim imprint on Porter. Never would he forget its strange vagaries and its vast complexities. It also confirmed his earlier fear. "I do not think we can ever successfully invade," he wrote two weeks later, "the ammunition question alone being enough to prevent it. Moreover our army is not large enough to stand the casualties even of a victory in the enemys country." [30]

Shortly after dark on the 3rd Lee withdrew his line to Seminary Ridge, and there he stood defiantly on the defensive all the next day. Having

failed in his consummate effort he had nowhere to go but home, and it was
a long road back to Virginia. The men were exhausted, the animals few
in number and feeble, and the wagons inadequate to handle the wounded.
Meade's army might pursue and try to pin Lee against the Potomac. There
was much to consider and little time to do it.

He elected to divide the army. John Imboden's cavalry had arrived
on the afternoon of the 3rd; his fresh troopers could lead all trains, including the wagons, across the mountains via the Chambersburg Road, ford
the river at Williamsport and go on to Winchester. He could take the
Washington Artillery and a few extra guns to augment his command and
Hampton's cavalry with one battery would protect the rear of his column.

Organization of the train began next morning but went slowly because
the wagons were scattered so widely. The artillery made a hasty inspection
of the reserve trains and found barely enough ammunition for another
fight. By 4 p.m. Imboden's train, fully seventeen miles long, got underway. But early that afternoon the rains began, first a light shower and then
torrential sheets. Meadows became swamps and the roads turned to soggy
quagmires. Harmless creeks leaped from their beds to sweep away fences
and outhouses.[31]

In no time the retreat became a nightmare. Plagued by the rain and
mud, Lee's army slowly groped its way back towards the Potomac. Alexander's battered battalion suffered terribly on the march, the worst handi-
cap being an acute lack of horses. The officers resorted to impressing
animals from neighboring farms, and in desperation Porter dismounted
his lieutenants and put their horses into teams. By July 7 the entire army
had reached Hagerstown, but the constant rains had rendered the Potomac
unfordable. Bridges would have to be built, but meanwhile no food or
ammunition could be obtained from the opposite shore and the Union
army might make an untimely appearance.[32]

For three days the engineers struggled to erect a bridge. On the 10th
Lee heard that the enemy was approaching and threw up a hurried line.
Still in charge of Longstreet's artillery, Porter prepared a superb if hasty
line of his own. In this task he had the help of a new staff member,
Captain Stephen Winthrop. An Englishman, Winthrop cared nothing for
the politics of war. He had come to fight and had heard the Confederates
were the best fighters. Originally he had been assigned to Walton but they
did not get along well and on June 6 he was reassigned to Alexander. His
brusque cheerfulness did much to strengthen the confidence of the gunners, and it came at a sorely needed time. Lee himself seemed strangely
grim and concerned as he toured the First Corps position, and the men
sensed his uneasiness.

Federal troops appeared on the 12th but did little more than fortify their position. On the 13th the bridge was completed but another heavy rain impeded the crossing. At one point during the black night the bridge broke, and two hours were lost repairing it. Alexander's guns took up vigil in nearby pits to protect the engineers while they worked. By 9 A.M. Longstreet's Corps had crossed. The skies cleared on the 14th and the army remained in camp. Next day the First and Third Corps marched to Bunker Hill and rested for five days.

Still they were not completely safe. Lee wanted to bring his army toward Culpeper, but the Federals tried to get to the Blue Ridge passes first. They beat Longstreet to Ashby's Gap and were racing the First Corps to Manassas and Chester Gaps. Meade's route down the eastern slope threatened Lee's vital railway connection to Gordonville and Richmond. With Porter's guns behind him Longstreet occupied the two gaps only minutes before the Federals arrived and withstood minor skirmishing until a pontoon bridge could be thrown across the Shenandoah for his main force to cross.

On the 24th the First Corps finally reached Culpeper, and Lee would require the rest of July to reunite his scattered army along the Rapidan. He did not complete his task until August 4, precisely one month after the army began its retreat from Gettysburg.

Chapter VIII

Once again the discussion was renewed in higher circles. In the East Lee's repulse had produced another stalemate, but in the West Federal troops were driving steadily into the heart of the South. Two months of good campaign weather remained, and Lee could ill afford to sit idle. He must make a decisive move, but where should he attempt it?

Longstreet renewed his argument in favor of using the interior lines to strike a decisive blow in the West. Let Rosecrans be the target, he urged, since his army posed the gravest threat to the Confederacy. Lee could remain on the defensive while Longstreet took his corps to Tennessee to reinforce Braxton Bragg; together they could overwhelm Rosecrans before he could be reinforced. Confident and ambitious, Longstreet pressed his point vigorously, and in the end it prevailed. All would depend upon prompt movement and swift execution of the plan, but at once the Confederates were undone. The question of which troops to send provoked an exasperating correspondence with the War Department before resolving upon Hood's and McLaws's divisions and Micah Jenkins' fine brigade. The reserve artillery would accompany these troops and all would be moved to Chattanooga by rail.[1]

After a week at Culpeper Porter had moved his battalion to Orange Court House where supplies could be brought up by rail. Once more the vital process of recuperation commenced. The army received better rations than it would ever see again. Fresh horses arrived, and even replacements in the form of recruits, conscripts, and returning sick. By early August the battalion lacked only two howitzers of its full armament and only two batteries were short of men. Morale revived quickly as Porter put his men to drilling and experimenting with fuzes and projectiles. He devised a method for raising howitzers on skids, propping the tails in the ground and using them as mortars.[2]

Nor did the pleasant countryside dampen the gunners' spirits. Not very far from Milford, where Bettie was staying, Porter got a furlough for the last six days of August. On September 8 orders reached him to march leisurely for Richmond with both reserve battalions. The possibility of friction with Walton remained, but he was in Richmond with Longstreet and in fact had already applied for some duty at Mobile to be nearer his home. Later that day new orders held the Washington Artillery in camp while Alexander's battalion proceeded. Porter had his own plans; the eventual destination was Petersburg, where the troops would be put aboard the trains for the West. Porter could easily reach Petersburg by rail from Milford; why make the march? He got cheerful permission from Long-street's headquarters, turned the battalion over to Huger for the march, and hurried to Milford to surprise Bettie with another visit. He did not rejoin the battalion until September 14.[3]

In Petersburg confusion reigned supreme. On September 14 orders were issued to ship Alexander, Dearing, and the Washington Artillery to Bragg. Four days later the order was amended to include only Alexander's guns. Then a vexatious argument arose over the question of whether to take the artillery horses or procure other animals in Tennessee, and it took the intervention of Davis to settle the issue. The days ticked off unnoticed. Originally Longstreet had allowed two days travel time for his entire command to reach Chattanooga, but on the very day he began loading his troops Cumberland Gap fell to the Federals. Since Knoxville had already fallen to Burnside a few days earlier, the direct rail line west was cut, and Longstreet would have to use the much longer route via Peters-burg, Wilmington, Augusta, and Atlanta.[4]

The infantry began its departure on the 14th. The artillery entrained last and did not get away until the 17th. The trip was a miracle of im-provisation. The one-rail line handled all the traffic between the eastern and western Confederacy. Equipment was scarce, gauges uneven, and the single track laid mostly with unreliable "stringer" rail. The tedious journey of 843 miles consumed a full week and seven hours.[5]

But the point had been lost. The momentous battle of Chickamauga had been fought on September 20, and only five of Longstreet's brigades arrived in time to take part. Porter's guns did not reach Ringgold Station, twelve miles from Chickamauga, until 2 A.M. on the 25th and found only the residue of battle. Bragg had stumbled into victory, but his failure to pursue Rosecrans had allowed the Federals to withdraw into Chattanooga. Porter's guns arrived just as Bragg was planning to attack the city, and Longstreet ordered him to find positions on Lookout Mountain. By the 29th he had posted thirty rifles and had run thirty howitzers up on skids to fire as mortars on the main sector of the enemy works, but that same night Bragg cancelled the bombardment. No new plan materialized.[6]

Time passed slowly, with Bragg seemingly content to wait for Rose-crans to do something. Porter's batteries remained in position on the moun-tain but did little service. The inactivity quickly soured his temper. He found most of the officers equally disgusted with Bragg's inactivity. Longstreet himself confided that the rout of the enemy at Chickamauga compared favorably with that of First Manassas, yet what had come of it? Nor did the western front please him. The place was choking in dust and stripped of any food but army fare. As for his new associations:

> This army is far inferior to the Army of Va. in organization & equipment & spirit, & I regret very much that I ever left the latter—tho of course I could not help it. We have no horses yet for my Battn & there seems little or no prospect of getting any so that my Battn cant fight very soon.[7]

Only one piece of news brightened the season: on October 4 Woolfolk, still recovering from his wound, telegraphed that Bettie had given birth to twins. She was well and the children received the names Edward Porter Jr. and Lucy Roy. She had been shocked to learn she had produced twins, but she would not complain:

> I have determined to make the best of it & just give myself up entirely to *baby-raising* for I see no other prospect in view for me until after I am forty-five. . . . Having three children makes me feel as if I was getting along in years. How do *you* feel old fellow? [8]

October passed with little more than random dueling and some partridge shooting to interrupt Porter's routine. A proposed movement against Bridgeport on the 10th came to nothing. On the 21st Longstreet formally appointed Porter his acting chief of artillery, but Walton had not yet been found a place and so the position could not be made permanent or a promotion granted. Inert and disgusted, the First Corps began to wonder if it would ever see Virginia again. Meanwhile Ulysses Grant had replaced Rosecrans and was fast turning Chattanooga into a powerful citadel. Clearly he hoped to take the offensive.[9]

Confederate command circles remained divided. Longstreet and Bragg developed a mutual hatred that grew daily, and a visit to the army by Davis only worsened matters when he refused to relieve Bragg despite the unanimous plea of the corps commanders. Internal dissent and external pressures forced Bragg to cast about for a plan. In desperation he decided to send Longstreet to wipe out Burnside's isolated force at Knoxville, hoping that a swift victory would enable Longstreet to return in time to thwart a Federal attack on Bragg's lines.

The plan was unwise. It divided Bragg's already weakened command for a venture that hinged upon too many intangibles. Success depended upon a quick victory and swift return; yet Longstreet was given but fifteen thousand troops to oppose Burnside's twenty-two thousand and in vain did he plead for more. Transportation and supply would be totally uncertain, and the artillery was notoriously deficient in horses, forage, and ammunition. Bragg was dividing his forces but refused to strip them too far; he was in effect going halfway on a long gamble. But the plan did have the conspicuous merit of separating Bragg and Longstreet for awhile, and orders for the expedition were promptly issued.[10]

On November 3 Porter received orders to remove his guns from Lookout Mountain in complete secrecy and take them to Rossville. Immediately he reported a shortage of ammunition; Longstreet asked Bragg for a supply but none arrived. Next day he continued on to Tyner's Station where Leyden's battalion of twelve guns joined him, making a total of thirty-five cannon. From Tyner Longstreet's troops were to entrain for Sweet-water Station, but the train proved unable to handle the huge load. As usual the infantry went first, and the gunners marked time for six days. Unfortunately they had rations for only half that time, and the men, nearly beserk with hunger, scrounged the countryside in illegal foraging raids.[11]

Finally, at noon on November 10, Porter's command embarked. It was a wretched trip. Riding in open cars, the men suffered greatly in the cold night wind. Fuel for the engine was scarce, and every few miles they had to leap from the train to chop fence rails or bail water for the overtaxed engine. The sixty-mile journey consumed twelve hours. Two more days passed in Sweetwater while Porter and the engineers searched for a place to cross the Tennessee River. They selected a point near Loudon mainly because a pontoon bridge was to be delivered there and no wagons were available to carry it elsewhere. Unfortunately Burnside had an outpost directly across the river. Longstreet quietly marched two miles below Loudon and commenced laying the bridge at night under protection of Porter's guns. He then ferried some infantry across the river to surprise the pickets but failed, and the Federals quickly fled to spread news of the crossing.[12] In pondering their next move the two commanding generals came to rather interesting decisions. Burnside decided to withdraw slowly toward Knoxville in hopes of luring Longstreet farther away from Bragg; Longstreet determined to bag Burnside before he could reach his Knoxville fortifications.[13]

There followed a three-day footrace to Knoxville for which Long-street was ill-prepared. He knew nothing of the country, he was short of food and forage, and his animals were so few and feeble that oxen had to be used to pull some wagons. But on his columns marched over winding roads until they reached Lenoir's Station on November 15. There they found Burnside encamped and unaware of their approach. Longstreet ordered an immediate attack, but the short day ended before his flounder-ing troops could get into position on the boggy, unfamiliar ground. He then postponed the attack until dawn only to learn that Burnside had hurriedly departed. That annoyed "Old Pete," and he ordered pursuit down two separate roads that converged at Campbell's Station. Jenkins would take the right road and McLaws the left, with half the artillery accompanying each column.[14]

Burnside elected to make a stand at the station. Jenkins arrived before noon, found the enemy in position, and promptly deployed his troops. He ordered a battery to open on the Federals while he personally took Anderson's brigade to a position behind the Union left. Porter rode up soon after his departure and received the order to advance a battery. That was suicide, he protested; one lone battery would be cut to pieces. He countermanded the order and waited for more guns to come up. Jenkins, wondering why the battery had not opened, returned just in time to encounter Longstreet. Now they decided to delay the assault until McLaws arrived; meanwhile Jenkins could put Law's brigade on Anderson's right. McLaws could then deploy his brigades to overlap the Federal right and Porter's artillery, with two infantry brigades, could hold the center. The guns would shell the Federal position while McLaws struck the Federal right. Then Law and Anderson could fall upon the enemy left. It looked like a good plan.[15]

McLaws appeared about 2 P.M. and immediately took his position. Porter now had seventeen guns up, but when they opened fire the shells nearly all burst prematurely or not at all, and those that did burst tumbled so badly that they did no damage. Then one of his 20-pounder Parrotts burst just beyond its trunnion. The Federals had no such problems. From their line Lieutenant S. N. Benjamin's battery of 20-pounders delivered a blistering fire against the Rebel position. One of his shells passed lengthwise through a horse, took off both arms and a leg of the man holding the animal and ripped up a limber.[16]

The lopsided duel went on for half an hour. Jenkins was suffering from the shelling and wondered why McLaws did not attack. Then he discovered the Federals vacating their line and notified Longstreet. About that time McLaws advanced his troops only to be halted by Longstreet when he learned the Federals had retired. Daylight was fast fleeting; Longstreet ordered both McLaws and Jenkins to carry out their original plan of attack against the new Union position. Tempers grew progressively shorter as McLaws and Jenkins pushed their command forward. The difficult ground disrupted orderly movement. McLaws got into position despite occasional shelling, but Jenkins soon found that Law's position made it impossible for Anderson to take his proper place. In desperation Jenkins ordered Law to attack alone only to learn that Law had obliqued so far to the left that he missed his line of assault.

Darkness intervened to spare the Confederates, and it was a group of distinctly morose generals that put their men into bivouac. That night Burnside withdrew to Knoxville while Longstreet charted his course. He had already soured over the whole venture, and now an acrid feud between Law and Jenkins rose to plague him. Law had deeply resented being passed over in favor of Jenkins for command of Hood's division anyway. Aware of Law's hostility, Jenkins insinuated that the sulking Alabaman had bungled the attack to prevent Jenkins from reaping any credit. The hot-tempered Law naturally denied the charge but tensions only deepened. Alexander, bitter over his faulty ammunition, thought only of relieving Benjamin of his fine guns if Knoxville fell.

Early on November 17 the Confederates reached the outskirts of Knoxville and found themselves opposed only by a brigade of Federal cavalry. Longstreet encamped and spent the day reconnoitering. He discovered that the advanced Federal position rested behind a line of fence rails on a hill. Porter ran two of Taylor's Napoleons up to a house about 250 yards from the Federal line and put Moody's 24-pounders in rear and left of Taylor. Then he called up two of Kershaw's regiments to make the assault.[17]

About 3 P.M. Taylor suddenly rolled out his Napoleons and opened with solid shot. The heavy balls sent rails flying in all directions and threw the Federals into panic. The Confederates advanced smartly until they had come within thirty yards of the enemy line where, misunderstanding their orders, they took cover and opened fire. Winthrop, perched in his high English saddle, his elbows squared and his sabre drawn, spurred his horse forward to rally the troops.[18] Under his orders the men swept forward with a yell and carried the line, though Winthrop himself took a ball in the collarbone. Hurriedly Porter and Huger followed up the skirmishers and helped chase the Federals into Knoxville.

Longstreet had penned the Federals up in their fortifications but he still faced a formidable task. He had to maintain a long, irregular line with considerably fewer troops than the enemy possessed; he was expected to produce a quick victory with this outnumbered force against a well-fortified enemy over ground totally unfamiliar to him; and he lacked even maps of the city. His reconnaissance showed but one weak point in the Federal line: a salient on the northwest corner. The fort itself, originally built by the Confederates during their occupation and later renamed after the slain General W. P. Sanders, was a rectangle about 125 by 95 feet with the side facing Knoxville open. The salient, lying in a valley between two creeks, had been unwisely planted since undulations of the ground would allow large bodies of troops to approach unseen and unexposed to within 150 to 400 yards of the fort.[19]

That was Longstreet's attack, and he consumed two days in preparing his line. Porter deployed his guns to repel any sudden Federal movement and also to enfilade most of the Union line adjacent to Fort Sanders. He converted four howitzers into mortars by running them up on skids. By the 20th Longstreet was ready to attack, but now came the delays. First Jenkins proposed a scheme to break the Federal line and a day was lost rejecting it. Another day passed when McLaws objected to a night attack ordered by Longstreet. Then, on the 22nd, Major John Fairfax of Longstreet's staff reported excitedly that he had found a high hill across the river from which artillery could enfilade most of the Federal line. Longstreet ordered Alexander to take a battery across and dig pits on the hill.[20]

The hill stood some twenty-four hundred yards from the fort, much too far for Porter's inferior ammunition to have any effect, but Longstreet postponed the attack until the battery was located. Taking charge personally, Porter had to cut a road, dig the pits, and haul all of Parker's equipment across the river on a makeshift ferry. The brigades of Law and Robertson also crossed on the 24th, and diligent work readied the gun pits by noon of the 25th. Longstreet then announced his attack for the next day but soon wavered. Uncertain all along of where to attack, he had settled reluctantly upon the salient. With Law and Robertson gone he felt the need for more troops, and a timely telegram announcing the approach of two brigades under Bushrod Johnson induced him to postpone the attack until the 26th.[21]

The delays steadily eroded Porter's patience. He considered the salient to be the best, indeed the only feasible point of attack, and throughout these delays he noted bitterly that the Federals were "working working working day & night" to improve their position. But the worst was yet to come. That same night saw the arrival at camp of General Danville Leadbetter, Bragg's chief engineer. The oldest Confederate engineer, he had been in Knoxville when the Rebels held the city and to Porter's chagrin Longstreet now eagerly sought his counsel. Rumors of a great battle at Chattanooga were already floating through camp but still Longstreet hesitated. Since Johnson had not yet arrived he would postpone the attack so that Leadbetter could reconnoiter.

Next morning Longstreet took Leadbetter, Porter, and other officers for an early reconnaissance ride. Leadbetter at first favored the attack on Fort Sanders, but a later hurried examination convinced him that the attack should be made against Mabry's Hill on the extreme Union right. Porter exploded at the suggestion and argued that Mabry's was the strongest part of the Federal line, but Leadbetter persisted until a bewildered

Longstreet finally agreed to postpone the attack again. He also ordered Parker's guns brought back across the river that night, and that disgruntled officer struggled to collect his command at the bottom of the hill and ferry them across to support the new attack.

Next morning Longstreet, Leadbetter, Porter, and Jenkins rode out to inspect the ground around Mabry. A careful survey convinced everyone that no attack could be made there, whereupon Longstreet reverted to his original plan. McLaws had noted earlier that the ditch surrounding Fort Sanders might be too deep for his men to cross. Porter argued that it could be cleared without difficulty, and on the way back he showed Longstreet a Federal trooper crossing the ditch easily. That satisfied "Old Pete" and he so informed McLaws. The assault would be delivered next day, the 28th, but that night the weather turned cold and stormy and Longstreet deferred the attack until later in the day.[22]

McLaws then worked out a schedule of attack with Porter. First the "mortars" would open and then the batteries, firing slowly for twenty minutes. While the guns found their ranges pickets and sharpshooters would seize the rifle pits before the forts. The main line would form behind the screen of pickets. At the end of twenty minutes Porter would open a rapid fire for ten minutes, during which the main force would press forward. A sound plan they both agreed, and McLaws assembled his officers to explain the details. Then, feeling pressed for time, he suggested to Longstreet that the attack be postponed until dawn. Longstreet agreed, and back across the river went Parker's bewildered gunners.

That evening about sundown Porter left Longstreet's headquarters and rode toward his camp. On the way he met Micah Jenkins, who stopped him and said, "Alexander, I want you to go back with me to Longstreets. McLaws troops are to form the storming column tomorrow, & I don't think McLaws has provided any ladders. I am going to urge Longstreet to order him to do so. . . . I want you to go back with me & add your influence to mine." [23]

Porter slumped wearily in his saddle. The whole fiasco had worn him down. He recognized Jenkins' point as important, but let the infantry officers do it! He was tired, the roads were wretched, and he wanted very badly to reach camp before dark: "Jenkins, your influence will be enough. The matter is very simple & obvious. And if my opinion is of any weight you can tell the general that you met me & discussed it & that I asked you to say that I most heartily concur."

Disappointment clouded Jenkins's face and he rode on his way. Immediately Porter regretted his inertia, but not enough to follow Jenkins. He soon realized the folly of his action, for at 9 P.M. he received notice that the attack plan had been altered. The artillery would not take part;

instead a surprise assault would be made that night. After all his efforts to post the guns he would be denied their use. He blamed not Longstreet but Leadbetter, who was spending the night at headquarters. But his fulminations were in vain; he would remain a dejected spectator of the attack.[24]

At 10 P.M. the Union pickets were easily seized and their pits occupied, but the troops within Sanders now braced for a dawn attack. Just before daylight the signal gun fired and the Confederates rushed forward. The leading units promptly got ensnarled in a network of telegraph wire wound about some stumps. In the confusion the three brigades of Wofford, Humphrey, and Bryan soon intermingled and approached the ditch more as a mob than organized commands. Anderson's brigade soon compounded the confusion by piling into the left of the lead brigades, but the men nevertheless jumped promptly into the ditch.[25]

There they met disaster. At the corner where the troops attempted to cross, the ditch was only four to six feet deep and about twelve feet wide, with a high parapet on the opposite side. Normally it would have been easily crossed, but two conditions rendered it impassable. The berm, a foot long notch used as a foothold, had been entirely cut away, which meant the troops would have to scale the opposite side without any foothold. But rain and ice had glazed the sides of the ditch slick. Men clutched desperately at the wall without making headway, and troops coming in behind them hesitated after seeing their plight. Several officers quickly jumped into the ditch to set an example and were soon followed by their men.

Despite heroic efforts chaos soon ensued. Some officers managed to scale the glassy wall only to be shot down and thrown back into the swarm of men trying to come up behind them. Federals inside the fort pelted the helpless Rebels with axes, sticks, and hand grenades made by lighting artillery shells. Increasing daylight exposed the milling ranks to an enfilade fire from Federal works to the South. For nearly twenty minutes the troops groped for a way to get at the Federals; then, finding none, they reluctantly withdrew. After hearing of the log-jam Longstreet halted the supporting brigades and suspended the attack. Porter opened fire on the fort to cover the retreat.

Jenkins begged permission for another try and Longstreet assented only to change his mind half an hour later when a telegram arrived with the news that Grant had routed Bragg. When the Federals offered a truce Longstreet gratefully accepted; he now had to find a way to rejoin Bragg as soon as possible. He wanted to withdraw that night but further dispatches revealed that Bragg had fallen back to Dalton, thus leaving Longstreet without communications or supplies. After holding a council of his officers he decided to ease the pressure on Bragg by remaining at Knoxville in hopes of enticing Union troops there. This policy bore fruit, for on December 1 a captured letter disclosed three Federal columns bearing down on Knoxville. Now all he had to do was find a way out of the trap.[26]

He chose a route leading toward southwest Virginia because it offered hope of obtaining supplies, provided choice ground for a possible engagement, and afforded a chance to strike the Federal column moving up from Cumberland Gap. The trains departed on December 3 and the rest of the army took up the march the following night. It was five months to the day since the dismal retreat from Gettysburg, but this time the weather was much colder and the country far more barren. And a fierce rain began late on the 4th. Porter would remember that first night as the worst march he ever experienced.

The First Corps paid a terrible price in suffering for their humiliation at Knoxville. The men had only summer garments and outworn shoes or rags to combat the cold, driving rain and frozen, muddy ground. Unground corn comprised the sole available ration, and the horses had no forage. The animals were weak from hunger, inadequate in number, and footsore from lack of shoes. At Knoxville the Confederates had scrounged for horseshoes by fishing dead Union animals out of the river. They could no longer shoot feeble beasts for shoes since all were feeble and badly needed.[27]

To provide shoes drivers gave their footwear to marching gunners and prisoners were "swapped" out of their shoes if the Confederates had anything at all to exchange for them. A frozen trail of blood marked the entire line of retreat. The pelting rains mired the roads and the night was pitch-black. Often guns or wagons bogged down in the muck and blocked the column until extra teams and men could be brought up to move them. The usual order to leave fence rails alone was disregarded, and all through the night the column marched by the light of burning rails.

About noon on December 5 the haggard lines reached Blain's Crossroads. There Porter bought himself a pig and chased off some infantry shooting other animals, but tempers were growing short: one of them fired back at him. Longstreet found no Federals near Cumberland Gap and trudged on. By December 12 the column had reached Bean Station, where Longstreet attempted to surprise a detachment of Federal cavalry and garner some needed supplies. Once more the plan miscarried, though a few captured wagons yielded some supplies. On the 22nd Longstreet crossed the river again and encamped at Morristown. There Porter's cannoneers found some welcome food and rest before pushing on to their permanent winter quarters at Russellville. Porter had lost only four men in the campaign besides Moody, who had fallen seriously ill at Knoxville and had to be left behind when the retreat commenced. But the battalion was in poor condition and would need much work.[28]

The campaign closed on a bitter note. A thoroughly disgruntled Longstreet preferred charges against Generals McLaws, Law, and Robertson and soon found himself snarled in a tedious harangue that would eventually drag in Alexander as well. Virginia and those glorious battlefields of bygone days seemed far away to the survivors of the First Corps in their wretched winter quarters.

A winter spent amidst the dreary confines of Russellville appealed to no one; yet it was by no means certain when if ever the First Corps would return to Virginia. Porter still had not seen his twins, and Bettie had returned to Fairfield. He obtained a sixty-day furlough from Longstreet and endured the long journey to Washington. When he reached Fairfield just after dark the family was still at supper. Suddenly the door opened and heavy footsteps echoed down the hallway. "Lor," Mammy Cynthia exclaimed, "that walks like Mars Porter." [29]

Conscious of his measured time, Porter wanted to devote it entirely to Bettie and the children. Adam chided him on his selfishness and urged him to run down to Savannah for a visit with relatives. Late in January Porter made the trip. During his absence a telegram arrived ordering him back to Russellville as a witness in McLaws' court-martial. Heartbroken and riddled with guilt, Adam promised to keep the telegram from Porter but he could not put down his conscience. Scarcely was Porter back from Savannah when he prepared to leave again, and he bemoaned his departure as "about the hardest farewell we had yet had to take." Nor did it help his disposition to learn upon his return that the trial had been suspended indefinitely.[30]

While the battalion rested and refitted from the rigors of the past campaign Porter pondered his future. The old question of his promotion had flickered anew. On February 8 Joe Johnston, now commanding the Army of Tennessee, asked Davis to make Alexander a brigadier and assign him to command all that army's artillery. Mindful of the dreadful state of his artillery, he argued persuasively that only an officer of Porter's abilities could put it in shape for combat. Bragg seconded the suggestion and Porter learned of it while in Richmond on his way back to Russell-

ville. Asked for his preference, he hedged uneasily and submitted himself
to Providence: he would go wherever the army needed him most. To
Bettie he confided that "I declined making any official choice of position
& leave it entirely with the President—tho of course I would prefer Johnston as being the more prominent & complimentary & as being nearer to
you."[31]

There followed a month of confusing maneuvers that succeeded in
embittering almost everyone concerned. The essential problem continued
to be Walton. Lee clearly wanted Porter's promotion and had recommended it as early as August 20. Longstreet agreed entirely but refused to
make the change until a place could be found for Walton. The position at
Mobile never panned out, and Lee's efforts to create a suitable command
somewhere in the deep South failed. In September he broached the subject to Longstreet again but to no avail. Again Longstreet affirmed his
desire to make Porter his artillery chief but not at the cost of wounding
Walton, whose shortcomings were after all a product of advancing years
and faltering health rather than incompetency. There the issue had rested
when Longstreet departed for Tennessee.[32]

But Lee was unwilling to drop the matter. In November he asked
Pendleton to draw up a list of recommendations for artillery promotions.
In the paper, dated November 20, Pendleton strongly urged that Porter
replace Walton as chief of artillery for Longstreet's Corps, that Huger
replace Porter with Jordan as his subordinate officer, and that some other
post be found for Walton. Still lacking a place for Walton, Lee refused
to be put off any longer. On January 16 he wrote a tactful letter to Longstreet in which he enclosed the proposed promotions. He had not yet sent
in the recommendations, for he did not want Longstreet's gunners to be
overlooked when promotions were approved. But campaign season was
approaching, and Lee wished his organization perfected. Longstreet must,
therefore, settle the promotion question at once.[33]

Carefully Lee noted that Longstreet had made Porter chief of artillery
in October. Was this, he asked, a permanent or temporary assignment? If
temporary, what were Longstreet's thoughts on the matter now? Finally,
Lee mentioned that the enclosed list of promotions assumed that Walton
could be given some other post but, he said with finality, "if he cannot,
he and Major Eshleman will be the field officers of the Washington Artillery." Unable to deter Lee's desires any longer, Longstreet assented to
the list as it stood.

Unaware of this complex negotiating, Porter read the matter in a
different light. He knew only that Lee had persuaded Davis, who had
remained on poor terms with Johnston for nearly three years, to refuse

Johnston's request for Porter's services. Ignorant of Lee's attempts to secure his promotion, Porter poured out his feelings to Bettie:

> The President refused Johnston's application & keeps me with Longstreet though he promises to promote me. It is a little unfair on me as neither Lee or Longstreet ever secured my promotion when I was not wanted elsewhere —Moreover there is no prospect of Longstreets ever rejoining Lee, but every prospect of his soon going to Johnston & then I will be in a subordinate position to the very office for which I am now recommended. However the matter wears its pleasant aspects also, for I will be able now to go on as I have done heretofore with the pleasantest associations that I have ever met in the Army. . . . I always feel better satisfied when my wishes are not consulted or gratified for I then feel sure that the whole matter is *providential* & that my path is chosen for me by a wiser judgment than my own—& could I now by a word of my own change my orders I should not think of doing it.[34]

Not everyone concerned reacted with Porter's temperance. Johnston regarded Davis' refusal of his request as yet another personal slight and promptly renewed his appeal. Bragg, now serving as the president's military advisor, again denied the request and suggested several substitutes; eventually Johnston received none other than Pendleton himself. Nor did Adam appreciate the overlooking of his son. Davis had in fact confided to Sarah Lawton that Porter was "one of a very few whom Gen Lee wd not give to anybody," but Adam gave the whole affair a less charitable interpretation:

> I still have my doubts of his immediate promotion, for he has before this been successively recommended for the same by Lee, Jackson & Longstreet . . . so if Davis was not unwilling to promote him, he has reasons enough for doing so, without waiting for a fourth application from Johnston. As a family we owe Davis *nothing*. He has treated both Lawton & Ed. with great injustice, & Gilmer's promotion was with him, a matter of necessity. . . . No! we owe Mr Davis nothing but to condemn his injustice & his disgusting favoritism to a long list of imbeciles.[35]

Late in February Porter returned to Richmond as a messenger for Longstreet, and there he remained during the final negotiations. By the 29th he knew that he would receive his promotion and become Longstreet's artillery chief. Sarah informed Adam that "I think he is very well satisfied to return to Longstreet tho we all thought he ought to have been sent to Johnston, & that both Johnston & he were unjustly treated in the matter." The promotion dated from February 26, and he left Richmond on March 2 pleased with his fate. There was even some talk of the corps returning to Virginia that spring.[36]

Chapter IX

Privation and discontent beset the Confederates at all levels. Longstreet, still quibbling with his subordinates, remained surly over the military situation and not even a resolution of thanks from Congress could slake his difficulties with the War Department. Between his troops and Johnston's army at Dalton lay two large Federal armies, one at Nashville under Grant, the other at Chattanooga under Thomas. Sherman held Memphis with a third force, and the Rebels desperately needed a plan of operations to avoid strangulation. Late in February Longstreet suggested sending his entire command on muleback into Kentucky to cut the vital Louisville & Nashville Railroad, but within a day he reluctantly acknowledged the logistic impossibility of his scheme. Still he argued in favor of it in modified form.[1]

For Porter the winter proved no less trying. For his new rank he had assembled a modest staff including Joe Haskell as adjutant, Winthrop as inspector, and seventeen-year-old William Mason as aide. Porter declined to add either a quartermaster or surgeon to his staff because they would only add to his already overburdened mess. No problem plagued him more than rations. At first officers had not been given rations but were allowed to buy them at cost from the commissary. Then Congress passed a law giving each officer a ration in kind but taking away his purchasing privilege. Since the officers required servants to cook, care for the horses, and perform other tasks, they had no choice but to divide their meager rations with their servants.[2]

Stripped of their purchasing privilege and faced with extreme food shortages, the officers responded with several devices. They tried to buy food from the countryside, and no sight became more familiar than a host of Negro servants scouring the surrounding houses and farms for food. Some were fortunate enough to receive boxes of victuals from home. Porter resorted inevitably to shooting game to enrich his fare. Sometimes he had to borrow powder and shot, but an arrangement with the Ordnance Department allowed him to receive shot in exchange for stray shot, metal, and shrapnel gathered on the battlefield. The army soon grew accustomed to Porter and his staff scavenging for stray metal, and once his mess turned in seven hundred pounds to exchange for seven bags of shot.[3]

In these dreary surroundings Porter's loneliness grew more acute than ever before. In past years he had staunchly purged his letters to Bettie of laments over his unhappiness; now he was remorseful over their separation:

> Oh darling you grow dearer to me every day of my life & the idea that you cant realize how much I love you even if I could try to tell you afresh every day is always troubling me for I do want you to know how entirely you possess my heart. . . . Oh how I long for the end of the war & then Darling Bessie my own beloved wife I'll never leave you again, & all our past happiness will fade before the bright days we will have together with our children growing up around us. . . .[4]

So acute did the lack of provisions and forage become that on March 24 Longstreet's Corps moved to Bristol. Deep snow and lack of forage killed many horses en route. Porter's command could not even carry its ammunition chests but sent them by rail instead. Conditions at Bristol were no better. The artillery arrived there March 31; two nights later a large crowd of soldiers, including several lieutenants, stormed the commissary storehouse and carried off bacon and flour until the guard fired on them.[5]

Finally, on April 7, the corps was ordered to Gordonsville by rail to join Lee, but inadequate facilities delayed arrival until the 22nd. Hunger still dogged Porter and his staff in Virginia. Showered with invitations to visit neighboring families, he accepted only those promising a good meal. His meat ration for April expired on the 24th, "& this morning we had none & would have been reduced to dry bread not even made up with grease but for a little hominy & irish potato . . . got from a friend in Charlottesville." [6]

Porter's command now numbered some five battalions with ninety-one guns and twenty-five hundred men. He could have put more guns in the field but for his acute shortage of horses. Yet the men seemed in high spirits and excited about the coming campaign. Porter confessed to feeling the same way, and he reported fewer absentees and sick in his ranks than usual. On April 29 Lee honored his restored First Corps with a review, his first since October of 1862. He selected a large open valley near Mechanicsburg, about six or eight miles south of Gordonsville. There two large square gateposts without gate or fence (the war had long since swept them away) marked a country road leading out of some tall oaks behind the meadow to an open knoll.[7]

The two thinned divisions with Porter's old battalion, some twelve thousand men and forty guns, assembled before the knoll. Through the thick posts came Traveller bearing Lee at the head of his staff. Slowly he rode onto the ground. The bugle sounded the signal, guns fired their salute, and Lee reined up before his proud, eager troops. He took off his hat and received in exchange a loud chorus of rebel yells. Now the field dissolved into shouts and cries and the furious waving of flags. It seemed as if Lee determined to look at each man personally as he rode in review. A vast wellspring of sentiment engulfed every man; Porter described it reverently as a "military sacrament."

When Lee had finally traversed the entire rank the proud lines marched smartly by him in review. Frank emotion broke through the leathery faces of the hardest veterans, for no man knew what lay ahead. No man knew that only five days hence lay the opening of the Wilderness campaign.[8]

Ulysses Grant had come east to try his luck against Lee, and he faced no less pressure than any of his predecessors. If he failed the northern cause might suffer a fatal blow, for elections were due that fall and discontent with war remained a key issue. The North still maintained her overwhelming physical supremacy over the South, but her will to continue the fight might collapse should Grant be beaten. Both sides entered the new campaign girded for a final decision: the South was fighting for its life, and the North to sustain her will to win.

Grant would fight a different kind of war. There would be no rest periods, no exchange of prisoners, and no gentlemanly agreements. He would emphasize the destruction of Lee's army rather than the capture of Richmond, and he would hammer away at his goal with the same tenacious ferocity that had characterized his record in the West. Simple and logical in his aims, he would stop at nothing to achieve them. His strategy called for a coordinated offensive by all the Federal armies. Sherman would go after Johnston's army; Banks, upon completing his Red River venture, would move against Mobile and thence toward Sherman; Butler would march on Richmond from south of the James River; Sigel would send two columns to occupy the Valley and destroy the East Tennessee & Virginia Railroad; Grant himself would accompany Meade's army as it went after Lee.[9]

Grant crossed the Rapidan on May 4 and covered twelve miles that day. Lee rose to meet the threat by sending Ewell's Corps up the Turnpike and Hill's Corps up the Plank Road. Since Lee had only about sixty-four thousand men to oppose Grant's one hundred and three thousand he hoped to neutralize the Federal superiority in men and ordnance by rushing to meet Grant before he could get clear of the entangling Wilderness.[10]

When the Federals crossed the Rapidan Porter was still hard at work trying to outfit his command with horses. He needed at least 130 more animals to put 60 guns in the field; as it was he barely managed 50. Orders arrived that day to march for Todd's Tavern, and the bustle of breaking camp went into full blast. The march commenced about 5 P.M. and pushed some thirty-three miles to Craig's meeting house by sundown of the 5th. Here Longstreet paused to rest his men, intending to start for Todd's at 1 A.M. That same day Ewell had stopped Grant's advance in a fierce battle.[11]

Now Lee had his battle where he wanted it. He ordered Longstreet to disregard previous orders and come instead to Parker's store, six miles distant, via the Plank Road. About 12:30 A.M. the column set off under a bright moon, Porter riding in the van with Longstreet although his guns brought up the rear. About 6 A.M. next morning they encountered Rebel troops filing down the road toward them. Joe Haskell cried out to a passing officer, "Major, whats the matter. Are not these men being marched back?" The officer shouted in exasperation, "No God damn em! . . . they are running!" Both Heth's and Wilcox's divisions had been thrown into confusion and retreated, and behind them came a whistling hail of Minié balls. Quickly Longstreet double-timed his lead brigades to the front. Porter ran into Lee and received orders to park his guns near Parker's store until some place could be found for them in the thick underbrush.[12]

By 10 A.M. Porter had his guns corraled. He rejoined Longstreet, who sent him to find Stuart near Brock's Road on the far right and search for possible artillery positions there. In leaving Porter passed Micah Jenkins with his brigade. He shook hands with the handsome South Carolinian and said, "Old man I hope you will win that next grade this morning." Jenkins smiled pleasantly. "Well," he drawled, "we are going to fight for old South Carolina today aren't we boys?" Porter found Stuart and they rode along the picket lines but could find no good openings in the thick, flat country. On the ride back Haskell spotted a surgeon he knew and stopped to talk for a moment. Suddenly he was galloping back down the road after Alexander with shattering news: Jenkins lay dying in the tent and Longstreet had been desperately wounded, both by Confederate troops in another tragic accident.[13]

Richard Anderson assumed command of Longstreet's Corps and Porter stayed close by him for the rest of the day. May 7th passed with only heavy skirmishing. When Grant did not renew the fight Lee became suspicious that he might be trying to slip around the Rebel right. To prevent this Lee ordered Anderson to march for Spotsylvania Court House with his corps at 3 A.M. By a stroke of luck Anderson chose to leave at 11 P.M. instead, and thus unknowingly found himself in a footrace with the Federals.[14]

Anderson got underway promptly. The artillery did not follow the infantry but went instead via the Shady Grove Road. It was a black night and the infantry had twelve miles to cover; by dawn they had reached the Po River and halted for an hour to rest and eat. In short order Haskell's battalion trotted up to join the column. When the troops reached the Block House at 7 A.M. they were met by pleas for help. Confederate cavalry had cleverly delayed the Union advance during the night but at daylight the troopers found themselves pressed from several directions. Rosser was being driven back from the court house, a mile and a half from the Block House, by Federal cavalry. Up the Brock Road about a mile Warren's Fifth Corps was putting heavy pressure on Fitz Lee's brigade.[15]

Despite Anderson's timely arrival the Confederates remained outnumbered and in danger all day. To meet the situation he split Kershaw's lead division, hurrying Humphrey and Kennedy to support Fitz Lee and Bryan and Wofford to relieve Rosser. Porter, who had ridden with Anderson, sent two of Haskell's batteries to support Humphrey and Kennedy and the third to the court house. Lee's men held some rail breastworks on the edge of a dense pine wood. When Warren's cavalry failed to break the line he ordered Robinson's division forward. As the Federal infantry formed, Kershaw's two brigades quietly relieved the troopers and Lee went off to help Rosser. Haskell's two batteries also wheeled into position.[16]

Then Robinson charged. He had expected to find only cavalry and planned to scatter them with the bayonet, but his cocky veterans bounded up to the rails to be repulsed. Robinson himself lost a leg leading the charge. Haskell's guns had reaped a bloody toll, though they suffered badly in the exchange. Field's division now came onto the field to the left of Kershaw and five of Huger's newly-arrived batteries unlimbered near the edge of the woods where Lee's troopers had made their stand. Furiously Porter located his guns. Meanwhile the Federal cavalry at the court house withdrew, freeing Kershaw's two brigades to rejoin their command on the Brock Road.

But it was by no means over. Gradually both armies arrived on the field and extended their lines. Griffin threw his division into two desperate assaults before intrenching on Robinson's right about four hundred yards from the Rebels. Soon Cutler's division took position on Griffin's right and then Crawford extended the line even farther. By noon Warren's Corps was busily digging in. On the Confederate side Haskell's two battered batteries had to be withdrawn during a lull in the firing.

Meade still wanted the Confederate position; he sent Sedgwick's Sixth Corps to reinforce Warren. The weary Federals finally advanced at 5 P.M. and soon overlapped the Rebel right, but darkness prevented any real gains. Crawford's division penetrated the line only to run into

Rodes' division of Ewell's Corps, which was just arriving. Quickly Ewell took up position on the right and continued the fight until after dark. In the battle Porter managed to use every one of his guns against the enemy line.

While searching for positions Porter paused to get a drink from an infantry officer's canteen. Suddenly three shells burst in front of them. Dixie shrieked and went down, nearly pinning Porter beneath her. Winthrop dashed up to extricate him and said the horse had a large hole in her neck. "She's mortally wounded," he shouted. "Shall I put her out of her misery?" Porter said yes and Winthrop drew his revolver. "Hold on Winthrop," he said on second thought. "I guess she will live to carry her own saddle to the wagon train & save our packing it." That saved Dixie's life, for a closer inspection revealed only a flesh wound; in six weeks the horse returned to duty.[17]

Heavy skirmishing and hasty entrenching consumed the 8th as the remainder of both armies filed onto the field. The Confederate line became a strongly-fortified bastion barely visible through the dense underbrush. Anderson's portion ran from the Po River across the Brock Road to a point just west of the Harrison house. Ewell's Corps held the center in a curiously formed salient shaped like a muleshoe; the rear of the salient was occupied by Gordon's division behind another line of fieldworks. To the right of the salient Early, commanding the Third Corps during Hill's illness, stretched his line about a quarter mile beyond the court house. One detached division, Mahone's, remained just below the Block House bridge on Anderson's left.

Porter used the lull to find strong positions for every one of his guns. Four of Cabell's Napoleons anchored the left flank, with the rest of that battalion posted along an interior ridge to cover the line in front of it. Haskell's battalion and Woolfolk's battery also went onto this ridge behind the main line to Cabell's right, while Huger's other five batteries remained on the front line across the Brock Road.

Unfortunately the Second Corps could not follow suit. Two battalions, Page and Braxton, were stationed on Ewell's line within the salient, but dense underbrush prevented the location of any more guns there. A gap in the artillery line extended from Braxton to the ground left of the court house, where some of Hardaway's and Nelson's guns were posted. Cutshaw had to be left in reserve. The Third Corps fared better. Poague's guns went onto the left of Early's line. To Poague's right sat Pegram's guns across the Fredericksburg Road beyond the court house. Cutts held the extreme right from a position just over the road to Massaponax Church.

McIntosh had been left with Mahone and Richardson remained in reserve. Little firing interrupted the gunners as they fortified their positions.[18]

Lee's hidden line and well-placed sharpshooters rendered Federal reconnaissance difficult; as a result the Federals were slow to grasp the basic features of the Rebel line. On May 10 Meade decided to strike the Confederate left again. He ordered an attack for 5 P.M. but Warren, after surveying the ground closely, elected to move at 3:30 P.M. Union artillery shelled the line for most of the day to soften it up. By creeping through some dense thickets Warren's troops managed to get close to the Confederate line unobserved, but Porter had thought of that too. He had arranged his guns to enfilade the thicket, and when he spotted movement there the guns blasted away with canister. The startled Federals emerged in disorder and, unable to reform their ranks in the face of a hot fire, stormed forward in straggled lines. Their repulse was swift and bloody.[19]

At 7 P.M. Hancock sent his corps forward only to meet the same fate. The attack had crumbled on the left but the center was another matter. There General Wright and his engineers had discovered the vulnerable muleshoe salient. Though still lacking full comprehension of the salient, he had found a path through some pine woods that led to within two hundred yards of the breastworks. He decided to attack through this thicket and ordered Colonel Emory Upton, a bright young brigade commander in Russell's division, to lead twelve regiments forward. Mott's brigade would support the assault once it got underway.[20]

Upton formed his command into four lines and issued detailed instructions. Under a covering fire of artillery he led his troops to the edge of the pine woods where, shortly after 6 P.M., the cheering Federals leaped forward. Doles' Georgia brigade and Smith's battery of Hardaway's battalion met the column with a vicious frontal and flank fire, but the Georgians were heavily outnumbered. They shot down the first blue wave and then held their ground with the bayonet. Fierce hand-to-hand fighting ensued as more Federals poured into the Rebel works. Sheer weight of numbers broke Doles' line as the Federals forced their way into the enclosure. When Smith's battery fell into Upton's hands the breach was complete and the Federals had only to wait for Mott to throw in his reinforcements.

But Mott didn't make it. Porter's guns scattered his brigades with a blistering fire, and Gordon's division and Battles' brigade hustled into the salient along with some of Hardaway's and Cutshaw's guns. Upton's isolated command could not long withstand the pressure and grudgingly gave ground in the growing dusk. Smith's cannoneers regained their guns and turned them on the fleeing Federals. As the line settled down the gunners found Hardaway slightly wounded and his major, David Watson, dying.

An uncomfortable night gave way to a rainy day. Amidst sporadic exchanges of fire Lee's and Grant's thoughts took curiously divergent paths. Grant at last realized the full significance of the salient and determined to crush it on the next day. Blaming Mott for Upton's failure, he was convinced that a well-supported assault could break the muleshoe. Hancock and Burnside were ordered to move into position with their corps at 3 P.M.; the assault would commence at 4 A.M. on the 12th.[21]

While the Federals quietly shuffled their troops, Lee found himself in a quandary. He well appreciated the weakness of the salient now, but a flux of incoming intelligence convinced him that the Federals were easing troops around the Confederate right toward Fredericksburg. If Grant was on the move again Lee had no intention of giving him a head start. Perhaps he considered the narrow margin of his successful race for Spotsylvania; whatever the reason he ordered all units to prepare for marching that night.[22]

The order held fateful consequences for the artillery. It specified that all guns on the front line not easily removed at night should be brought out of the line and readied for travel. This implicitly left a crucial choice to the artillery chiefs: if they could arrange their guns to move rapidly on call, they could leave them in position. If not, they must withdraw them to a more accessible location. The distinction proved vital, for of the two men most affected one understood the alternative and the other did not.

Puzzling over the order, Porter caught its broader implications. He did not relish removing his guns while still in the enemy's face, and so he visited every battery to make special preparations. He had the ammunition chests, normally placed in the pits near the guns, remounted on their limbers. He had every road carefully cleared and all equipment wagons and carriages lined up for a quick, noiseless withdrawal. By taking these precautions he felt justified in leaving his guns in place.[23]

Armistead Long, commanding the Second Corps guns within the salient, construed the order differently. He thought of the dark, rainy night ahead and the narrow twisting road over which his guns had to travel. Seeing no alternative, he pulled twenty-two of Page's and Cutshaw's guns out of the salient, leaving only eight of Cutshaw's guns in position. Several of Page's guns were then dispatched to Guiney's Station on escort duty. He also neglected to inform Edward Johnson, who commanded the division within the salient, of his actions.

That afternoon Johnson toured his line and noticed the artillery pulling out. When he learned the reason he demanded their return on the grounds that he could not defend the salient without them. Reports of a Union concentration on his front confirmed his anxieties; he swiftly informed Ewell of the Federal movements and asked that the guns be returned. Ewell issued the necessary orders at once but Long did not receive them until after 3 A.M. While Page spurred his confused gunners back through the darkness Johnson woke up his men for a tense vigil.

Both armies crouched shivering in the early morning dampness. Hancock was ready by 4 A.M. but a thick fog obscured the field. When the fog began to lift about 4:35 A.M. he sent his lines forward. They would have to go twelve hundred yards up a steep hill to the Rebel breastworks, and the last four hundred yards of clearing offered no protection. The Federals surprised and quickly seized the first Confederate picket line but the picket reserve at the Landrum house opened an annoying fire. About halfway up the slope the Federals gave a thundering cheer and broke into a run.[24]

Johnson's veterans braced for the onslaught. At three hundred yards they opened fire on the charging horde but could not slow them. Steuart's brigade, aided by two of Cutshaw's guns, splintered the first Union wave, but another blue wave poured into the other side of the salient held by Jones's undersized brigade. Glancing now to the rear, Johnson saw his wayward artillery galloping up. Quickly he dismounted and hobbled over to rally his troops. Brandishing his large club, he implored the men to hold their ground until the guns could open, but the pressure was too great. Thousands of Federals rushed through the gap once protected by Long's guns and overran the position. Johnson and Steuart with two thousand of their men fell prisoner, and Page had hardly unlimbered when the onrushing Federals swarmed over his guns before he could fire a shot. Only two cannon escaped, leaving twenty on the field including Cutshaw's.

Never had the war witnessed such close and savage fighting. Bodies filled the salient, many of them slain by bayonet, clubbed musket or bare hands, and more than once had to be cleared away. The triumphant Federals pushed onward until they unexpectedly bumped into a second line of works. A splendid delaying action there by Gordon checked the advance until reinforcements could arrive. Brigade after brigade of Confederates leaped into the holocaust—first Gordon, then Daniel, Ramseur, Harris, Mahone, McGowan, and in the afternoon Bratton and Humphreys from the First Corps.[25]

Incredible numbers of men from both armies piled into the narrow opening to rip each other to pieces. Sharpshooters climbed the parapets and poured a murderous fire into the enclosure while others took shelter in small pens. The trenches ran deep with blood and the incessant rain turned the soft ground into a slithery maroon swamp. The ground seethed with dying men trampled by comrades who fought savagely on top of them. There was no place for the wounded to go. As the Federals were finally forced back outside the breastworks they fought furiously through and over the logs.[26]

On the left Porter wheeled his guns about and delivered a blistering fire from the interior ridge. Federal batteries less than four hundred yards away opened a desperate counterfire with uncanny accuracy. Their shells burst just above the Rebel parapets and disabled three of Porter's guns by direct hits in the muzzle. In one case a Union shot went right down the muzzle of one of Huger's guns; he dug it out and fired it right back. A lieutenant in Moody's battery had his head taken off by a shell, Thompson Brown took a ball through both jaws, and Parker's nephew lost an arm. Still Porter's overall losses remained slight (*"miraculously* small" he noted), and his fire was devastating.[27]

To relieve the pressure on the salient caused primarily by Porter's guns, the Federals attacked his front about 8 A.M. Warren protested that the artillery would enfilade him, but when Meade insisted that he "attack at all hazards" he obediently sent his men forward: There would be no salient, for Porter's guns stood waiting for the Federals. Both infantry and artillery held their fire until the enemy approached within one hundred yards. Then a wall of fire staggered the Federals from front and flank, forcing them back with heavy losses. Porter reported that his guns had "butchered the yankees in piles." In the confusion that followed the Federals apparently fought each other for some time while Porter turned his fire back to the salient.[28]

Not until midnight did the grisly slaughter in the salient cease and Ewell's troops limp back to a new line some eight hundred yards to the rear. Both armies were exhausted and confined themselves to skirmishing on the 13th. The rain had filled trenches and made them virtually unliveable, but waiting sharpshooters forced the men to stay huddled in them. Porter continued to strengthen his line, but already Grant was on the move again. For four days the armies side-stepped southward, vying for key positions until the Confederate right rested on the Po River.

Discouraged by the failures of Banks, Butler, and Sigel, Grant grew increasingly convinced that the war would have to be won on his own front. Almost too eagerly he searched for an opening. Growing progressively impatient, he tried an unwise attack on the 18th and walked into an artillery trap. Alexander promptly strengthened that portion of the line but Grant now attempted to lure Lee out of his entrenchments. Lee declined the bait and the side-stepping began anew on the 20th. Two days later the Confederate line overlapped Hanover Junction. Porter deployed his battalions about the Telegraph Road to repel a Union attack. A. P. Hill had returned along with nine thousand reinforcements including Pickett's division. On May 22 Hill launched a furious attack but made little gain.[29]

Seeing no opportunity at Hanover, Grant next headed for the Pamunkey River. While he crossed the river Lee brought his army southward via

Half Sink. On the march Porter noticed that the infantry expected a great battle to be fought within days. By May 28 the two armies confronted one another at Totopotomy. Poised on a ridge between the Chickahominy and Pamunkey rivers, Porter himself expected a major battle on the 30th but got only a light skirmish in which a close childhood friend, Edward Willis, was killed. Curiously both Lee and Grant now decided to march for Cold Harbor. On the night of the 31st Anderson took the First Corps there in an attempt to flank Grant, who was heading for the same place with two corps.[30]

Grant was playing his trump card. One corps, the Sixth, was marching from the extreme Union right, while the Eighteenth Corps came by river from Butler's position at Bermuda Hundred. When Lee discovered that Butler was detaching troops to Grant he promptly wired Richmond for reinforcements from Beauregard, who had bottled Butler up in the Hundred. After an excited correspondence Hoke's division was put in motion, and the First Corps hurried to link up with Hoke before the Eighteenth Corps, under W. F. Smith, could reach the field.[31]

Another crucial race, and again the Confederates won. Fitz Lee's cavalry beat the Federal troopers to Cold Harbor crossroads and held on until Hoke arrived next morning. Anderson arrived soon afterward and quickly attacked the Union cavalry only to be thwarted when an inexperienced regiment broke. The attack ground to a halt as panic seized the entire brigade. Meanwhile the rest of his column waited impatiently. Annoyed by occasional sharpshooting, the idle troops began to scoop out shallow entrenchments with bayonets or tin cups. When Wright's Sixth Corps reached the field at 10 A.M. after an all-night march the Confederates set up a battle line behind their hasty works. Porter scattered his guns along the entire line but fortification with such crude tools went slowly.[32]

Wright's tired and scattered troops were in no condition to strike the exposed Rebels, and misfortune had also befallen Smith. Upon arriving at the White House he had been sent to New Castle instead of Cold Harbor through a blunder by Grant's chief of staff. After discovering the error Smith hurried his men back but did not reach Cold Harbor until 5 P.M. Even then his exhausted troops formed slowly.[33]

Grant desperately wanted to attack before the Confederates could entrench but Wright could not advance until late afternoon. When the Federals did strike they caught the Confederates by surprise. The Rebels dropped their tools and formed a line that soon checked the advance except at one point. The Federals found a fifty-yard gap between Hoke and Kershaw and penetrated deeply before reinforcements pushed them back. Darkness ended the fighting. Thick foliage had kept Porter's guns out of action, and he began searching at once for good positions.

On June 2 Grant determined to try again but delays in bringing up reinforcements and ammunition forced him to postpone the attack, first until 5 P.M. and then to 4:30 the next morning. Despite incessant sharpshooting the Confederates made good use of their time. They improved all fortifications and set up a new horseshoe-shaped line behind the gap. Meanwhile Lee ordered Early, now commanding the Second Corps, to attack Warren. The fighting lasted until nightfall and accomplished little. To divert Federal attention from Early's front Lee ordered Alexander to employ his guns aggressively. Huger promptly ran his battalion out in front of the line to get an enfilade fire and held his position despite intense sharpshooting. Before he pulled back young Clary Woolfolk fell with a fatal shell wound.[34]

The fighting of June 1 convinced Grant that the gap held the key to victory. At 4:30 A.M. Wright, Smith, and Hancock hurled their troops forward, but only minutes earlier the Rebels had slipped quietly back to the horseshoe where they waited eagerly for the Federals. Porter had carefully placed his guns to play freely along the old line, and the charging Federals ran into a devastating fire from the front and both flanks. Again and again they lunged vainly against the wall of fire, and only Barlow's men reached the Confederate line. He captured some prisoners and three or four of Porter's guns before reinforcements threw him back. Elsewhere Huger's guns and the infantry shot the charging columns to pieces with very little loss to themselves. At one point on the line Porter counted ninety-five dead Yankees where not a single Confederate had even been wounded. Kershaw informed Lee that he had repulsed fourteen assaults in about two hours and noted that "if they keep up this game long we will have them."[35]

At 12:30 P.M. Grant called off the debacle, and the armies settled down behind their powerful entrenchments while the generals pondered their next move. Confined to their stationary lines, the men endured a new and miserable mode of living. The incessant sharpshooting made every movement a hazard. The boiling sun forced the Rebel veterans to canopy their trenches with blankets, but they could find no way to ease the lack of water, the swarms of vermin, and the nauseous stench of rotting corpses. No less than other men did Porter complain over his living conditions:

> I have lost some very valuable men & officers by the sharpshooters—among them Capt McCarthy of the 1st Rich. Howitzers. . . . As an illustration of the severity & accuracy of their fire, I counted the other evening on the muzzle of one gun . . . eight dents from minie balls hit that day between 10 A.M. & 6 P.M. & about thirty more on the small portion of the carriage visible to the enemy & six had gone down the bore. . . . We are rather at a loss now to know what Grant means by lying so quiet & I wish he would do

something for I am very tired of stooping & crawling thro the trenches every day in the hot sun, with minie balls shaving the parapet above, & soldiers crowding the ground beneath covered with things that I wont mention but wh. I dread almost as much as a bullet sting.[36]

Grant came to a decision first. Tired of slugging it out without results, he devised a fresh plan that Alexander would later call "the most brilliant stroke in all the federal campaigns." He would cross the James River and approach Richmond from Petersburg. Strategically Petersburg held the key to Richmond; if it fell the Confederate capital could no longer be defended. Moreover, by straddling the James, Grant could alternately threaten Richmond to the north or Petersburg to the south, thus forcing Lee to divide his already meager forces. By possessing the interior line he could eventually extend his lines until the Rebels buckled under the pressure of having to stretch their own lines to meet the threat. And, if Grant could cross the James without Lee knowing it, he might get to Petersburg fast enough to capture the city before Lee could reinforce it.[37]

In his attempt to deceive Lee Grant succeeded entirely. He began his bridging of the James on June 12 and headed for Petersburg. Lee had meanwhile just sent Jubal Early off on his raid down the Valley in hopes of forcing Grant to detach troops to stop him. Hearing on the 13th that Grant had deserted his lines, Lee was at a loss to know where he had gone. On the 14th he suggested to Davis that the Federals might have crossed the James, but lack of reliable information caused him to hesitate. For three agonizing days Lee grappled with the question. Not until the 18th was he convinced that Grant had moved his entire army south of the James, and by that date a dramatic scene was already drawing to a close at Petersburg.[38]

Chapter X

While Lee puzzled over Grant's whereabouts, the Federal army gathered before Petersburg. From June 16 to 18 the Yankees slowly overran section after section of the elaborate Petersburg fortifications. Only a superb defense by Beauregard and some time-consuming blunders by the Federals averted the city's fall. Frantic pleas for reinforcements finally induced Lee to send the First Corps to Petersburg. Even then he did not know that Beauregard was fighting desperately for time. By 5 A.M. on the 16th Anderson had his men on the march, with Porter's artillery close behind. Crossing the James at Drewry's Bluff, the corps entrained to Bermuda Hundred, pushed Benjamin Butler's force back into the bottleneck, and joined Beauregard on the 18th. They arrived just in time to frustrate a quick Union capture of Petersburg.[1]

With Grant's hope of an immediate seizure foiled, the two armies planted themselves behind elaborate defenses to wait. The siege of Petersburg marked a new phase of the war, one in which the value of field fortifications was finally accepted. Every major engagement that year had involved mass assaults against powerful works, and each attack had failed after terrific losses.

Trench warfare brought incessant harassment and demanded infinite patience. The old gentlemanly modes of war, long fading, virtually disappeared as the two armies, facing one another at close range behind powerful works, tried to annoy each other constantly. Unremitting sharpshooting and artillery shelling became the daily routine all along the line. If this meant no more bloody battles it also meant no more peace of mind, for now every ordinary activity had to be restrained by the necessity of precaution. The most accidental or trivial exposure might bring instant death at the hands of a waiting sharpshooter. Grant had already eliminated the interludes between major engagements; now he succeeded in making daily living an insufferable hazard.

Confined to his rapidly proliferating entrenchments and drugged by the fierce heat, Porter wracked his brain for ways to get at the enemy. He persuaded the ordnance department to produce some mortars for him. They could prove effective in stationary warfare, and already the Federals were resorting to them. By late June he managed to put some Coehorn mortars in position. They had to be made of iron, since the Ordnance Department lacked copper, but they did satisfactory service. Unfortunately they could be manufactured only at the rate of three per week. The Ordnance Department hopefully experimented with wooden mortars— six or eight of them could be turned out a day—but they tended to burst in short order.[2]

Porter freely admitted his position to be precarious. His men had inherited the worst portion of the line. It required much work to complete and heavy sharpshooting forced them to do everything at night. The addition of mortar fire to daily living forced every man to construct a small "bomb-proof" in the side of the trenches for sleeping at night and ducking into during daytime bombardments. Before long the trenches became honeycombed with little caves and cellars. Though Porter had very few guns posted on the line he devoted no little time to scouting new positions. To augment his armaments he sent to Richmond for some hand grenades. These were to be thin iron shells about the size of a goose egg, filled with powder with a sensitive paper percussion fuze in front and a two-foot cord in back by which the grenade could be thrown sixty yards or more. In his spare time he continued to gather Minié balls and stray shrapnel to exchange for shot. The rate had gone down to four pounds for one, and he found a rich harvest of balls in the yards behind the Rebel breastworks where, he noted, "they are deposited like dew every night."[3]

The Federals worked no less diligently to improve their works, and Porter noted that "every morning there appeared fresh piles of red dirt." Grant had in effect constructed two sets of fortifications. In front an offensive system of trenches and redans zig-zagged ever closer to the Confederate works. In the rear a defensive system of enclosed forts connected by good parapets enabled a small force to hold the position while the remainder of the army marshalled at some strategic point for an attack. Well might the imprint of these works seem familiar to Porter; they had been supervised by his old friend Jim Duane, now Meade's chief engineer.

The offensive works seemed especially intent upon approaching a weak point in the Confederate line known as Elliott's salient. That the Federals harbored some plan for striking the salient seemed evident from the intense sharpshooting there—so fierce that it prevented the Confederates from getting a good look at the advancing enemy line. Colonel Walter Stevens, the engineer in charge of the Richmond lines, realized the futility of trying to steal a look over the parapet or even through a loophole. He resorted to the clever device of keeping his head below the top of the parapet and cautiously raising a mirror tilted so that it reflected the enemy line down to his eye. In one minute a bullet smashed the glass and behind it came the derisive taunt: "Set it up again, Johnny!"[4]

Convinced that the Federals would launch an attack at the salient,

Porter resolved to turn the position into a death trap. In so doing he devised one of his most ingenious positions of the war. The Jerusalem Plank Road ran some eight hundred yards behind the salient. Depressed about five feet below ground level, it offered a fine place for an ambuscade and on it Porter posted fourteen of Haskell's guns. He put another four cannon in a small hollow to the right and two more near the path leading out from the road. These last guns could enfilade the Confederate trenches should the enemy get into them and fire into the flank of any force moving out of them.[5]

Then he found the choicest position of all:

> . . . a beautiful place for a whole battery to give the same sort of flanking fire which had been so effective at Cold Harbor—a random fire which did not directly see the enemy (& consequently he could not reply to it) but every shot from which would come bouncing & skipping along exactly parallel to the front of his brigades, killing bunches of them when they hit & demoralizing the troops . . . even when they went clear. . . . It could see little or nothing in front, little knolls in front on each side of the winding creek cutting off the direct view down the course of the stream, but every shot fired over them would rake the dead space in front of Elliotts salient.

The main problem would be convincing the gunners to ignore what they could actually see to their right and to fire exclusively at the blind front of the salient. Putting Davidson's battery in the position, Porter ordered him to build high, narrow enclosures about the guns so that the men could see only to the front. When the next day Porter inspected the enclosures and found them looking too far to the right, he tore them down in a rage and threatened to arrest Davidson unless he built them exactly as specified.

At any sudden battle firing, Porter ordered sternly, Davidson would fire every kind of ammunition he had as rapidly as possible straight down the valley "& let them go where they would." As a final support, he located another battery within a small salient just to the right of Elliott. These guns also built enclosures shaped to give them a raking fire along the right flank of Elliott while protecting the cannon from all direct fire. They belonged to Hampton Gibbes' battalion and could be relied upon. Now Porter felt ready for Grant's entire army; the only question was when they would come.

During that sultry June fresh administrative duties intruded upon construction of the line. After conferring with Alexander, Long, and Walker, Pendleton submitted to Davis a new and far-reaching reorganization of the artillery. The plan, dated June 8, attempted to complete modernization of the long arm. In addition to providing a standard of organization it proposed two crucial changes designed to strengthen leadership. The first made the number of guns in a corps the determining factor in fixing its quota of artillery field officers—a vast improvement over the existing practice of allotting the same number of officers to each corps regardless of the strength or condition of its armament. The second removed the harmful restriction that prevented artillery officers from rising above the grade of brigadier.[6]

The plan received approval from both Lee and Bragg. Both felt that the artillery had become an independent arm deserving recognition as such, and Lee pointed out that a brigadier commanding all the artillery of an army corps had a far more difficult job than a brigadier commanding a brigade of infantry. It was a splendid plan, and its acceptance represented the final step in the evolution of the artillery during the war. Unfortunately it came along too late, for the Confederacy by June of 1864 lacked the time and means of putting it into effect.

By the end of June Federal trenches had approached to within a hundred yards of Elliott. Lee ordered Alexander to examine the position carefully. After fixing himself an observation post some five hundred yards behind the salient, Porter slowly studied the ground. Suddenly on the 30th an idea struck him: "they were coming . . . but they were coming underground. They were mining us!" That would explain their entire pattern of behavior, and he resolved to inform Lee at once. The previous day he had joined DuBose's nearby Georgia brigade in the trenches to take a shot or two at the distant Federals. While there he had hit a man in the leg from about eight hundred yards, amidst great cheers from the Georgians. Coming back to the path now, he determined to save time by cutting across this same ground. Sharpshooting had mostly died away there, and he did not think it systematic anyway. Walking rather nonchalantly down a path facing the enemy line, Porter suddenly heard the pop of a distant musket. The ball hit the hard ground in front of him and glanced up into his arm, lodging just under the bone of the armpit. "It benumbed the arm & staggered me a little," he informed Bettie the next day with grim satisfaction, "but I walked straight on to keep the rascal from knowing that he hit me." [7]

At a nearby gun pit Porter summoned a cannoneer to accompany him lest he faint before reaching his horse. The wound bled freely but he managed to ride to his camp, where his staff put him beneath a pine tree on some clean blankets. More than his wound plagued him. He had been seized with alternating chills and fever for over a week, his eyes were pumpkin yellow from jaundice, and his gums bled from the onset of scurvy. Dorsey Cullen, chief surgeon of the First Corps, arrived to examine the wound. The ball had narrowly missed both artery and joint, he announced, and soon removed it after dousing Porter with chloroform. Though still weak and groggy, Porter was in good spirits. The wound would mean a furlough, and rapidly pain gave way to bliss.[8]

He obtained permission to leave the very next day, but the question of a Federal tunnel still troubled him. Before departing he dropped by Lee's headquarters. The general was absent but Colonel Venable of his staff was there conversing with a correspondent from the London *Times*. When Porter informed Venable of his suspicions the reporter asked how long the tunnel would have to be to reach the salient. Porter estimated five hundred feet, whereupon the correspondent assured him that the longest military tunnel ever built was a four-hundred-foot gallery constructed during the siege of Delhi. It was impossible, he added, to ventilate a tunnel of any greater length.

Military precedent could be ignored, Porter replied tersely. The Federal army had Pennsylvania coal miners capable of ventilating tunnels of indefinite length. Alexander asked Venable to give Lee the message and left to catch his train. Lee took the warning seriously and ordered countermines, but they were begun too late and dug too far back. Porter never learned who had charge of the digging, but it went slowly and aimlessly. On July 30 the Federals mined Elliott and followed with a badly-bungled attack. In repulsing the assault Porter's meticulously placed batteries, under Huger's command, did splendid service, as did his Coehorn mortars. John Haskell had in fact run one of the mortars right up near the lip of the crater and lobbed shells into it.[9]

Only Davidson, whose battery he had placed with such care and pride, marred his joy. The old captain was not seasoned to combat; a fierce Yankee counterfire had unnerved him and he fired only about twenty rounds.

A restful month at Fairfield gradually restored Porter, though the wound proved troublesome and he was forced to apply for a twenty-day extension of his leave. It was not so much the wound as his general condition: he was badly run down. An improved diet soon banished the scurvy and the jaundice slowly disappeared, but he could not shake the chills and fever. By August 14 he was back in Petersburg and ready for duty. Except for the giant crater he found the situation little changed, and to prevent another such attack he helped strengthen the line behind the crater. It proved unnecessary. The crater fiasco had confirmed Grant's conviction that direct assault was not the solution. He resorted instead to his original two-point program. First, he would extend his lines and force Lee to follow suit. Second, he would keep Lee's army committed to the Petersburg line by constant skirmishing and occasional minor assaults to prevent him from detaching reinforcements to other Confederate commands.[10]

Grant's strategy was sound. It forced Lee to weaken his already thin lines, and while he might hold Grant in check the other Federal armies would not stand still. Sherman was pushing relentlessly into the heart of the South, and Sheridan would soon chase Early out of the valley. It seemed only a matter of time before the Confederacy collapsed from this combination of pressures. For the remainder of the year Grant struck first at one flank and then the other. Slowly the Confederates extended their lines and tried desperately to bolster them. Already in August Federal shells were falling in Richmond itself, and the Confederates raged at their helplessness to prevent it.

Doggedly Grant struck at the vital railroad arteries feeding the capital. When he seized the Petersburg & Weldon Road near Globe Tavern below Petersburg Lee tried desperately to recover it. On August 19 and 21 he launched furious assaults that achieved local successes but failed to dislodge the Yankees. Porter accompanied Lee with a reserve battalion but did not see action. It was just as well, for his chills beset him; on that torrid day he burned in the heat and shook violently in the shade with a cold ague. Back he went to strengthen the main line near the crater while both sides continued to extend their flanks.[11]

On September 29 Grant delivered a surprise attack upon Battery Harrison near Chaffin's Bluff. He took and held the position and quickly threw up a line extending back to the James River near Dutch Gap. The fort itself was of little consequence but it gave Grant a crucial foothold in the Richmond lines. Unsettled by the threat, Lee hastily moved his headquarters to the vicinity and laid plans to recapture the fort. Anderson brought his headquarters over as well, and Porter with him. Lee decided to strike the fort across the Darbytown Road and ordered Porter to send two battalions there at once. On the afternoon of October 6 he issued final instructions. To reach the Darbytown Road the troops would have to take a crossroad; therefore Lee would meet Porter and the other officers there at 2 A.M.[12]

The attack started according to schedule. Porter drew up his guns to soften up the Federal position. Over a stretch of open ground he used the only chance he ever had for a "Fire advancing by half battery." Half a battery stood to fire while the other half advanced a short distance, unlimbered and opened. On its first shot the first half quickly limbered, galloped past its mates and took a more advanced position to repeat the maneuver. Everything worked to perfection as Porter advanced his long line of batteries over half a mile under Lee's approving eye. His superior number of guns largely silenced the Union fire, and when a Federal caisson blew up just as the infantry rose to charge, the veterans gave a loud cheer and pressed forward. But something went wrong: Hoke's men mysteriously failed to charge on schedule. The assault quickly aborted and all hope of recovering Harrison faded.

The defeat upset the normally imperturbable Lee, and Porter remarked that he "was more worried at this failure than I have ever seen him under similar circumstances." Nor had he ever seen the general as cross as he had been that morning. But in no time Lee had recovered and seemed unusually gracious in his demeanor to his officers. After the Darbytown attack the Confederate line lapsed back into its helpless inertia to wait.[13]

With the enemy having breached the exterior Richmond line Lee reluctantly extended his position farther to the left. Ultimately it ran from the Chickahominy on the left to a point below Petersburg, a distance of about thirty-seven miles by the shortest route. As autumn waned Porter found the going progressively tougher. He now commanded all the artillery from the Chickahominy to the Appomattox River—a twenty-four mile line with ninety field pieces, fifty heavy guns, and the mortars. Setting up permanent camp on the left, he toured his lines daily to check positions and give instructions. To one inexperienced gunner he gave a solemn order to shoot at everything "a yard high a foot wide or a year old."[14]

The wound had healed but often nagged Porter with a rheumatic ache. The fever and chills tandem continued to come and go, forcing him to draw a steady supply of pills from the dwindling Confederate medical rations. A siege of dysentery led him to devise his own cure—a compound of chloroform, brandy, peppermint, and laudanum. Rations too were dwindling but had not yet become critical; Porter could still buy a few potatoes and tomatoes in the local market. His standing breakfast became bacon and hominy while dinner usually consisted of "Hopping John"—okra soup or rice peas boiled with bacon. More important, a wealthy local resident named Cameron constantly showered the officers and men with gifts of food and drink. His larder seemed endlessly stocked with delicacies despite the privations of war (he operated a successful blockade runner), and on one occasion he presented Porter with seven bottles of fine wines and some English pickles.[15]

That fall Porter received a genuine compliment when his old battalion applied successfully to be known permanently as Alexander's battalion. The lines remained quiet although a series of minor engagements steadily sapped the strength of Lee's army without noticeably affecting his position. Distant Georgia came more and more to occupy Porter's mind. He brooded constantly over Sherman's unopposed progress, and as late as November 27 still feared that Sherman might go through Washington. In camp he had lost the services of Winthrop, who had quarreled with some other officers, grown disgusted, and wanted to return to England.[16]

Grant had commenced building a canal across Dutch Gap but Porter determined to stay ahead of him. The Darbytown fiasco had convinced him that the confused tangle of Richmond lines needed to be made stronger and more compact. Since no Confederate map clearly delineated the lines, he began riding out with Gilmer to explore and survey them. Afterward they would return to Richmond and mark in improvements on a map. His most basic change was to construct a line running from the spur line across to the exterior line near the Charles City Road. When he had completed his map Porter took it to Lee, who promptly approved orders to construct the new works.

"That was the beginning," Porter noted proudly, "of the most beautiful line of intrenchments which I saw during the whole war." Almost entirely unbroken by salients, the line featured long sweeps where artillery could enfilade all assaults. Troops could be shuffled quickly and easily in any direction, and the whole front bristled with abatis. He had placed isolated heavy batteries to fire upon Union vessels across Dutch Gap and in the river below the Howlett line. If the Federals completed their canal they could turn these batteries but Porter placed mortars to shell the canal at all hours and filled the river with torpedoes hidden in concealed stations. The layout was for the most part his own handiwork and he was immensely proud of them. They offered yet another demonstration of how far the techniques of waging war had evolved by the autumn of 1864.[17]

But fortifications alone could not turn the tide. Lee was losing a war of attrition. There were few actual engagements, but it was the deadliest challenge he had ever faced. Three Federal armies were gradually strangling his forces by cutting off sources of supply, and as a result the winter of 1865 would prove the bleakest yet faced by the Rebels. Food and clothing were meager, ammunition was dwindling, the supply of muskets insufficient, and the number of horses inadequate. Lack of copper caused an acute shortage in percussion caps, and an attempt to cheer the men with a big New Year's dinner fizzled for want of provisions. Porter's entire command of fifteen hundred men on the northside received only 182 pounds of meat, a little bread, and four or five bushels of turnips and potatoes. Gloom and discouragement descended upon Lee's shivering ranks, and desertion sapped his forces at an ever-increasing rate. Nine of Cabell's men deserted in one forlorn afternoon; the infantry rate was much higher.[18]

The meaning of attrition came home to Porter in quite personal ways. On December 10 he purchased a flannel shirt for $9, a pair of drawers for $3, and a pair of socks for $1. To acquire these treasures he had to swear that he had not made similar purchases in the past year. Later he would consider himself fortunate to acquire a fine pair of cavalry boots for $450, and in buying Bettie a scarce pound of green tea he paid out $125. In camp the theft of provisions and clothes from tents became commonplace.[19]

But Christmas did not pass uncelebrated. Cameron's larder remained bountiful, and he hosted a luxurious dinner of salmon, oysters, turkey, pig, beef, mince pies, plum pudding, fruits, nuts, candies, champagne, egg nog, and other delicacies. Porter stayed until 2 A.M. laughing, singing, and playing cards. And when he encountered Joe Johnston in Richmond that December the general greeted him with the cordial remark that Porter was the only young officer he knew whom the war had not made to look ten years older.[20]

The severe trials of that dark winter demanded the triumph of in-domitable will over reason, and so Porter pursued his duties more zealously than ever. He continued to experiment with new weapons, improve his line, and deal with the ever-increasing output of paper work. On March 7 he wrote a lengthy response to a circular requesting opinions on the punishment of deserters, and as late as March 24 he submitted a list of recommendations for promotion within his command.[21] His own mounting anxiety Porter revealed only indirectly. He admitted the growing de-spondency of both troops and the civilians in Richmond, but he con-sidered them still optimistic about foreign intervention or some favorable turn in the war. His meager rations and the shortage of supplies he dismissed as mere inconveniences:

> We are now living on corn meal made from what ought to go to our horses, & the horses—poor things have to fill up with only four lbs of hay a day & are pretty nearly starved. When we are lucky we draw bacon & have for each meal—two a day one slice of bacon a piece & as much corn bread as we want. This may *sound* like poor living but it is very healthy & I really enjoy these meals as much as I ever did any in my life. . . . They are now issuing liquor—apple jack to us.

In his letters to Bettie he tried to encourage her with assurances that he was in fine condition and with admonitions to bear up under the strain. He began to delve uncharacteristically into religion:

We must look upon our separation, Darling, as a merciful dispensation to draw us nearer to God that we may not fail to meet where partings are unknown. . . . I was much struck a few days ago with an idea from a verse in the Bible wh. I never noticed before viz. "There is joy in the presence of the angels of god over one sinner that repenteth." I think it teaches us clearly that the occupation of the angels is the watching over of mortals—what I have always *wished* to believe, & I love to think that whichever of us is taken first will always watch over the other & the dear children.[22]

Nowhere did his letters betray any sign of some impending disaster, and everywhere did they portray the agonizing sorrow of his predicament. In mid-March he unleashed briefly the bittersweet loneliness that had come to torment him so:

Oh Darling how I wish I could just take you in my lap this morning for one hour to tell U all that is my heart, & to hear what is in yours for I know & feel that U are thinking of me this very minute. I feel too such a longing this morning to hear you *laugh* . . . the pleasant happy times of our Courtship & engagement when we always had so much to laugh about —or at least *thought* that we did. Ah Well! Well! Those careless happy days are gone, but they have left a green memory. . . .

Early in March it became evident that the fate of Richmond hung precariously in the balance. Sherman continued to advance relentlessly through the Carolinas to close the ring about Lee. On the 25th Lee attempted a desperate attack against Grant's line in hopes of stunning him long enough to effect a retreat to the Carolinas, where he could combine with Johnston's army. The attack failed miserably and the plan was abandoned. Late in March Sheridan rejoined Grant and prompted the latter to commence his decisive move.

To weaken the already thin Confederate line Grant sent a sizeable force to Five Forks. Lee countered by sending Pickett's emaciated division to reinforce the cavalry already there. On April 1 Sheridan's attack shattered Pickett's troops, whereupon Grant immediately ordered an attack upon Lee's works. After some bitter fighting the Federals carried the Rebel position on the 2nd. Lee's last chance now was to reach Johnston before Grant could cut his escape route. Sadly he notified Davis that Richmond would have to be evacuated.[23]

That same day found Porter preparing torpedoes in a swamp near the James. When he returned to camp shortly after sundown he learned that the army was in full retreat, and soon orders came for him to withdraw his artillery southward toward Amelia Court House. Riding down his long line, he ordered the stationary cannon spiked and muskets given to their gunners. By 10 P.M. his wagons were packed and moving. Porter rode ahead into Richmond where he found to his relief that Sarah Lawton and Louisa Gilmer had already left the city.[24]

In the streets chaos reigned supreme. Long ragged lines of troops, trains, and guns filed through continuously while civilians frantically packed bags, papers, supplies, or anything else they could carry for the evacuation. Every house was open and filled with light. Women and children could be seen on the steps crying or standing silently on the streetcorners. On Main Street a provost guard was emptying barrels of liquor into the gutter. Already stragglers had begun to loot Mitchell & Tyler's and most of the other prominent stores on the street, and running gun battles between the looters and the provost guard took their toll of casualties. Government stores had been thrown open to the public, and Porter watched "thousands of hideous irish & dutch & negroes men women & children . . . carrying off bacon corn leather saddles harness & every variety of army stores."

Fires raged everywhere. Near Drewry's Bluff the blowing up of the few remaining Rebel ironclads shook the city only to be exceeded by the tremendous explosion of the Richmond Arsenal. Porter hurried back to the bridge to await the arrival of his command. Still the streets swarmed with people. Near the bridge Porter noticed that the Richmond & Danville depot had caught fire. Walking over to it, he saw that it bulged with supplies. These were the provisions that were supposed to meet Lee at Amelia; instead they had been mistakenly sent to Richmond where the flames rapidly consumed them. Charley dodged into the depot to grab some clothes for himself and a saddle, harness, bridle, and blankets for Porter. He also seized a side of bacon.

At 5 A.M. Porter's battalions reached the bridge. The span had caught fire, and the caissons rattled across before it collapsed. As they hurried on Porter took one last look at the dying city. The sight appalled him. "I dont know that any moment in the whole war impressed more deeply with all its stern realities," he recalled later. His command covered twenty-four miles that day and bivouacked near Tomahawk Church. Scarcely had he dismounted when orders arrived for him to help find a route for the guns and trains. The column floundered through mud all night and kept their path only by waking local residents to ask directions.[25]

Next day the train proceeded across the Appomattox River on a railroad bridge and encamped at sundown near Amelia. There Porter intended to unpack his wagon. He had brought back a new uniform in February, and he wanted to put it on now along with his sword. But sixty-two hours of labor had exhausted him; he fell asleep at once. In the morning he was discovered by members of a nearby family who claimed to be Bettie's cousins. They whisked him off to their home and fed him a "Virginia breakfast." Afterward he joined Lee at Amelia to reorganize the retreating force. One column under Lee and Longstreet would take the road to Jetersville to secure a line of retreat; with them would go Porter and thirty-six guns. Another column, including trains, impedimenta and the remainder of Porter's command, would march directly for Lynchburg.

The march commenced about 1 P.M. but within a few miles encountered two Union corps blocking the route. Quickly Lee countermarched his column toward Rice's Station in hopes of skirting the Federals. A tiring all night march of sixteen miles brought them to Amelia Springs, where they spent the night. Porter had run into Lawton and Gilmer and rode a distance with them only to separate again at the springs. Next morning he went ahead to Rice's Station to select a line of battle. In his absence some Federal cavalry cut the rear of Lee's column and captured most of Porter's old battalion. Taylor had managed to unlimber three guns and, ignoring demands to surrender, fired steadily until a trooper shot him dead. Huger wrathfully shot through the cheek a major who invited him to surrender and gave up only when a trooper repeated the invitation with his carbine jammed against Huger's head.

Since his command wagon with all equipment and supplies was in the column, Porter sent Charley back to get some food—unaware that the column had been attacked. Charley rode into the melee wearing a haversack containing Porter's command flag. Fearing that the Federals would hang him if they found the flag, Charley panicked. He abandoned the haversack and returned to Porter without rations and bearing the sad news that wagon, tent, baggage, cooking utensils, all rations, uniform, and all other personal possessions had fallen into enemy hands along with Abram.

At Rice's Station the column encountered only heavy skirmishing. Lee arrived there at sundown and determined to resume the retreat via the Lynchburg road. Crossing the Jamesville River that night, the army headed for Farmville. The miserable march scarcely covered six miles. The roads were deep in mud from a heavy rain, and both men and animals were exhausted. At sunrise the procession crossed the Appomattox River beyond Farmville, where the men received a small supply of rations. Joining Porter for a scant breakfast and a look at the map, Lee pointed to a spot on the road three miles ahead and ordered Porter to send artillery there to prevent the Federals from blocking the road. He also directed Porter to burn both bridges at Farmville after all Confederates had crossed. Porter took one, Willie Mason the other, and both destroyed their bridges and retreated under a hail of fire.

As the march resumed Porter rode alongside some wagons and ambulances. Suddenly he heard a cheer and saw Union cavalry charging across the fields. Quickly he spurred Dixie for some nearby woods but the sound of a rebel yell caught his ear. He turned to see some Confederate cavalry strike the Federals in the flank, break up the charge, and capture several prisoners including the brigade commander. The rest of the day passed in quiet marching, and Porter slept that night in a pine thicket unaware that Lee had received his first note from Grant.

Next day the march proceeded without raids. Porter had procured some utensils from a major who generously divided his belongings. Some of the servants had already fled their masters but Charley remained steadfast. Porter rode for a time with Pendleton, who expressed the opinion of several generals that Lee be asked to surrender. He had already asked Longstreet to approach Lee but "Old Pete" had refused indignantly, whereupon Pendleton went personally to Lee only to receive a decided rebuff. Lee was shouldering the responsibility himself. That day another exchange of notes with Grant took place, in which Lee proposed a meeting for the next day, April 9.

Porter rose early on the 9th and trotted toward the little village of Appomattox. On the way he passed his idle artillery. The men had heard rumors of an impending surrender; they pleaded with Porter to avoid it, saying that they had carried their precious ammunition from the James River line with loving care. In looking over his command Porter reckoned that he could field forty guns with one-hundred rounds apiece. He loathed the thought of surrender because it might mean an indefinite term in prison, and he vowed to make a run for it if Lee should accept terms. But first he had a plan to offer Lee.[26]

He found the General and his staff atop a small hill. The sound of battle echoed in the distance, a sign that Gordon's advance corps was engaged. He did not know that Gordon had just sent Lee a note describing the hopelessness of his situation, and that Lee had resolved to talk to Grant. As they sat upon a felled oak tree Lee pulled out the same worn map he and Porter had studied on the 7th. "Well, we have come to the Junction and they seem to be here ahead of us," the General said quietly. "What have we got to do today?"[27]

Porter replied that his guns were ready to fight. Lee answered that he could scarcely muster eight thousand muskets for battle. That was Porter's opening. With great passion and energy he bared his plan to Lee:

Then, general, we have only choice of two courses. Either to surrender or to take to the woods and bushes, with orders either to rally on Johnston,

or perhaps better, on the Governors of the respective States. If we surrender
this army, it is the end of the Confederacy. I think our best course would
be to order each man to go to the Governor of his own State with his
arms.[28]

Lee asked what Porter hoped to accomplish by this plan. The response
was immediate:

> In the first place, to stand the chances. If we surrender this army,
> every other army will have to follow suit. All will go like a row of bricks,
> and if the rumors of help from France have any foundation, the news of
> our surrender will put an end to them.
>
> But the one thing which may be possible in our present situation is to
> get some sort of terms. None of our armies is likely to be able to get them,
> and that is why we should try with the different States. Already it has been
> said that Vance can make terms for N. C. and Jo [sic] Brown for Ga.
> Let the Governor of each State make some sort of a show of force and then
> surrender on terms which may save us from trials for treason and confisca-
> tions.

The more Porter talked the more reasonable it all seemed. He was
wrought up, his logic seemed irrefutable, and his listener remained silent
and attentive. Confidently he went on:

> But, general, apart from all that—if all fails and there is no hope—the
> men who have fought under you for four years have got the right this
> morning to ask *one* favor of you. We know that you do not care for
> military glory. But we are proud of the record of this army. We want to
> leave it untarnished to our children. It is a clear record so far and now is
> about to be closed. A little blood more or less now makes no difference,
> and we have the right to ask of you to spare us the mortification of having
> you ask Grant for terms and have him answer that he has no terms to offer.
> That is 'U. S., Unconditional Surrender.' That was his reply to Buckner
> . . . and to Pemberton . . . and that is what is threatened us. General,
> spare us the mortification.

Lee heard these words in such reflective calm that Porter felt inwardly
elated over his success. Lee then asked how many men could escape
should he follow Porter's advice. Porter had a ready answer: "Two-thirds
of us. We would be like rabbits and partridges in the bushes, and they
could not scatter to follow us."

Porter waited for Lee to nod agreement, but instead the General now
spoke his own mind:

> I have not over 15,000 muskets left. Two-thirds of this divided among
> the States, even if all could be collected, would be too small a force to

accomplish anything. All could not be collected. Their homes have been overrun, and many would go to look after their families.

Then, General, you and I as Christian men have no right to consider only how this would affect us. We must consider its effect on our country as a whole. Already it is demoralized by four years of war. If I took your advice, the men would be without rations and under no control of officers. They would be compelled to rob and steal in order to live. They would become mere bands of marauders, and the enemy's cavalry would pursue them and overrun many wide sections they have never had occasion to visit. We would bring on a state of affairs it would take the country years to recover from.

And, as for myself, you young fellows might go to bushwhacking, but the only dignified course for me would be, to go to Gen. Grant and surrender myself and take the consequences of my act.

But I can tell you one thing for your comfort. Grant will not demand an unconditional surrender. He will give us as good terms as this army has the right to demand, and I am going to meet him in the rear at 10 A. M. and surrender the army on the condition of not fighting again until exchanged.

Porter stared at Lee in abashed silence. The answer to his argument was pitched on such a lofty plane that he felt a twinge of shame for having even suggested the plan. He rode to his comrades whom he knew to be planning an escape. Hearing that they would be allowed to go home upon surrender, all of the men elected to remain.

But procedural difficulties hampered the surrender, and meanwhile the two armies inched closer to each other. Longstreet ordered Porter to prepare a line of battle behind the village should Gordon have to fall back. Porter selected a line about one thousand yards from the village and crowded his guns with some five thousand infantry along it. It was the last line of battle ever formed by the Army of Northern Virginia.

Soon Meade rode forward and arranged a truce until negotiations could be completed. Once this was done Lee wandered back to an apple orchard in front of his lines, where Porter fixed him a seat of fence rails beneath an apple tree. When the general invited him to sit for a time Porter did so long enough to roll a cigarette. Soon a member of Grant's staff came forward with a note agreeing to the conference. In short order Lee rode forward to the village while Porter sat idly with his staff on a nearby grassy knoll. As he watched the riders trot into the village a wave of despair suddenly overwhelmed him:

A great feeling of strangeness came over me. It was as if I had suddenly died & waked up in an entirely new & different world. . . . There are no words to tell how forlorn & blank the future looked to me. I could not imagine myself making a living in any civil occupation.[29]

Porter summoned his officers to form the cannoneers along the return route where they waited tensely for Lee. When he approached, Porter ordered, the men would uncover their heads in silence. About 4:30 P.M. they saw Traveller in the distance but now the infantry, seeing the gunners up to something, swarmed down to investigate. They swallowed up the artillerists and all pressed close around Lee. Someone started to cheer and the rest took it up. Lee stopped and spoke briefly to his men. He had done his best for them; now they must go home and become as good citizens as they had been soldiers. Slowly the cheers gave way to tears. It was a moment none of them would ever forget. The war was over, all over but the paperwork.[30]

Paroling began the next day, with officers and men being allowed to retain private horses and baggage. Porter kept his four horses, and his parole read thus:

> Brig.-Gen. E. P. Alexander, chief of artillery, 1st corps, A. N. V. of Ga., a paroled prisoner of the Army of Northern Virginia, has permission to go to his home and there remain undisturbed with four private horses.

On April 11 Porter prepared his command for formal transfer of arms to the Federals. He lined his guns in a mile-long column along the road. The feeble horses, most of them starving, stood unattended behind the silent row of guns. The sight broke Porter's heart but no forage could be found.[31]

As he rode into the village to confer with General John Gibbon he spied the familiar face of Major Wilmer McLean, who had owned the farm on which the skirmish at Blackburn's ford had been fought in July of 1861. He had dropped out of Porter's sight early in 1862; now here he was in the very yard where Gibbon made his headquarters. "Hello Mc-Lean!" Porter shouted. "Why what are you doing here?"

McLean turned his short stout body in Porter's direction. "Alexander," he replied gravely, "what the hell are you fellows doing *here?* I stood it on Bull Run, backwards & forwards, between you, my whole plantation was ruined & I sold out & came way off here over 200 miles to this out of the way place where I hoped I never wd see another soldier of either side, & now just look at this place." Porter surveyed the yard full of tents, the trampled fields, and burnt fences and nodded sympathetically. Poor McLean! He had opened the war and he would close it down.[32]

On his parole lists Porter counted 84 officers and 1,116 men present for the surrender. Huger was there along with Parker and Jordan. Taylor had been killed and Gilbert captured on the 6th. Woolfolk had recovered slowly from his wound and was last on duty in Richmond. Moody had been captured, exchanged, recaptured, exchanged again, and had fled south with Davis. Near Federal headquarters an old West Point classmate that Porter hardly knew stopped him and offered delicately to lend him $200 or $300 to get home on. Porter thanked him but declined; he had already borrowed $200 in gold from Hampton Gibbes.[33]

On April 12 the formal surrender ceremony for the infantry took place. Porter stayed to watch his comrades lay down their arms and their precious battle flags. When it was over he rode down to bid them farewell. That was the hardest task of all. The army had been his home for four long years, and now the invisible threads of comradeship he had so cherished were to be broken forever. Then he headed slowly down the road toward Burkesville, the nearest site where a train could still be caught. In his saddlebags he carried letters of recommendation from Lee, Longstreet, Gilmer, and Pendleton. But which train would he take, where would he go, and what would he do after he got there?

Part Three

A SINGED PHOENIX

Chapter XI

Porter now confronted the bitter fruit of his momentous decision in 1861. He had taken his gamble and lost. The door of the past closed irrevocably upon him; he could never return to the United States Army. Cut off from the only career he knew, he would have to begin again at 30. The distinction he had won as a soldier would count for something, but reputation alone would not feed his family. He had in fact two alternatives, neither of which looked promising at the moment: he could abandon his homeland and seek employment in some foreign army, or he could return to the ruined South and try to find a place in its restoration.

His first impulse was to remain a soldier. Hearing that Brazil might go to war with Paraguay, he went first to Washington to sound out the Brazilian minister. But the capital was inflamed with excitement over the assassination of Lincoln, and the minister offered little encouragement. Porter went on to New York to see the Brazilian consul there, but that too came to nothing. After that failure his mood shifted quickly. There seemed little reason to stay in New York. He had no prospects there and Bettie, in Washington, was expecting a child any day. He took the better part of Gibbes's gold, converted it into New York bills, and stuffed them into a valise. He boarded the steamer *Arago* that very night for Hilton Head, South Carolina. Docking there on April 26, he roamed through the city's shops, buying for Bettie all the clothes he could carry. Then he boarded another steamer and reached Savannah on the 27th. There he made a brief stop to visit his uncle Anthony Porter, who had handled all of Porter's financial affairs during the war. Porter had insisted upon converting all his stocks into Confederate notes and bonds. His uncle had carried out his wishes except in one instance: he had kept a small block of Southwestern Railroad stock for Porter. With the Confederate paper—about $20,000 worth—now worthless, the railroad stock comprised Porter's only potential source of income, though it would pay no dividends until the road had been rebuilt.[1]

Not until May 5 did he reach the Washington depot and Fairfield. There he found that Bettie had given birth to a girl on April 7.

Federal troops arrived in Washington on May 5. Not until early August did the feverish excitement of occupation subside. "Washington is becoming nothing but a small, dull country village again," Eliza Andrews noted gloomily. "Everything relating to the dear old Confederate times is already so completely dead and buried that they seem to have existed only in imagination. . . . I feel like one awaking from some bright dream to face the bitter realities of a hard, sordid world." And what, after all, did these bitter realities offer but "a sense of grinding oppression, a deep humiliation, bitter disappointment for the past, and hopelessness for the future." [2]

No less gloomily did the Alexanders lament their fortune. All the men had survived the war but most of them, like Porter, faced the dilemma of trying to find new occupations. Restless and uncertain, Porter spent the summer doing chores about the plantation and pondering his future. The thought of service in a foreign army still tickled his fancy and a brief correspondence with Beauregard revived the Brazilian prospect, but by mid-September he had dismissed it and resolved to stay at home. From Josiah Gorgas came a glowing letter of recommendation ("I consider him as I have often stated in conversation," he wrote, "the most accomplished officer in the Confederate Service") and congratulations: "I am heartily glad to hear of your change of views, and that you will go to work here. It is best." [3]

As a trained engineer Porter's best bet might be a position with one of the Georgia railroads, then in the process of repairing war damage. He applied first to the Georgia Railroad and included letters of recommendation from Lee, Longstreet, Gorgas, Beauregard, Pendleton, and Gilmer. Nothing came of the matter. Gilmer then proposed that they go into business together as civil and practical engineers. Adam warmly approved the idea, but Porter showed no interest and the matter lapsed.[4]

Early in October Alexander received an offer to become professor of chemistry at the reviving Virginia Military Institute.[5] Here finally was a concrete offer but Porter hesitated. The prospect of teaching pleased him, but the compensation seemed scant and not likely to increase. And since he considered himself an engineer rather than a chemist, he tended to regard the position as a waste of his talents. Because it offered some immediate security Bettie favored the job, but Porter sensed he would soon tire of it. He harbored too many ambitions (half-formulated, to be sure), too many ideas. He could not bring himself to abandon them for a job promising a drab if reasonably secure future. Afraid to disavow the position entirely, he deferred decision while he scouted other possibilities. Hearing that the National Express Company needed a supervisor for Georgia, he tried unsuccessfully to obtain that post.

To eke out support while looking for a job, Porter sold one of his horses and performed odd jobs, one of which took him away from

Bettie for several weeks. To console her in his absence he unfolded new schemes. They might find some small plantation, lay in some provisions, plant the land in cotton, and accumulate some money to invest. Or he might borrow about $1,500 and "go shares with [Gilmer] in a grits mill with power perhaps to apply to something else after a while." Bettie endured the uncertainties with patience, but occasionally her disposition wore thin. "I do trust with all our schemes we may eke out a living," she wrote her husband that October. "I suppose after a while you will get *something* to do." [6]

Much of Bettie's anxiety stemmed from having to depend upon Adam for support. She longed to have a home of her own for Porter and the children, though Adam generously provided for his dispossessed children. November approached with no sign of improvement. Then early in November Aleck Haskell informed Porter that the University of South Carolina had reorganized and would reopen in January. Haskell had declined a chair in mathematics and civil and military engineering, preferring to practice law instead. He put Porter's name up for the job, and urged him to accept it. Getting word of the new offer, Bettie hastened to endorse Haskell's plea:

> I am delighted beyond measure to hear of the offer you had of a professor in S. C. & am exceedingly anxious for you to accept it. I don't care how small the salary is for a year or so. I am more opposed than ever to your making Georgia your home. I want you to go where you are known and appreciated & don't believe you would ever get anything to do here if you remained till the end of time.[7]

Porter gave the matter considerable thought. He still harbored vague hopes for a position in California. The job at V. M. I. remained open but Porter regarded it as inferior to the South Carolina post. He decided to accept it and was promptly given the chair. The post would pay $1,000 a year plus a good dwelling house. In addition he would receive $25 for each student in his classes (assuming, of course, that the student could afford to pay). "The number of students will this year be small—scarcely exceeding fifty," Haskell warned. "I hope that the reconstruction of the town and recovery of the state will make it much more than double this number in the succeeding years." [8]

In accepting the post Alexander displayed the fundamental practicality of his attitudes. Many of his former comrades had not yet adjusted themselves to the conditions of a defeated South. They withdrew wrathfully from participation in state or local affairs and spoke of themselves as men bereft of country, allegiances, or prospects for the future. Custis Lee, still in Lexington, found it a hard job to set down roots in the ruined South.

"Theoretically, I am strongly in favor of our people remaining in the country and seeing the thing out," he wrote Porter, "but practically I find it very difficult to do." [9] In Porter's own mind the trial of arms had settled the issue—however unfavorable the result. Times pressed hard upon him. Having lost his life's work he must take up something else. He could not afford the luxury of bitterness. It tended eventually to become self-consuming and he could not spare the time or energy. The future held the key to everything; why dwell morbidly upon the destroyed past.

When Porter arrived in Columbia on February 11, 1866, he found much of the campus in disarray. Federal authorities still occupied the northern tier of buildings and would continue to do so until June of 1869. The southern range of dormitories housed troops. Outside the walls, the chapel had become an army post and the field adjoining it a parade ground. Hastily built barracks flanked the chapel-post, and above it fluttered the stars and stripes. The drilling infantry, some six companies strong, with its military band often attracted spectators and did nothing for the lectures going on within the classrooms. [10]

Haskell had predicted that the number of students enrolled would scarcely exceed fifty; the actual number turned out to be forty-eight. As Porter took up his class he noted a striking lack of preparation in mathematics. No students were prepared to undertake engineering, and none could tackle the higher branches of mathematics. New students arrived continually and drifted into his class. At last he divided it into three separate sections—advanced, average, and beginner—and drilled his charges until they climbed towards a common level of achievement. He soon became a highly popular instructor apt at spicing his lectures with pungent similes and pointed stories. That he knew his business thoroughly no one doubted in the least; one of his collegaues labeled him "a kind of genius in mathematics, and especially in engineering." [11]

Columbia society proved to be affable and genial. The Alexanders immediately drew close to John and Joseph LeConte and their families. The brothers were both scientists of growing repute. The university's president, Robert W. Barnwell, impressed everyone with his vigor and ability. Society as a whole in the city abounded in gaiety—the necessary rebound, Joseph LeConte thought, "from the agony and repression of the war." Since the war had impoverished most people, social standing counted far more than wealth. Lack of means put no damper on gatherings: the ladies furnished cake and lemonade, the young men brought along a Negro fiddler, and the party spun merrily on.

Though he had by no means closed his eyes to other offers, Porter grew increasingly optimistic over the university's future. Fall enrollment in 1867 climbed to 108, and most of the students chose mathematics as one of their fields. At mid-term Porter counted 78 students in his class, 60 of whom were paying their way; that added $1,500 to his income. Confident that enrollment would continue to grow, he turned down an offer from the University of Georgia to head a school of civil engineering even though the guaranteed salary doubled that paid by South Carolina.[12]

Life drifted along pleasantly for the Alexanders in Columbia. Steeped in work and enjoyable associations, the taste of ashes slowly faded from Porter's mouth. He might almost have forgotten that there had been a war or that the South still choked on the bile of defeat. He had struck out upon a new road for himself, and it would not have surprised him if the rest of the country followed suit. But he could not shake free of the past. In Washington the venomous struggle between President Johnson and Congress finally resulted in a devastating victory for the latter in the fall elections of 1866, and by winter a new reconstruction policy would make its imprint upon South Carolina.

The First Reconstruction Act of March 2, 1867, fell like a thunderbolt upon South Carolina. The South would be divided into five military districts subject to martial law. Every state would be obliged to call a constitutional convention, elected by universal suffrage, and then form a new state government guaranteeing Negro suffrage and ratifying the Fourteenth Amendment. No ex-Confederate disqualified by the terms of the amendment could take part in the voting. With the freedmen now enfranchised, the state moved rapidly to form a new government under the requirements of the act. By November 19, 1867, some 127,758 voters had been enrolled in South Carolina, of whom 80,832 were Negro. A constitutional convention, summoned by an overwhelming vote, proceeded to draw up a state constitution on the basis of "equal rights to all, regardless of race, color, or previous condition." By mid-April it had won ratification, and election of a state legislature soon followed. Of its 157 members 84 were colored and 72 were white. In part these figures proved deceptive, for the white members split sharply between Radical and Conservative views. The first legislature listed seven known Conservatives in the Senate and sixteen in the House. At all time the Radicals held a commanding majority.[13]

Porter and his colleagues watched this turn of events uneasily. The fate of the university hinged upon the disposition of the legislature, and the new state constitution expressly stated that "all the public schools, colleges, and universities of this State, supported in whole or part by the public funds, shall be free and open to all the children and youths of this State, without regard to race or color." What this provision meant in concrete terms for the university's future no one yet knew, but rumor had hordes of impoverished but eager freedmen descending upon the school. The result was a drop in white enrollment from 113 to 65 despite efforts to dispel the rumor. When the legislature opened debate upon the university's future, several faculty members began searching for new positions. Porter gathered a fresh supply of recommendations and applied to the University of California. A raise in salary to $2,000 a year induced him to remain through the term ending in June of 1869.[14]

Porter planned to resign that coming August, but he had no new position as yet. California had fallen through, as had a possible job with the Central Railroad. These discouragements did not sting so badly as those of a few years before, since Porter no longer hovered on the brink of poverty. He had put money aside regularly and invested it in stock, a cotton mill in Georgia, and Columbia real estate. His speculations achieved some success; a Columbia lot he purchased for $973 in March of 1868 fetched $1,200 in cash the following winter. Later he acquired North Island, one of the sea islands in the mouth of Georgetown harbor. He paid $766 for the 10,000 acre island and was soon offered $1,000 for it. But he refused to sell, thinking that northerners might later offer at least $3,000. The island, he admitted, seemed good only for "cattle range, live oak timber & fishing grounds—sea bathing, hunting, etc." Though he did not realize it then, the island would in time prove to be one of his most significant investments.[15]

That same spring Porter became intrigued by another scheme—the potentiality of cottonseed oil. Cotton seed had long been thought an utterly worthless by-product; in fact the great mounds of seeds that accumulated about every gin proved such a nuisance that many a planter simply relocated his gin rather than cart off the unwanted seed. A verse from a song popular among Negro tenant farmers bore testimony to its worthlessness:

> Go to de big plantations
> Whar de hawgs an' cattle feed;
> De white man gits de cotton 'an corn
> De nigger gits de seed.

Since seed existed in abundance and normally went to waste, it could probably be obtained cheaply and in quantity. If uses could be found for its by-products, a lucrative business might be developed. "I do know that enormous profits are being made in the business out west," he reported to his father, "& that the prospect here is certainly good enough to investigate. . . . I am writing in every direction to collect information on different questions." [16]

Within a month he had plunged headlong into the venture. The real difficulty, he learned, lay not in finding uses for cottonseed oil and the other by-products; they could be utilized in a number of ways. But transportation and supply proved to be the historical drawbacks to the industry. One would first have to teach the planter to save his seed, then find some way to transport it cheaply. Finally, a market would have to be cultivated for the products. A failure to solve these problems accounted for the lack of oil mills in the South, but Porter believed that these obstacles could be surmounted. "A $40,000 mill would certainly pay for itself in a year," he insisted, "if seed could be had at a cent a pound." He began to travel through the South, culling information from every source on seed, on the building and operating of mills, and on production techniques. Convinced that his thinking was sound, he lined up other businessmen to join him in the investment.[17]

In October Porter and his partners incorporated the Columbia Oil Company "for the purpose of extracting and manufacturing oil from cotton seed, and other seeds or grain." [18] Porter assumed the presidency of the company. The new factory, built near the South Carolina Railroad line basked in a $30,000 capitalization and an unlimited reservoir of optimism and enthusiasm.

Chapter XII

The attempt to cull a profit from cottonseed dated back to the eighteenth century and had been tried in America as early as 1804. The invention of new machinery in succeeding decades stimulated efforts to maintain profitable mills, but always the problems of transportation and supply arose to frustrate entrepreneurs. By 1860 only seven mills produced cottonseed oil in the United States; by 1867 the number had shrunk to four.

The Columbia Oil Company, despite all efforts, failed to conquer the old problems. Salvaging of cottonseed continued to lag pitifully behind cotton production. The difficulty lay not only in educating the planter to save his seed but also in buying and transporting it. The price of cottonseed, buoyed by British buyers who kept a lively hand in the market with their purchases of sea island cottonseed, exceeded Porter's original estimates. Transportation, too, cost the mill dearly. The whole business was too new to the South; it possessed no seed warehouses and no fixed techniques of transportation. No agencies devoted to obtaining and handling seed for oil mills existed, for the simple reason that no oil mills existed. Profit in such a new field required a favorable commercial atmosphere and some timely educating of the public. Neither of these factors prevailed. The diverse uses of the oil and its by-products remained outside common usage. Even worse, an adequate seed supply still proved elusive, for farmers and planters alike remained indifferent or ignorant to the possibilities for selling their seed.[1]

Uncertain supply and indifferent demand told the tale. Oil prices, catering helplessly to the whims of an uncertain market, remained low. Too late the Columbia Oil Company discovered the heavy price for plowing new ground. It prophesied a thriving southern industry of the future, but it lacked the necessary circumstances to earn dividends for its investors. Though the mill struggled on for several years, it failed to climb out of the red. A disenchanted stockholder unwittingly coined the firm's epitaph when he made the astute observation that the company failed because the price of seed was too high and the price of oil too low.[2]

Brooding once more over his future, Porter again cast out his nets for whatever offers they might snare. His inclinations leaned towards a railroad job, but no promising opening had yet appeared. In March of 1870 he received an unexpected chance to renew his military career. Feelers reached him from the Near East, where the Khedive of Egypt was struggling to organize an effective army. Charles P. Stone, the capable Federal general who had been imprisoned without charge after the battle of Balls Bluff in 1861, had gone to Egypt to become chief of staff for the Khedive's army. Needing a talented engineer to head that service, he offered Porter the post with rank of brigadier general and pay and allowances (in gold) equal to that rank in the American army.[3]

Further encouragement came in June from Beauregard, who had also been offered a post in the Khedive's army. "As I always remember with great pleasure your able & valuable services in the late war," he wrote Porter, "I have thought that you might perhaps desire to accompany me." Clearly tempted, Porter pondered the offer. Then the situation grew foggy. To Beauregard the Khedive tended an offer only to withdraw it later. Porter's status remained nebulous until the following February, when Stone formalized his original offer. "If possible," he concluded, "I should like to have you leave America within two months."[4]

The old pressures assailed him once more. He loathed the burden of such a decision. The prospect of military service whetted his appetite, and he certainly had no important interests to keep him at home. But the thought of pulling up all roots, leaving the South, and removing his family to a foreign land repelled him. No doubt Lee's frequent plea to stay at home and help rebuild haunted his mind. Bettie would care nothing for the move, and the children would suffer for it. On the other hand, what future awaited him here? The South still lay in ruins (spiritually, if not physically), his own prospects were flagging, and the future looked conspicuously blank. He had floundered for six years—why not take a gamble now? He penned a careful letter of acceptance to Stone.

Then the forces of reaction gathered about him. Plagued with doubts, Bettie sought counsel from other members of the family. From most of them came emphatic pleas not to go. In Columbia Aleck Haskell (he had married Porter's sister Alice the previous year) and other close friends plied him with arguments for declining the offer. Beauregard had not gone after all, the situation in Egypt remained ambiguous, and prospects at home would certainly improve. Slowly but surely Porter gave ground. Ambivalent from first to last, he finally relented when a new prospect appeared at home and telegraphed Stone to ignore his earlier letter.[5]

The new prospect involved the superintendency of the Charlotte, Columbia & Augusta Railroad. When he obtained that position in May of 1871 he promptly resigned as president of the oil company and turned enthusiastically to learning the railroad business. Though he could not know it at the time, he had reached another crucial juncture in his life. The long and frustrating search for a new career was over.

For a man who thrived on shouldering many duties at the same time the superintendency of a railroad posed an appealing challenge. Porter would spend at least half his time inspecting the road. He would need precise knowledge of the entire track, the bridges and their trestlework, the masonry, the depots and all other buildings. He would have to decide questions of repair or renewal, both for the track and for a rolling stock that totalled 18 locomotives and 152 cars. He would have to know each employee, his pay and duties, and see that all new men received proper instruction in their jobs. Minute variations in the schedules, train movements, freight volume, and location must all be kept at his fingertips. A flood of reports, requisitions, correspondence, and other paperwork besieged him in his office, and traffic department officers, agents from other lines, customers and employees clamored incessantly for his attention.[6]

The job, Alexander learned quickly, was no sinecure. His first responsibility, that of supervising the roadway, he found befitting his skills as an engineer. Maps of all key stations and junctions, scale drawings of all bridges, trestles, depots, tanks, switches, rails, fastenings and signals cluttered his office. These he used as guides in examining the real objects before assigning repairs to the field or bridge gangs who roamed the track in service cars. Every morning saw a report placed before him on the business traffic along the road, important events of the night, train movements for the day, and the volume of freight to be handled. A similar report greeted him every night, and it was a notorious fact in the profession that superintendents could ill afford to be heavy sleepers.[7]

But Porter felt quite at home under such pressures. Within a year he had mastered his trade and absorbed a shrewd and intimate knowledge of railroad operation. He found it a fascinating business and one not unlike the running of an army. Of the higher arts of management and finance Porter knew little as yet, but a new opportunity would soon open up these fields to him.

In 1870 an ambitious plan was launched to build a railroad from Opelika, Alabama, to Corinth, Mississippi. Given the misnomer Savannah & Memphis, the new road completed only 42 of its projected 263-mile route in two years. The company's president resigned, and in October of 1872 the directors elected Alexander to fill the place. The new position promised to extend his education into the complex arenas of finance and policy. With the Savannah & Memphis he would deal with both the strategy and tactics of railroading, for he would be both president and superintendent.[8]

Though the offer sounded encouraging, Porter could not allay his anxiety. The war had ended some seven years before, and still he had not found his place. He longed to take root somewhere and settle down in a home of his own. A migratory life could impose only hardship upon the children—now five in number after the birth of Adam Leopold in 1867 and William Mason in 1868. Bettie would not protest openly, for she knew that Porter was doing his best to get established. Nevertheless he could not help but sense her uneasiness, and sometimes gnawing fear about the future dogged his thoughts.

Alabama, no less than the rest of the South, had been seized with railroad fever shortly after the war. In 1867 the provisional legislature passed an act authorizing the governor to endorse railroad first mortgage bonds at the rate of $12,000 a mile for each twenty-mile section built. The following year's reconstruction legislature upped the ante to $16,000 a mile, reduced the section requirement from twenty to five miles, and promised aid to any company going twenty miles beyond the Alabama boundary. Another bill on December 31, 1868, authorized counties, towns and cities to subscribe to railroad stock. Public opinion in Alabama (and elsewhere in the South) demanded new roads; now public law made the building of new lines deliciously attractive to promoters. Fledgling towns and villages imagined themselves transformed overnight into thriving centers of commerce by the coming of the railroad. Rushing eagerly to embrace every new project, they found no dearth of promoters ready with tantalizing schemes. Among these enthusiastic towns Opelika stood foremost. No less than two ambitious lines had been launched with the town as their terminus: the East Alabama & Cincinnati and the S & M.[9]

Taking charge of the road early in October, Porter realized immediately that the road would be virtually useless until completed. So far it had been laid only to Sturdevant (forty miles), just short of the Tallapoosa River. The route across the river had been surveyed, and the roadbed located to Youngsville. Construction could not continue without capital, and financially the road remained in tenuous shape. The state had authorized a funded debt of $640,000 for the line, and of this amount about $400,000 in 8 per cent mortgage bonds had already been sold. County and individual subscriptions had added another $1,000,000, but financial prospects for future construction remained vague.[10]

The course seemed obvious to Porter: construction must be pushed along to meet the necessary requirements for the state subsidy, and more financial backing must be found. Before October's end he let contracts for the next ten-mile section towards Youngsville. He discovered that three neighboring roads were interested in joining the S & M to their lines as a feeder: the Central of Georgia, Mobile & Ohio, and the St. Louis & Iron Mountain. By patient dickering Porter persuaded them in August of 1873 to underwrite a $6,500,000 construction mortgage. In return 25 percent of the road's gross earnings would be set aside to purchase its bonds with a minimum allotment for this purchase of $150,000 a year. In addition, each of the three larger roads would take $50,000 worth of the bonds, thus cementing their stake in the S & M's future.[11]

On paper the transaction seemed promising. It appeared to guarantee completion of the line without surrendering immediate control, and it left open the pleasant possibility of a future lease or outright purchase by one of the three participants. But Porter and his associates failed to include fate in their reckonings. Scarcely had they left the negotiating table when the September 18 failure of Jay Cooke & Company brought a speedy halt to the rampant speculation in railroads and triggered a general financial panic. The most solvent roads struggled desperately to stay afloat; the more vulnerable lines succumbed one after another to default and receivership. Smaller roads, born in a flush of optimism and launched with inadequate capital, especially felt the pinch of hard times. In Alabama over half the larger lines and practically all the smaller ones toppled into default. The remaining roads either retrenched frantically or depended upon some major line for financial support. None of the Alabama roads paid dividends in 1873 or 1874.

Alexander surveyed the growing wreckage. At first the S & M withstood the panic, but in November the company finally defaulted. Realizing that the road could never recover if construction were not finished, Porter pushed through a plan to fund five coupons or enough to meet interest through May of 1876. Undesirable as it might be to borrow money for meeting fixed charges, the stockholders saw little choice but to accept. Receivership would bring them no relief and more likely a heavy loss. By 1876, moreover, the depression might be lifting, and the three major lines underwriting the S & M could then fulfill their obligations.

Since part of the company's financing derived from a state subsidy that depended upon completed construction, Alexander drove his crews to finish the necessary twenty-mile section. He succeeded in opening the line from Opelika to Atkins Gap, a distance of sixty miles, by November of 1874. That achievement garnered the road an $80,000 subsidy in Alabama state bonds. Though Porter had staved off disaster and put the S & M on relatively solid footing again, his job had brought neither prosperity nor security. Even if the road did eventually thrive it would offer him no chance for advancement. That winter he began scouting for new possibilities.[12]

One intriguing situation developed on a neighboring line, the Western Railroad of Alabama. Born of an 1870 merger between the Montgomery & West Point and the Western of Alabama, the company operated three routes totalling 160 miles: a main stem running 88 miles from Montgomery to West Point, a 28-mile branch from Opelika to Columbus, and the 44-mile line between Montgomery and Selma. Despite increased efficiency after the merger the Western failed consistently to pay its way. The Western could not survive the Panic of 1873. Early in the year it defaulted and headed toward receivership.[13]

The Western's deteriorating situation did not go unnoticed by its competitors. Both the Central and the Georgia railroads quickly involved themselves in its affairs. The Central in fact had already invested heavily in the road by mortgage guarantees; it also held some $164,500 in Western bonds and 5,256 shares of Western stock. Both lines recognized the uncomfortable truth that the Alabama road would be a long time paying its way and might never achieve stability. But both realized, too, that acquisition of the Western by some major competitor might prove fatal. The new Western board, elected late in December of 1873, included William W. Wadley, president of the Central, and John P. King, president of the Georgia. Shortly afterward the rival presidents agreed to buy the Western and operate it for their joint benefit.

If their efforts were successful the two Georgia roads would need someone to operate the road, and Porter let it be known that he desired the post. He tried first to be appointed receiver for the road prior to its sale, but the court named the incumbent president instead. The setback left Porter deeply discouraged and caused him to look elsewhere for a position. Pressed for cash, he tried to sell North Island for $4,500 but found no buyers; mockingly he dubbed the island his "Barreny." Soon, however, the Western reclaimed his attention. It became known that appointment of the old president as receiver meant no immediate change in policy, and that the court proceedings looked forward to early foreclosure and sale. Wadley and King had perfected their plan for purchasing the Western, and both let it be known that they favored Porter's appointment. Lawton, who served as Wadley's private attorney and as general counsel for the Central, confided to Porter early in April that arrangements had been completed.[14]

On April 19, 1875, Wadley and King purchased the Western, though King encountered such opposition from his minority stockholders that he had to beat down a court injunction restraining the purchase. The whole debate over the Western had so deeply split Georgia stockholders and directors that final decision would have to be deferred until the Georgia's annual meeting in late May. More than the Western would be at stake, for King had also decided to endorse the bonds of the Port Royal Railroad to the tune of $500,000. In a February meeting the minority stockholders had reacted bitterly against two enabling acts passed by the legislature, which amended the company's charter to allow purchase of the Western and the Port Royal. Now, in the annual board elections, they opposed King with their own candidate, banker Charles H. Phinizy of Augusta, but the crafty veteran won reelection by a narrow margin. Even then the minority did not give up but wrangled sharply for several days before reluctantly conceding the directors' power to act.

Not until May 26 was the sale confirmed. The Central would control the route from Columbus to Opelika, the Georgia would have the West Point to Opelika line, and the two roads would share the remaining portion from Opelika to Selma. The joint line would be run by a board of six directors with Porter as president. The long wait over, Porter and his family gathered up their belongings again and hurried to Montgomery.[15]

It did not take Porter long to realize that the Western would be a difficult problem at best. Its huge funded debt would require, by Wadley's calculations, a net annual income of $204,240 to avoid becoming a drain upon its owners. But in 1874 the Western netted a paltry $60,808, and the ratio of operating expenses to income stood at a staggering 87.4. Formidable competition menaced the road on every side despite its new connections. Along with these obstacles Porter had also to contend with the impatient directors of both parent roads. Neither could stand much loss with the Western.[16]

Feeling these latent pressures, Porter wasted little time. In his first year he renovated the physical plant of the road while rigidly paring down expenses. Dwindling traffic and rapacious competition hampered his efforts as southern roads dueled savagely for whatever traffic remained in the depressed country. Many southern roads deplored the competition and groped for some means to control it. In October 1875 twenty-nine southern carriers convened in Atlanta and created the Southern Railway and Steamship Association. The new pool, largely the work of Louisville & Nashville executive Albert Fink (who became its first commissioner), pledged itself to reducing the evils of competition by securing a fair distribution of business. Enthusiastic over the pool's possibilities, Alexander followed the Georgia roads into the organization. No innocence of business practices prompted his decision; he knew well the limitations of pools that depended for success upon the integrity and voluntary coopera- tion of every member. The railroads of the South (and of the nation for that matter) had shown no real ability to eschew the tempting short- term gains of rate wars for the long range benefits of stable rates. Yet Porter also believed that the only hope for the future lay in such coopera- tive pools, and that they must be tried until something better could be devised.[17]

In his first year Porter managed to double the previous year's net revenue. He had done this primarily by slashing the operating expense ratio from 87.4 to 75.2; gross earnings showed only a modest increase. But business in general had not recovered, and Porter knew he could not maintain the pace. Passenger traffic had been unusually brisk in 1875, and local crops had picked up over the previous year. He could not hope for these bounties to continue another year, and in fact they did not. In addition, the need for physical improvements frustrated his efforts at strict economy. He had, for example, to expend $36,494 for new rails— twice as much as the previous year. Two new depots went up, a pair of water stations, and three turn-tables. Even so Porter managed to cut operating expenses by about $3,000, but gross earnings, hampered by poor crops, dropped some $24,000 in 1876.[18]

Under his management the line had netted $207,701 in two years, a healthy improvement over past performance but not enough to satisfy the parent roads. The Western barely earned in two years what Wadley had estimated it would have to earn annually to pay its own way, and the Central president did not mask his disappointment in his annual report. But no one blamed Porter; it was acknowledged that he had done all he could with a struggling line. Instead the tracks of suspicion led straight to the question of whether or not the line should have been purchased in the first place. At the Central Wadley squelched what little opposition to his policies appeared, but in Augusta King did not fare as well. His discontented stockholders singled out the Western as one more example of King's poor judgment and tried again to oust him, but at the May meeting he beat the rebels down again.[19]

Porter's third year with the Western opened in fine style. Earnings picked up considerably, and the future seemed promising not only for the road but for the country in general as improved crops and re- vitalized business brought growing revenues. Porter had shown what he could do with a railroad. He had demonstrated both a mastery of tech- nical detail and a flair for management. The habit of command came second nature to him; he saw no reason why a railroad, complex organization that it is, should be any less efficiently run than an army. He no longer harbored grave doubts about his future, and partly for that reason he was not overly surprised at the budding of a new opportunity.[20]

Five long years the bitter fight within the Georgia Railroad had raged, and now time was running out on the old president. Slight, grizzled and well past seventy, King had served as president since 1841 after leaving a seat in the senate. His lined, bewhiskered face masking an indomitable will, King had long defended his policies and opposed his enemies with undeniable skill and consummate stealth. He presided over a system that included the 171-mile main stem from Augusta to Atlanta and three branches: Carmak to Warrenton, 4 miles; Barnett to Washington, 18 miles; and Union Point to Athens, 39 miles. In addition it shared the lease on the Western and leased the 74-mile Macon & Augusta running from Warrenton to Macon. Quick to recover from the war, the company paid consistently high dividends from 1866 to 1872 and established an enviable reputation for stability and conservatism. Then the reconstruction boom in railway expansion caught up with the Georgia, and a combination of increased competition and the Panic of 1873 steadily reduced net earnings. In 1874 the Georgia paid no dividend.[21]

For all his cunning King could not long conceal the harsh statistics that pointed to a stagnating financial situation. Though earnings rose in 1875, he announced that no further gains could be counted on. He spoke angrily against the competition for through freight and called for a policy favoring local business with its moderate but steady rates in preference to the uncertain returns of through business with its rapidly fluctuating rates. That same year he tried to strengthen the Georgia's hold over its territory by purchasing a half interest in the Western, by extending loans and endorsements to the Macon & Augusta, and by endorsing the bonds of the Port Royal.

The terrific struggle that ensued involved two more subtle issues than the simple issue of expansion versus contraction. First, King's opponents charged that he had the right idea at the wrong time. He advocated risking the company's credit just when money was tight, credit expensive and hard to obtain, and business conditions such that any railroad (especially one already insolvent) would have a hard time paying its way. To buy such a railroad would saddle the Georgia with a financial obligation that could not possibly be offset by its removal as a competitor. Secondly, King had made it perfectly clear that for him the future lay in preserving and cultivating local traffic rather than in any connection or consolidation with other lines. On this point his detractors bitterly disagreed, and into King's attitude they might read either the set ways of an old man clinging to the past or the slipping hand of an aging executive who had lost touch with the changing realities of the business climate. In either case the result spelled disaster for the Georgia's future, and so the rebels combed the ranks of the stockholders for support.

Whoever was right in the continuing debate, it appeared as if fortune had clearly cast her lot against King. Fires, floods, shriveling traffic and labor disputes plagued the Georgia in 1876. Net earnings for the year slumped over $50,000 to $500,017. In January of 1877 the directors declared a modest 3 percent dividend, but King remained steeped in gloom over future prospects. In his report for 1875 he had characterized southern and western railroads as having two common features: "reduced business by the poverty of the people . . . and reduced receipts from a ruinous competition. . . . It cannot be . . . denied that the future of the railroad interest, especially in the South and West, is very discouraging." Now, in his report for 1876, he repeated his dark prophecy for the southern carriers.[22]

The handwriting was on the wall. Georgia stock, solid and stable at 97 throughout 1872, dropped slowly until it reached 67 by June of 1876. Already King had decided that the first step toward the Georgia's salvation lay either in leasing or purchasing outright both the Port Royal and M & A lines. To accomplish this aim he proposed to issue $1,000,000 worth of new 7 percent bonds to pay off all outstanding obligations. Late in February the state legislature obliged him with three acts authorizing each point of his plans. That put the issue squarely up to the annual meeting. On May 18 King confronted the stockholders with his program.[23]

The rebels denounced his proposals as ruinous and ill-considered and tried desperately to drum up support from the rank and file, but once more the old fox outflanked them. He still commanded a narrow majority among both the directors and stockholders, and he had come to the meeting well-prepared for the fight. After a bitter struggle he pushed through his program by slender margins.[24]

It proved a Pyrrhic victory. Furious over their defeat and alienated beyond reconciliation, the dissenters vowed to break King once and for all at the next meeting. As the months went by they scrutinized the fruits of his triumphant policies. Fortune favored their efforts, for 1877 proved to be King's most trying year. Heavy replacement expenditures, accidents, and a slight decline in traffic reduced net earnings 42.8 percent from $500,018 to $286,012. The M & A operated consistently at a small deficit all year, and Port Royal bonds continued to drain the Georgia's earnings. Reluctantly King announced that the December dividend would be passed and braced for the oncoming storm. Jubilant over King's embarrassment, the rebels now needed only a good candidate to oppose him. Led once again by Phinizy, they went straight to Porter Alexander.[25]

Under the circumstances Porter could not very well decline the offer. The presidency of the Georgia represented a healthy promotion, and while he had no desire to fight King personally he did disagree sharply with the old warrior's philosophy. Phinizy and his cohorts promised Porter unflinching support; with his acceptance in hand two months before the meeting they launched an extensive canvas of the stockholders.

King readied his defenses. In his report he took great pains to justify his policies. The statement of net profit he dismissed as an unfair test of the company's management and attributed its decline to a costly accident and the purchase of steel rails. "Great efforts are made by some persons to stir up discord among the stockholders because the last dividend was passed," he asserted. "True, it was made, but was well appropriated in payment of debts." What other road pays regular dividends, King asked his stockholders: "I know of but one at the South, and that is the creature and *protege* of the Georgia road." The future of the company depended upon factors beyond human control, he concluded pessimistically. "Everything is abnormal and shrinkages still continue, and no business prospers on a declining market."

The stockholders converged on Augusta in great numbers. The meeting convened on May 9 and the bitter struggle broke out almost at once. King fought his usual shrewd and stubborn battle, but this time the odds were against him. His argument against the paying of regular dividends seemed reasonable except to stockholders long accustomed to receiving them; in that ironic sense his own past record of success betrayed him now. The opposition, tightly organized, exploited every opening. They played cunningly upon the smaller stockholders' resentment over passed dividends; they harped on the wasteful sapping of Georgia funds by the Port Royal; they pointed up the M & A as another unwise venture; they hinted broadly that perhaps King, after thirty-six years as president, had lost his grip, grown too old to handle his demanding job; they chanted the theme that fresh blood was necessary to keep the company attuned to fast-changing times. "Active, bitter, and unsparing," one correspondent labeled the campaign. When the final tally was announced, Porter had a 4,081 vote majority out of 37,491 ballots cast. Even the victors professed surprise at the size of their majority.[26]

Alexander had not been present at the election; his official notification came the next day. As he prepared to leave Montgomery he savored his moment of triumph. The sense of dislocation had almost gone. It seemed now that he had risen rapidly, almost spectacularly to his important post, but he knew better. He could not have done it without the financial help of his father and the constant advice of Gilmer and Lawton. He leaned especially upon Gilmer and drew closer to him than any other member of the family. Just turned forty-three, a swiftly retreating hairline enlarged Porter's already high forehead. His cheeks had filled out, his glowing grey eyes sank deeper and his once formidable moustache now thatched only the span of his lip. He had five healthy children, the oldest of whom would soon be seventeen. She had been born in Virginia on a bleak November day in 1861. Porter remembered it well: by it he could measure the age of a time long past.

Chapter XIII

Once arrived in Augusta Porter launched a survey of the Georgia's affairs. In addition to its 232-mile roadway, the company controlled the Atlanta & West Point, owned half interest in the Western, and sponsored by bond guarantees the Port Royal and the M & A. Capitalized at $4,200,-000, the company had no mortgage outstanding and only $399,000 in bonds. Thus most of its fixed charges lay in underwriting other roads— the Western, the M & A, and the Port Royal. Porter soon discovered these tributaries to be heavy burdens.[1]

The Port Royal provided the most baffling problem. The Georgia had already invested over one-half million dollars in it, hoping to develop at Port Royal a sea outlet for a steamer traffic to northern ports. But Port Royal was no Savannah and could not boost the Georgia as the Ocean Steamship Company had done for the Central. Even worse, the Central had no intention of allowing the Georgia to develop a rival sea outlet, and Wadley possessed the means to block any such attempt. King had won the authority to buy or lease the Port Royal outright, but he could do neither because the Central controlled a majority of the road's stock. The situation had become untenable: involved in the company with nearly $1,000,000, the Georgia could neither control the line nor develop Port Royal as a commercial center without a further prohibitive investment.[2]

The old specter of competition continued to menace the Georgia's traffic and earnings, and now a new potential menace appeared. The restoration of home rule for Georgia in 1877 had brought with it a new constitution. To the convention held that same summer in Atlanta came Robert Toombs with two obsessions: to obliterate the constitution of 1869 and to ram through some provision for abolishing state aid to railroads and allowing the state to regulate railroad rates. To oppose Toombs the railroads mustered some powerful advocates of their own, notably Lawton and ex-governor Joe Brown, now president of the Western & Atlantic. But by sheer force of personality Toombs crumbled all opposition and planted his resolutions in the final draft of the constitution.[3]

Article IV (sections 2–6) of the new constitution clearly marked the success of Toombs' efforts. The legislature received the power to regulate all railroad passenger fares and freight tariffs to prevent "unjust discrimination." All rebates and bonuses were declared illegal. No legislative act could authorize any corporation to buy stock in any other corporation *if* the purchase served to lessen competition or encourage monopoly. Railroads and other corporations granted privileges or exemptions by a previous constitution would not be subject to contrary provisions of the new one *except* where the privileges pertained to buying stock in another company or the building of branch roads. The last point preserved the status of the older lines, but even that proved ephemeral. According to a further proviso, if the railroad voluntarily applied for some special law or amendment to its charter, that change constituted a new charter and therefore subjected the corporation to *all* the provisions of the new constitution. In broad terms the new constitution posed three basic threats to the major Georgia systems: it threatened indirectly to remove the immunity from taxation, it blocked efforts at consolidation designed to reduce competition, and it struck a lethal blow at the formation of self-regulatory pools by investing the legislature with the power to regulate rates.[4]

What difficulties these provisions promised for the Georgia's future Porter could only guess; as yet the legislature had not convened to enact them into specific laws. For the present Porter faced the more immediate task of pumping new energy into the sluggish Georgia system. The company's stock had toppled to a low of 60 that February and showed no inclination to recover. Porter first shuffled his personnel, filling several positions with men from the Western. He had forty-five miles of new steel rail laid on the main stem, approved an experiment begun two years earlier of using coal for fuel in place of wood, absorbed the M & A into the parent system, and finally forced the troublesome Port Royal into a foreclosure sale.[5]

Porter had the good fortune to take office just when economic conditions were improving; business took a marked upturn in 1878 that continued into the next year. Even so the sting of competition caused a slight decline in Georgia earnings, but Porter slashed operating expenses so effectively that net earnings rose 18.3 percent to $338,392. He paid a 6 percent dividend his first year, paid all fixed charges and expenses, and emerged with a surplus balance of $4,124. The Alabama Supreme Court dealt the Western a blow by declaring it liable for outstanding bonds of the old Montgomery & West Point Railroad. That forced the Georgia to pay $132,217 to the bondholders, and Porter estimated the amount would eventually reach $250,000. Despite the setback he pronounced the Georgia system in fine shape: for the coming year it would have to pay interest obligations totalling $242,375. Receipts from sources other than the bank and parent system were estimated at $159,620. Therefore the bank and railroad need net only $82,755 or less than two percent of capital stock to meet all charges. Any amount above that sum could be applied to dividends or to retiring obligations.[6]

Porter's annual report prophesied a good future. The company's stock had climbed steadily all winter and touched 85 as the meeting convened. Georgia bonds stood at 114, a rise of ten points since Porter's accession. In the report he warned against the threat posed by excessive competition and ruthless rate wars, arguing that the only hope lay in "some method of arbitration by which reasonable compromises of the claims of rival lines and rival markets can be arrived at." He praised the Southern Railway and Steamship Association as the best hope for stabilizing rates. To be sure, the pool had achieved only partial success; the first year of its life had witnessed several fierce conflicts among the member roads. But new pooling and payment amendments in 1877 and organizational improvements in 1878 had increased the association's effectiveness, and Porter believed it held the key to the future.[7]

He made his point well. The stockholders promptly reelected him along with the incumbent directors. Porter felt more than content with his lot. Life in Augusta proved pleasant. Phinizy had developed a deep attachment for Porter and supported his every move. Porter welcomed his friendship and never ceased to appreciate his loyalty. Socially, the Alexanders mixed quickly and easily with Augusta's finest; they were not exactly strangers to the city or its society anyway.

The increasing tempo of prosperity persisted. Business in general improved steadily, and bumper crops were sprouting all across the South. On the Georgia freight traffic showed modest gains over the past two years. Through passenger revenues had suffered a steep loss of nearly one-third in 1879; now they showed a modest increase. Local passenger traffic had increased steadily since 1878, but Porter decided to experiment with reduced fares to boost it even more. Response came quickly in the form of a 30 percent increase in revenues. Even the resurging Western caught the mood by running up a surplus. Stock prices languished briefly in late summer but marched steadily through the eighties as the year drew to a close.[8]

The threat posed by the new constitution had not yet fully materialized. The newly assembled legislature opened early hearings in both house and senate on proposed bills to regulate railroads. At the legislature's invitation the entire spectrum of interests from railroad executives to implacable anti-monopolists poured out their suggestions on how the bill should be framed. Most of the discussion soon centered about the proposal to create a railroad commission. Though the new constitution did not specify the creation of such a body, it appeared to be the most feasible alternative even to the railroad executives themselves.[9] Several key questions disturbed both houses as proceedings got underway. Should a commission be created, and if so what powers should be granted it? To what degree should the state attempt to regulate the railroads? How stiff should the penalties be, and how enforced?

In response a flood of bills swamped the house. In scarcely a week the house committee had reported out a bill whose provisions could match those of any similar law in the country in scope. The bill made five basic points. It created a railroad commissioner whose judgment fixed and enforced the other provisions. Secondly, it outlawed as extortion any railroad rate that was not "fair and reasonable." A third provision aimed to prevent discrimination in rates by eliminating all differences in long- and short-haul rates. For passenger fares it stipulated that every passenger must be charged exactly the same rate per mile; for freight traffic it forbade a road to carry any article a given distance at the same price it received for carrying the same article a greater or lesser distance. Rates must be the same per mile between any two points, for traffic going in either direction. A further set of provisions flatly banned pools, drawing upon article IV, section 2, paragraph 4 of the new constitution as its source. Finally, several provisions spelled out the penalties for violators.[10]

The bill passed the house easily and headed for the senate, where it soon ran into strong opposition. The senators in committee asked a number of railroad executives to testify, including Alexander. He welcomed the opportunity and prepared his case carefully. On the subject of railroads he had read a wide range of literature. No work impressed him more than Charles Francis Adams's recently-published essay, *Railroads: Their Origins and Problems.* Adams had defined the Railroad Problem (as it had come to be called) as a conflict between the stupendous impact of the railroad upon civilized life and the utter inadequacy of existing laws of trade to deal with such an innovation. The railroad, he asserted, "has not only usurped, in modern communities, the more important functions of the highway, but those who own it have also undertaken to do the work which was formerly done on the highway." Time had shown that

> recognized laws of trade operate but imperfectly at best in regulating the use made of these modern thoroughfares by those who thus both own and monopolize them. Consequently the political governments of the various countries have been called upon in some way to make good through legislation the deficiences thus revealed in the working of the natural laws.[11]

Drawing heavily upon Adams's ideas, Porter sought to apply them (as well as some of his own) to the specific situation at hand.

Alexander appeared before the senate committee on September 22 and argued that the house bill, if passed, would produce results quite unexpected by its supporters and compound rather than remedy existing evils.[12] He divided the bill into sections according to the evils each tried to remedy. The provisions against extortion or positively high rates he found no fault with; they were, he quipped, "fair and reasonable." He offered no objection to giving the commissioner power to determine what constituted fair and reasonable rates: "I assume that the Railroad Commissioner will be honest, intelligent and impartial, and . . . will take the time and trouble to fully investigate the subject."

Against the next section, designed to prevent unjust discrimination, Porter levied his sharpest attacks. That unharmful discriminations must and do exist cannot be denied, he noted, and the bill implicitly recognizes this by prohibiting "unjust" discriminations. In this instance the complaint becomes not that the rates are *absolutely* too high, but that they are *comparatively* too high to one destination as opposed to another. The question involves a conflict between two different methods of determining a fair and reasonable compensation for any service: the first is based upon the actual *cost* of rendering the service, the second upon the *value* of the service to the recipient. The second method quite naturally involves discriminations, but even a hasty consideration will show this to be the only practical method for some businesses. For example, the government charges three cents to carry a letter three thousand miles but will carry a newspaper four times the weight and ten times the bulk for only a penny. It does this not because the cost to send a newspaper is less (it is actually greater) but because at the three-cent rate very few newspapers would be mailed.

Now the railroad is a machine providing transportation and must therefore charge a certain sum to support itself. The cost of carrying one hundred pounds of silk is the same as for one hundred pounds of corn, but the value of each article differs greatly. If the railroad were required to charge the same rate for both silk and corn, the effect would be not a reduction of price on silk but a prohibitive rate on corn. The charter of the Georgia Railroad prevents the raising of prices—even on high priced goods that could afford higher rates—above a prescribed average, but the company itself has seen fit to discriminate by introducing some twenty different classes of freight at gradually reduced rates. The silk makers have lost nothing; the corn shippers have made an important gain simply because if their rate were not lower they could not afford to ship their corn, the railroad would lose its business, the planter his profit, and the public its corn. The discriminations become a net to catch more business, and the more business there is the lower rates can go.

Freight charges provided an illustration. Nothing, Porter insisted, is more misunderstood than the rationale behind long and short haul charges. The reason for the confusion lay in a failure to distinguish between the cost of providing a service and the value of that service to the recipient. If the bill becomes law, then no railroad will be allowed to charge as much or more for any article carried a given distance than he does for carrying the same article a greater distance. That would declare every existing tariff in the state illegal. A farmer at Thomson, 37 miles away, pays twelve cents per hundred pounds of fertilizer; the farmer at Stone Mountain, 155 miles away, pays the same rate. If discrimination were removed, the latter would have to pay a much higher rate than his Thomson counterpart, but the value of the fertilizer is the same for both men's land. The result might be that the Thomson farmer could afford to buy fertilizer while the Stone Mountain farmer could not. That, too, would be a kind of discrimination, and of a much less fair and reasonable sort than that already in existence. Nor could the railroad solve the problem by simply lowering the rates to fit the scale, for then it would lose money and be forced to quit carrying fertilizer.

The question becomes not discrimination versus no discrimination but rather who shall be favored by whatever form of discrimination is suffered to exist. Here Porter went to great pains to show the senators how existing tariff discriminations worked for the greatest good of the greatest number. Through freight provided an excellent example. The term actually meant four things: freight traversing the entire length of a single line (such as Augusta to Atlanta on the Georgia); freight originating in another state that stops at the terminus of some Georgia road (New York to Atlanta); freight going from a Georgia terminus to some other state (Atlanta to New York); and freight passing through Georgia from one state to another (Boston to Houston). The proposed bill not only prorates local freight tariffs but forces carriers to accept the same rate as any through freight. But the price of through freight depends, as does local freight, solely upon its value to the shipper. For traffic involving other states the result would be disastrous. Georgia roads could not raise through freights to fit local rates, for then non-Georgia shippers would simply reroute their business on one of the many competing non-Georgia lines. On the other hand, to base local rates upon through rates would be equally ruinous, for through rates are at the mercy of changing business conditions at distant and uncontrollable points. And they are subject to the whims of competing non-Georgia lines. Georgia roads have no choice but to fit their through rates to existing rates if they want any business; to base local rates upon these fluctuating rates would be to render them equally unstable.

Nor are the bill's provisions without discriminations. Some parts of the provisions seemed to Porter clearly designed to protect Atlanta and other major terminal points in the state. These cities do not cry out against discrimination, for they benefit from it. The protests come from mercantile interests of other cities, who want to share Atlanta's or Augusta's prosperity. Seen in this light, the cry of discrimination becomes one of partisanship based not upon right but upon commercial envy. The merchants of East Point and Belair would not object to discriminations in the least if they worked in favor of those cities rather than Atlanta or Augusta. To this struggle for commercial supremacy, Porter surmised, the railroad must come as an impartial force.

Having done with discrimination, Porter turned next to the anti-pool section of the bill. He felt certain that these provisions were aimed specifically at the Southern Railway and Steamship Association on the assumption that it served to defeat competition and promote monopoly. Nothing could be further from the truth, Porter argued: "this railroad bill is, to some extent, a chess board where opposing interests of cities and towns are moving to gain or maintain advantages over each other, and unless I am very much mistaken, this section is one of the moves in the interests of the large cities and large shippers against smaller communities and small shippers." The whole theory behind the bill consisted of the fact that three basic kinds of evils had grown up within the transportation system and needed correction. These were: unjust discriminations wrought not by differences of geographical location or laws of supply and demand but by artificially exaggerated rates; unjust discriminations between individuals, usually in the form of rebates; and fluctuating rates, which left railroad and merchant alike uncertain of income and future prospects.

The curing of these evils comprised the Railroad Problem, and that was precisely the object of the Southern Railway and Steamship Association. The public cried for free competition, but no one could deny that in such competition the larger and wealthier roads could eventually grind their weaker rivals into the dust, or that such competition produced the unsavory rate wars. The Southern pool sought not to defeat competition but to restrain its worst abuses. It did not promote monopoly but instead allowed weaker roads to survive by assuring them a fair share of existing markets. It worked ruthlessly to destroy the system of rebates and exaggerated rate differences. It existed not as a secret pool but, as Adams said, "in the full light of publicity." Every transaction made by it could be observed by the public.

Rather than working against the public interest, the pool strove to achieve the same end as the railroad bill now being considered. Instead of being prohibited by law it ought to be granted full legal recognition. Alexander lauded the legislature's desire to create a railroad commission. That step should be the very first to be taken—not the passing of the present bill. The Railroad Problem is one of enormous complexity, he warned; it is too interlaced with subtle nuances and overlapping interests ever to be solved by rigid and inflexible legislation:

> That the Legislation cannot lay down any rigid rule for the construction or regulation of tariffs, removing all inequalities and protecting and harmonizing all interests, is clear from the present bill, which is a sort of drawn battle between the opposing interests of the cities and the towns, and in which they have about succeeded in slaughtering every other interest in the State. And this result was only to have been expected, for no complicated system of transportation ever has been, or ever can be, comformed to such an inflexible thing as a law and fulfill the requirements of modern commerce. Should this bill become law, it is my sober conviction that public opinion would soon force the Governor to call an extra session of the Legislature to repeal it.

Porter had delivered a telling blow against the bill. Other voices pressed similar arguments home to the committee, and there is no way of knowing whose words each senator took most to heart. But the final product turned out to be much as Porter had advocated. The senate produced a much milder version than the house bill.

The final legislation, approved on October 14, differed radically from the original house bill. The provisions against unjust discrimination shrank to one general statement forbidding the practice. Only extortion remained explicitly prohibited. Most important of all, the new law heeded Porter's advice to create a strong commission rather than a rigid and detailed set of regulations. It called for a three-man commission, of whom one should be a lawyer and one an expert in railroad affairs. The three commissioners received virtually unprecedented powers. They could make any necessary rules and regulations to prevent unjust discrimination. They could also fix joint rates for connecting roads on thirty-days notice, and could create regulations to prevent rebates. They could investigate the books and papers of any company and summon any employee to testify. They could inspect all contracts and written agreements between railroads.[13]

The commissioners also received full power to fix rate differences on long and short hauls, but the law contained a crucial proviso rendering it inapplicable to through freight even if carried at lower charges than local freight. Thus the lawmakers accepted Porter's defense of long- and short-haul discriminations as necessary and often beneficial. They fixed the basic responsibility for regulation upon the commission, and as such the bill represented a triumph of the senate bill over the house version. Nearly all interests hailed the measure as a workable solution to a thorny problem. Governor Alfred Colquitt appointed ex-governor James Smith, Samuel Barnett, and Major Campbell Wallace as the commission's first

members. None of the three had even applied for the post, and their selection, the *Atlanta Constitution* proclaimed, was "received with un-
qualified satisfaction all over the state." [14]

Porter had no intention of letting his notions on the future of railroads
remain idle theory. He sensed that the vise of competition would squeeze
the smaller lines to death unless they worked in harmony with the larger
companies. He knew that the ultimate downfall of the railroads would be
laid at the feet not of the public but of the railroads themselves. He
would not let the Georgia and its stockholders be devoured in the brutal
struggle for survival among the carriers; instead he practiced a doctrine
of cooperation and consolidation. During the winter of 1879–1880 he entered into a cooperative five-year alliance with the Louisville & Nashville,
the Central, and the South Carolina roads for moving traffic along their
combined systems. He, Wadley, and President Horatio Victor Newcomb
of the L & N discovered themselves to be genial companions who agreed
essentially on most railroad questions. During the late winter and spring
they huddled for long and frequent conferences concerning their roads.[15]
In mid-April Porter and Wadley leased the Montgomery to Selma branch
of the Western to the L & N for five years.[16]

The following month Porter faced his stockholders at the annual
meeting. His report was impressive. Total earnings had jumped 17.2 percent and net earnings 19.1 percent. The company had paid another 6 percent dividend, and even the Western returned a surplus for the first time.
Company stock had risen to 103, a gain of 43 during Porter's two years
in office. Porter compared the firm's financial condition to that of other
Georgia lines and noted that it had the highest dividend rate and smallest
funded debt in the state. He praised the new alliances with the Central,
the L & N, the South Carolina, and the steamer companies operating out
of Charleston and Savannah. "The new business for our lines," he observed, "is the direct business between the West and New York and other
Eastern ports." The L & N brought the Georgia traffic from the West, and
the steamers carried it on to eastern ports in as good time as all-rail
connections could provide. A good increase in through traffic could be
expected if the alliances worked well.[17]

He won his stockholders' approval with little effort. The improvement
in the company could be seen tangibly in its regular dividend checks.
The stockholders did not always understand Porter's policies, but they
knew enough to see that they worked. They stood ready to reelect him
and his entire board for another year. Then he announced that he would
not stand for reelection, that he was resigning his office as president.

Chapter XIV

In his two years with the Georgia Railroad Alexander had demonstrated his mastery of railway management. He had in some respects reached the pinnacle of his career and certainly could have remained president of the Georgia indefinitely. But in typical fashion success had only whetted his appetite for some greater challenge, and he could not find it in Augusta. In his conference with the L & N he had been introduced to the dynamic Victor Newcomb, the young vice-president who had launched that company onto a program of breathtaking expansion. The two executives deeply impressed one another. Newcomb, who became president of the L & N in March of 1880, needed a new second vice-president. He wanted not only a man of considerable talent but preferably a Georgian who might help popularize the L & N's recent entrance into that state. Seeing both qualities in Alexander, he offered him the job late in April.

The stockholders and directors of the Georgia pleaded with Alexander not to accept. Phinizy added a deeply personal plea: "I have become very much attached to you personally, and for that reason am truly grieved that you think of quitting Augusta." [1] The directors plied him with added financial enticements, but to no avail. The great challenge posed by the L & N intrigued Alexander, and he had already struck a strong rapport with Newcomb. He explained his decision in simple language:

> I would have accepted a similar offer from no man except Mr. Newcomb. I have such absolute confidence in him and in the outcome of his plans which, though gigantic, are so simple and logical to me, that I did not feel justified in declining. I feel that I can do more for my country with him than elsewhere.

Observers agreed that Newcomb had done well to acquire Alexander's services. One Savannah correspondent noted astutely that Porter's entry into the L & N management "strengthened more than anything else could have done, the position of the Louisville & Nashville in Georgia." From that gruff, laconic Wadley of the Central came the highest tribute: "Well, Mr. Newcomb has made the best selection that America afforded." [2]

Alexander's accession to the L & N thrust him into even broader realms of railway management. The Georgia would be the last purely regional company he would ever serve. Already the L & N was rapidly coming under northern influence, and Porter would join it at a crucial juncture in its history.

The history of the L & N since the Civil War had been an unbroken tale of expansion. Partly because of its Nashville terminus and partly because of its location on the Ohio River, the company had developed most of its new lines southward. By 1880 it controlled a 1,840 mile system with a capital stock of $9,059,361 and a funded debt of over $16,000,000. The chief architect for the company's expansion had been Newcomb, whose father had been president of the road until his death in 1874. Succeeding to that office himself in 1880, the younger Newcomb manipulated his company with finesse and brilliance. By 1880 he had defeated rival entrepreneur Edwin "King" Cole by secretly buying out control of Cole's own Nashville, Chattanooga & St. Louis Railroad. It was this victory that gave Newcomb entry into Georgia and led to his alliance with the Georgia roads.[3]

The alliances reflected Newcomb's desire to cooperate with the Central and Georgia roads, though this real ambition was to control them either by lease or outright purchase. The acquisition of Alexander as a vice-president would doubtless mean close harmony with the Georgia, and on the Central Wadley could ill afford to fight so formidable a foe as the L & N. With the two Georgia roads and the L & N system cooperating under a ten-year agreement, the result would be a heavy interchange of traffic, stable rates, and lower tariffs on many items. Henry W. Grady applauded the agreements, announced on April 7, 1880, and spoke of Newcomb as "the Moses that leads Atlanta out of bondage." [4]

But the survival of the alliances depended in large part upon Wadley of the Central, who took pride in his road as a Georgia corporation and regarded the invasion of an outsider like Newcomb with grave suspicion. In truth Newcomb faced a similar problem within his own company, for northern interests had been buying into the L & N since 1874 and were already grappling with the president for control. Their struggle for power would have a decided influence upon Alexander's future.

Porter assumed his new position amidst a fresh burst of expansion by Newcomb. One of his first tasks was to negotiate a rate war between the L & N and the Chicago, St. Louis & New Orleans, a subsidiary of the powerful Illinois Central. Provoked originally by a fight over passenger fares, the war soon spread to freight rates and dragged on through most of the summer. When it threatened to consume most of the profits of a good year, Newcomb sent Alexander to work out a settlement based on concessions by the L & N. His skillful negotiating helped ease the tensions and led to a final settlement in August.[5]

As he gained mastery in his new position Porter became increasingly fascinated by the complexities of such a giant system. He wanted to master every detail. At forty-five he showed no less energy than he had at twenty-five, and in some ways he felt he had reached the height of his powers. Already his reputation was beginning to spread beyond the South, where he had long been recognized as a future railroad king. One Georgia historian, noting that Wadley and Cole were nearing sixty, called Alexander "the young Napoleon of the railways." [6] But the railroad proved a jealous and demanding mistress; she gave Porter little time for other pleasures. The boys were already going off to school, and the girls were preparing for a trip to Europe. He begged all of them to write from time to time. "I get awfully lonesome sometimes," he confessed to little Bess, "& the letters are the only things that enable me to stand it." Bettie, too, travelled a lot and fretted anxiously over her husband. "I know you must be busy," she scolded in early September. "Please dont sit up late at night. I know your failing & am afraid to trust you. You can smoke your cigarette in bed as much as you choose until I come home if you will only go to bed early." [7]

But Porter found little time to relax, for Newcomb in rapid order purchased some more small lines and announced a new $20,000,000 mortgage to finance the whole L & N system. His lightning expansion had earned his system the bitter epithet of "Newcomb's Octopus"; it had also cost a lot of money. In his carefully composed annual report Newcomb wrote an elaborate defense of his policies. The burden of preparation fell equally upon Porter, who shared Newcomb's vision and warmly approved his course. [8]

When the annual meeting opened in Louisville on October 6, Newcomb played his cards carefully. [9] He listed the new additions to the L & N system in the last year and readily conceded that they had swollen the company's funded debt from $16,546,770 to $23,902,820 (a shrewd comparison, since these figures stopped at June 30, the close of the fiscal year, and did not include more recent acquisitions). But he hastily underscored the fact that the company netted 14 percent on capital stock and paid an 8 percent dividend for the year. Newcomb argued confidently that all newly acquired properties, once put in good physical condition, would pay their own way and eventually turn a profit for the parent company. Then he went on to propose his new $20,000,000 bond issue which, he asserted, would place the company "financially in a position of strength and independence never before enjoyed, probably, since its organization."

Newcomb gained reelection with little effort only to announce that he wished to resign at the earliest possible date. What motives prompted his decision remain obscure. He advanced ill health as his reason, yet he stayed on as a director of the company and exerted no little energy that year organizing the United States National Bank in New York. Perhaps he had tired of the railroad game; perhaps he sniffed some impending disaster; or perhaps the bank had simply absorbed his attention. Whatever the reasons, the stockholders voted to relieve him on December 1 and elected Edward Green, the first vice-president, to succeed him. One other change resulted from the election: James T. Woodward, president of the Hanover National Bank in New York, replaced a Louisvillian on the board. Porter did not like this drift. He sensed overtones of changing policy that could only hurt the company. He had come to the L & N largely because of Newcomb, and soon Newcomb would be gone. But he liked Green well enough personally, and when the New Yorker assumed the presidency Porter would certainly replace him as first vice-president. He would bide his time.[10]

The late fall hatched one annoying crisis after another. Though gross earnings perked up considerably for the first half of the year, expenses spiraled upward as well. More important, a modest rebellion erupted within the company itself. A minority of L & N stockholders, fearing an unfavorable shift in control, filed suit to block the transfer of any new stock but lost the case. Internal dissensions, the impending change in management, and hazy reports of unsound policy all played havoc with L & N stock late in the year, and it was whispered in some circles that the new northern members of the board took more interest in speculation than in the welfare of the company. Newcomb stepped down as expected on December 1. Green took his place, and Porter acceded to the first vice-presidency. But stories of dissension within the board persisted stubbornly, as did rumors of a further change in management at the board meeting on February 26, 1881.[11]

At that meeting Porter's worst fears were confirmed. Green tendered his resignation as president and was replaced by Christopher Columbus Baldwin, a New York financier. Porter disliked Baldwin and distrusted his intentions. Baldwin fully appreciated Porter's value to the company, however, and successfully urged him to remain as first vice-president. The board now included four Louisville men, George Washington of Nashville, Clarence Clark of Philadelphia, and five New Yorkers. Of the group Green was said to be the company's largest stockholder, and behind him stood his formidable wife, Hetty Green, supposedly the richest woman in America.[12]

Once in office Baldwin launched an expansion program of his own. A choice opportunity turned up in Georgia and involved none other than the Georgia Railroad. Phinizy, though still basking in prosperity, fully appreciated his precarious position of being surrounded by three ambitious giants: the L & N, the Richmond & Danville, and the Central. The simplest assurance of a guaranteed income for his company, he reasoned, would be a lease to one of these competitors, and early in the winter he let it be known that the Georgia would consider leasing proposals. All three major systems snapped at the bait, but Wadley quickly got the inside track despite strenuous opposition within his own board. He proposed to Phinizy a ninety-nine-year lease to the Central at a guaranteed rate of 8 percent a year on capital stock. After a long and complicated set of negotiations Wadley acquired the lease in his own name and soon sold half interest to the L & N. This move forced his reluctant directors to accept the other half for the Central.[13]

Encouraged by this sudden turn of events, Baldwin accelerated his expansion program. He purchased the strategically-located Louisville, Cincinnati & Lexington Railroad. This 175-mile addition extended the L & N northward to Newport, across the Ohio river to Cincinnati, and eastward through Frankfort to Lexington.[14] He acquired a majority of the Pensacola & Atlantic Company and planned to build a 170-mile road to link the L & N's existing Florida subsidiaries. He consummated an agreement with the East Tennessee, Virginia & Georgia Railroad whereby the L & N would extend its Knoxville branch to the Tennessee state line to meet a similar extension by the East Tennessee of its Knoxville & Ohio branch. The new line when finished would give the L & N through connections to eastern Tennessee, North Carolina, and Virginia. It also opened up a potentially rich coal and iron area.[15]

Baldwin paused long enough to assemble a glowing annual report. Sliding casually over a mortgage debt that now totalled a staggering $46,991,840, he depicted the year past as a trial period whose results promised accelerating prosperity for the coming years. He lingered fondly over the manifest signs of national prosperity, dwelled poetically upon thriving crops and burgeoning mineral resources. He showed how the proliferating L & N system could not help but reflect this pyramiding affluence by increased traffic and revenues. He won speedy reelection along with the incumbent slate of directors.[16] As winter neared he unfolded new projects.

In all of Baldwin's schemes the burden of negotiation, contracting, and arranging final details fell upon Porter. Never had he been so busy. Operating out of a private railroad car, he whirled up and down the tracks like a rail-bound Flying Dutchman. When Bettie complained of ill health in August he sent her off to White Sulphur Springs but could not accompany her. Louisa Gilmer promptly suggested that she console her loneliness with a Savannah visit. "Who knows," she teased, "perhaps the wandering *Gentile* might come with you for half an hour—wh. is the longest I believe he ever stops in one place." [17]

In truth Porter relished his strenuous pace. Moreover, he had been funneling his earnings into stock investments, including the purchase of three hundred shares of Central stock to participate in a proposed special 40 percent dividend.[18] And no one appreciated the value of his services more than Baldwin, who thoughtfully provided Alexander with a third vice-president and traffic manager to relieve part of the burden. As company for Porter's rare leisure moments, he welcomed a restored and cheerful Bettie back from her southern sojourn. "And do you know," he confided slyly to the girls in Europe, "she & I alone are so much company to each other that I'm afraid it is selfish in us to be so well satisfied. I can spoon as much as I please now that Lula is not here to reprove me— & Mother likes it." [19]

Winter. The year of good fortune had slipped away, and hard times seemed clearly in the wind. Baldwin had calculated wrong. The financial structure of the nation had again overextended itself, and during the coming months symptoms of weakness appeared in the form of deteriorating stock prices. On the L & N board friction rose again. The dissenting faction, centered around E. H. Green, had never really approved of Baldwin's frenetic expansion; nor did they trust him personally. Whether or not he actually speculated (some said he did so on company funds) remained a moot question, though suspicion tainted his every dealing. But as long as he kept the road solvent and paid regular dividends he could not very easily be assailed.

Swiftly Baldwin began to reap the inevitable harvest of his expansion program. Many of his purchases proved to be poorly constructed and inadequately equipped. Few of the new roads paid their way, and some displayed an utterly inadequate traffic to offset their obligations. Even the coveted Georgia failed to earn its keep, netting only $449,521 the first year of its lease. New construction projects ate up their share of earnings, and for those recently acquired roads in dilapidated shape the L & N had no choice but to sink more money into repairs and renovation. The swollen funded debt added another sizable drain, and rumors of a large floating debt persisted stubbornly in the face of repeated denials.

Alarmed at the L & N's deteriorating financial structure, Green and his friends vowed to oust Baldwin. When Louisville mayor Charles Jacob decided to sell 10,000 of the city's 19,132 shares of L & N stock, Green outbid all contenders to claim the whole lot. Baldwin knew he had troubles;

in March he was forced to buttress his crumbling financial position with a $10,000,000 issue of debenture bonds.[20] Porter was disgusted with the whole business. He sided wholeheartedly with Green and saw little hope for the L & N unless Baldwin could be replaced. He also looked for a new position.

In March Albert Fink dangled an attractive possibility before him. Now commissioner for the eastern Trunk Lines, he had recently submitted to his executive committee a plan to reorganize their board of arbitration and suggested that Porter head the new board. Porter considered the offer a compliment and expressed frank interest in the position, but nothing came of the proposal.[21] Then Porter, backed by Green and his associates, tried to persuade Fink to resign his commissionership and oppose Baldwin for the L & N presidency. Fink had served eighteen years with the L & N, and no man save former president James Guthrie had done more for the company. Would it not be fitting for him to return now and rescue the L & N in its time of troubles? Fink entered gingerly into the discussion and soon added a new aspect to the situation: if he accepted the presidency of the L & N then he would certainly recommend Porter to replace him as Trunk Line commissioner. Porter jumped at the suggestion. He could wash his hands of the whole messy L & N affair, move to New York, and bid farewell to railroad politics.

Early in June reports announced that Fink had already accepted the L & N presidency, but they proved unhappily premature. "Mr. Fink could not get the Trunk Lines to agree to his resigning," Porter observed sadly on June 3, "& so all prospects of our going to N. Y. to live are gone. . . . What we will do is *very* uncertain but I feel very much disposed to move *somewhere*." He told little Bess not to worry, "for every move I have ever made has bettered things & I hope the next may do so too." [22]

Dissatisfied as he was, he could not very well stay put. Inklings of the L & N's dissension had already affected its stock, which had stood at 100 in January and wobbled steadily downward to a low of 61 in July. Baldwin announced that the company would pass the August dividend. Porter expressed his discontent to Gilmer, who was quick to sympathize: ". . . now may be the proper—the appointed time, for you to make your farewell bow, and return to Georgia, where you are so much needed." And he went on to describe the complex situation that had evolved on the Central.[23]

The problems of the Central involved an awkward situation that had arisen within the management. Ever since the Civil War Wadley had ruled the Central with an iron hand. Gruff, rugged, and taciturn, Wadley brooked no opposition to his policies; yet workers and associates alike regarded him as a fair man and a keen judge of talent. He valued power above wealth, lived modestly, and never speculated in Central stock.[1]

The Central's main line, consisting of two divisions, the 192-mile Savannah to Macon and the 103-mile Macon to Augusta, had pyramided into a 709-mile system by 1877. Wadley's most important acquisition had been the sprawling Southwestern Railroad system, whose branches totalled 306 miles by 1877. He understood only too well the necessity for annexing competitors and working harmoniously with those feeder lines he could not control directly. As early as 1872 he warned against the fierce competition for traffic "that has resulted from the construction of competing lines in a section of the country where there is but a limited amount of business to be had."[2]

Much as he disliked it, Wadley caught the drift of changing times and swam with the current. To make the Central invulnerable to damage from competitors became his fixed ambition, and he pursued it with a shrewd and relentless hand. His attention focused on the Central's strategic location at Savannah. "New York is, and will continue to be, the great commercial centre of the country," he observed in 1874. "This being recognized, and the fact that there are numerous land routes from the South and Southwest, terminating at New York, the question to be settled is whether an all rail or rail and ocean transportation is the cheapest." He was willing to gamble on the latter, and in 1872 purchased controlling interest in a company of six steamships plying the northern route out of Savannah. Since the Central's charter did not permit it to own ships directly, Wadley created in 1875 an independent corporation, the Ocean Steamship Company, with himself as president and other Central directors as the officers. The Central sold its ships to the new company and received in exchange all its stock, which then became an asset of the parent company.[3]

Under Wadley's iron hand the Central prospered, paying 10 percent dividends from 1870 to 1873. When depression settled in he kept the road solvent despite falling earnings by the simple expedient of plowing all earnings back into the company. For three years he stubbornly refused to pay a dividend and worked to consolidate the Central's position. In 1879 he obtained a controlling interest in the Vicksburg & Brunswick and arranged for the purchase of the foreclosed Montgomery & Eufaula. The following year he picked up the Columbus & Western (formerly the S & M) in foreclosure sale. Uneasy over the L & N's keen interest in Georgia, he entered into agreement with that line for an interchange of traffic. A year later he joined the L & N in leasing the Georgia Railroad, and added the Port Royal & Augusta as well.[4]

Once more he pared dividends down to provide funds for the new properties. Devoted to his task of building and Spartan in his habits, he expected his directors and stockholders to follow suit. Those who objected he brushed aside with a heavy hand, and in so doing incurred enemies on his own board. No one questioned his ability and integrity. Those directors who opposed him did so not because he had built poorly but because they resented his arbitrary domination of the company's management. Some of them thought Wadley too conservative. He was sixty-seven and in declining health.

In 1881 discontent became open rebellion. Since December of 1873 Wadley had paid only 27 percent in dividends even though net earnings had consistently increased. He offered a reasonable defense for this policy, insisting that surplus funds could be better used in retiring old obligations and placing new acquisitions on a firm basis. But this explanation failed to appease those stockholders anxious for income. At the heart of the dividend problem lay the Southwestern lease, which guaranteed stockholders in that company an 8 percent dividend for every 10 percent declared for Central stockholders and a minimum 7 percent dividend whether the Central declared one for itself or not. As a result, Wadley's policy of deferring or reducing annual dividends in favor of reinvestment meant that the Central could not make up for these lost dividends without cutting Southwestern holders in for an 80 percent slice. And every time Wadley passed a dividend for the Central he still had to pay the Southwestern its 7 percent. Thus, for the eight year period 1874–1881 Central stockholders received only 27 percent in dividends while Southwestern holders reaped a fat 56 percent.[5]

To compensate for the dividends they claimed to have lost, the dissatisfied directors proposed a plan to create a special 40 percent dividend by issuing certificates of indebtedness to the stockholders. If this were done, however, the directors would also have to issue another 32 percent in debentures for the Southwestern. Wadley cringed at the thought of creating $4,600,000 worth of debentures, but he found himself blocked by a majority of the board. Reluctantly he signed the certificates and then hastened in his annual report to defend his decision from the inevitable charge that he had merely watered the Central's stock.[6]

During the debate Alexander had involved himself by purchasing some three hundred shares in anticipation of the dividend and personally urging Wadley to issue the debentures. Later he claimed that his interest in Central affairs arose during the attempt by Wadley to lease the road to Cole in 1880. Gradually his study of the company's affairs convinced him that Wadley and his supporters were deliberately undervaluing Central stock in order to maintain their control over the company and especially to avoid attracting the interest of outside investors. The dividend policy was to Porter and the other dissidents only a part of the plan to keep the stock depressed. Occasionally, Porter charged, Wadley made gloomy predictions about the stock and advised the company bank not to accept it as collateral at any price.[7]

As dissension widened on the Central board the anti-Wadley forces slowly coalesced around Porter. They included Gilmer and other members of the family, long-standing enemies of Wadley, some of Savannah's younger financiers, disenchanted stockholders, and a growing number of L & N officials who had bought into Central stock. Together they represented a faction opposed to the old entrenched management and its conservative policies, and especially to Wadley's one-man rule. They insisted that even the 1881 certificates did not provide dividends large enough to reflect the Central's true earning power, and they put forward a new scheme. A further dividend could be declared on the earnings of the Ocean Steamship Company, either by distributing that company's stock to Central holders or by issuing certificates of indebtedness upon it. Since it was an entirely separate company owned by the Central, the courts might consider it outside the Southwestern lease and thus no division of dividend would have to be made.[8]

In December the rebels broached the scheme to Wadley. The old president exploded at the idea and argued that the proposal watered the company's stock by converting $795,000 worth of assets into debentures. He flatly rejected the plan and prepared to face his tormentors in the January stockholders' meeting. Porter and his supporters insisted that no stock would be watered and that the proposal only guaranteed that all Ocean earnings above expenses and a $150,000 sinking fund should be turned over to the Central for dividends. They accused Wadley's supporters of trying, as Gilmer phrased it, "to depreciate the stock for sinister & party purposes." In the board election they put up a slate of candidates pledged to issuing the Ocean certificates.[9]

Wadley still had too much strength to be displaced as president, but he could find no way of stilling his opponents. Already several of the smaller stockholders who had supported him for years had begun selling out at the attractive prices offered by outside buyers known to be in sympathy with the dissenters. Wadley had always been proud of the fact that the Central had remained over the years a Georgia road controlled by Georgians. Now he saw among the rebels ample evidence of a growing infiltration by the L & N. Baldwin himself had purchased 1,772 shares of Central stock, and other L & N figures lesser lots. The thought of L & N domination only intensified Wadley's resistance.[10]

The stockholders expectantly assembled early in January. Rumors in Savannah had Wadley on the point of resigning or the rebellious directors powerful enough to unseat him or Alexander about to run for the presidency against him. No such contest materialized, but the rebels put four of their men on the board including Alexander and Gilmer. Nine incumbents kept their places, some of them known supporters of the Alexander faction. Wadley retained his place, as did his vice-president, staunch supporter, and son-in-law William G. Raoul.[11]

Entrenched upon the board though not possessing a solid majority, the pro-certificate faction quickly won support for their plan. They pushed through a proposal to issue $5,000,000 in 6 percent bonds on the Ocean Steamship Company, of which $3,500,000 would be used for the certificates and the rest for three new steamers and some other improvements. Though his health continued to worsen, Wadley refused to budge. Presented with the certificates on February 7, he protested loudly, refused to sign them, and resigned as Ocean's president. One of the pro-certificate directors, E. C. Anderson, replaced him but found his attempt to issue the certificates blocked by a court injunction.[12]

As the case moved slowly toward the Georgia Supreme Court both factions searched for a way out of the deadlock. The main issue still revolved around the question of whether or not Alexander's position represented a sincere concern for the Central's financial condition. Was it a genuine attempt to make the company's dividends reflect its true earning power or was it simply a raid for the benefit of speculators and outside interests? Most of the major Georgia newspapers thought the latter and castigated Porter for trying to wreck the Central. Others reminded their readers of Porter's reputation as a railroad man. The *Savannah Morning News*, though against the certificates, noted that "General Alexander occupies too prominent a position in railroad circles to be willing to recklessly jeopardize his reputation merely for the sake of a speculation." [13]

In mid-February Porter abruptly called for a conference on the dispute and offered a compromise. He expressed the willingness of his supporters to accept increased dividends on some basis other than the certificates, such as quarterly cash dividends, but no agreement could be reached. It became increasingly obvious that the certificates were losing popularity. Meanwhile Wadley's position continued to deteriorate. Fresh rumors of his impending retirement appeared as his health grew worse and his position more untenable. Even his supporters talked privately of replacing him but could not agree upon a suitable candidate. In June the Central's longtime New York director, Moses Taylor, died and was replaced by E. H. Green of the L & N. Wadley eyed his accession with grim suspicion. He saw his enemies gathering about him, and he would not suffer to see the Central delivered into their hands.[14]

As Gilmer explained it early in July, Porter could easily become the key to the situation. No one wanted an open war with Wadley for the presidency; all held him in great esteem, and it would hurt the company's stock. But Wadley had made no bones about his desire to keep the Central free of L & N influence, and to achieve that end he wanted Raoul to succeed him. During the past few months Raoul had taken over most of the ailing Wadley's duties. He had bound himself closer to Wadley by marrying one of his daughters. Wadley knew he could trust Raoul to carry out his wishes; for that reason he might, Gilmer feared, stand for reelection. If Wadley won and got his own board elected, then he could resign and have them elect Raoul in his place. And he might win if he ran again.[15]

"To avoid all *risk*," Gilmer offered a compromise plan. Wadley realized that Raoul could not be elected president on his own. "I am inclined to think, that Mr W. would agree to 'a compromise or amicable adjustment' that retained Raoul as V. P. & made you President." True, the plan would saddle the board with Raoul, "with his sins of commission and omission—merits & demerits all of which are *great*." But the board could put up with Raoul if Porter became president, and Wadley might be appeased by retaining him in his office "with the hope of succession."

Porter agreed completely with Gilmer's prognosis. So far his Central activities had not interfered with his duties for the L & N; now he saw the opportunity to leave his distasteful position in Louisville. He had represented the L & N well on the Central board and could count on its support in a campaign. He could rely, too, on the wide influence of his family and his many friends. But this support alone could not swing an election. Control could not be bought; it would have to be won by a gathering of proxies and already Gilmer and friends were contacting key holders. Late in June Porter placed his resignation in Baldwin's hands and turned a deaf ear to pleas for him to withdraw it.[16]

Then fate intervened. Wadley had gone to Saratoga Springs for some rest. There on August 10 he succumbed to an apoplectic stroke. The reassembled board promptly elected Porter to fill his place, but the hope of compromise had vanished. Raoul might be inclined now to try for the presidency on his own by portraying himself as Wadley's personally groomed heir apparent. He lacked sufficient votes on the board to be selected now, but he could make a fight of it in January. In public Raoul maintained an inscrutable silence, but he had already made his decision. Even before Alexander's election Raoul wrote a confidant: "I regard this as the most critical epoch in the history of the Central Railroad. . . . I am writing honestly in the interests of the Company, and I believe we ought to have an able and conservative board next January." [17]

Gingerly Porter stepped into his new position. Wadley's death had disrupted routine and thrown the company into confusion. The annual report had been delayed and Porter had to put it in shape as quickly as possible. The tables told an unhappy tale. Gross earnings had dropped over 6 percent, and steadily increasing expenses had slashed net earnings nearly 25 percent. Yet surplus earnings, though down nearly 18 percent, still equalled 5 percent on capital stock. In the report Porter reviewed Wadley's past dividend policy and stressed the importance of regular dividends. By plowing surplus earnings back into new investments the old president had doubtless done the company a good service, but the peculiar nature of the Southwestern lease had forced him to pay, over an eight-year period, only 27 percent dividends on Central stock compared to 56 percent on Southwestern stock. Even the 40 percent certificate dividend in 1881 had only narrowed the gap to 67 percent for the Central and 88 percent for the Southwestern.[18]

Once in control of the presidency Porter and his supporters no longer needed the steamship certificates. Since they now controlled both companies and could formulate their own dividend policy, they tried to reconcile their opponents by nullifying the certificates. But the conservatives were not mollified. Early in December Raoul resigned as vice-president to campaign openly for the presidency. He denounced the current board as a tool of the L & N and proclaimed himself the true inheritor of the Wadley tradition. Raoul had a powerful and emotional theme to play on—that of L & N domination. He could speak movingly on his vision of a great Georgia railroad owned and operated by Georgians, and easily link himself to that vision. Chauvinism it might be, but it made potent campaign medicine and Raoul knew it.[19]

Behind the facade of emotion and rhetoric, however, lay some genuine issues. The Wadley tradition represented by Raoul meant a policy of plowing most earnings into improvements and expansion. Its conservatism appealed greatly to the smaller stockholders and those who considered the Central a native corporation devoted to the commercial aspirations of the state. Though Porter was a native Georgian, his meteoric career with several companies had given him the reputation of representing not so much investors as brokers and speculators. He had come up a little too fast and moved a little too quickly. His critics distrusted his glib facility for manipulation; ignoring his genuinely fine managerial talent, they tended to see only a career steeped in ambiguous financial activities. That he possessed such a reputation among many Georgians is beyond dispute. The Griffin *News* put the matter baldly: "There can be no doubt that General Alexander is the candidate of the speculators and Captain Raoul of those persons who desire a good, safe and profitable investment." [20]

Such objections usually crystalized in the charge that Alexander, if elected, would run the road more in the interest of outsiders as opposed to state interests. This accusation implied in part that outside interests, involved in many vast projects, would manage the Central only as a part of the larger whole of their affairs and, if necessary, sacrifice the road (and thus the minority holders) whenever their larger interests required it. In part, too, the charge reflected a much more basic factor ever lurking behind the election rhetoric: the fiercely competitive and conflicting commercial aspirations within the state. In the long run Georgians cared less about outside domination than about which interests or locales in the state itself would benefit from the chosen management. Though portraying the conflict as one between Georgia and outsiders, the economic realities shaped it as one between rival interests within the state.

Under these circumstances the Alexander forces worked against difficult odds. They could not very well deny their ties with the L & N, but they did minimize them. They stressed Wadley's alliance with the L & N, and his realization that to survive the Central needed to work harmoniously with connecting lines. They obtained from Albert Fink a glowing testimonial to Porter's ability:

I would consider it a great mistake of the stockholders . . . if they should not re-elect . . . Alexander. . . . His high character and his ability as a railroad manager, and his peculiar acquaintance with the Southern railroad system should, I think, make his services invaluable to the company. . . . It is the short-sightedness and arbitrary policy that has so much prevailed with railroad managers in the past, that has led to so many difficulties with the people, resulting in hostile legislation and in reduced dividends. . . . I always considered General Alexander peculiarly qualified, while guarding the interests of the companies with which he has been connected, to act upon broad and liberal views, to secure the good will of the people with whom he has to deal, and thereby advance the interests of the railroad companies more than by arbitrary methods.[21]

Before December the struggle had confined itself largely to in-fighting. Now it grew hot and fierce. Raoul held the better cards and he knew it. Gilmer fumed bitterly because, as his wife complained, "it is being represented, and by people who shd know better, that Ed is acting the part of an ingrate—that he was as it were dug out of a dunghill by Mr Wadley, and wd never have been anybody but for him." As January 1 approached, rumors appeared that a crucial part of the L & N stock had sold out to Raoul. The sixty-two hundred shares supposedly owned by E. H. Green but actually controlled by his wife had gone over to the Raoul camp. Some sources said that Senator Joe Brown had purchased the shares outright for his friend; others claimed he had merely "paid a bonus for the privilege of voting them in this election." Whatever the case, loss of the Green or Cisco stock meant defeat for Alexander. The transfer took place only three days before the election, at which point Porter was reported to have a lead of about two thousand proxies. News of the transfer plunged the Alexander camp into gloom.[22]

No company election in Georgia had ever raised such intense ex-citement. Stockholders and proxies representing 66,378 of the Central's 75,000 shares assembled in Savannah, more shares than had ever been voted. Voters waited patiently outside the bank building to cast their ballots, and wagers on the outcome could be heard everywhere. The steady stream of voters kept the poll open a full hour past the six o'clock closing time, but the Alexander men had glumly conceded defeat early in the afternoon. The final tally showed Raoul's entire board elected by 4,211 votes. It was a crushing defeat and Porter took it hard. "I have not yet recovered from the bitter blow of . . . Ed's defeat," his sister Hattie wrote. "The sight of his face almost broke my heart." [23] Hurt and be-wildered, he left Savannah to go on a trip, to rest for a while and to think about where next to go.

At forty-seven Porter suddenly found it necessary to seek new prospects again. It was not, as it had been at thirty, a struggle for survival; his investments had ensured that. Rather it was that he could not bear to remain idle. And, too, the postwar struggle had left its scars, for he never ceased feeling uneasy over his financial security. When the disappointment had worn off he took to scouting for a new job. In the fall he accepted a post on the commission to build a new capitol building in Atlanta,

but that would occupy only part of his time. He spent some time converting North Island into a resort area and by 1885 began to consider
buying nearby South Island as well.[24]

Two new possibilities appeared in 1885. The new Democratic president, Grover Cleveland, would need a railroad commissioner and Alexander's name went into a crowded hat. The second opportunity involved
a position as one of the government directors for the Union Pacific Railroad. Caring little for political office, Alexander displayed no regrets when
Cleveland chose the aging Joe Johnston as commissioner. The UP
position was another matter, for Charles Francis Adams had recently
accepted the presidency of that road. Determined to restore it from Jay
Gould's rapacious manipulations, Adams urged Porter to accept the job as
director. Alexander readily agreed, since it would consume only part of
his time and thus leave him free to pursue his other interests.[25]

On the side Porter dabbled in Florida real estate, bought and sold
stocks, loaned a little money out at interest, and did a prodigious amount
of reading and writing. He spent at least part of every winter on North
Island to make repairs, supervise his fisheries there, and go hunting for
duck and wild game. In April of 1886 Cleveland reappointed Porter to
the UP, along with Franklin MacVeagh and James Savage. A new
member had joined the board earlier in the year and also retained his post:
Marcus A. Hanna. He and Porter soon became fast friends.[26]

The "railroad problem" had come to be a very familiar topic to Porter. As
a brilliant and articulate man with a reputation for honesty and fairness,
he had often been summoned to testify in hearings pertaining to railroad
legislation. In 1879 he had addressed the Georgia senate committee, and
in 1881 he made a similar appearance before the Alabama senate.[27]

In these and other appearances Porter gradually formulated his concept
of the railroad problem and possible solutions to it. Asked to contribute
a volume to the Putnam's "Questions of the Day" series in 1887, he con-
densed his ideas into a succinct sixty-page summary on the theory and
practice of railroad management. To the task he brought a wide background of reading, experience, and personal observation. He understood
the vast social and economic transformation going on about him. He felt
deeply the impact of the railroad upon American life, and appreciated the
roots of complaint against it. He readily admitted that railway management
was liable to abuse and corruption, but he showed no sympathy for
popular attempts to regulate the railroads. He despised especially what he
called "theoretical reformers." Alexander was a pragmatist to the core. He
cared nothing at all for ideas that could not be put to use, and he liked

nothing better than pursuing the ramifications of what he considered to be a practical idea.[28]

Lack of practicality was his principal objection to the many proposed reforms circulating in 1887. The question was in fact being discussed everywhere. Congress seemed finally on the verge of passing the long delayed Reagan bill. Reform seemed to be winning its way, but reformers had trouble agreeing upon a common plan or program. Porter disputed current proposals because none accepted the reforms instigated by the railroads themselves. Yet who should know more about the question? "Surely after fifty years of experiment, and a development covering all civilized countries," he chided, "there must be to-day a few principles, settled by actual test, and put beyond question or dispute, making what we might call the present state of the science of railway management." In his book and before the committee Porter advocated the pool as the only practical solution. It undermined the proffering of rebates in the only possible way: by removing the temptation to give them. It eliminated the ruinous railroad wars that kept rates unstable and crushed smaller competitors by promoting an orderly division of traffic. It did not stifle competition but on the contrary encouraged it. Yet, Porter noted, by an ironic twist public opinion had come to picture the pool as a leviathan of monopoly. The Reagan bill, in prohibiting pools and forbidding unequal long- and short-haul rates, sought to promote competition but would end up destroying it by its failure to distinguish between reasonable and ruinous competition. Unfettered competition among railroads led invariably to rate wars and consolidation. The pools existed to curb this ruthless competition. If they were banned by law, Porter predicted, "consolidation must be the inevitable result," and nothing did the public dread more than monopolies. But outlaw the pools and they would come: "It may be temporarily checked in any manner that theorists think good, but it will have its way in the end."

Porter admitted the shortcomings of the pools in practice and criticized the railroads' distrust of one another. He asserted that pooling should be legalized except that the country would be afraid of it: "For the interests of the roads I would like to see that done. I would rather that you would regulate competition, so that we could not cut each other's throats as we do now."

The crux of Porter's principles rested in his belief that "the greatest good to the greatest number is subserved by making no exception to the law of freedom of individual action." The struggle for existence inevitably favored those who best suited changing times. The railroad represented a striking example; it had fashioned thriving commercial centers out of once isolated villages (Atlanta furnished a perfect example), and destroyed once prosperous coastal towns whose commercial superiority vanished when the iron horse prevailed. Someday, Porter added, flying machines and Keeley motors may destroy the value of railroads, "but, for all that, the field must be left open for the utmost freedom of individual action."

It was Darwin who dominated his thinking. He had diligently absorbed the theory of evolution and, fascinated, assimilated it into his world view ("There are but two possible theories for this world," he would later write, "one of wh is 'Chance' & the other is 'Blue Print.' I am a Blue Printer").[29] As early as 1876 he had put his Darwinian ideas into some delightful children's verse called the *Catteral Ratteral Doggeral*. To the Reagan committee he offered this summation:

> It is the history of creation that development is going on everywhere; that old things are passing away, to be succeeded by newer and better. No political system, no city, no trade, no manufacture, no individual business has any divine right to be protected or to protect against the growth of any other system, or city, or trade, or individual which is able to gain a foothold and make its way in the world. Let the struggle for existence go on, and let the fittest survive. This is my political and commercial creed.

To what extent he impressed the committee cannot be ascertained, but Fink wrote him that one member praised Porter's testimony as "the clearest statement that had been made before the Committee." [30]

In most of his attitudes Porter personified the ideology of the late nineteenth-century businessman, except that he was more articulate and precise in his meaning. His concept of the railroad problem may be fairly considered as an archetype of the stance of thoughtful railroad executives. That his views are not without error is obvious; he tended, for example, to put too much faith in pools as the only solution to the railroad problem, though he expressed serious doubts as to whether they could actually do the job. Some historians have been all too willing to dismiss the arguments of the railway executives as partisan rationales of self-interest while portraying the arguments of anti-railroad interests as selfless, enlightened doctrines. Historians resorting to this approach tend to reduce the struggle to a morality play with the "people" as the hero and the railroad men as the villains.

A biographer of Reagan, for example, has dismissed the arguments of Alexander, Albert Fink, Charles Francis Adams, and others as the mouthings of "paid experts." To delay Reagan's progress, he avows, the railroads "sent their highly-paid 'siege guns' . . . to create confusion and uncertainty, and to criticize and to defeat their greatest antagonist, Reagan." By this approach Reagan emerges as a legislative St. George, the railroads as dragons with no justification for their dragonhood save greed and short-sightedness.[31]

This is poor history. The railroad problem was one of immense complexities, and the history of late nineteenth-century attempts at railroad regulation bears out the truth that the "people" never quite understood or mastered the problem well enough to deal with it successfully. In his analysis of the railroad and its effect upon economic life Alexander provided an essentially accurate and honest portrayal. That he was defending a personal interest does not in the least diminish the validity of his arguments; it may be held that many railroad men were not lacking in integrity and took a broad view of the problems of their industry. Porter was probably right in asserting that only the railroad men really understood the intricacies of railway management, but his trenchant logic still avoided the heart of the matter: the dual nature of the railroad.

Porter's formulations would have been correct for any honestly capitalized railroad, but few such railroads existed. He made no mention of rates being excessive because they had to cover not honest expenses but watered stock and bloated funded debts. His argument emerged as a true analysis of how a railroad meets its expenses but could say nothing about the degree to which those expenses were fraudulent products either of financial manipulation or poor management. The fundamental problem lay in the railroad's role as an engine of finance capitalism, which made it a prime target for speculators. As long as businessmen found it more lucrative to make their profits from the railroads by speculation and financial manipulation rather than by sound operations, no real reform could occur from within. Yet the complexity of the problem and the lack of specialized knowledge by the public made reform from without equally difficult, and the result was a persisting railroad problem down to the present day.

Chapter XVI

It was known as early as August of 1886 that outside interests were trying to gain possession of the Central. Most of the whispering identified the L & N as the company behind the movement, and for that reason knowing observers usually singled out Porter as the logical candidate to be pitted against Raoul. Early in autumn word leaked out that the candidate being promoted by the New York syndicate was none other than Porter Alexander. The financiers, led by John and Patrick Calhoun, H. B. Hollins, and Isaac Rice, had come to Porter and asked him to run. He needed little persuasion. He still smarted from his earlier defeat, and he wanted the Central back. But he refused to run unless the financiers promised him enough stock to assure victory. The syndicate agreed and began buying up stock.[1]

Many of Porter's backers held large interests in the Richmond Terminal, a holding company whose officers had attracted much attention by their attempts to weld together a vast system of southern railroads. They also possessed a reputation for financial manipulation and stealthy maneuvering. It seemed obvious that if the syndicate got Alexander elected, their next step would be to bind the Central to the Terminal system. Yet that gave Porter no immediate cause for alarm. So far the Terminal representatives had revealed no ambitions beyond the natural desire to bring the Central into harmonious relationship with their own roads. Cooperation could only mean prosperity for everyone. Porter saw real promise in the relationship; on paper it typified his own philosophy of railway management.[2]

As stock prices continued to climb, Raoul sensed the drift of things and readied his defenses. On November 1 he issued a circular asking for proxies. The notice made no reference to Porter's opposition and in fact declared that the board knew of no desire to change the company's management. Halfway through November Porter formally announced his candidacy. Though his supporters continued to remain anonymous, observers began to shift emphasis from the L & N to the Terminal as the probable source of his backing. Raoul supporters countered with charges that the unknown buyers represented "wreckers" who were out to cripple the company.[3] On December 1 Raoul surprised the opposition by declaring a 4 percent dividend. Still opposition against him increased. The *Commercial and Financial Chronicle,* in advocating Porter's candidacy, condemned Raoul for his skimpy annual reports and his refusal to issue monthly earning reports:

> We think the election of General Alexander, who has special qualifications for the office, would mark a distinct step forward. . . . He is an able man of liberal views.[4]

Like his mentor Wadley, Raoul tended to be high-handed and arbitrary in his policies, and now, in the heat of battle, he overreached himself. Knowing that Raoul had already started gathering proxies, Porter's men went to the Central's offices and asked for a list of the company's stockholders. On Raoul's orders the cashier refused to give out the list. Quickly Porter's attorneys filed suit to have the books laid open for inspection. The court as expected upheld the right of any stockholder to examine the company books so that he might confer with his fellow holders on questions of policy. Then Raoul's lawyers appealed the case to the Supreme Court, which would not convene until January 10, a full week after the election. For this hollow victory Raoul paid a dear price, for his tactics offended many stockholders.[5]

In the last election Porter had lost because of Hetty Green's stock. This time he insured the Witch of Wall Street's support by negotiating with her personally. After an exasperating conference Hetty agreed to surrender her proxies for a stiff fee. Again and again Porter defined the issue in terms reminiscent of 1883:

> The real issue is whether Central railroad stock will longer submit to be slaughtered. [It] has been slaughtered by suppression of information concerning the value of the stock and sometimes even by active efforts to depress it in the market. . . . Secrecy as to the real value of the stock has been the thing that slaughtered the stockholders and kept their property down far below its real value. . . . It was the policy of Mr. Wadley and has been intensified by the present management.

Repeatedly Porter denied the charge that he was the agent of outside interests: "The sole and only interest in which I am running for is the Central stockholder, whether he lives in Georgia, New York or California." [6] The Alexander forces hammered away at the charge of wrecking and emphasized Raoul's unwillingness to give out the list of stockholders.

On election day Porter arrived an hour early in order to cast his vote first. It was a shrewd move. By 10 a.m. a throng of voters had arrived, and five minutes later the balloting began. For nearly five hours Porter rattled off his proxy lists; when he had finished some of his supporters followed with their votes. At 3:15, when the first vote for Raoul was cast,

Porter had 40,145 votes, a clear majority. He finished with a 13,893 majority out of 69,439 votes cast.[7]

Observers pondered the significance of the results. The *New York Times* noted that Porter's victory "is considered a 'scoop' of the road by New York capitalists" and added that "the final result will be a merging of the Richmond and Danville and the Georgia Central systems." The Danville, as the heart of the Terminal system, stood to gain much more from the proposed merger than did the Central. The latter road derived much of its profits by hauling freight to Savannah and sending it north from there by its steamships. Any alliance with the Danville could only mean a diversion of this traffic northward by rail on the Danville and a subsequent loss of business for the steamships.[8]

Porter and his supporters firmly denied such rumors, but they would not disappear and soon Porter would have to confront them directly. His return to the Central opened the final phase of his business career.

Porter found the Central to have changed little in his absence. The main system now comprised 1,282 miles including a 300-mile estimate for the steamship lines. Thirteen auxiliary lines added another 1,252 miles, making a total of 2,534 miles. Finding the whole system awkward and unwieldly, he devised a new structure of three divisions to weld it into a more efficient and economical administrative unit. Mindful of Raoul's past failures, he issued monthly statements on earnings. After a slow start earnings picked up sufficiently for him to pay a 4 percent dividend in July. In his first report he noted proudly that the Central system had a capitalization of only $20,485 per mile, over $2,000 less than in 1861. "So low a capitalization on such an extensive and well equipped system," he concluded, "can scarcely be paralleled." [9]

In very little time he felt completely at home. The Central's future looked bright. Under intelligent management it could continue to prosper indefinitely. Early in 1888 Porter outlined his hopes to Lawton:

> My plans for the Central—to protect her exposed points, & develop new & occupied fields & to finance the whole system & provide money for offense & defense & for engines, cars & steamers.

The reference to "exposed points" revealed Porter's main fear—that of rapidly proliferating and consolidating competitors. In his mind future success lay in shoring up the Central's weaknesses by a program of careful expansion, not unlike that attempted by Newcomb on the L & N. He would eliminate competitors and protect Central territories by extending her feeder lines deeper into the mineral fields of Alabama and other untapped regions. He would also try to reduce fixed charges by refinancing all outstanding obligations at lower interest rates.[10]

Alexander had reached the height of his ambitions. He wanted nothing more than to be left alone to run the Central, mend its weak points and keep the system flourishing. But he could not operate in a vacuum. He had gained office by the support of financiers who controlled a majority of Central stock, and their conflicting ambitions would do much to dictate the company's future. In the summer of 1888 a syndicate composed mainly of Porter's supporters and some Richmond Terminal directors formed a new holding company known as the Georgia Company, which had for its capital forty thousand shares of Central stock. No one knew exactly what plans the Georgia Company harbored, though a series of conferences made it clear that they planned no immediate change in the Central's management. By December it had become apparent that the new company owed its origins to a highly complex power struggle within the Terminal.[11]

The Terminal embraced two distinct railroad systems, the Richmond & Danville and the East Tennessee, Virginia & Georgia, in addition to its interests in the Central. One faction of Terminal directors wished to operate the entire system without favoring any one component of it. Another group, holding large interests in the East Tennessee, wished to use the Terminal as a vehicle to increase the business of that company. Since the Danville and East Tennessee systems paralleled one another to an embarrassing degree, directors with large personal holdings in one of the two systems usually advocated Terminal policies that favored their system. As a further complication, those directors having an interest in the Georgia Company wanted the Terminal to purchase their stock. The Terminal would thus acquire a third system of railroads, and the Georgia Company founders would realize a tidy profit on the transaction.[12]

The power struggle within the Terminal could not help but affect Alexander. He was completely at the mercy of the Georgia Company as majority stockholder, and that company's attitude in turn depended upon events within the Terminal board. During the winter of 1888 the complex intrigues of the Georgia Company firmly ensnared Porter. Hollins, now president of the company, and some of his associates asked Porter to run for presidency of the Terminal. The current president, Alfred Sully, was about to resign, and unless a compromise candidate could be found there would be a fight for the position. The right man could avert ruinous conflicts and iron out all differences. Porter would not even have to surrender the Central but could run it along with the Terminal.[13]

Porter balked at once. He explained his feelings to Lawton:

> I have been greatly distressed over it all & reluctant to touch anything
> else but the Central. I have taken the measure of that & *I know what I
> can do with it*. I can make it worth 200 in less than 5 years. I dont want
> any big salary but ... peace & security.... Our friends say to me that
> what they wish is not idle ambition ... & that I happen to be the only
> man available to be put in control of the whole & I must submit.

And submit he did, with great reluctance. The campaign opened early
in March, though no official mention of Porter's candidacy was made.
Sully resigned as expected in a stormy meeting on April 5 and threw his
support behind Alexander, whose supporters charged the present Terminal
management with inefficiency and corruption. In publishing a list of
fraudulent transactions carried out by the incumbent directors they concluded that "the property should be managed by an experienced, practical
railroad man of recognized ability, aided by an efficient Board of Directors." The fight grew progressively hotter, and reports singling out
Porter as the opposition candidate began to emerge openly. Fifteen of
the Terminal's directors published a statement opposing any change to
the present management and accusing Porter's backers of acting as agents
for rival railroads. In reply Hollins and his group printed a pamphlet
refuting the charges against them and detailing a lengthy indictment of
the incumbents' actions as directors of the Terminal.[14]

That scorching tract evoked howls of protest; yet within a few days
the conflict lapsed into mysterious silence. The Hollins group had demanded a general meeting to elect a new board; the incumbents had
been forced to accede and scheduled the meeting for May 31. Possession
of stock and proxies would be vital for both sides, but movement of
Terminal stock remained quite normal and even quiet. The *New York
Times* sneered, "That Richmond Terminal contest for control is lost,
strayed, or stolen."

Then, on May 13, the Hollins group suddenly announced their
candidate to be not Alexander but F. B. Clarke, a veteran railroad manager
in the Vanderbilt system. No one proffered an explanation for the switch.
Perhaps Porter withdrew of his own accord, or perhaps the opposition
thought Clarke a suitably neutral candidate, since the Georgia Company
had become a prominent issue and Porter, as president of the Central,
might not seem sufficiently lacking in self-interest. Whatever the reason,
Porter showed no regret. He watched the meeting convene in an anti-
climactic atmosphere that saw the incumbents win an overwhelming
victory.[15]

Once free of that unpleasant obligation Porter could devote his full
attention to the Central. His plan to expand the system and seal it off
from competition had crystalized into two projects: completion of the

Columbus & Western line to Birmingham, and the building of a through line linking the Columbus & Western to Savannah via a cut-off route from Columbus through Americus and Eastman to Eden, only a few miles outside Savannah. The first project was completed by July 1. He hailed the Central's entry into Birmingham as an important prize. It opened up the rapidly developing iron and coal regions and promised a lucrative traffic in subsidiary goods. At Birmingham the Columbus & Western would connect with the Kansas City, Memphis & Birmingham, which gave the Central direct lines to Memphis, Kansas City, and points north. To feed his new road Alexander bought a small Alabama line and pushed extensions on two other Central branches.[16]

But Porter knew that the new line meant nothing if the Columbus & Western did not have an efficient route eastward to Savannah; this was the purpose of the second project, the Savannah & Western. The present route east of Columbus contained a cumbersome dogleg running up to Macon via Fort Valley and then down to Savannah. Porter's new line would route traffic down a straight stretch to Americus and then across a 180-mile nearly-straight stretch to Eden. He planned to consolidate it with the other Alabama lines in one general system known as the Savannah & Western. That summer he took preliminary steps to commence construction; by year's end he had let the first contracts.

At mid-summer the Central, under Porter's guidance, stood at the peak of its strength. The rapidly expanding system now contained nearly three thousand miles and earnings were increasing steadily. Though the new construction would require some financing, capitalization of the system remained an impressively low $17,357 per mile. The few existing problems Porter saw as minor and easily disposed of. He believed the Central to be basking in prosperity, and most observers agreed. The *Chronicle* applauded his record and complimented his administration as (no small feat this) "a liberal and progressive, yet safe and conservative management." In his report Porter sounded the call for continued growth and warned against slacking the pace:

> There is much to be done which will yield large returns by enabling us to handle business more economically and rapidly, and by attracting new business. . . . With the natural advantages of our location, the valuable local business which has grown up along our lines during many years, and the new facilities we are offering for through business between the West and the East, the condition of the Company should improve rapidly every year.[17]

In October the Richmond Terminal startled the railroad world by purchasing all outstanding stock of the Georgia Company. Later it would be discovered that the deal was tainted with fraud and impropriety; at the time most observers saw the transaction as a poor one for the Central and asserted that no better sign of good faith could be given than the continuation of Porter Alexander as president.[18]

News of the transaction could not have pleased Porter. He wanted to shape the Central's destiny himself, and believed that he could if left alone. Yet he knew perfectly well that it was not his company to run, and he could not formulate its policy. Like it or not his fate hinged upon the unpredictable pleasures of the Terminal, and his choice of a policy beneficial to the Central might be overruled in favor of one more amenable to the Terminal system as a whole. Porter was, in effect, a Terminal employee now, and no amount of popularity or reputation could protect him if the directors decided that he was expendable.[19] The once budding Napoleon of the rails had been reduced to a figurehead. His motives for staying on with the Central can only be guessed at. A cynic might dismiss him as a kept man but that seems unfair. Someone, after all, would have to strengthen the Central system and shield it from raids by either its enemies or its supposed friends. Who could better perform that duty than Alexander? If he left, the Terminal would simply replace him with their own man who might well have little sympathy or concern for the company's future welfare. It is reasonable to suppose that Porter felt a genuine loyalty toward the Central. He had come into office pledged to protect the stockholders. Even with his hands tied he could still serve.

With grim determination Porter pushed his pet expansion programs. But these cost money, and no one question created more friction among Porter, his board, and the Terminal management than the raising of funds. The Central's minority holders feared that further indebtedness would imperil the company's financial stability and destroy its proud dividend record; the Terminal interfered with Porter's financial policy by constantly borrowing money for its own use or sketching out plans that did not fit in with his own. From start to finish it proved an explosive network of relationships. Still he managed, with some difficulty, to procure new mortgages to finance the Savannah & Western construction and pay off debts incurred by completion of the Columbus & Western.[20]

But sluggish earnings, a severe flood in Augusta, a yellow fever epidemic in Florida, a decline in the cotton crop, an invasion by six small but ambitious competing lines, and rate reductions by state railroad commissions in Georgia, Alabama, and South Carolina all helped undermine Porter's expansion program. The result was a persistent floating debt that Alexander could find no cash to relieve. The very efficiency of his management left him no loose ends or unswept corners from which to garner cash in tight moments. Nor could he reduce the dividend rate without arousing shrieks of protest from every quarter. The squeeze for money would get worse, too, for 1887 had been a flush year for earnings and would not often be repeated.[21]

The basic facts stood out with brutal transparency. Porter had come into office with a program and backing geared to prosperous times. He could only assume that intelligent management of the Central would parlay that prosperity onto a steadily upward course. Thus, to maintain his delicate position he desperately needed a continuation of those good business years. But that seemed unlikely in 1889.

Every year it cost more to operate and maintain a railroad system, especially if management wished to keep high standards. The regulation of rates by state and federal commissions combined with increasingly organized competition to keep rates low or at least slow to rise. The protection of a system's existing territory demanded the acquiring of an auxiliary system to feed the main system and choke off competition with it. But auxiliary systems rarely paid their way, for they usually drained less profitable regions or were constructed in untapped locales and required time to develop a regular traffic. This made the auxiliary system a drag on the earnings of the parent road, since its earnings could rarely cover both the fixed charges spawned by its acquisition and the cost of its operation.

Therein lay the origins of a persistent floating debt. But to dodge the question by not taking on an auxiliary system succeeded only in leaving those roads and the regions drained by them as dangerous competitors to the main system. It also left the unguarded territories open for invasion by some other budding colossus. Therefore the question of expansion by acquiring auxiliary roads presented most railway executives with a "damned if you do and damned if you don't" choice. The inevitable decision to shoulder the financial burden of such roads, however optimistic the language of official justification, derived as much from selecting the lesser of two manifest evils as it did from motives of clandestine profit or buoyant dreams of empire.

Porter realized these facts and strove to make his peace with them. In his annual report for 1890 he wrote:

> To protect our business and to occupy our legitimate territory we have been compelled during the past three years to extend our mileage over 30 percent. Of course the newer roads . . . have not the business over them of the older trunk line portions. But their value as feeders to the latter, and their satisfactory growth, is indicated by the increase of nearly $500 in the average earnings per mile of the entire system. . . . every dollar spent in bringing the property up to high condition will be an investment returning a large interest in an increased, a cheaper and a more satisfactory service.[22]

Beneath these words lay the implicit assumption that business conditions would prosper long enough for all the lines to pay their way. To many observers that might seem like a rather naive profession of faith, but it was not at all uncommon to the late nineteenth-century American business executive. Besides, what other policy could offer a feasible alternative?

By early 1890 a floating debt of about $2,000,000 had accumulated on the Central. Porter announced the issuance of a new $13,000,000 mortgage on the main system to retire old bonds, call in the 1881 certificates of indebtedness, and pay off the floating debt. But the new bonds could not meet immediate needs, and net income for the year, including a $523,515 surplus from the previous year, could not be stretched far enough to meet all expenses and still pay the usual 8 percent dividend. If the dividend were not paid or even reduced, the consequences would be an angry blast from the minority holders and a glaring blemish on the Terminal annual report, some of whose directors depended heavily upon full and regular dividends to justify their purchase of the Georgia Company. There was only one way out. The Ocean Steamship Company had accumulated a sinking fund of $600,000 to retire a $1,000,000 bond issue scheduled to fall due in 1892. With the Central's endorsement the steamship company replaced the old bonds with a new $1,000,000 issue, enabling the Central to put the $600,000 sinking fund in its surplus fund instead of using it to redeem bonds. It also added another $600,000 to the funded debt.[23]

Of course that sort of maneuver would not be available every year, and the most interesting question remained unanswered: who had made the decision to transfer the fund? Was it Alexander or did he merely follow orders from the Terminal management?

As Porter pursued his course he was betrayed not so much by hard times as by the complex machinations within the Terminal. The struggle for power there raged on unchecked, with individual financial speculations playing no small part in the intrigue. By 1890 the Terminal's president, John H. Inman, had split deeply with the East Tennessee representatives on his board and was hard pressed to maintain his position. He, too, had overextended himself in acquiring new lines for the holding company, which itself had grown so vast and complex in its intricate labyrinth of interrelated leases, holdings, and obligations that no one person could possibly fathom the entire structure. When the stock market broke unexpectedly in October of 1890 and sent Terminal stock falling, Jay

Gould bought a large lot and moved onto the board. His sinister presence added a further complication to the struggle already in progress.[24]

Pressed by the need for strict economy to reduce the Terminal's obligations, Inman hit upon the idea of leasing the Central to the Danville. The Georgia constitution prohibited a railroad from leasing any competing road, but Inman skirted that obstacle by leasing the Central to the Georgia Pacific, which in turn was leased to the Danville. This would simplify lines of control and, as Inman put it, "simplify traffic matters very much and enable us to retire many expensive men." The Central lease, signed early in June, was to run for ninety-nine years and guaranteed a 7 percent dividend on all Central stock, the majority of which was, of course, owned by the Terminal.[25]

The lease offered a potential solution to Porter's dilemma if the Terminal remained true to its obligations, and he must have welcomed its signing. He wanted to leave the presidency of the Central and take on only a few obligations so as to have time to tend to North and South islands and his other affairs. But when Inman asked him to stay on Porter did so. Mindful that many minority stockholders distrusted the Terminal and thus the lease, he realized the delicacy of his position. If something went wrong he would bear the brunt of the minority's wrath, for by remaining as president he had in their eyes associated himself directly with the Terminal and its policies. But he believed the lease would hold.[26]

The lease was scarcely two months old when a crisis arose. On August 8 the *New York Herald* published a devastating indictment of the Terminal system and its management. Based upon an extensive analysis by New York broker F. L. Lisman, the lengthy article gave itemized examples of fraud and mismanagement within the company and asserted that "the system is so vast and complicated that the average investor is utterly unable to form any idea of its financial status for himself." Since the Central was included in the charges, Alexander joined Inman in rushing rebuttals to the paper. Porter's reply exceeded Inman's in frankness and detail, but neither sounded convincing and neither responded to the main issues. Whatever the degree of truth in the charges, they succeeded in worsening the Terminal's already-serious financial crisis; by mid-September Inman admitted large floating debts on all three Terminal systems.[27]

The persistent Central debt required two sizable loans to abate. Throughout the fall Inman struggled to retain control of the Terminal, but time was running out on him. He won reelection in November only by announcing that he had formed a committee of financiers to help perfect a plan for readjusting the Terminal's whole financial structure. When his committee failed to produce satisfactory results, a faction of minority holders formed their own committee to draw up a separate plan. Meanwhile the struggle between Inman and the East Tennessee men continued, and one of its first fruits was to bring about a default on the Central lease.[28]

The Danville was scheduled to make its first dividend payment under the lease in December. Coupons presented in Savannah received proper payment, but in New York the window remained closed, and both Terminal and Danville officials declined comment. News of the default apparently caught Porter by complete surprise. Just back from a trip to New York, he conferred hurriedly with his board and returned to that city. There he discovered that the Danville had filed a claim amounting to more than $800,000 against the Central and refused to pay any dividends until the claim was honored. Porter denied the validity of the claim but agreed to arbitrate and to put Central assets equal to the claim in escrow until the question was settled. Shortly after this settlement had been announced, however, the Danville abruptly reversed its stand and demanded that Porter surrender custody of the securities he had placed in escrow. Indignantly he refused and appealed again for arbitration. "The issue is so simple," he commented, "that I think there is really some misunderstanding . . . which only needs to be cleared up." [29]

At this point Inman stepped forward, explaining that illness had confined him to his bed and prevented news of the default from reaching him. Declaring the whole thing a simple misunderstanding, he sent Porter a telegram in Savannah affirming that "all payments will be made by Danville under the lease, including Central dividends. I am greatly gratified to be able to give matters this turn." He added that the disputed claim would be arbitrated. Whatever his personal feelings, Porter hailed the announcement as putting an end to the controversy. Payments were resumed and tension in Savannah eased noticeably. But the internecine warfare within the Terminal only grew worse. The East Tennessee men, who had prompted the default in hopes of breaking the Central lease, now demanded a shakeup of the Central board to make it more cooperative. Their efforts met with some success, for results of the Central election on January 4 showed the absence of several familiar members, all known to be Inman supporters. The most conspicuous absentees were the Calhoun brothers, who had served as Inman's most trusted lieutenants on the board.[30]

Still Alexander remained as president. Caught in the controversy, he seemed uncertain as to which way to turn. He could expect only trouble from the Terminal fight and hence chose to defend the Central as best he could. But the minority stockholders, unnerved by the whole bewildering squabble, had already begun to funnel their wrath onto him. During the winter of 1892, amidst rumors of Inman's impending resignation, a group of disgruntled stockholders led by Mrs. Rowena Clarke of Charleston filed suit in Circuit Court to have the lease annulled.[31] The suit charged that the Central lease had violated the Georgia constitution; the lessees had mismanaged the property; and the proposed plan to reorganize the Terminal would be detrimental to Central holders. Mrs. Clarke asked that a permanent receiver be appointed for the company, that the lease be annulled and that the Terminal be enjoined from voting its 42,200 shares of Central stock in company elections. Judge Emory Speer deferred arguments for ten days until March 14 and appointed Porter temporary receiver for the company pending a final decision.[32]

The charges carried not only serious but bitter import as well. The mismanagement allegation in effect accused Porter and his board of managing the company more for the Terminal's behalf than the Central's. He could not but take it personally, since as president he bore responsibility for the Central's policies however little they were of his own making. In terms of real power he could have done nothing that did not suit the Terminal. But he could ameliorate the Terminal's policies wherever possible to favor the Central, and he had conceived of the lease as a genuine service for his stockholders. It guaranteed them a good dividend even in hard times unless flagrantly violated. No holder in fact objected to the guaranteed dividend; they objected only to the Terminal's management of the property.

But if the Terminal collapsed so would its ability to honor the lease. Mrs. Clarke's suit implied that Porter had chosen (or rather defended) the wrong policy and had seriously erred by putting all his eggs in the Terminal's basket. Porter refused to tolerate such an attack upon his judgment. He would not resign under fire, even though the minority holders and key financial figures representing the bondholders had already agreed that he had to go. In his mind the appointment of a receiver held the key to a decent solution. If the court named him as permanent receiver it would in effect constitute a vindication of his management against all charges. He could then resign without stigma.

Final hearings opened March 24 and continued for over a week. The eventual decision declared that the Terminal had no right to vote its Central stock, but it made no final ruling on the lease and gave little comfort to the charges of mismanagement. The court appointed Porter permanent receiver pending a new company election. To be sure the decision seemed more of a salve than a cure, for under the circumstances Porter would have no chance of winning another election. And the verdict did not dissociate him from the whole complex story of the Central's marriage to the Terminal. To what degree he bore responsibility for the company's fate could not be assessed by even the most astute observer without unravelling five long years of hopelessly tangled events.[33]

That Porter felt no philosophical remorse was evident in an article he published during the court battle. In it he reiterated his earlier ideas and reaffirmed that the only hope for the nation's railroads lay in some enlightened policy of consolidation. But the Terminal had proved a poor example for his ideas. Immediately after the hearing he resigned his presidency and gladly threw the whole burden aside. He did not relish the circumstances of his departure, but there was nothing more for him to do. None of the Terminal's tainted scent followed him, and even his worst critics accused him of no more than bad judgment.

Later that summer Porter accepted a post as member of a board to investigate obstructions in the Columbia River. Taking Bettie along, he turned the trip into a nostalgic vacation to old Fort Steilacoom. Porter could appreciate the irony in the fact that the grounds had been given over for an insane asylum after the war. The pristine charm of the past had almost fled the Steilacoom forests and soon it would vanish entirely. But it would remain no less fresh and inviting in his memory. He wandered out to the small lake where he and Bettie once strolled so often and carved their initials on a tree together with the dates 61 and 92.[34]

Chapter XVII

Porter's retirement from the Central, rather than slowing his pace, succeeded only in diverting his still prodigious energies into other pursuits. He maintained rigorously his lifelong pattern of rising at six and going to bed late. Freed from the press of business, he read even more and informed himself on a wide spectrum of subjects ranging from poetry to storm behavior to politics and finance. His mind conceded nothing to the passing years, and he remained an engaging conversationalist. "He was a delightful companion," one acquaintance recalled, "had read and observed much, and talked well and to the point, interesting, instructive, amusing." [1]

Despite his many activities Porter maintained his interest in business affairs and especially in stock investment. His fascination with stocks grew steadily through the years, and derived largely from his impulsive quest for financial security. By no means a poor man, he never quite shook free from the helpless despair he had felt during the first lean years after the war. No accumulation of income and property seemed adequate to provide for his descendents. Then, too, he had very little liquid capital on hand, for his islands and other projects consumed most of it. In stocks he became something of a plunger, inclined to gamble on unusual long shots that caught his imagination. His penchant for eccentric, picturesque investments increased as the years passed and did nothing to stabilize his financial condition. He obtained a decent income from the rice crop of his island, but the amount fluctuated with the season's harvest. To avoid depending upon dividends or even the erratic return from his sea island crops, Porter went looking for some position that would assure him a guaranteed salary. He moved in circles that offered a rich variety of possibilities. The friend destined to gratify Porter's ambition was no less than President Grover Cleveland.

An ardent sportsman, Cleveland had for some years been making an annual winter pilgrimage to South Island to hunt ducks. Porter found the Cleveland group congenial company and delighted in arranging their outings. Cleveland for his part deeply appreciated Porter's unaffected hospitality during a period that had been anything but pleasant for the president. "He is wonderfully kind and generous," he once wrote of Alexander. Early in 1897, on the eve of his departure from the White House, Cleveland chanced upon a happy means to repay Porter.

During his first term in office, Cleveland had arbitrated a boundary dispute between Nicaragua and Costa Rica, the origins of which traced back to the Treaty of Limits signed by the two republics in 1858. Nicaragua denied the legality of the treaty and insisted therefore that Costa Rica had no right to put warships or revenue vessels in the San Juan River running between the two countries. Costa Rica declared the treaty legitimate and demanded her rights of navigation. Reluctantly the republics signed a treaty on December 24, 1886, agreeing to submit the question to Cleveland.[2]

The arbitration actually involved two points. First the question of the treaty's validity had to be settled. If Cleveland ruled the document valid he then had to decide upon Costa Rica's right of navigation, and this in turn meant fixing a more precise boundary line between the two republics than the one stipulated in the 1858 treaty. Cleveland sent Assistant Secretary of State George Rives to investigate the whole affair, and on the basis of his report delivered the award on March 22, 1888. In it he rejected Nicaragua's objections, upheld the treaty's validity, and allowed Costa Rica passage of the San Juan for revenue purposes but not for ships of war. He also fixed a boundary line originating in the mouth of the San Juan at a point called Punta de Castilla and defined the rights of both parties pertaining to any interoceanic canal constructed in that region.[3]

Cleveland had tried to make the boundary line specific and concrete, but in this worthy aim he failed. When the two governments undertook a survey of the line they were utterly baffled by the award's references. Cleveland had fixed the starting point as Punta de Castilla in the mouth of the San Juan River "as they both existed on the 15th day of April 1858," but no one had the slightest notion of how they existed on that day. The harbor sands had shifted considerably in thirty years, as had the mouth of the river itself. The surveyors could not therefore agree on the location of Punta de Castilla; nor could they decipher the rules laid down for fixing the center of Salinas bay on the Pacific coast.

For several years the republics tried unsuccessfully to mark a boundary; meanwhile the canal question grew increasingly more important. By early 1897 the United States had secured rights to build a canal in the disputed area, but nothing could be done until the boundary question was settled. Still baffled over the meaning of Cleveland's award, the two presidents, Jose Zelaya of Nicaragua and Rafael Iglesias of Costa Rica, signed a new convention on April 8, 1896. Each republic would appoint two engineers to survey the boundary line according to Cleveland's award. Whenever the two teams disagreed on a point of interpretation, they would submit their arguments to a fifth engineer appointed by Cleveland. The American engineer would have complete authority to decide the issue, and both republics bound themselves to accept his verdict.[4]

In filling the engineer's post Cleveland thought first of Alexander and offered him the job. The time required would be between three and twenty months, and for his services Porter would receive $1,000 a month in gold plus expenses.[5] Attractive as this offer was, Porter might well have hesitated to accept. The position meant a prolonged stay in a foreign climate; however vigorous his constitution at sixty-two, it might not stand the strain successfully. He would have to run his other affairs from a distance and, worst of all, he would be separated from his family for an uncertain duration.

But he could not resist. The post meant financial security with little effort on his part, and it included some travel and adventure. Family affairs could keep Bettie occupied during his absence, and his foreman on South Island could supervise planting and other activities there. He wrote a letter of acceptance and hurriedly put his affairs in order, for he would have to sail on May 1. If any regrets nagged him they did not show; he radiated only enthusiasm for the venture. Apart from any other consideration, the lure of gold persuaded him that he had chosen wisely for himself and his family. Hereafter he would refer to the post as his "little Klondyke." [6]

Separations had never come easy for Porter even though he had seen many of them. "It was like our partings in the war," he wrote Bettie after his steamer had left New Orleans, "& after I could not wave to you any longer I had to put my handkerchief to another use." [7] Arriving in Greytown on May 13, he received quarters in the provincial governor's mansion, which would serve as headquarters for the boundary commission meetings. On his first morning Porter rose at six as usual and set out to explore the town. He learned that the population numbered about fourteen hundred "of all shades of color," and that the place had virtually wilted since the canal company failed a few years back. Several attractive two-story houses stood as vacant monuments to the yet flickering dream of canal prosperity. Four times a day the street car clattered noisily up the avenue, not so much to handle traffic as to keep the company's charter alive in case the canal project did revive.

It did not take Porter long to realize how seriously both republics took the dispute. They sensed that ownership of the outlet for any future canal lay at stake, and neither intended to abandon its claim. Only the commitment to arbitration, Porter thought, prevented them from going to war over the question. At their first joint session the commissions ground to a stiff deadlock within two hours and agreed to adjourn until they received further instructions from their governments. Porter sighed assent. "I am entirely willing," he wrote Bettie cheerfully, "either to stay here, on salary as long as they want or to take one years salary & return to you."

On June 5 the commissions reconvened and agreed to submit written arguments to Porter on the 14th and adjourn until the 30th, at which time they would hand in rebuttals to the first set of arguments. The opposing arguments and rebuttals arrived on schedule and Porter prepared to have them translated so he could get down to work. At the meeting both commissions agreed that the arguments and rebuttals should be not only translated but printed as well, and they adjourned until August 1 to complete the task.

To occupy his spare time Porter entered into Greytown society, hunted, fished, and collected plant specimens. He read anything he could find and spent much of his time writing long letters to Bettie and the children. He kept a close account of his rice crop at South Island and other business affairs. One project especially occupied him. For some time his children had beseeched Porter to write down his personal recollections of the war. Porter finally agreed to try. "I . . . try to do something every day when there is no special work in hand," he reported. But he found the going rough and marvelled at the crowd of memories clamoring for recognition on paper. "When I start writing in those times," he confessed, "I hardly know where to stop."

The fear that an alien climate might undermine his health had long since vanished. He remained robust and energetic, and a hearty appetite boosted his weight to an unprecedented 183 pounds. Clearly he was thriving, but he never ceased to feel uneasy at being so remote from news. Information from home he got two or three weeks after the fact and often in painful form. A belated newspaper in early July informed him of the death of a close friend. "Oh—how it distresses me to hear of Frank Huger's death!" he cried. "In Richmond last July he was the very picture of health."

Not until September 10 did the commissions reassemble in full strength with documents in hand. While they surveyed some unmapped ground Porter pondered their arguments and rebuttals. By the 24th he had resolved the main question of his award and needed only to work out some details. Then a sudden revolution against Zelaya threatened to confuse the proceedings until a telegram from the interior reported that the revolt had been crushed. Relieved of that complication, Porter had his final award ready by September 30.[8] In it he took great pains to justify his decision beyond dispute, for he realized that the main problem would be to get both sides to accept the award. In the first paragraphs he defined the whole purpose of his mission as the interpreter of the 1858 treaty *"in the way in which it was mutually understood, at the time, by its members."* That treaty had not been made hastily or carelessly, he insisted; it had been created to avert a war already declared by Nicaragua. The final compromise declared Costa Rica's boundary to be the southwest bank of the San Juan River starting at Punta de Castilla. She also received the right to use the river as a commercial outlet, but Nicaragua would have sovereignty over these same waters, all islands in the river, and the northwest bank and headland.

A boundary line thus drawn, Alexander continued, would cut across both the Taura and Colorado branches of the San Juan River; yet it could not follow either branch since neither owned a harbor at its mouth or could be considered an outlet of commerce as called for by the treaty. Therefore the line had to follow the remaining branch, known as the Lower San Juan, through its harbor and into the sea. The natural terminus of any such line, Porter noted, would be the right or east headland of the harbor mouth, and the precise language of the treaty confirmed this conclusion. In their argument Costa Rica claimed the western headland of the harbor as the boundary while Nicaragua insisted upon the east headland not of the Lower San Juan but of the Taura branch.

Carefully Porter dismantled both claims. The major problem lay in the starting point, Punta de Castilla. No one knew where it was, and not a single map of the region made reference to it. Obviously, Porter deduced, it possessed no political or commercial importance or it could not have achieved such thorough obscurity. That description alone would place it on the rather barren eastern headland, but if further proof was needed, the treaty itself provided it. In Article V Costa Rica agreed to permit Nicaragua temporary use of her side of the harbor without charge of port dues, and the area so designated was Punta de Castilla. Furthermore, Porter continued, there is an island in the bay important enough for both sides to have mentioned it in their arguments and rebuttals. During the dry season, when the bay received little water, sandbars normally submersed by the tide emerge above the water's crest. On these occasions a man can walk across the sandbar to the island without getting wet. The whole Costa Rican claim derived from the assumption that such a condition connected the eastern headland to the island on the day the treaty was signed. This converted the island into a part of the mainland and thus transferred the boundary's starting point to the western extremity of the island—remembering always that the boundary was to be determined by the conditions existing on the day the treaty was signed.

Porter tactfully set aside the claim. No one could determine exactly what conditions did exist that day, he concluded, but "it would be unreasonable to suppose that such a temporary connection could operate to change permanently the geographical character and political ownership of the island." Follow this principle and every island linked to the mainland by a sandbar would fall to Costa Rica, "but throughout the treaty the river is treated and regarded as an outlet of commerce. This implies that it is to be considered as in average condition of water, in which condition alone it is navigable." Secondly, and more important, no one could deny that the western extremity of the island, known as Puntas Arenas, was the most "important and conspicuous point in the bay." It housed the wharves, workshops and offices of the old Vanderbilt steamship line, and in their invasion Walker's filibusters went after it first. If the treaty-makers had intended this prominent place as the starting point, why did they not so designate in the treaty instead of referring constantly to Punta de Castilla as the starting point?

On this basis Porter rejected the Costa Rica claim, but for similar reasons he dismissed those of Nicaragua as well. He could not conceive of Costa Rica agreeing to the Taura as the boundary, he explained, without having it mentioned at least once in the treaty. But it does not appear, and so Porter declared the Lower San Juan's eastern headland as the point intended both by the original treaty and by Cleveland's award. He then went on to project the line westward across the isthmus to the Pacific. The major obstacle had been hurdled. The line would have to be surveyed and marked, and doubtless minor points of dispute would arise for him to resolve. But for the first time they would at least have a certified boundary line to debate.

The printed award strove to placate ruffled sensibilities. Privately Porter dispensed with niceties. "Costa's claim was simply *outrageous*," he admitted. True, the award seemed to deny both claims, "but really the Nics never *expected* to get what they asked for—they only made an extravagant claim to match the Costas wh was very exaggerated, tho based on what seems a reasonable proposition, that anywhere you can walk is land." But the crucial question remained: how would Costa Rica accept her defeat? Porter received a pleasant surprise. Admitting the loss to be a blow, the Costa Rican commission still confessed that the award had been both just and unanswerable. "I quite fell in love with them for being such perfect gentlemen," Porter wrote, and thereafter he referred to them as his "dear beautiful little Costa's." Nicaragua promptly launched wild celebrations over the decision. Both sides agreed to adjourn for a month before taking up the actual marking of the line.

The outcome boosted Porter's spirits immensely. Not that he was foolish enough to believe a crisis had been permanently averted. Nagging rumors persisted that Costa Rica, denied the mouth of a future canal by Porter's award, might find some pretext for war in order to seize it by force. "She believes she could whip Nicaragua & I believe so too," he admitted, "so we may all break up in a row down here yet." Still the whole venture into Central America seemed to be working out beautifully. "If there is any happier situation on this earth," he told Bettie, "than for you all to be . . . happily fixed while I work a little Klondyke for the joint benefit, my mind has never conceived it." Only one nagging item marred his happiness: Bettie had confessed to not feeling well lately.

The season of good cheer soon vanished, to be replaced by a black autumn. Porter received gloomy reports of deteriorating conditions in both Nicaragua and Costa Rica. Having already snuffed out three revolutions, Zelaya moved to tighten his grip. He threw his leading opponents into jail, levied stiff assessments against them, and conscripted their plantation laborers into the army. In Costa Rica Iglesias had a budding revolution of his own to cope with, and the temptation to divert giddy minds into a war with Nicaragua grew more irresistible than ever. News from abroad gave him even less comfort. "The World I think is getting worse every day," he grumbled to Bettie. "Murders, suicides, & NY City politics is just the whole business." The frenetic campaign of 1896 and the Democratic repudiation of his friend Cleveland left him despondent, as did the ominous quarrel with Spain over Cuba.

Insecurity had seized Alexander again. His personal finances continued to fluctuate uncertainly, and his proclivity for overextending his investments did not help. Hopeful about the increasing price of rice, he bought two plantations adjacent to his own, Maxwell and Whitemarsh, to prevent a consolidation by some other planter. But the transactions plunged him deeper into debt and sent him in search of buyers for St. Vincent, an island lying close to North and South Islands that Porter had purchased some years earlier. Apart from the trials of long distance business, Porter learned in November that his sister Sarah had died. Two years earlier he had stood the blow of Louisa's death fairly well, but he had always been especially close to Sarah.

The commission members began returning around November 20, and Porter determined to put them to work before their governments toppled into war. But the sessions dragged terribly. After translating

Porter's award into Spanish and copying it into the official books, the commissions disagreed over surveying and mapping the first eighty-mile stretch to Castillo. Then Costa Rica insisted that the proposed monument marking the boundary's starting point be carved with the proper longitude and latitude, but Nicaragua would not have it. The Costa Rican commissioner thought his rival's objections to be pure caprice and threatened to have Porter arbitrate every trivial point however long it took.

Patiently Alexander composed an award for the marker dispute. This time the decision favored Costa Rica. "I dont know whether the Nics take it hard, or whether the Costas are triumphant or not," he confided, "but I dont think my argument can be shaken about it." Once again both sides accepted the verdict gracefully. The presence of a canal commission from the United States coupled with a peaceful acceptance of Porter's latest awards gave rise to a jolly Christmas. Porter's guide, an Englishman named Kattengell, hosted the festivities and surrounded his ample table with commissioners and local dignitaries. At dessert Kattengell proposed a toast to Porter's absent family. Drowsily nostalgic, he could not help thinking of Bettie. "Oh Miss Teen I could hear you & see you this morning," he wrote later that night. "Couldn't you see me? I was just outside the window—looking thro the glass—I couldn't get the window up, & oh but for that glass what a hug you would have had."

Offshore the steamer *Newport* signalled Greytown a sketchy report that the battleship *Maine* had exploded in Havana harbor. Not unexpectedly the news stirred some long dormant embers in Porter. "I want to keep a sharp lookout," he wrote Bettie, "& if we have war with Spain make an immediate push to get into the army—Regular if possible, but somewhere, & I'd do a couple of years hard fighting for that." Not that he approved of the war; on the contrary he declared it unnecessary and denounced the newspapers for trying to bring it on. Porter dreaded the prospect of a free Cuba, "for she will only become another Hayti—or we will be having her in the Union with two mulatto senators." Still, he toyed with the idea of going home and seeking a berth in the regular army. He asked Longstreet to submit his name, and the old general complied, but nothing came of it.

The boundary marking had dragged on for nearly a year. Anxious for a vacation at home, Porter knew he could not leave until the line reached Fort Castillo, where it left the San Juan River and plunged into some woods. Beyond the forest it skirted the southern shore of Lake Nicaragua, then turned southward into Salinas Bay on the Pacific coast. Only two major points remained for Porter to settle: the lake boundary and Salinas Bay. With Bettie's health declining steadily and his own affairs at home in need of attention, Porter wanted desperately to wind up the job, but the commissioners moved slowly. Incipient revolutions and the threat of war continued to interfere with the work.

Worn down by the bickering, Porter paused long enough that spring to honor a favorite memory. The date April 9 always retained a special significance for him, not only because of Appomattox but because of his departure from Steilacoom: "To write this date puts all Central America out of mind & calls up times & events in the long-ago, wh seem as if they belong to some other planet." He recalled vividly the old *Massachusetts* rolling alongside the wharf, the sharp tang of salt air tickling his nostrils, and the doleful howl of his pointer Nat as the ship pulled out to sea. "I have lived in the most interesting generation which has ever had its day on this planet—or ever seems likely to have a day," he confessed to Bettie, "And of all the possible happenings of my generation I wd not exchange my lot with any other man who has lived."

Spring brought no end to the round of crises. Costa Rica presented Zelaya with a demand for a new arbitration of the whole boundary question and hinted broadly at war if she received no satisfaction. Zelaya shrewdly countered by submitting the issue to the people. Town meetings throughout Nicaragua boisterously rejected the proposal; in Greytown a Nicaraguan commissioner delivered a belligerent speech denouncing the demand as an insult to the *"ingeniero norte americano."* The aroused audience then flooded into the streets behind an undersized brass band and paraded until midnight, shouting "viva Nicaragua" and "viva General Alexander." Braced for the worst, Porter did not fret unduly. The treaty provided that one party could, with Alexander's approval, complete the line if the other defected, and both would be bound by it. The defector would also stand responsible for Porter's salary as well. "So let the heathen rage & the people imagine a vain thing," he thundered. "I know not what course others may take, but as for me, give me my salary and let them rip!"

Rip they did not. Costa Rica soon recanted, disbanded her frontier army, and signed a peace treaty aboard an American warship. But the new treaty had by no means evaporated all tensions. As the line crept near Salinas Bay Porter knew that the pressure would increase on both parties. "This question is just the very apple of its eye to *each side*," he noted, "& has been for 50 years & the US and Spain are not half as bitter enemies as Nic & Costa are." A newspaper from the interior told the tale: in it a cartoon caricatured Costa Rica as a small cat trying to snatch the San Juan River from under the paw of the lion Nicaragua.

But the woods would occupy the surveyors for a time, and both re-

publics seemed anxious to avoid any open clash. The time had come for
Porter to take his well-earned vacation. On July 6 he sailed for New York.
From there he rushed to the family cottage at Flat Rock, where he swept
all the children and grandchildren together for a grand reunion. Only
one thing marred his bliss—the extent of Bettie's illness. And in his
presence she grew weaker—an ironic contrast to his own robust health.

He had hoped the leave would last through Christmas, but it fell nearly a
week short. The two commissions came to loggerheads again and
summoned Porter to return. On December 23 he climbed aboard the
Altar in New York and promised Bettie to come back in little more than
two months. Back at work he learned that the Costa Ricans had rejected
the forest line indicated by Porter and asked for an award on the lake
boundary. "I will have to arbitrate the lake shore and perhaps at several
places," Porter reported, "& I am likely to be kept a good long time at it." [9]

Despite another revolution against Zelaya, Porter pushed work forward.
He prepared the lake award and began to draft his decision on Salinas
Bay in advance. Still work lagged badly. It soon became apparent that
Porter could not go home that summer. To make matters worse, Bettie
suffered a sharp setback in Augusta and made the summer pilgrimage to
Flat Rock with great difficulty. Harassed and distraught, Porter begged
her to rest and be patient. "We must turn our prophetic eyes toward next
July," he pleaded, "when everything must surely be over, & *then* we will
be together to stay together." In July the formal arguments on the lake
boundary were presented to him and he made his award. With that
question resolved he insisted upon his right to go home that fall for a short
visit, and prepared to leave by September 30.

But he reckoned without the spirit of Nicaraguan hospitality. Zelaya
had no intention of letting him go without a fitting sendoff. "On Sept 7
I start for the Interior," he wrote to Bettie. "I will reach Managua the
capitol [sic] on Sep 11 where for four or five days I will be a martyr to
all the possible courtesies & civilities of these excellent & generous people."
Reinforced by favorable news about Bettie's condition, he braced for the
ordeal. It proved to be a long triumphal procession, with huge crowds
turning out to cheer him at every stop. In the capital Porter encountered a
great welcoming ceremony headed by select officials, a fifty-piece band,
four hundred infantry, and throngs of public school children in trim blue
and white uniforms. He called on Zelaya and was given a tour of schools,
museums, churches, and public buildings. For a few days he moved about
the countryside poking into everything that intrigued him from volcanic

craters to a mountain railroad. A New York newspaper noted that his presence in Managua was "causing immense enthusiasm among all classes." [10]

If the Nicaraguans roared their undying affection for Porter, he did no less for them. At the culminating banquet on September 16 he groped for words to express his gratitude, insisting that all the honor heaped upon him had gone to the wrong man. It was not he who had averted war and appealed to arbitration but Zelaya and the president of Costa Rica. Both sides had preserved their agreement despite awards that went against them. To take credit for the success of the work done, Porter averred, would make him feel like a receiver of stolen goods. But undeserved as the affection might be, he would not relinquish a particle of it. His triumph was completed. He need only settle the Salinas Bay issue and prepare to sail home.

But anxiety drained his hour of glory. A fresh packet of letters from Bettie on the 24th distressed him: "One thing you write disturbs me," he replied, "that you only weigh 100 lbs! How & when did you lose that other 14? I'm afraid you've been keeping things back from me! I hope you will go right on to NY & put yourself under Dr Garmany *without waiting for my return*." Early in October Nicaragua submitted her argument on Salinas, and Porter quickly asked Costa Rica for her statement. Shortly after that document reached his impatient hands he announced his award and managed barely to catch the October 14 steamer. In New York, striding down the gangplank looking hopefully about the wharf for Bettie's face, he received the news that she was dying. [11]

She had taken a turn for the worse at Lula's house in Augusta and been put to bed by her daughter. There Porter hurried as soon as he learned of her condition. His spirit cringed at the sight of her emaciated body, but she lingered on for nearly a month. Steeped in remorse, Porter scarcely left her room. Early in the morning on the 20th the watch ended. Her great suffering left deep scars on the family; long afterwards one of Porter's sisters described her passing as "a terrible death." After the burial Porter shook off the anxious pleas of his children to come stay with them and retired in seclusion to "The Dunes" on South Island. In his life he had seen much death and suffering, but from this sorrow he rallied very slowly. [12] He received a further blow the following April when his daughter Lula succumbed unexpectedly to pneumonia. The double loss almost broke Porter's heart. "My first loss seemed more peculiarly my *own* loss & so I seemed more able to bear it," he wept. "But *this*—this falls with even more crushing weight & overwhelming desolation on others as well & it seems to me just unspeakable." His own health faltered briefly and caused his other children to keep watch over him.[13]

Personal affairs now absorbed his attention. "I am here all alone," he wrote his sister, "& do not see a white person to speak to once a week, but I find a very great deal to occupy my time." The yet unfinished boundary question might call him back to Nicaragua at any time, and until that assignment was complete he had no heart for new projects. For the first time the weight of years began to betray him. He raged at trivialities and an uncharacteristic peevishness crept into his letters. On more philosophical matters his opinions grew sharper, almost cranky. In a letter to his sister he scoffed at her appeal to the old theology of their parents:

> Belief—I sometimes feel *indignant* at the stress laid on belief! It ought to be preached *against*. It has been at the bottom of half the sin & misery & wickedness in the whole round world. And it is so *unnecessary* and *foolish*. ... You can no more make children born since the war & educated to *know* something of Gods work in Creation & Nature, believe now in a personal devil & physical hell & in a whole lot more of the delicately adjusted & complicated scheme of man's being condemned for one thing he never did & given a chance for pardon for another than you could make them believe the folklore stories . . . of the Romans.[14]

Porter rebuked the old theology for trying to explain the world in such simplistic terms. No one aware of the findings of science could possibly accept such a fairy tale, he insisted; it was not aging ministers but aging theology that rendered religion obsolete and impotent. Yet the attitude spawned by the new science differed little in its practical effects from the old theology. Porter, like his father, had always been something of a fatalist, singularly reluctant to challenge the gods in their weaving of his destiny. He differed from Adam not so much in principle as in interpretation: where the father accepted the course of things as a working out of the Divine will, the son saw it more as the inexorable product of Darwinian evolution.

Fatalism had thus mutated into determinism, but the two interpretations, the old theology and the new, bred strikingly similar attitudes. True, the theology of evolution breathed more of a spirit of progress (if one equated fitness with progress) than did Adam's more orthodox reliance upon the will of God as sufficient justification for any change or upheaval. But did not both approaches stress the helplessness of man to deflect or alter the awesome forces of transformation at work in the world? Did not both compel his acceptance of these forces and demand that he follow a path that would best square himself with them? For Porter no less than Adam the faith in his inability to swerve the course of destiny (whatever name one assigned its author) left him immune to pining over lost causes and quick to accept the verdict of history as not just the *only* possible end but the *best* possible one as well.

Though still not feeling well, he prepared to return to Nicaragua for the celebration that would mark completion of the boundary line. He sailed late in June. At Greytown a huge gathering greeted him. He remained there over a week before beginning the trip to Managua. Once again he wearily but happily submitted himself to the boisterous fanfare that surrounded his every move. On July 24 the commission books were formally signed by Porter and the commissioners, making the boundary line official. At once a joyous celebration commenced, and that night Porter was honored at a large banquet. Near the end of the evening Porter made a short speech that helped endear him to the two republics. The banquet broke up shortly before midnight with Porter admitting that "I really believe now that the Nicaraguans like me as much as I like them." [15]

He had finished at last the "beautiful & delightful job" that Cleveland had given him nearly three years earlier. The next steamer left on August 4 and he would be on it. Iglesias sent him a lavishly complimentary telegram and beseeched him to visit Costa Rica, but Porter politely declined. The pleasant ordeal at Managua had worn him out, and he disapproved of such displays however enjoyable they might be. He reached Greytown on the 30th and indulged himself in some nostalgic wandering. "In all these closing ceremonies I have thought so much of your mother," he wrote to the children, "& believed that she was present." He ambled serenely along the banks of the San Juan, gazing at the waters "with the consciousness that I'll never see it again, after three years of familiarity with it."

Chapter XVIII

When Porter arrived in New York on August 14 he had already decided what he must do: "The work of the rest of my life is to be to sell the Islands or get them ready for sale, & to write over my recollections." He went immediately to "The Dunes" and plunged into both tasks. He would devote nearly nine years to improving the islands. They would be his legacy to his children, for he already believed that his own life was about finished. More and more he felt the biting loneliness of having outlived his generation. Reporting the death of Moxley Sorrel to a friend, he added, "Like yourself all of my intimate friends nearly have died." [1]

The task of writing over his recollections was but the revival of an old project. Throughout the years since the war Alexander had written articles, books, and pamphlets on a variety of subjects ranging from railroads to "The Origins of Animal Instincts" to the behavior of weather patterns. His penetrating analysis and lively style won him praise from no less a critic than E. L. Godkin, who remarked that Porter could earn his living with the pen if he chose. By the late 1880s he had become a familiar sight at the editorial offices of *Harper's, Century, Forest and Stream,* and other magazines. He could not always find immediate takers for his railroad and other specialized articles, but he invariably found requests for another type of material—war recollections. [2]

As early as 1866 Porter, at the urging of Longstreet, had begun work on a history of the First Corps. While at South Carolina he collected a mass of materials, but the job proved long and unrewarding. Old comrades encouraged his effort but were slow or careless in responding to Porter's inquiries and detailed questionnaires. Soon the project took a back seat to Porter's accelerating business career. The pressures of railroading, the fires of postwar controversy, and the elusiveness of documents helped drive the idea into abeyance, but it never disappeared. Porter grew more deeply fascinated by the purely military development of the war. He never let his correspondence on the subject lapse, and during the 1880s it underwent a vigorous renewal. Once more he began to study the campaigns, and inevitably his studies led to the writing of an article. [3] To the Southern Historical Society he contributed a sketch of Longstreet's division, a paper on Confederate artillery service, and accounts of the Seven Days campaign, Fredericksburg, and Gettysburg. For the *Battles and Leaders of the*

Civil War series he prepared narratives of the artillery fight at Gettysburg and the Knoxville campaign.

In these articles and the recollections written in Greytown Porter relied heavily upon his own memory. Indeed the very strength of his memory impressed his associates as his most remarkable quality. Charles Francis Adams later recalled his amazement at the

> singular tenacity of his memory. He seemed to forget nothing; nor was he less accurate in matters of detail than in generalities. He delighted in reminiscence of the great war, and he recalled its incidents with the particularity of a trained officer of the general staff.[4]

Nor could a return to the now tranquil seat of war shake his rigid sense of perspective. In April of 1893 he joined Longstreet and Billy Mahone for a nostalgic visit to the Gettysburg battlefield. A few other survivors, including O. O. Howard, Howard Slocum, and Benjamin Latrobe, also joined the party. It marked Alexander's first visit to the field since the war's end, and he defied a driving rainstorm to inspect the Federal line carefully. He led the others to a small knoll halfway between the ruins of the old Codori house and the edge of some woods near Seminary Ridge. Here, he announced, Lee stood to receive the shattered fragments of Pickett's division. Slowly he surveyed the route taken by the charging divisions, and later he walked about the field to search for alternatives to it. Coming down the Fairfield Road in a carriage, Porter amused his companions with the wry observation that the last time he had travelled this road it was at a faster gait and in the opposite direction.[5]

In the articles published during the 1880s Porter based his narrative largely upon his own experiences. As time went on, however, the formal military problems posed by the campaigns increasingly absorbed his attention. His own role faded into but a single aspect of the larger canvas; his approach shifted from that of a participating observer to that of a genuine student of war. In Greytown he had conceived of the recollections as a personal legacy for his family, and so he had woven into the narrative a rich stock of personal experiences and anecdotes. Yet even then he had begun to evolve his narrative into a critical analysis of the campaigns. "I have written along with my own little doings, a sort of critical narrative of the military game," he wrote in October of 1899. "I have not hesitated to criticise our moves . . . no matter what General made them." [6]

At the time he did not contemplate preparing his manuscript for publication. For one thing, he lacked the necessary scholarly apparatus—books, documents, records and other materials—for a formal study. In addition, he seriously questioned whether the public would accept his rigidly analytical approach. "I doubt whether our people," he confided, "are yet prepared to have it said that either Lee or Jackson ever made a military mistake." Personally loyal but critically impartial to his old comrades living or dead, he pursued his studies with a fierce objectivity. Controversies detained him only when they shed light upon the course of things on the battlefield. He had no mistakes to justify or reputations to defend; his impartial eye penetrated the personal allegation to get at the raw facts of strategy and tactics. He proved a harsh critic, but when he attacked he did so on purely military grounds. He might call old General Pendleton "as utterly unfit and incompetent for the position of Chief of Artillery . . . as man could be," but no one who knew Porter doubted his personal affection for his former comrade. "I want to tell the story *professionally*," he explained to a friend in 1901, "& to comment freely on every professional feature as one wd comment on moves at chess, even tho' it may seem to reflect on Lee or Jackson or any body else." [7]

Only once did he allow himself to be drawn into a postwar controversy. In 1877 Porter contributed a letter on "Causes of Confederate Defeat at Gettysburg" to the *Southern Historical Society Papers* and referred to his role in the fight as "chief of artillery for the action." Strictly speaking, of course, he did not hold that position, since Longstreet had passed over Colonel Walton in assigning command to Alexander. On the battlefield Walton had concealed his resentment at being overlooked, but Porter's letter reopened the wound. He wrote a rejoinder defending his role as chief of artillery and accusing Porter of seeking to usurp the title. Stung by the charge, Porter solicited letters from surviving officers of the corps and marshalled a crushing rebuttal. All the letters supported Porter's position and most expressed astonishment that Walton had raised the issue in the first place. After Porter's detailed reply had been published Walton let the matter drop. [8]

In finishing the Greytown recollections Porter had crystalized most of his own ideas on the crucial questions of the war. His approach to secession and the coming of the war revealed no startling insights, no unexpected shifts in his thought. In an earlier encyclopedia article on the Confederacy he declared that secession would have been achieved peacefully had it come earlier. But time had passed the South by; when she made her attempt existing conditions would no longer countenance it:

> In all human affairs there are silently but forever at work, forces which make for the survival of the fittest & the passing away of the unfit, and

these forces, when, at last, a crisis has been reached declare themselves, & operate with a volcanic power, against which the barriers of no constitution can prevail.

The South, he argued, had fought not for slavery but for the *"sovereignty of the states* which is practically the right to resume self government or to secede."* Slavery had served only to raise this more basic issue of sovereignty, and Porter insisted that "the South wd never have united as it did in secession & in war had it not been generally denied at the North & particularly by the Republican party." [9]

This unoriginal, even shallow, interpretation reflected Porter's innate uninterest in the political world. It also betrayed his innocent readiness to accept a narrowly political or legal explanation of the sectional crisis, especially when it could be so neatly fitted into the broader framework of Darwinian theory. Apparently it never occurred to him that the reverse might be true—that the deepening struggle over slavery had itself raised the sovereignty question (as indeed the tariff and other issues had done earlier) as a last defense of the southern position. For why need sovereignty even be debated unless a conflict over some more compelling issue had forced it out?

An overview of the government, its aims and its purpose, Porter never achieved, probably because he had little interest in such matters. It was far more convenient to attribute the whole spectacle to the inexorable if mysterious workings of evolution. To him the South had warred to uphold an honest, eternal principle of self-government, and he would broaden the issue no further. Into his preface would go the assertion that the war had been fought "for that right of self-government which the Englishman has claimed, and fought for, as for nothing else, since the days of King John." But the verdict of history had gone against the South and proven its stand to be anachronistic.[10]

This stance Porter could easily reconcile with his interpretation of the war. State sovereignty had served the nineteenth century as a valuable doctrine, but the new era of the telegraph, the railroad, and the steamboat rendered it obsolete. Just as the sweeping climatic changes of past geological eras had wrought profound alterations in flora and fauna, so must political institutions evolve to fit emerging geographical, social and commercial relations. The industrial revolution, the great strides in transportation and the rise of rapid communication had pulled the nation together, "have gradually made what may almost be called a new planet." The ruthless progress of evolution, dictating such change as unavoidable, rendered state sovereignty extinct because it was not compatible with the new order of things. "Briefly," Alexander summarized, "we had the right to fight, but our fight was against what might be called a Darwinian development—or an adaptation to changed and changing conditions so we need not greatly regret defeat." [11]

On a more personal level Porter pondered the weighty choices he himself had made in those uncertain hours. The decision to resign and come home to fight he had never regretted. Sometimes he thought wistfully of the carefree life he had forsaken, but he had after all survived the hardships with a precious store of experiences as his reward. But would he do it again? That question troubled him. He could take chances easily enough when he was a young man, because he did not yet appreciate how much depended upon his choices—not only for himself but for his family as well. "I did not then as fully realize as I now do," he confessed, "how inexorable are the *consequences* of mistakes." He thought soberly of other southern officers who had made a similar choice. Not one in a hundred escaped as fortunately as Porter. A host of them met death while many others reaped only personal tragedy after the war. He acknowledged his incredible luck readily and gratefully, conceding that "if I had now to take for my wife & children the tremendous chances of overwhelming disaster which I took in 1861 there would at least be much more deliberation about my choice."

Porter isolated himself on South Island and dug into his writing, but he found his isolation there untenable. During family gatherings, his wife's niece, Mary Mason, frequently came down to keep house. She had always been fond of Porter, and he in turn grew more dependent upon her presence. In the fall of 1901 he startled his children by announcing that Mary had consented to be his wife.

The news produced mixed reactions. Outwardly the children expressed approval and conceded that she would be a valuable companion for their father. Privately most of them harbored some doubts. A tall, rosy complexioned spinster of about forty, she was scarcely older than Bessie Ficklen; as late as the previous summer she referred to Porter as "Uncle Ed." Although she was terribly nearsighted and wore thick glasses that made her eyes look very small, her youthful appearance belied her age. She lacked Bettie's impish humor and would always suffer in comparison to Porter's first wife. Yet she charmed the observant and critical Frederic Bancroft with her "rare good fellowship," her merry laugh, and her broad knowledge of books and events. She was a gracious hostess and a competent housekeeper.

The flurry of discreet titters over the engagement did not escape Porter's notice. Obviously sensitive to the reaction of his friends, he justified his decision to one correspondent in curiously pragmatic language: "I am *compelled* to live here on this property until I finish improving it &

can sell it. And I cant live here entirely alone & I need a home in which my friends can come & see me." For their part the parents of the prospective bride expressed passive doubt. "I think that I will follow your wise example," a friend wrote to Mrs. Mason, "and not commit myself." [12] The small wedding took place on October 1, and Porter immediately took his new bride off on a honeymoon trip through the eastern states and Canada. By early November the Alexanders had installed themselves on South Island, where their friends and relatives descended upon them.

While still entertaining his guests Porter received an invitation to deliver an address at the West Point centennial celebration. He accepted the bid as a genuine compliment, for he would be representing the Confederate army and would be the first ex-Confederate invited to speak at the Academy. The speech he wrote had for its theme the notion that history had justified the South's defeat. In his Darwinian vocabulary he argued that the South had fought for a just and honorable but wrong cause, and she would do well to be grateful for her defeat instead of cursing it as an indelible scar. The people of the South, crushed by four years of war, had overcome their grief to rebuild their country. In time the war generation passed away. The smoke of civil strife drifted upward, too, and beneath it rose a great and thriving nation rendered indivisible by four years of mortal combat. "Whose vision is now so dull," Porter declared, "that he does not recognize the blessing it is to himself and to his children to live in an undivided country?" [13]

The right of secession, he continued, would now be rejected as an invitation to suicide. The diverse states, once little more than independent agricultural communities, had evolved into a closely-interrelated commercial nation. The transportation and communication revolution had made national life incompatible with the doctrine of state sovereignty, and so the latter had perished. True, the South had once believed deeply in that doctrine, and she would have been worse than cowardly not to have fought for it. Posterity owed her gratitude for having fought to the bitter end, but the South in turn ought now to realize the profound benefits of her defeat. She had placed great faith in Patrick Henry's immortal credo, "Give me liberty or give me death," but Henry spoke for an age ignorant of Darwinism and its implications. Porter asserted that he now understood the limited range of Henry's plea: "I want neither liberty nor death; I want conformation to environment."

The nation had emerged into an age of universal civilization, Porter insisted. National commerce had become international commerce; science and technology had laced together the loose ends of a crowded planet. "Neither states nor nations can longer dwell to themselves," he warned. "An irrepressible conflict is on between barbarism and civilization." After

Appomattox the hope for a generous and harmonious reconciliation had been dashed by the act of a madman, but an equally senseless act, the sinking of the *Maine,* had provoked a war that once more joined the sections in common cause.

Porter's family did not entirely share his feelings. "Leopold has been heard from" Porter wrote in exasperation of his son, "& the 'speech' has been returned & with it an earnest appeal for the Lords sake to write another! What do you think of that?" His objection, shared more reticently by Mary and the other children, was not to the theme; rather he feared that Porter's delivering of it at an important public ceremony would antagonize many southerners. Porter fumed at their timidity. "I cant but think," he replied, "that you all exaggerate the sensitiveness certainly of all reasonable people, in this matter." [14]

He did not change the speech. When he delivered it on June 9 it met with the longest and loudest applause of any address given. In the receiving line President Roosevelt wrung Porter's hand enthusiastically, and of all the speakers only Porter received a corps yell from the cadets. Later a Cleveland printing firm printed ten thousand copies of the speech for free distribution. Eventually the implications of the speech would be distorted by some southerners into a defection from the Sacred Cause, but none of the veterans in the audience misunderstood its tone. Union and Confederate soldiers alike showered Porter with congratulations. [15]

Pleased and content, Porter returned to South Island and his memoirs. They were beginning to absorb most of his time; as early as April he confessed to putting in "18 hours a day on writing & studying." He had reached the peninsular campaign of 1862, and often lugged his books to the table for perusal during meals. To a friend he described the difficulties of his task:

> It is very slow studying the different points out of the War Records & books published by six different authors all *specially* qualified to tell something. And after I have worked out something and written it some little fact pops up as some unexpected place and changes a whole aspect & then I have to go back & rub out & fit in a new story.

As the memoirs broadened in scope they gained in objectivity, for Porter realized he could not write both a personal account and a detailed military critique. Ruthlessly he began to delete the anecdotes that filled his Greytown recollections, and descriptions of his personal role survived only when they fitted the general survey of the campaign. More and more he donned the robes of scholar, formalizing the instinctive approach he had always taken in his writings. Isolated at "The Dunes" from major libraries and depositories, he bombarded Fred Colston in Baltimore with letters requesting information, statistics, and books. When stymied he did not hesitate to turn to professional scholars for assistance.[16]

Porter had in fact moved into a circle of scholarly acquaintances that included William A. Dunning, J. Franklin Jameson, and Frederic Bancroft. He began to spend more time in Washington to be near his friends as well as the archives and libraries there. Of these acquaintances none developed a closer friendship with Porter than Bancroft. In 1902 Porter invited him to visit South Island. When Bancroft decided upon a general tour of the South Porter promptly furnished him with letters of introduction to all his kin. The two men still had not met personally, and upon his arrival Bancroft recorded his first impression of Alexander:

> On a slight dock stood a man of little over medium height, with a white moustache, dressed in brown corduroy and a brown felt hat. A more genial face one rarely sees. . . . He received me with all the cordiality of an old friend.[17]

The island entranced Bancroft at once. For three days the Alexanders entertained him. Alternately the conversation ran from the serious to the comic and roamed across the war, history, the old South, famous persons, and a host of other topics. Bancroft took his leave with genuine regret.

Late in September a small blood vessel in Porter's brain burst and threw him into a convulsion. During his recovery aphasia and dizziness seized him, and the doctor warned against prolonged, intellectual activity. By February Alexander had abandoned his reading of unrelated books and newspapers; yet he still complained that "I am always behind in my writing." On March 1 he finally completed the Antietam campaign and celebrated the event with a bottle of wine at dinner. Still interruptions harassed him. Restless over his finances, he plunged into debt again to buy another nearby plantation. As an aside he devised and printed a universal calendar which he hoped to sell in quantity at twenty cents a copy.[18]

After Bancroft departed the two men struck up a lively correspondence that lasted until Porter's death. In the spring of 1903 they joined some of Porter's former comrades to tour the battlefields around Richmond including Petersburg, the Wilderness, Manassas, and Fredericksburg. In 1904 they returned to Manassas, and the following year went on to Gettysburg. Eagerly Bancroft prodded Porter for his collections about specific incidents or events. In their correspondence the two men exchanged views and criticisms of each other's work.[19]

Still the memoirs proceeded at an achingly slow pace. Porter complained to a friend in 1904 that "I have been at it two years, and am just half through." When he reached the tangled complexities of Gettysburg, Bancroft suggested that he suspend further writing until he had completed a final revision of the manuscript already done. Porter did so and mailed the chapters to Bancroft, who had them typed. He read one chapter—the Second Manassas campaign—and pronounced it "surprisingly lucid concise & comprehensive without being technical & hitting the happy medium the first shot." But Porter continued to find time a precious and elusive commodity. He had renounced unrelated reading, social calls, and other distractions, and he abandoned his plan to attend the St. Louis Exposition. "I am *so* anxious to push ahead with my writing," he explained, "& with such work as that that no one but myself can ever finish if it ever is to be finished." He cultivated a new patience for piecing together conflicting reports; no longer did contradictory testimony by sworn witnesses exasperate him. "No two a/cs of any event will ever come out exactly right together," he philosophized. "They are like Joe Brown's ideas of honestly kept bank a/cs They will *always* disagree." [20]

No one portion of the memoirs better exemplified Porter's approach than the chapters on Gettysburg. He treated the Pennsylvania invasion more thoroughly than any other campaign, and in the end he levied some of his most pungent criticisms at it. He declared the decision to invade a mistake and argued that Lee should have utilized his advantage of interior lines to relieve Pemberton at Vicksburg; he deplored the confused and divided command over Confederate troops in the eastern theater; he scored the fatal lack of coordination in the army's command system and, in one of his most astute insights, attributed it to Lee's pitifully inadequate staff; he challenged the decision to turn Stuart loose on his fruitless raid behind the Federal army; he detailed the tragic warping of Lee's original plan to fight a defensive battle into one that threw the Confederates on the offensive; most of all, he raked over the tactics applied in battle as among the worst exhibited by the Confederates during the war. The Confederates, he insisted, never really understood the Federal position from start to finish. They chose unwisely to assume the offensive, and they never located the only point in the enemy line capable of being assailed with some hope of success. Of the second day's fighting he concluded tersely that "few battlefields can furnish examples of worse tactics," and similarly did he condemn the next day's attack on the impregnable Federal center.[21]

Porter did not come easily or automatically to these conclusions, and he couched them in the language of cold military logic. He tried earnestly to delete personal opinions that did not seem relevant to the constructive purpose of his analysis. He had long felt, for example, that Pickett's name should not be associated with the famous charge, "as he himself bore but a small share in its dangers," but the manuscript omitted any reference to the point. In an earlier article he had described General Garnett, shivering and ill, leading his troops into the charge on horseback. Challenged on this story by a veteran and unsure of his own recollection, he dropped it from his narrative. His thorough inspection of the field in 1893 convinced him that the charge had been made in the worst possible place. It seemed so obvious once he examined the ground; yet to his knowledge no student of the battle had called attention to the fact. He himself had not realized it at the time. "When I wrote the Century Article," he admitted to a friend in 1899, "I had never been upon the field since the war, & I had a very vague conception of the enemy's position." Now he knew differently, and the visit to Gettysburg with Bancroft in 1905 only confirmed his opinion.[22]

The Federal line, that unforgettable fishhook, had been struck by Lee on its long shank. The Confederates had to advance across fourteen hundred yards of open field under a murderous fire not only from the long shank but from the enfilading positions atop Cemetery Hill on the left and the Round Tops on the right. But suppose, Porter mused, the Confederates had attacked Cemetery Hill instead? It could have been reached in less than a thousand yards and could have poured a much less devastating fire upon the assault troops, none of it by enfilade. In fact Cemetery Hill, as the bend in the fishhook, could itself have been enfiladed by Confederate guns massed on opposite sides of the town. Moreover the salient seemed weak, and a sheltered position lay within five hundred yards of its western face (Rodes's troops had actually occupied that position the previous night). There the attack should have been launched if it were to be made at all, Porter concluded, and into his analysis went this summarizing paragraph:

> As long as Gettysburg stands and the contour of its hills remains unchanged, students of the battlefield must decide that Lee's most promising attack from first to last was upon Cemetery Hill, by concentrated artillery fire from the north and assaults from the nearest sheltered ground between the west and northeast.[23]

The fierce engagements of the second day gave him equal pause for second thought. In his original recollections, written before the publication of the *Official Records,* he surmised that Longstreet's delay in launching his attack had robbed the Confederates of a possible victory. But once Porter gained access to the Federal reports he realized that the delay had meant little. In his narrative he judged that "It hardly seems probable . . . that in this instance the delay influenced the result of the battle." Similarly, he once thought that Sickles possessed sound reasons for his controversial shift of position to the peach orchard. Reflection led him to think otherwise. While explaining that Sickles had probably been motivated by his recollections of the advantage gained by the Confederates at Chancellorsville when they seized Hazel Grove, he concluded that "it was, nevertheless, bad tactics. It exchanged strong ground for weak, and gave the Confederates an advantage not otherwise possible." The day's attack had little to recommend it anyway; only Sickles's inadvertent blunder had provided a choice opening. But swift, precise direction by Meade and atrocious tactics by the Confederates destroyed that one frail chance.[24]

And on the dissection went. The most difficult problem was scope. So detailed had the work become that Porter was forced to rewrite and condense most of his chapters. That spring he accepted an invitation to lecture on Gettysburg at the Army Staff College in Leavenworth, Kansas. He began to read up on Chickamauga, pausing only long enough to receive Cleveland for a short visit. Once past Chickamauga, Mary sighed hopefully, "I shall feel the end is in sight at last." Porter felt the same way. "I do feel now," he informed a friend, "that I have gotten my work where if I had to abandon it I could leave it where any one else could finish & publish." Feeling chipper and confident, he closed down the house late in May and took Mary off to Kansas.[25]

Leavenworth treated the Alexanders in royal fashion, and Porter returned in high spirits. Carrying his materials with him, he went not to South Island but to Flat Rock to resume work on Chickamauga. There he confronted an old and familiar adversary:

> It was not a *sudden* attack which I . . . could drive off in a few minutes with a little ice on my head. It was so *very* gradual that I was not sure it was any attack for over a week & then it lasted 2 or 3 weeks & now it has just as gradually gone entirely.

The attack forced Porter to suspend all work for two weeks. He loafed a little in the warm Carolina sun, played some golf, and resolved to close out some of his business affairs once back on South Island.[26]

On January 9 Alexander gathered his materials and plunged into the baffling corridors of the Wilderness campaign. Steadily he plodded onward until, by the end of March, he had finished the Crater fiasco. He refused to ease the pace and spoke of reaching Appomattox by June. By early

April he was predicting that "I think 60 more days can now finish it." True to his word he wrote the last paragraph on May 23. The task had consumed nearly six years, and the exhilaration of cheating mortality overwhelmed him. When Porter finished revising he took off for Flat Rock to enjoy a genuine vacation. By early October he had negotiated a contract with Scribners. Publication would be scheduled for the coming spring.[27]

The final product was impressive. In his beautifully efficient preface Porter set the tone for what followed. The raison d'être had not been a vindication of Confederate arms or a defense of Confederate generalship:

> These are as they may be, and must here take their chances in an unpartisan narrative, written with an entirely different object. That object is the criticism of each campaign as one would criticise a game of chess, only to point out the good and bad plays on each side, and the moves which have influenced the result.

He sought to dissect and analyze every campaign not just for the benefit of general history but for the particular instruction of military students and staff officers. No one had yet done this, he noted; indeed it had not been possible to do even approximately until the *Official Records* were published. But now the *Records* were public, and the time had come to sweep out the half-truths, eliminate the distortions and contradictions handed down through the years by incomplete and inaccurate accounts, and throw the full light of comprehensive scholarship upon the subject.

He might have stopped there, but his unerring sense of the special significance implicit in his task prompted him to go further. He denied the old accusation of treason as a matter of course and briefly attributed the Confederacy's fight to the ageless quest for self-government. He refrained from drawing out his arguments on these complex questions, concluding that "the South may be content to leave all such questions to the final verdict of history, admitting itself too close to the event to claim impartiality." Then, painfully conscious of the reaction his position would evoke in the South, he penned three concise, deeply-felt paragraphs repeating the sentiments he had expressed at the West Point centennial. The world had not stood still in those rushing years since Appomattox. The South enjoyed now the rare privilege of examining her cause in retrospect. No longer did it seem desirable: "It would now prove only a curse. We have good cause to thank God for our escape from it, not alone for our sake, but for that of the whole country and even of the world."

These propositions Alexander confidently believed would be accepted by any rational southerner, but he harbored no such optimism for his military judgments. His severe analysis had spared no one, and comradeship went by the boards in his vigorous efforts to play no favorites. The venerated Lee came in for his share of criticism, but (as would later be true of Lincoln) the renting of his deistic cloak by the cold light of minute scrutiny only reinforced his claim to greatness. No general received a sharper examination than Stonewall Jackson and the inescapable conclusion appeared to be that his abilities had been overrated. Yet even with Jackson, Alexander had been judicious; the memoirs reflected a much more objectified appraisal than the earlier recollections.[28]

No one who knew Alexander could deny his deeply felt devotion to the Army of Northern Virginia.[29] But the memoirs inevitably criticized the Confederates in greater detail because he had a more intimate knowledge of their intentions, operations and leaders. The southern reader browsing casually through the book would no doubt resent the apparent castigation of Lee, Jackson and other of his fondest heroes, and Alexander's style would do nothing to ease the affront. His prose moved with crisp, infuriatingly precise logic across the campaigns in a tone that seemed more than once to verge upon arrogance or mockery, and the genuine humor of many passages could easily be misread as a smirking superiority. More likely than not such a reaction would be widespread once the book came out.

The reaction to Alexander's book confirmed both his hopes and his fears. Many general readers in the South rebuked its general thesis, and wrathful veterans deluged the *Confederate Veteran* with letters condemning Porter for his censure of Lee and Jackson and especially for his apparent desertion of the Holy Cause.[30] Some stigmatized him bitterly as a latter-day Longstreet; others protested what they considered to be wholesale distortions of the truth and offered as evidence their own recollections of details and events. Porter's fellow officers, however, endorsed the book almost unanimously. T. M. R. Talcott wrote that "it comes fully up to my expectations as the first real history of the war," and Colston thought the book would become a text for those who "wish to read a work that will give a clear account . . . within the compass of a single volume." No aspect of the book impressed the old soldiers more than its objectivity, for they, unlike more general readers, understood the crucial distinction between critical analysis and partisan censure. An old friend on the other side, General O. O. Howard, pronounced the *Memoirs* "the fairest of anything I have seen. In fact, you seem to have eliminated all prejudice, something I have earnestly tried to do for many years, but I fear not so successfully." [31]

Professional scholars, too, hailed the work as a landmark. William

A. Dunning, whose significant volume on Reconstruction appeared that same year, wrote Bancroft that he found the *Memoirs* a "fascinating book ... I have been through it two or three times already, and never fail to find something more of interest in it." James K. Hosmer, whose two volume history, *Appeal to Arms,* had just been published, wrote an enthusiastic review and sent a copy to Porter. A friend of long standing, Charles Francis Adams, considered the book to be one of the most important ever to appear on the subject.[32]

And finally that most exuberant of critics added his unrestrained plaudits. From Oyster Bay came the enthusiastic admission that "I have so thoroly enjoyed your 'Military Memoirs' that I must write to tell you so." Roosevelt pressed upon Porter an invitation to dine at the White House, so that they might discuss some of the points developed in the book. "Being in many matters a good follower of Burke," the president confided, "I am much less concerned with merely academic or technically legal rights than I am with duties, and with expediency in its largest and ultimately moral sense." [33]

Rid of the discipline imposed upon him for so long by the *Memoirs,* Porter resumed a more modest schedule of activities. He tended meticulously to island affairs and searched for a buyer. He followed the sales record of his book closely; in the first six months the *Memoirs* sold 1,503 copies and netted Porter $901.80. Apart from these diversions Porter pursued his voluminous correspondence. The *Memoirs* had thrust him squarely into the scholarly world as an oracle of information on the war, and more than one writer intruded apologetically upon his time to ask for information.[34]

Above everything, however, loomed the lengthening shadows of age and sorrow. He had completed the two projects he set for his later years, the *Memoirs* and the islands, and the former had proved a brilliant capstone to his career. The erosion of his powers, stubbornly resisted for so long, now began to have its way. His letters lost their crispness and clarity. His interest in the stock market grew keener and his judgment more erratic; he developed a marked taste for gold mine schemes. Worst of all, his tenacious memory began to desert him. The attacks increased in size and frequency; when one struck him late in September he shrugged it off as minor.[35]

When the American Historical Association, scheduled to meet December 28–31, invited Alexander to deliver a paper on Grant's conduct of the Wilderness campaign, Porter overruled Mary's objections and accepted. But when he sent a draft of his paper to Bancroft, the latter realized that Porter no longer possessed his former resources. Fearful that a public discussion of it might embarrass Porter, Bancroft wrote Jameson to hold the paper until he could persuade Mary to have it revised or withdrawn. To his chagrin, however, Jameson wrote Porter an enthusiastic letter of praise, and Bancroft could do nothing but let events proceed on schedule. Since the convention would open in Washington and move on to Richmond, he invited the Alexanders to a little "military luncheon" along with the Dunnings, Livermores, Swifts, and Boyds. Bancroft planned to discuss some of the controversial Gettysburg questions with Alexander as guest of honor, but he saw at once it would not work. Porter's mind was far too hazy to grasp the questions and answer them precisely. He had in fact warned Bancroft earlier that he was in poor shape to deliver the paper, and now the historian conceded sadly that "he had passed over the border into the domain of timid old age." Tactfully the questions ceased and Porter regaled them with his unbeatable stories.[36]

The final session Thursday evening proved to be the highlight of the convention. As expected his topic excited much local interest, and a capacity crowd filled the auditorium to hear the papers. Porter looked well, by Mary's own admission, and got through the paper despite some minor mishaps. Afterward he tramped off to a splendid New Year's eve banquet. He returned shortly after midnight feeling fit and in high spirits; even Mary had to admit that he had shown only a few signs of strain or fatigue. Reluctantly they parted company with old friends and returned to South Island, where Porter continued his lively pace. The convention seemed to have breathed a fresh vitality into his system.[37]

Three days later Porter suffered a severe paralytic stroke. He could not be left alone, and the doctor advised that he ought not remain on the island so far from medical care.[38] The Alexanders made the decision to dispose of the islands at once and move to Savannah. A buyer turned up conveniently and purchased everything but the household effects for $125,000. They left for Savannah on April 23 to stay with Leopold until other arrangements could be made. In early May they took a house on Liberty street east. Mary brought in another nurse and retained her until late June.[39]

That summer Mary decided to take Porter north to visit her family in Hagerstown and spend some time at Johns Hopkins in Baltimore. He checked into the hospital for a week and submitted to a thorough examination. The summary diagnosis surprised no one: severe arterio-sclerosis. He must stay calm, lead a quiet life, and take the greatest care of himself. Another mild attack in July passed quickly but left him weak.

During that long summer Porter sat upon the veranda and quietly recited jingles to a neighboring boy. No longer could he find the words for ordinary conversation. Occasionally he would mumble a stray stanza of verse, but never could he get out the whole piece. In October Bancroft came up for what proved to be their last meeting. The sight of Porter crushed his spirit. He tried to keep the conversation simple but Porter could not follow it. Yet he was no less cheerful and affectionate. For all his frailty the tired grey eyes still shone, the old smile and soft tones still remained. He leaned heavily on Bancroft and smoked two cigarettes before Mary took him away to catch the train for Savannah.[40] Once home he enjoyed a round of visits from his family. No more attacks seized him; he seemed in fact to be scarcely sick. But the entire family knew it was merely a matter of time.

Thursday, April 28. The rising sun hovered behind a dull haze. In distant Mobile depleted ranks of Confederate veterans were forming for their march through the city's streets to celebrate their annual reunion. Porter knew nothing of their ceremonies. Nausea had seized him at about 10:30 P.M. on the 21st and left him wretchedly ill. With great effort he remained conscious until the afternoon of the 27th, when he slipped peacefully into a coma. Now it seemed certain that his time had come. Mary sat motionless near the bed. Bessie was there, too, along with Leopold and Willie. They shuffled nervously in and out of the room, talking in muffled tones and showing visible signs of strain. In the bed Porter breathed heavily. He appeared to be in no pain.[41]

The clock edged past eight and Porter's breathing suddenly became more labored. If any thought or fantasy flashed through his mind no one would ever know of it. Many of his old comrades had died with some immortal or revealing phrase, some inspiration of delirium falling from their lips. Porter had none. In that harsh light of reality he so cherished, he looked only like a dying old man whose breath came harder with every passing moment. At 8:35 it stopped. And shortly afterwards, in her prim, matronly hand, Mary wrote a brief epitaph to the "Sea Island Log," that capsule summary of so many good times past:[42]

The strife is o'er, the battle done
Alleluia!

Footnotes

Chapter I

1. This description of the Alexander ancestors, unless otherwise indicated, is based upon the correspondence in the Alexander-Hillhouse papers, Southern Historical Collection, University of North Carolina. A selection of these letters is published in Marion A. Boggs, ed., *The Alexander Letters* (Savannah, 1910). Other relevant printed sources include M. P. Hillhouse, *Historical and Genealogical Collections Relating to the Descendence of Rev. James A. Hillhouse* (New York, 1924), Charles T. Hazelrigg, *James A. Hillhouse* (New York, 1953), Grace G. Gilliam, comp., *Early Records of Georgia: Wilkes County* (Macon, 1932), and George R. Gilmer, *Sketches of Some of the First Settlers of Upper Georgia* (New York, 1854).   2. See for example Eliza Bowen, *The Story of Wilkes County, Georgia* (Marietta, 1950), p. 98; Gilmer, *First Settlers of Upper Georgia*, p. 222; and Aaron G. Stephens to Alexander Stephens, July 30, 1831, in possession of R. P. Graveley, Jr., Martinsville, Va. I am indebted to Professor James Z. Rabun for showing me a copy of this letter.   3. See the pamphlet "In Memoriam" in Alexander-Hillhouse papers.   4. See the sketch in the Edward Porter Alexander papers, Southern Historical Collection, University of North Carolina, hereinafter cited as Alexander papers.   5. Boggs, ed., *Alexander Letters*, p. 69. Contrast this with the following quotation from Porter Alexander: "She perpetually scanned her whole horizon for new duties as astronomers do the skies for new comets. . . . It was the simple natural story of daily life, a life devoted to the good and happiness of husband, children, friends, neighbors, servants, and the poor." *Ibid.*, p. 68.   6. Sarah Alexander to her husband, January 18, 1824, in Alexander-Hillhouse papers.   7. Adam Alexander to his wife, April 21, 1831, in Alexander-Hillhouse papers.   8. *Ibid.*, January 21, 1838. The children along with year of birth were: Louisa Frederika 1824, Sarah Gilbert 1826, Harriett Virginia 1828, Mary Clifford 1830, William Felix 1832, Edward Porter 1835, Charles Atwood 1838, James Hillhouse 1840, Marion Brackett 1842, and Alice Van Yeveren 1848.   9. Edward Porter Alexander, "Personal Recollections of the War," 1:13–16, in Alexander papers.

10. Alexander, "Recollections," 1:6–9; Boggs, ed., *Alexander Letters*, 122. See Wright's obituary in the *Easthampton News*, January 29, 1904.   11. Sarah Alexander to her husband, January 15 and January 27, 1838, in Alexander-Hillhouse papers.   12. Sarah Alexander to Louisa Alexander, March 28, 1842, in Alexander-Hillhouse papers.   13. Alexander, "Recollections," 1:17.   14. Sarah Alexander to her husband, January 26, 1848, in Alexander-Hillhouse papers.   15. Alexander, "Recollections," 1:1–4.   16. *Ibid.*, 1:5; Jeremy Gilmer to Adam Alexander, June 15, 1850, in Alexander-Hillhouse papers.   17. Robert Toombs to Adam Alexander, February 22, 1853, in Alexander-Hillhouse papers. Such appointments were coveted and consequently owed much to influence. The competitive examination had not yet been put into use at West Point. See Morris Schaff, *The Spirit of Old West Point* (New York, 1907), p. 2.   18. Porter Alexander to "sister," June 12, 1853, in possession of Mrs. Elizabeth Hilton. For the physical measurements see Alexander, "Recollections," 1:11.   19. Schaff, *Old West Point*, pp. 25–29; Felix Alexander to Adam Alexander, July 23, 1853, in Alexander-Hillhouse papers.

20. Schaff, *Old West Point*, p. 38, says that the entrance examination was thorough yet quite simple. But a number failed owing to a lack of basic schooling.

There was some feeling that, in general, southern applicants were handicapped by a poor educational background and consequently had a harder time of it academically. For detail on this point see Sidney Forman, *West Point* (New York, 1950), pp. 113–114. See also the Board of Visitor's Report, *Executive Documents*, No. 1, Pt. 2, serial 778, p. 130.   21. See the roster in Report of the Secretary of War, 1, Pt. 2, serial 778, pp. 124–125; Sarah Alexander to Porter Alexander, June 20, 1853 and Adam Alexander to Porter Alexander, September 5, 1853, in Alexander papers; Alexander, "Recollections," 1:11.   22. Adam Alexander to Porter Alexander, November 30 and December 24, 1853, and Sarah Alexander to Porter Alexander, December 8, 1853, in Alexander papers.   23. W. T. Sprole to Sarah Alexander, December 12, 1853, in Alexander-Hillhouse papers.   24. Alexander, "Recollections," 1:11–12; Adam Alexander to Porter Alexander, February 14 and February 24, 1855, in Alexander papers.   25. Porter Alexander to Adam Alexander, April 1 and April 23, 1855, in Alexander-Hillhouse papers.   26. Adam Alexander to Porter Alexander, October 22, 1855, in Alexander papers.   27. Ibid., December 17, 1855.   28. Porter Alexander to Adam Alexander, January 14 and February 8, 1856, in Alexander-Hillhouse papers.   29. Ibid., May 8, May 15, and May 30, 1856, in Alexander-Hillhouse papers.

30. Ibid., May 8, 1856; Sarah Alexander to Porter Alexander, January 28, 1854, in Alexander papers. For other examples of sectional incidents about this same time see Schaff, *Old West Point*, pp. 29, 139–140; John M. Schofield, *Forty-Six Years in the Army* (New York, 1897), p. 3; O. O. Howard, *Autobiography* (New York, 1908), 1:52–54.   31. Porter Alexander to Adam Alexander, March 9, 1857, in Alexander-Hillhouse papers.   32. Adam Alexander to Porter Alexander, March 16 and April 2, 1857, in Alexander papers.   33. Report of the Board of Visitors, *Senate Executive Documents*, 35th Congress, 1st Session, No. 11, Pt. 2, serial 920, p. 203; Porter Alexander to Adam Alexander, June 5, 1857, in Alexander-Hillhouse papers.   34. Alexander, "Recollections," 1:16; G. W. Cullum, *Biographical Register of the Officers and Graduates of the U. S. Military Academy* (Boston, 1891), 2:674–699.

Chapter II

1. See the daguerrotype in Boggs, ed., *Alexander Letters*, p. 218.   2. For the most thorough and balanced account of the dispute see Norman F. Furniss, *The Mormon Conflict 1850–1859* (New Haven, 1960), especially chaps. 1–4. See also General Orders No. 4, January 16, 1858, in Alexander papers.   3. Alexander, "Recollections," 1:17, 18. (Through a numbering error Alexander made two page 18's in his MS. This refers to the second); Edward Porter Alexander, *Military Memoirs of a Confederate* (Bloomington, 1962), p. 2. See also Furniss, *Mormon Conflict*, pp. 101–105.   4. E. P. Alexander to Adam Alexander, February 8, 1856, in Alexander-Hillhouse papers.   5. For details of Alexander's buffalo hunt see his "Recollections," 1:20–24, and Bessie A. Ficklen, *Stories Told by General Edward Porter Alexander* (privately printed pamphlet, 1927).   6. For Alexander's movements during the trip see his "South Platte to Fort Bridger Diary," in Alexander papers.   7. Ibid.; George Andrews to Samuel Cooper, August 5, 1858, and F. J. Porter to George Andrews, August 2, 1858, both in *Messages and Documents 1858–1859*, 35th Congress, 2d Session, pt. 2, serial 998, pp. 137, 215; Alexander, *Memoirs*, p. 2; Alexander, "Recollections," 1:25.   8. Alexander, "Recollections," 1:24; Alexander, *Memoirs*, p. 3.   9. Boggs, ed., *Alexander Letters*, pp. 211–212; Jeremy F. Gilmer to Adam Alexander, January 6, 1859, in Alexander-Hillhouse papers.

10. Frederic Bancroft, "Southern Notebook," 2:122, in Frederic Bancroft papers, Columbia University.   11. Adam Alexander to Marion B. Alexander, September 14, 1859, in Alexander-Hillhouse papers.   12. Porter Alexander to

Adam Alexander, March 6, 1860, in possession of Mrs. Elizabeth Hilton.   13.
Dictionary of American Biography, 13:374–375; J. Willard Brown, *The Signal Corps U. S. A. in the War of the Rebellion* (Boston, 1896), pp. 20–21.
14. Alexander, *Memoirs*, p. 3; James D. Reid, *The Telegraph in America* (New York, 1879), pp. 646–653.   15. Alexander, "Recollections," 1:28–29.   16.
Porter Alexander to Mary Clifford Hull, November 10, 1859, in Alexander-Hillhouse papers.   17. Porter Alexander to Adam Alexander, December 28, 1859, in Alexander-Hillhouse papers; Report of the Secretary of War, 36th Congress, 1st session, *Messages and Documents* (abridged), serial 1025, p. 218.   18. Porter Alexander to Adam Alexander, December 28, 1859, in Alexander-Hillhouse papers.
19. Ibid. For a panorama of this period see Allan Nevins, *The Emergence of Lincoln* (New York, 1950), 2: chaps. 3–7.

20. Samuel Cooper to Porter Alexander, February 20, 1860, in Alexander papers; Porter Alexander to Adam Alexander, March 4, 1860, in Alexander-Hillhouse papers; Special Orders No. 44, March 8, 1860, and No. 56, March 21, 1860, in Alexander papers; Boggs, ed., *Alexander Letters*, p. 216; *Congressional Globe*, 36th Congress, 1st session, Appendix 489.   21. Porter Alexander to Adam Alexander, July 10, 1860, in Alexander-Hillhouse papers; Porter Alexander to Adam Alexander, June 10, 1860, in possession of Mrs. Elizabeth Hilton.   22. Porter Alexander to Adam Alexander, July 10, 1860; Alexander, "Recollections," 1:30.   23. For the account of the journey to Steilacoom see Alexander, "Recollections," 1:30–35; Porter Alexander to Adam Alexander, September 16, 1860, in Alexander-Hillhouse papers, and Alexander, *Memoirs*, p. 4.   24. Details and descriptions of life at Steilacoom, unless otherwise noted, are drawn from the following sources: Alexander, "Recollections," 1:34–44; Boggs, ed., *Alexander Letters*, pp. 218–220; Porter Alexander to Adam Alexander, September 16, 1860, and October 14, 1860, in Alexander-Hillhouse papers.   25. Alexander, "Recollections," 1:36.   26. Ibid., 1:37; Boggs, ed., *Alexander Letters*, pp. 219–220.   27. U. B. Phillips, ed., *The Correspondence of Robert Toombs, Alexander H. Stephens and Howell Cobb* in *Annual Report of the American Historical Association 1911* (Washington, 1913), 2:502.
28. Alexander, "Recollections," 1:49.   29. Ibid., 1:49–50, 45; Alexander, *Memoirs*, pp. 4–5; *The War of the Rebellion: A Compilation of the Official Records of the Union and Confederate Armies* (Washington, 1880–1901), ser. 1, vol. 50, pt. 1, p. 453, hereinafter cited as *Official Records*. Unless otherwise indicated, all citations are to series 1.

30. Alexander, "Recollections," 1:53–54; Alexander, *Memoirs*, p. 5.   31.
For the scene with McPherson see Alexander, "Recollections," 1:59 and Alexander, *Memoirs*, pp. 5–7.   32. Alexander, "Recollections," 1:70.   33. Ibid., 1:66.
34. Alexander, "Recollections," 1:91; Alexander, *Memoirs*, p. 8.   35. Felix Alexander to L. P. Walker, March 2, 1861, in Alexander folder, Confederate Records, National Archives.

Chapter III

1. Porter Alexander to Bettie Alexander, June 2, June 4, June 6, June 7 and June 8, 1861, in Alexander papers.   2. Ibid.; *Official Records*, ser. 4, 1:531; Alexander, *Memoirs*, p. 13; Edward Porter Alexander, "The Battle of Bull Run," *Scribners Magazine*, 41 (1907): 81.   3. Porter Alexander to Bettie Alexander, June 21, 1861, in Alexander papers; Special Order 205, in Alexander folder, Confederate Records; Alexander, *Memoirs*, p. 14.   4. *Official Records*, 51(2):150; Porter Alexander to Bettie Alexander, June 29 and June 30, 1861, in Alexander papers; Alexander, *Memoirs*, p. 14. It is not at all clear what Alexander's ideas on artillery were at this time. Jennings C. Wise, *The Long Arm of Lee* (New York, 1959), pp. 74n., 141, asserts that Alexander persistently advocated the formation

of battalions while organizing Richmond batteries in April. This is obviously an error since Porter had not yet left California in April. No other evidence has appeared to support this idea, and Alexander himself never claimed credit for such an early attempt at innovation. He did insist that the Army of Northern Virginia was the first army ever to organize its artillery by the battalion system. See Alexander, "Recollections," 2:106. 5. Porter Alexander to Bettie Alexander, July 1, 1861, in Alexander papers. 6. *Official Records,* 51(2):150, 175; Alexander, "Recollections," 1:97–98; Alexander, *Memoirs,* pp. 15–16; Alexander, "The Battle of Bull Run," 81. In his *Memoirs* Alexander refers mistakenly to the Van Pelt house as the "Van Ness" house. Wise, *Long Arm of Lee,* p. 74, notes the unusual thoroughness of Alexander's reconnaissance and points out the fatal lack of such work during the Peninsular campaign. For the size of the battlefield see Douglas S. Freeman, *Lee's Lieutenants* (New York, 1942), 1:46–47n. 7. Porter Alexander to Bettie Alexander, July 10, 1861, in Alexander papers. Of course the signals could not be transmitted directly to officers in the field because none of them could read the wig-wag code. See G. T. Beauregard, *The Battle of Manassas* (New York, 1891), p. 83. 8. Porter Alexander to Mary Hull, January 21, 1862, in Alexander papers; *Official Records,* 2:500; R. U. Johnson and C. C. Buel, eds., *Battles and Leaders of the Civil War* (New York, 1887–88), 1:205. The guns were signal guns from the force of General Daniel Tyler, who was commencing his demonstration against the Confederate left. The Federals thought Alexander's signal tower was a command post. See L. Van Loan Naisawald, *Grape and Canister* (New York, 1960), p. 5. 9. Alexander, *Memoirs,* p. 30; Alexander, "Recollections," 1:143–145.

10. *Official Records,* 2:474. 11. Alexander, *Memoirs,* pp. 32–34. The trains proved to be Johnston's own, coming in from the valley. 12. Ibid., pp. 41, 44–45; Freeman, *Lee's Lieutenants,* 1:74–76. The brigade spotted by Alexander was Howard's brigade of Heintzelman's division. 13. *Official Records,* 2:446, 500. 14. Alexander, "Recollections," 1:150. 15. Alexander, *Memoirs,* p. 52; Special Orders 159, July 24, 1861, and Porter Alexander to Bettie Alexander, June 6 and July 27, 1861, in Alexander papers. 16. For a description of this activity see Alexander, "Recollections," 1:159–160 and *Memoirs,* pp. 52–53. 17. See *Official Records,* 2:571. 18. Ibid., 51(2):255–256; *Augusta Daily Constitutionalist,* August 21, 1861; Porter Alexander to Bettie Alexander, August 5 and December 11, 1861, and Porter Alexander to G. T. Beauregard, December 18, 1861, in Alexander papers; Porter Alexander to Adam Alexander, August 31 and September 4, 1861, in Alexander-Hillhouse papers. For the rocket battery see Special Orders 353, General Orders 34 and G. T. Beauregard to Porter Alexander, October 14, 1861, in Alexander papers. 19. *Official Records,* 51(2):205, 323; S. P. Lee, ed., *Memoirs of W. N. Pendelton, D. D.* (Philadelphia, 1893), pp. 154–157. Again the question arises as to what extent Alexander tried to impose the battalion system upon his command during this short period. Wise, *Long Arm of Lee,* pp. 140–141, insists that Alexander was "persistently" advocating the battalion system, but he cites no source and Alexander himself leaves no corroborating evidence. See also W. M. Owen, *In Camp and Battle with the Washington Artillery* (Boston, 1885), pp. 334–335.

20. Alexander, "Recollections," 2:6–9; T. Harry Williams in Alexander, *Memoirs,* p. 624. 21. Alexander, *Memoirs,* p. 55; Alexander, "Recollections," 2:6–9. 22. *Official Records,* 51(2):340–341; Porter Alexander to Mary Hull, January 21, 1862, and Judah P. Benjamin to Porter Alexander, November 10, 1861, in Alexander papers; Porter Alexander to C. C. Buel, April 6, 1892, in possession of Mrs. Elizabeth Hilton. 23. Porter Alexander to Adam Alexander, November 2, 1861, in Adam Alexander papers; Alexander, "Recollections," 2:11–15. For the fake letter and other relevant materials see Alexander papers. 24. James Hillhouse to Adam Alexander, October 14 and December 27, 1861, in Adam Alexander papers. 25. *Official Records,* 53:215 and ser. 4, 1:687; Judah P. Benjamin to Porter

Alexander, November 10, 1861, in Alexander papers.   26. Porter Alexander to Adam Alexander, January 10, 1862, in Alexander-Hillhouse papers. For Beauregard's situation see Freeman, *Lee's Lieutenants,* 1:49n., 99–110. See also Felix Alexander to Adam Alexander, January 30, 1862, in Alexander-Hillhouse papers. Albert Sidney Johnston had already made an effort to acquire Alexander's services but was denied. See *Official Records,* 4:426–427.   27. Joseph Johnston to Porter Alexander, January 18, 1862, in Alexander papers; Alexander, "Recollections," 1:169–170.   28. For the retreat from Manassas see Porter Alexander to Adam Alexander, February 10, March 7, and March 20, 1862, in Alexander-Hillhouse papers; Porter Alexander to Bettie Alexander, March 18, 1862, in Alexander papers; Freeman, *Lee's Lieutenants,* 1:137–147; J. E. Johnston, *Narrative of Military Operations During the War Between the States* (New York, 1874), pp. 98–116; Alexander, *Memoirs,* pp. 61–62. The letters contain considerable detail on the movement.   29. Porter Alexander to Adam Alexander, March 20, 1862; Alexander, "Recollections," 2:18. For Charley see Porter Alexander to Frederic Bancroft, July ?, 1905, in Bancroft papers; Alexander, "Recollections," 2:31–32; Charley Crowley to Porter Alexander, December 18, 1887, in Alexander papers.

30. *Richmond Examiner,* February 17, 1862; Porter Alexander to George Randolph, April 12, 1862, in Alexander folder, Confederate Records; George Randolph to Porter Alexander, April 18, 1862, in Alexander papers.   31. Alexander, *Memoirs,* pp. 64–69; Alexander, "Recollections," 2:43–50; *Official Records,* 11(2):568; Johnston, *Narrative,* p. 120.   32. The Federal trap involved catching Johnston's army between McClellan's main army and another force landed at Eltham's Landing. See Freeman, *Lee's Lieutenants,* 1:192–200.   33. Alexander, "Recollections," 2:51–66.

Chapter IV

1. Freeman, *Lee's Lieutenants,* 1:264–265; Alexander, *Memoirs,* pp. 110–111; Porter Alexander to Frederick Colston, February 9, 1905, in Bancroft papers. The letters to Colston in the Bancroft papers are all copies.   2. Alexander, "Recollections," 2:151; Alexander, *Memoirs,* p. 172.   3. R. H. Chilton to Porter Alexander, June 23, 1862, in Alexander papers; Joseph Barnwell to Porter Alexander, May 17, 1907, in Alexander papers; *Battles and Leaders,* 2:513; Alexander, *Memoirs,* p. 172; Porter Alexander to Adam Alexander, July 24, 1863, in Alexander-Hillhouse papers; Alexander, "Recollections," 2:144–150.   4. George Randolph to Porter Alexander, July 17, 1861, in Alexander papers. The promotion dated from December 31, 1861.   5. *Official Records,* 11(3):616, 629, 634, 677; Alexander, "Recollections," 2:160–173.   6. Freeman, *Lee's Lieutenants,* 1:614–619. Wise, in his *Long Arm of Lee,* denies that Pendleton lost face here but this does not fit either later criticism or the contemporary reports of his subordinate officers. See *Official Records,* 11(2):498, 547, 551.   7. Porter Alexander to Bettie Alexander, July 13, 1862, in Alexander papers. Wise, *Long Arm of Lee,* pp. 342–344, attempts to refute the allegations against Pendleton's conduct under fire but his argument is unconvincing. He blames Alexander for lending credence to Pendleton's critics but admits that Alexander never directly accused Pendleton of cowardice. Ironically, Alexander declared in private that Pendleton "was as *utterly* unfit & incompetent for the position . . . as a man could be . . . The old man could not stand fire & on the battlefield was a complete zero." Porter Alexander to Frederic Bancroft, September 21, 1902, in Bancroft papers. Doubtless this is too harsh a judgment and shows that Alexander did not fully appreciate Pendleton's redeeming talent as an administrator. Wise's problem arises from his assumption that the charge of inability to stand enemy fire was in effect a charge of cowardice. I don't think Alexander or Pendle-

ton's other critics meant this at all.   8. *Official Records,* 15(3):634; A. P. Mason to Porter Alexander, July 5, 1862, in Alexander papers.   9. Alexander, *Memoirs,* p. 219; Edward Porter Alexander, "Second Manassas," 8–12, in Alexander papers.

10. Porter Alexander to Adam Alexander, August 16, 1862, in Alexander-Hillhouse papers.   11. Alexander, *Memoirs,* p. 232; Freeman, *Lee's Lieutenants,* 2:166–183.   12. Alexander, "Sharpsburg," 25–26; Alexander, *Memoirs,* pp. 232, 242; Wise, *Long Arm of Lee,* pp. 292–293; Lee, ed., *Pendleton Memoirs,* pp. 218–219.   13. Alexander, *Memoirs,* pp. 242, 272–273.   14. Ibid., p. 281; *Official Records,* 19(1):153–156.   15. Alexander, "The Fall of 1862," 8–12.   16. Alexander, "The Fall of 1862," 11–12; *Official Records,* 19(2):703–704 and 21:1046. 17. Stephen Lee to Porter Alexander, November 30, 1862, in Alexander papers. For the sketches of the battery commanders see Alexander, "The Fall of 1862," 13–23 and the folder of each man in the Confederate Records. See also Frederic Bancroft, "Southern Notebook," 4:331.   18. Rhett was promoted and transferred by his own request to Beauregard's staff. He was replaced first by Lieutenant Elliott, who soon joined Stephen Lee's staff, and then by Gilbert. See the sheet on Rhett's battery in the Alexander papers. For more on Parker and his battery see the memoir written by one of its members, R. W. Figg, *Where Men Only Dare to Go* (Richmond, 1885).   19. Figg, *Where Men Only Dare to Go,* pp. 192–193; Alexander, "The Fall of 1862," 23 and "Recollections," 2:174.

20. Wise, *Long Arm of Lee,* 356; *Official Records,* 21:563, 1020 and 51(2): 649–650, 1020; G. M. Sorrel to Porter Alexander, November 22, 1862, in Alexander papers.   21. *Official Records,* 21:563–565; Alexander, "Fredericksburg," 3–4, in Alexander papers.   22. Alexander, "Fredericksburg," 3–4; *Official Records,* 51(2):652–654. See also the series of notes with early December dates in Alexander papers.   23. *Battles and Leaders,* 3:79; Wise, *Long Arm of Lee,* pp. 372–373.   24. *Official Records,* 21:563–565 and 51(2):653–654; *Southern Historical Society Papers* (Richmond, 1876–1930), 10:387, hereinafter cited as *SHSP*; Figg, *Where Men Only Dare to Go,* p. 80.   25. Alexander, "Fredericksburg," 6–9; Alexander, *Memoirs,* pp. 290–291; Boggs, ed., *Alexander Letters,* p. 243.   26. Alexander, *Memoirs,* p. 291 and "Fredericksburg," 10–11.   27. Boggs, ed., *Alexander Letters,* pp. 243–244; Alexander, *Memoirs,* pp. 291–292. 28. Figg, *Where Men Only Dare to Go,* p. 80.   29. *Official Records,* 51(2):662.

30. Ibid., 21:575–577; *SHSP,* 10:449–451. Parker, from the Stansbury house, greatly aided the volley since his position enfiladed the federal line.   31. Alexander, "Fredericksburg," 20–22. Confederate ammunition, too, turned in a dismal performance. See *SHSP,* 5:387–388.   32. Alexander, "Fredericksburg," 19–20; Figg, *Where Men Only Dare to Go,* p. 85; Boggs, ed., *Alexander Letters,* p. 247. 33. Alexander, *Memoirs,* p. 306; Naisawald, *Grape and Canister,* pp. 264–266; F. W. Palfrey, *Antietam and Fredericksburg* (New York, 1889), pp. 170–171. 34. J. B. Walton to Porter Alexander, December 12, 1862, in Alexander papers. The note is incorrectly dated and was written at 3:25.   35. Alexander, "Fredericksburg," 22–23; *Official Records,* 21:575–577; Boggs, ed., *Alexander Letters,* pp. 243–247; *SHSP,* 10:455; Wise, *Long Arm of Lee,* p. 396. Palfrey, *Antietam and Fredericksburg,* pp. 170–173.   36. *Official Records,* 21:575–577; Boggs, ed., *Alexander Letters,* pp. 245–247.   37. See for example, *Official Records,* 21:555–556, 571, 576.   38. Alexander, "Fredericksburg," 36.   39. *Official Records,* 21:1077; Porter Alexander to his wife, May 26, 1898, in Alexander papers; Jeremy Gilmer to Louisa Gilmer, December 25, 1862, in Jeremy Gilmer papers, Southern Historical Collection; Alexander, "The Winter of 1863," in Alexander papers. Rhett's battery remained on the line at Fredericksburg.

40. R. E. Lee to Secretary of War, December 5, 1862, in Alexander folder, Confederate Records; *Official Records,* 21:547, 555–556, 571, 576, 1046; Alexander, "Fredericksburg," 4–5.

Chapter V

1. Alexander, "The Winter of 1863," 3–4; Bancroft, "Southern Notebook," 4:325; Figg, *Where Men Only Dare to Go,* p. 100; Porter Alexander to Adam Alexander, April 25, 1863, in Alexander-Hillhouse papers.   2. Lee, ed., *Pendleton Memoirs,* p. 256; Porter Alexander to Adam Alexander, January 18, 1863, in Alexander-Hillhouse papers; Alexander, "The Winter of 1863," 1–2.   3. *Official Records,* 5:1086; Freeman, *Lee's Lieutenants,* 2:477.   4. General Orders No. 71, June 22, 1862, in Alexander papers; *Official Records,* 11(3):612.   5. Freeman, *Lee's Lieutenants,* 2:447–448; Wise, *Long Arm of Lee,* pp. 257–259.   6. *Official Records,* 19(1):803–810 and 19(2):660–662; *Battles and Leaders,* 2:600–603; Wise, *Long Arm of Lee,* pp. 279–281, 336.   7. Wise, *Long Arm of Lee,* pp. 198–202, 344, 357–359.   8. *Official Records,* 25(2):614–620. Crutchfield was Jackson's chief of artillery.   9. Ibid., 616.

10. Ibid., 625–626, 651, 680–681, 709, 727–730.   11. See Alexander, "Recollections," 2:112–113 and Naisawald, *Grape and Canister,* pp. 274, 328–329. 12. Thomas Seddon to Porter Alexander, March 3, 1863, in Alexander papers; *Official Records,* 21:1051 and 25(2):640; Porter Alexander to Adam Alexander, March 11 and April 25, 1863, in Alexander-Hillhouse papers. Alexander's promotion dated from December 5. It came not as a result of the reorganization but rather from Lee's efforts to promote him, which dated back to November 1862. Lawton had been severely wounded at Sharpsburg.   13. Porter Alexander to Adam Alexander, March 11 and April 25, 1863; *Official Records,* 25(2):628, 640. 14. *Official Records,* 25(2):320; Alexander, *Memoirs,* pp. 320–323.   15. Alexander, "Chancellorsville," 1–3; *Official Records,* 25(1):809.   16. Alexander, "Chancellorsville," 5–11; *Confederate Veteran,* 5:258, 287; *Official Records,* 25(1): 809, 820, 865.   17. Bancroft, "Southern Notebook," 4:343; *Official Records,* 25(1):809, 820, 865; Lee, ed., *Pendleton Memoirs,* p. 258; Freeman, *R. E. Lee,* 2:514–516 and *Lee's Lieutenants,* 2:528–532.   18. *Official Records,* 25(1):525, 729, 821, 865, 883; John Bigelow, *The Campaign of Chancellorsville* (New Haven, 1910), p. 245. Alexander, *Memoirs,* p. 325, explains that the Wilderness was originally a forest cut for charcoal many years earlier. No care was given it, and the area soon became an impassable jungle of undergrowth broken by occasional clearings. Troops could not be moved in order except on roads, and artillery was virtually neutralized except at certain key points. Moreover, a unit broken by attack could rarely be regrouped in less than a day.   19. Alexander, "Chancellorsville," 12; *Official Records,* 25(1):307, 311–312, 525–526, 670, 729. The reasons for Hooker's mysterious withdrawal have long been debated. Alexander, *Memoirs,* p. 327, argues forcefully that Hooker lost his nerve but still was fully justified in electing to play the safest game.

20. Alexander, "Chancellorsville," 13–14; Freeman, *Lee's Lieutenants,* 2:538– 541.   21. Alexander, *Memoirs,* pp. 329–330; Bigelow, *Chancellorsville,* 274 and map 16; *Official Records,* 25(1):992. The most detailed account of the march is Freeman, *Lee's Lieutenants,* 2:543–553.   22. *Official Records,* 25(1):386, 408, 443; SHSP, 25:110; Bigelow, *Chancellorsville,* pp. 275–277.   23. *Official Records,* 25(1):821, 940; *Confederate Veteran,* 5:287; Frederick Colston to Porter Alexander, June 2, 1909, in Alexander papers.   24. Alexander, "Chancellorsville," 14–24; *Official Records,* 25(1):798, 821.   25. Bigelow, *Chancellorsville,* pp. 317–319; Freeman, *Lee's Lieutenants,* 2:566–567.   26. *Official Records,* 25(1):484.   27. Ibid., 822, 887 and (2):769. There is variation on Stuart's time of arrival. Alexander's report, ibid., 822, says Stuart had arrived by 10 P.M., which is too early. In his *Memoirs,* p. 342, he says between 10 and 11. Fitzhugh Lee, in his *Robert E. Lee* (New York, 1894), p. 252, says Stuart was summoned at 10:30. Bigelow, *Chancellorsville,* p. 339ff., accepts the midnight estimate of H. B. McClellan, *Life and*

Campaigns of Major General J. E. B. Stuart (Richmond, 1885), pp. 235, 247–248. Finally, Stuart himself said 10 in his report.   28. Alexander, "Chancellorsville," 29–31.   29. For these descriptions see *Official Records*, 25(1):822–823.

30. Alexander, "Chancellorsville," 31–33. Forty years later Alexander's discovery of Hazel Grove prompted this comment from his former ordnance officer: "How did you ever find that position: it is very much out of the way and in a very obscure position, with a long road from the Plank Road to it." Bancroft, "Southern Notebook," 4:343–344.   31. *Official Records*, 25(1):823, 938.   32. Ibid., pp. 390, 887ff.; Bigelow, *Chancellorsville*, pp. 344–346.   33. *Official Records*, 25(1): 887, 941; Alexander, *Memoirs*, pp. 346–347. The fight that followed is impossible to unravel in correct sequence. For its difficulties see Freeman, *Lee's Lieutenants*, 2:586.   34. *Official Records*, 25(1):823, 887, 938; Alexander, "Chancellorsville," 35–37.   35. Alexander, *Memoirs*, pp. 346–347; Wise, *Long Arm of Lee*, p. 509; *Confederate Veteran*, 5:287.   36. *Official Records*, 25(1):249, 675; Bigelow, *Chancellorsville*, p. 362.   37. *Official Records*, 25(1):879, 1000; Alexander, *Memoirs*, p. 348; Freeman, *R. E. Lee*, 2:540; Alexander, "Chancellorsville," 37–39.   38. *Official Records*, 25(1):824, 888; Alexander, *Memoirs*, p. 349. 39. Alexander, "Chancellorsville," 39, 53 and *Memoirs*, pp. 348–349; *Official Records*, 25(1):800, 824. For Sedgwick's success see Freeman, *Lee's Lieutenants*, 2:603–628.

40. *Official Records*, 25(1):801, 821; Bigelow, *Chancellorsville*, p. 379. Alexander had with him fourteen guns: the whole of Moody's, Woolfolk's and Taylor's batteries, four guns each, and two of Parker's guns.   41. Alexander, "Chancellorsville," 60. On the battalion system see Stuart's comment in *Official Records*, 25(1):887–888.

Chapter VI

1. *Official Records*, 25(2):810.   2. Ibid., 840. Heth, Pender and Johnson were all new division commanders, and there were numerous new faces in charge of brigades and regiments.   3. Ibid., (1):804, 1001–1002. Notice Lee praised only the batteries not their commander, as is usually the case. Even Pendleton's later attempt to justify his difficulties on Maryes drew a blank response from Lee. Ibid., 29(2):724–725. See also Lee, ed., *Pendleton Memoirs*, p. 272.   4. *Official Records*, 25(2):850–851. See Special Order 130, May 13, 1863, in Alexander papers and Wise, *Long Arm of Lee*, pp. 654–670.   5. Freeman, *Lee's Lieutenants*, 2:706–707.   6. Porter Alexander to Adam Alexander, June 14, 1863, in Alexander-Hillhouse papers. Of course Alexander *did* have influential friends in Richmond.   7. *Official Records*, 25(2):808, 828, 837–839.   8. *Battles and Leaders*, 3:245–246; James Longstreet, *From Manassas to Appomattox* (Philadelphia, 1896), p. 327.   9. Freeman, *Lee's Lieutenants*, 2:714; *Official Records*, 27(2): 439 and 51(2):719; Porter Alexander to Adam Alexander, June 14, 1863, in Alexander-Hillhouse papers; Alexander, "Gettysburg," 6, in Alexander papers.

10. *Official Records*, 27(2):306, 340, 429, and 27(3):888; Porter Alexander to Adam Alexander, June 14, 1863. The purpose of Lee's cautious maneuvering was to pull Hooker's army away from the Confederate rear and line of supply and communication.   11. Alexander, "Gettysburg," 9–12. For the attitude of his officers see their letters in the Alexander papers. Huger noted in 1878 that "I shall never forget how often I have sat at the head of our column, waiting for W. A. to pull by & get the Road & how I used to *cuss*."   12. Ibid., 18–19; Bettie Alexander to her husband, June 17 and June 24, 1863, in possession of Mrs. Elizabeth Hilton. 13. *Official Records*, 27(2):307, 358, 692. Stuart had left on his highly controversial raid behind the Federal rear on the 24th.   14. Alexander, "Gettysburg," 19-20; *Official Records*, 27(2):358.   15. Porter Alexander to Adam Alexander, July 17,

1863, in Alexander-Hillhouse papers; Parker's report, July 25, 1863, in Alexander papers; *SHSP*, 4:100; *Battles and Leaders*, 3:358; Alexander, "Gettysburg," 29. Alexander, in different accounts, contradicts himself on the time the march began, but his earliest account gives 2:30 and this is corroborated by Parker's report.   16. Porter Alexander to James Longstreet, February 5, 1878, Pichegru Woolfolk to Porter Alexander, January 28, 1878, W. M. Owen to Porter Alexander, January 29, 1878, and Frederick Colston to Porter Alexander, January 31, 1878, all in Alexander papers. These accounts differ in details but agree on essential points.   17. For this complex controversy see Freeman, *Lee's Lieutenants*, 3:106–120.   18. *Official Records*, 27(2):353, 429; *Battles and Leaders*, 3:358; Porter Alexander to Adam Alexander, July 17, 1863; Longstreet, *From Manassas to Appomattox*, p. 365.   19. *Official Records*, 27(2):358; *Battles and Leaders*, 3:319–320, 342, 359; Longstreet, *From Manassas to Appomattox*, pp. 363–364. See also *SHSP*, 4:101.

        20. *Battles and Leaders*, 3:358; Alexander, *Memoirs*, pp. 391–392; *SHSP*, 4: 101; *Official Records*, 27(2):433. The exact route of march is unknown. The account given here is based upon a careful study of the reports, several maps, and the valuable estimations in Glenn Tucker, *High Tide at Gettysburg* (New York, 1958), pp. 232–234.   21. *SHSP*, 4:101; Alexander, *Memoirs*, pp. 391–392.   22. *Battles and Leaders*, 3:331.   23. Longstreet, *From Manassas to Appomattox*, pp. 358–359, 366; *SHSP*, 5:183 and 7:69, offer three contradictory versions of the situation.   24. Again the sequence of events is uncertain. Since Alexander later rode back to inquire about the infantry, he must have picked up the guns here. He specifically states that he had all three battalions in position before the infantry arrived. For relevant information see *SHSP*, 4:101; Alexander, *Memoirs*, pp. 391–392; *Battles and Leaders*, 3:358.   25. *Battles and Leaders*, 3:331; *SHSP*, 4:101–102 and 7:69; Alexander, *Memoirs*, p. 392 and "Gettysburg," 32.   26. *Battles and Leaders*, 3:332; Longstreet, *From Manassas to Appomattox*, p. 366.   27. *Official Records*, 27(2):350–351. Alexander could not have been far from the column since Kershaw, *Battles and Leaders*, 3:332, says the infantry crossed the run near the schoolhouse. The sequence here is necessarily uncertain because Pendleton's report is confused, conflicting, and distorted.   28. *Battles and Leaders*, 3:332; *SHSP*, 7: 70–71. For detail on the controversial Federal movement see Tucker, *High Tide at Gettysburg*, pp. 236–245.   29. *Official Records*, 27(2):351; *Battles and Leaders*, 2:359; Porter Alexander to Adam Alexander, July 17, 1863; John B. Hood, *Advance and Retreat* (New Orleans, 1880), p. 58; Freeman, *Lee's Lieutenants*, 3: 118–121.

        30. Porter Alexander to Adam Alexander, July 17, 1863; *Battles and Leaders*, 3:359–360; Alexander, "Gettysburg," 36. In the last source cited Alexander commented, "I dont think there was ever in our war a hotter, harder, sharper artillery afternoon than this."   31. Alexander, *Memoirs*, p. 399; *Confederate Veteran*, 5:287.   32. *Official Records*, 27(2):368–369; *SHSP*, 7:73; *Battles and Leaders*, 3:325; Longstreet, *From Manassas to Appomattox*, p. 370.   33. *Official Records*, 27(2):429–430.   34. Naisawald, *Grape and Canister*, p. 376; Figg, *Where Men Only Dare to Go*, p. 140.   35. *Official Records*, 27(2):430; *Battles and Leaders*, 3:360; Alexander, "Gettysburg," 37.   36. *Official Records*, 27(2):415, 428; *Battles and Leaders*, 3:360; Alexander, *Memoirs*, p. 399; Report of Captain O. B. Taylor, August 3, 1863, in Alexander papers.   37. *Official Records*, 27(1):593, 654 and 27(2):430.   38. *Battles and Leaders*, 3:361.

Chapter VII

        1. Longstreet, *From Manassas to Appomattox*, p. 385; *Battles and Leaders*, 3:342; Freeman, *Lee's Lieutenants*, 3:144–145.   2. A. L. Long, *Memoirs of Robert E. Lee* (New York, 1887), p. 288; *Official Records*, 27(2):320.   3. *Battles*

and Leaders, 3:361–362; *SHSP,* 6:102; Alexander, "Gettysburg," 44–45.   4. *Official Records,* 27(2):351–352, 434; Alexander, *Memoirs,* pp. 418–419; Willie Mason to Porter Alexander, August 16, 1866, H. C. Cabell to Porter Alexander, February 5, 1878, and H. H. Carlton to Porter Alexander, February 3, 1878, in Alexander papers. The letters make it clear that Alexander personally located most of the guns.   5. Parker's report, July 25, 1863, and B. F. Eshleman to Porter Alexander, February 5, 1876 and February 4, 1878, in Alexander papers; Alexander, "Gettysburg," 44–45.   6. H. H. Carlton to Porter Alexander, February 3, 1878; *Battles and Leaders,* 3:361.   7. Alexander, *Memoirs,* pp. 418–419 and "Gettysburg," 57–58; *Battles and Leaders,* 3:361–362; *SHSP,* 6:103.   8. *Official Records,* 27(2):360, 385, 615; *SHSP,* 6:103–104; *Battles and Leaders,* 3:343, 362; Alexander, "Gettysburg," 58–59; John Haskell to Porter Alexander, January 2, 1878, in Alexander papers.   9. *SHSP,* 6:104; Figg, *Where Men Only Dare to Go,* pp. 143–144; Porter Alexander to Adam Alexander, July 17, 1863; *Battles and Leaders,* 3:363; Alexander, "Gettysburg," 59–60.

    10. The text of the following notes is taken from the Alexander papers, Library of Congress. The original notes from Longstreet are preserved and are of course accurate. While Alexander made no copy of his own replies, he remembered their content so vividly that his various accounts written at different times all bear identical content with only minor variations in phrasing, punctuation and abbreviations. The text of Alexander's replies as written in his own hand alongside the Longstreet originals is the text used here.   11. For some varying interpretations of the notes see Wise, *Long Arm of Lee,* pp. 670–672; Freeman, *Lee's Lieutenants,* 3:151–153; Tucker, *High Tide at Gettysburg,* pp. 347–348; G. R. Stewart, *Pickett's Charge* (Boston, 1959), pp. 110–114. See also the comments of T. Harry Williams in Alexander, *Memoirs,* p. 632.   12. Alexander, *Memoirs,* pp. 421–422; *SHSP,* 6:104; *Battles and Leaders,* 3:362; Porter Alexander to Frederic Bancroft, May 13, 1904, in Bancroft papers. See also the appraisal of Alexander in G. Moxley Sorrel, *Recollections of a Confederate Staff Officer* (New York, 1917), pp. 76, 127, 272–273.   13. *Battles and Leaders,* 3:363; *SHSP,* 6:105.   14. Alexander, "Gettysburg," 61.   15. Ibid.; *SHSP,* 6:106.   16. *Battles and Leaders,* 3:362–363; Owen, *Washington Artillery,* p. 248. In both places the time is incorrectly given as 1:30.   17. Ibid.; Alexander, "Gettysburg," 61–65.   18. *SHSP,* 6:106; *Official Records,* 27(2):352, 388. Later Alexander learned that Pendleton had moved four of the guns without notifying anyone and Richardson, finding himself exposed to enemy fire, had shifted the other five to better cover.   19. Alexander, "Gettysburg," 65–66 and *Memoirs,* p. 423; Boggs, ed., *Alexander Letters,* p. 256. Originals of these notes are not preserved but copies in Alexander's own hand are in the Alexander papers, Library of Congress. The question of how long this cannonade lasted has been the center of constant controversy. A study of the reports on both sides shows a variety of estimates ranging from thirty minutes to four hours, with many of them claiming about two hours. Alexander himself always believed the time to be about forty-five minutes; in fact he never mentioned the existence of a time question even though he made a careful study of the battle. Most historians, however, reject his figure and support the two hour estimate. T. Harry Williams, in Alexander, *Memoirs,* p. 638, argues that "He could not have exhausted his ammunition in that short a period. . . . Moreover, the Confederate attack began around 3 P.M., whereas by Alexander's schedule it started an hour earlier." But Alexander, as the narrative indicates, kept close track of the time involved, and there are sound reasons for accepting his figures. These are, briefly: 1) unlike most of the other observers, he had important reasons for keeping close watch of the time, and he did so; 2) he possessed a general reputation for accuracy in such matters and referred often to his watch that day; 3) since the infantry did not mask his guns at once, the actual firing time was probably closer to an hour; 4) he could have exhausted all his *relevant* ammunition in that time. According to Alexander, "Gettysburg," 48, "The average gun carries in its limber & caisson about 125 rounds. This includes canister

... & all varieties of shell, shrapnel & solid shot ... Now a gun in action will easily fire some 30 carefully aimed shots in an hour to 100 hurriedly aimed." And, of course, such ammunition as canister could not be used for long range dueling. For the sources of Alexander's estimates see Porter Alexander to Adam Alexander, July 17, 1863; Alexander, *Memoirs,* pp. 422–424; *SHSP,* 6:106–108; *Battles and Leaders,* 3:364–365. See also James Garnett to Porter Alexander, December 1, 1903, in Alexander papers.

20. *Official Records,* 27(2):352, 389.   21. For this entire scene see Alexander, "Gettysburg," 71–72 and *Memoirs,* p. 424; *Battles and Leaders,* 3:344–345; Longstreet, *From Manassas to Appomattox,* 392; Freeman, *Lee's Lieutenants,* 3: 155–156.   22. *Battles and Leaders,* 3:346, 365; Alexander, *Memoirs,* p. 424; *Official Records,* 27(2):435; John Haskell to Porter Alexander, September 7, 1901, and B. F. Eshleman to Porter Alexander, February 4, 1878.   23. Hugh Garden to Lloyd Collis, July 18, 1901, in Alexander papers.   24. H. H. Carlton to Porter Alexander, February 18, 1878, and John Haskell to Porter Alexander, September 7, 1901, in Alexander papers.   25. *Battles and Leaders,* 3:365–366; *SHSP,* 6:108; *Official Records,* 27(2):620.   26. Alexander, *Memoirs,* pp. 425–426 and "Gettysburg," 79–81; *Battles and Leaders,* 3:366–367; Walter Lord, ed., *The Fremantle Diary* (Boston, 1954), p. 215. Alexander and his visitors were sitting on horseback on a slope behind the guns where they were not visible from the Federal line. 27. *Official Records,* 27(2):360, 376, 389, 432, 435.   28. Reports of Captains Parker and Taylor; J. Thompson Brown to Porter Alexander, June 3, 1902, in Alexander papers; Alexander, "Gettysburg," 82.   29. *Official Records,* 27(2): 378, 389, 428, 430, 436; Alexander, *Memoirs,* pp. 443–445.

30. Porter Alexander to Adam Alexander, July 17, 1863.   31. *Battles and Leaders,* 3:423; Alexander, *Memoirs,* pp. 435–436. Alexander estimated that four inches fell within twelve hours.   32. Alexander, *Memoirs,* pp. 435–441; Porter Alexander to Felix Alexander, July 26, 1863, in Alexander-Hillhouse papers; *Official Records,* 27(2):309–310, 361, 376–377, 389–390, 428, 430 and 51(2):734–735.

Chapter VIII

1. Longstreet, *From Manassas to Appomattox,* pp. 433–434; Alexander, *Memoirs,* pp. 447–448; *Official Records,* 29(2):683, 700–702, 706, 773. Pickett's shattered division was still unfit for field service and was left to defend the Richmond line. For the negotiations over the decision to send Longstreet west see Freeman, *Lee's Lieutenants,* 3:219–225.   2. *Official Records,* 29(2):637 and 51(2):741, 746; *Battles and Leaders,* 3:745; Alexander, "Chickamauga," 3–4, in Alexander papers; Owen, *Washington Artillery,* pp. 334–335.   3. *Official Records,* 30(2):762–764, 766; Alexander, "Chickamauga," 5.   4. *Official Records,* 29(2):719, 725; 30(2):607; 51(2):766–769; and 52(2):528, 533; Alexander, *Memoirs,* p. 449. 5. Alexander, *Memoirs,* p. 449 and "Chickamauga," 8; *Battles and Leaders,* 3:746; Sorrel, *Recollections,* p. 185; Figg, *Where Men Only Dare to Go,* p. 154.   6. Porter Alexander to Adam Alexander, September 30, 1863, in Alexander-Hillhouse papers; Alexander, "Knoxville," 1, in Alexander papers.   7. Porter Alexander to Adam Alexander, September 30, 1863.   8. Pichegru Woolfolk to Porter Alexander, September 24, 1863, in Alexander papers; Bettie Alexander to her husband, October 4, 1863, in possession of Mrs. Elizabeth Hilton; Alexander, "Knoxville," 3. 9. L. Blackford, comp., *Letters from Lee's Army* (New York, 1947), pp. 213–214; *Battles and Leaders,* 3:746; Figg, *Where Men Only Dare to Go,* pp. 56–57; Longstreet to Porter Alexander, October 10, 1863, in Alexander papers; General Orders No. 4, October 21, 1863, in Alexander folder, Confederate Records.

10. *Official Records,* 31(1):680; Alexander, *Memoirs,* pp. 480–481; Longstreet, *From Manassas to Appomattox,* p. 482.   11. *Official Records,* 31(1):477–478 and

626; *Battles and Leaders,* 3:746; Longstreet to Porter Alexander, November 3, 1863, in Alexander papers. 12. *Official Records,* 31(1):456–457, 478 and 31(3):687; *Battles and Leaders,* 3:746. The bridge was carried to Huff's Ferry by hand. 13. Alexander, "Knoxville," 33; *Official Records,* 31(1):273, 457; *Battles and Leaders,* 3:746. 14. *Official Records,* 31(1):457, 478; *Battles and Leaders,* 3:746; Longstreet, *From Manassas to Appomattox,* p. 486. 15. The Campbell Station episode is pieced together from *Official Records,* 31(1):458, 478, 482–483, 525–526 and Longstreet, *From Manassas to Appomattox,* pp. 492–494. 16. Figg, *Where Men Only Dare to Go,* p. 163. See also Alexander's account of the battle in Alexander papers, Library of Congress. 17. *Battles and Leaders,* 3:746; *Official Records,* 31(1):483. 18. Alexander, "Knoxville," 43–47. 19. Alexander, *Memoirs,* pp. 483–484; *Battles and Leaders,* 3:747–748.

20. *Official Records,* 31(1):459, 484; Alexander, "Knoxville," 51–53. For the delays see the sequence of notes in Alexander papers. 21. *Official Records,* 31(1):458, 460–461, 479. Johnson did not arrive until late on the 28th. 22. Ibid., pp. 460, 479, 484, 486–488. 23. Alexander, "Knoxville," 58–60. 24. Ibid. In this passage Alexander succinctly summarized his views: "There never was a more complete fiasco than the attempt to find a favorable point for the attack.... I will go to my grave believing that Leadbetter devised it [the new plan] & imposed it upon Longstreet & he afterward preferred to accept the responsibility rather than plead that he had let himself be so taken in." 25. *Official Records,* 31(1):343, 460, 479, 487, 521, 746; *Battles and Leaders,* 3:749–750. 26. *Official Records,* 31(1):342, 461–462. 27. Ibid., 480; *Battles and Leaders,* 3:750; Figg, *Where Men Only Dare to Go,* p. 169; Alexander, *Memoirs,* p. 491. 28. *Official Records,* 31(1):463–465, 479–480; *Battles and Leaders,* 3:750; Alexander, "Knoxville," 72, and *Memoirs,* p. 490. 29. Special Orders No. 38, December 28, 1863, in Alexander folder, Confederate Records; Alexander, "Knoxville," 78.

30. Samuel Cooper to Porter Alexander, February 8, 1864, in Alexander folder, Confederate Records; Alexander, "Spring of 1864," 1–2, in Alexander papers. 31. *Official Records,* 32(2):697; Porter Alexander to his wife, February 21, 1864, in Alexander papers. 32. Longstreet to Robert E. Lee, August 21 and September 5, 1863, in Alexander folder, Confederate Records. 33. *Official Records,* 29(1): 839–841 and 32(2):567. A copy of Pendleton's paper in his own hand may be found in Manuscript 2143, Confederate Records. 34. Porter Alexander to his wife, February 27, 1864, in Alexander papers. 35. Adam Alexander to Marion Alexander, February 21, 1864, in Alexander-Hillhouse papers. Alexander, "Spring of 1864," 4–5. 36. Sarah Lawton to Adam Alexander, February 29, 1864, in Alexander-Hillhouse papers.

Chapter IX

1. *Official Records,* 31(1):549 and 32(2):790–792 and 582, 587, 590, 598. See also Freeman, *Lee's Lieutenants,* 3:299–314. 2. Alexander, "Spring of 1864," 8–12; Porter Alexander to his wife, March 17, 1864, in Alexander papers. 3. Alexander, "Spring of 1864," 13–14; *Battles and Leaders,* 3:750–751; Porter Alexander to his wife, March 23, 1864, in Alexander papers. 4. Porter Alexander to his wife, March 17, 1864; Mary Alexander to Mrs. A. S. Mason, n.d., in Alexander papers. 5. Porter Alexander to his wife, March 23 and April 1, 3, 1864, in Alexander papers. 6. Ibid., April 10, 23, 1864. 7. Ibid., April 11, 20, 23, 1864; *Official Records,* 36(1):1036, 36(2):945–946 and 37(1):716; Owen, *Washington Artillery,* pp. 308–310. Alexander temporarily lacked the Washington Artillery, still on duty in Petersburg, but he had received two batteries from J. F. King's battalion. 8. Alexander, *Memoirs,* p. 492. 9. *Official Records,* 36(1): 14–17.

10. Ibid., 18, 1028; Alexander, *Memoirs,* pp. 496–497. The figures include only the opposing forces in the Wilderness.   11. Porter Alexander to his wife, May 2 and May 4, 1864 and Porter Alexander to Adam Alexander, May 29, 1864, in Alexander papers; Alexander, *Memoirs,* p. 498; *Official Records,* 36(1):1054 and 36(2):947.   12. Porter Alexander to Adam Alexander, May 29, 1864; Alexander, "Wilderness," 46–49, in Alexander papers.   13. Alexander, "Wilderness," 49–50. Since Alexander normally rode with Longstreet, the mission to the right probably saved him from the fatal volley.   14. *Official Records,* 36(1):19, 1041, 1056 and 36(2):968.   15. Ibid., 36(1):1037, 1041; Alexander, *Memoirs,* pp. 510–511; Porter Alexander to Adam Alexander, May 29, 1864. Anderson used a road cut through the forest that day.   16. *Official Records,* 36(1):541, 1041–1042. The narrative of the ensuing engagement is drawn from Alexander, *Memoirs,* pp. 511–512 as the only detailed Confederate eye-witness account. For an important correction see Freeman, *Lee's Lieutenants,* 3:385n. See also Porter Alexander to Adam Alexander, May 29, 1864.   17. Porter Alexander to Adam Alexander, May 29, 1864 and Porter Alexander to his wife, May 13, 1864, in Alexander papers; Alexander, "Spotsylvania," 62–64.   18. *Official Records,* 36(1):1042–43.   19. Ibid., 331, 541.

20. Ibid., 191, 490, 667–668, 1043–1044, 1072.   21. Ibid., 334, 1072 and (2)628; U. S. Grant, *Personal Memoirs* (New York, 1885), 2:228.   22. *Official Records,* 36(1):1044, 1072, 1079–1080, 1086 and 51(2):916–917; SHSP, 6:74. 23. *Official Records,* 36(1):1044, 1079–1080, 1086; Alexander, *Memoirs,* p. 518. 24. *Official Records,* 36(1):335, 358, 1044, 1072, 1080.   25. Ibid., 335–336, 1057, 1072–1073, 1079.   26. Alexander, "Grant's Wilderness Campaign," 6–9, in Alexander papers.   27. Porter Alexander to his wife, May 19, 1864, in Alexander papers; Porter Alexander to Adam Alexander, May 29, 1864.   28. *Official Records,* 36(1):541, 1066 and 36(2):662–664, 668–669, 671; Alexander, *Memoirs,* pp. 523–524.   29. *Official Records,* 36(1):1030, 1046–1047, 1087–1088 and 36(2):864–865, 871, 881, 1019–1020; Alexander, *Memoirs,* p. 530; Porter Alexander to his wife, May 19, 1864.

30. Porter Alexander to his wife, May 28, 1864, in Alexander papers; Porter Alexander to Adam Alexander, May 29, 1864 (fragment), in Alexander papers; *Official Records,* 36(1):1049; Grant, *Memoirs,* 2:264–265.   31. Grant, *Memoirs,* 2:262–265; *Official Records,* 36(1):998 and 36(2):40 and 36(3):320, 850, 857–858 and 51(2):969, 971. Lee had estimated Smith's force to be only half its real strength of sixteen thousand men and sixteen guns.   32. *Official Records,* 36(1): 794 and 36(3):858 and 51(2):974; Grant, *Memoirs,* 2:264–265; Alexander, *Memoirs,* p. 536; Robert Stiles, *Four Years Under Marse Robert* (New York, 1910), pp. 273–274.   33. *Official Records,* 36(1):998–1000, 1005, 1049; Alexander, *Memoirs,* pp. 537–539, Porter Alexander to his wife, June 10, 1864, in Alexander papers.   34. *Official Records,* 36(1):1001–1002, 1049 and 36(2):478–479; Grant, *Memoirs,* 2:268; Porter Alexander to his wife, June 10, 1864.   35. *Official Records,* 36(1):345; *Battles and Leaders,* 6:217, 225; Porter Alexander to his wife, June 10, 1864 and J. B. Kershaw to R. E. Lee, June 3, 1864, in Alexander papers. 36. *Official Records,* 36(2):624–626; *Battles and Leaders,* 4:217–218; Porter Alexander to his wife, June 10, 1864. For a drawing of a typical Confederate trench at Cold Harbor see the Alexander papers.   37. Alexander, "Passage of the James River," 156–158.   38. *Official Records,* 30(2):599, 662, 747–749, 754–755; 30(3):884–885, 889, 896; 36(1):1035, 37(1):346; 40(2):667 and 51(2):1003–1004; D. S. Freeman, *Lee's Confidential Dispatches to Davis 1862–65* (New York, 1915), pp. 227–232. For detail on Lee's gradual discovery of Grant's plan see Freeman, *R. E. Lee,* 3:402–424.

Chapter X

1. Porter Alexander to his wife, June 19, 1864, and R. E. Lee to R. H. Anderson, June 16, 1864, in Alexander papers; *Official Records,* 40(1):760–761 and 40(2):655–656; Alexander, *Memoirs,* pp. 552–556; Freeman, *Lee's Lieutenants,* 3: 530–537.   2. Porter Alexander to his wife, June 27 and July 1, 1864, R. E. Lee to Porter Alexander, June 27, 1864, and Captain Ronin? to Porter Alexander, June 21, 1864, in Alexander papers; Owen, *Washington Artillery,* p. 334.   3. Alexander, "Petersburg," 194, 208.   4. Ibid., 192–193. Elliott's South Carolina brigade occupied the salient.   5. Ibid., 204–207. A color map of the Confederate lines about Petersburg with the positions of Alexander's guns sketched in, can be found in the Alexander papers.   6. *Official Records,* 36(3):880–882.   7. Porter Alexander to his wife, July 1, 1864; Alexander, "Petersburg," 209–210.   8. Alexander, "Nicaragua Journal No. 1," in Alexander papers.   9. Alexander, "Petersburg," 211–241; Alexander, *Memoirs,* pp. 564–572; Porter Alexander to his wife, August 14, 1864, in Alexander papers; Bancroft, "Southern Notebook," 4:392.

10. Special Orders No. 153, July 2, 1864, and Porter Alexander to G. M. Sorrel, July 26, 1864, in Alexander folder, Confederate Records; *Official Records,* 42(2):1183–1184, 1208.   11. Alexander, "Fall of 1864," 254–256; Freeman, *Lee's Lieutenants,* 3:588–590.   12. Alexander, "Fall of 1864," 262–274. The Richmond lines consisted of two separate works. The exterior line comprised about eleven miles of breastworks from Chaffins Bluff to the Chickahominy River near New Bridge. Most of the seven miles north of Newmarket Road were but the abandoned trenches of 1862, and the exterior lines lacked abatis and gun platforms. The interior line, about one to two miles from the city, linked the James and Chickahominy rivers and included about a dozen forts near the city with permanent garrisons and stationary guns manned by local troops. A spur line of intrenchments ran from the interior line to the exterior line so as to embrace Chaffins Bluff and Osborn Pike. This spur line joined the exterior line at Battery Harrison—thus the significance of the latter's loss. See Alexander, "Fall of 1864," 258–260, and his own maps in the Alexander papers.   13. Porter Alexander to his wife, October 3, 1864, in Alexander papers.   14. Alexander, "Fall of 1864," 256 and "Winter of 1865," 284; Alexander, *Memoirs,* p. 585.   15. Porter Alexander to his wife, August 28, September 7, September 15, September 20, October 3, October 19, October 25, November 11, and November 27, 1864, in Alexander papers; Porter Alexander to Adam Alexander, September 22, 1864, in Alexander-Hillhouse papers.   16. Porter Alexander to his wife, September 7, November 10, and November 27, 1864, in Alexander papers. For the battalion's petition see the Alexander papers. For some of the minor affairs that fall see *Official Records,* 42(3):1186, 1229, 1232, 1250, 1257–1258, 1261, 1265, 1273 and Alexander's diary, in Alexander papers.   17. Alexander, "Winter of 1865," 281–284; Porter Alexander to his wife, November 27, 1864. The canal never opened for ships but was scoured out after the war and became a regular channel for navigation.   18. Alexander, *Memoirs,* p. 585; Porter Alexander to his wife, January 3, 1865, and Willie Mason to Porter Alexander, January 22, 1865, in Alexander papers.   19. Manuscript 6701, Confederate Records; Porter Alexander to his wife, n.d., December 25 and March 2, 1865, in Alexander papers.

20. Porter Alexander to his wife, December 14 and December 25, 1864, in Alexander papers.   21. *Official Records,* 46(2):1266–1267, 1293, 1296, 1300–1303 and 46(3):1322–1324, 1330, 1344, 1368.   22. See the various letters from Porter Alexander to his wife for February and March, 1865, in Alexander papers. In his later accounts Alexander emphasized repeatedly the blinding effect of the South's deep religious impulse upon any realistic consideration of political

and military alternatives: "I can only account for it in the general religious character of our people. They believed in a God who ... in the end brought the right to
prevail. They *knew* they were right, & they were! It was only waiting on God, a
little more or less." Alexander, "Winter of 1865," 308.   23. Sarah Lawton to
Adam Alexander, March 5, 1865, in Alexander-Hillhouse papers; *Official Records,*
46(1):382–383 and 46(3):1343, 1351–1352, 1368, 1378–1379; Grant, *Memoirs,*
2:439–440, 447; Alexander, *Memoirs,* pp. 591–594. As late as April 1 Porter wrote
"everybody is convinced now that Richmond is going to be evacuated. I dont begin
to believe it myself, however, for our army is able to give some hard blows in its
defense." Porter Alexander to his wife, April 1, 1865, in Alexander papers.
24. Alexander, *Memoirs,* p. 594 and "Appomattox," 343–348; Edward Porter Alexander, "Lee at Appomattox," *Century Magazine,* 63(1902), 922; Porter Alexander
to his wife, April 3, 1865, in Alexander papers.   25. Porter Alexander to his
wife, April 8, 1865, in Alexander papers; Alexander, "Appomattox," 349–355 and
"Lee at Appomattox," 923–925; Alexander, *Memoirs,* pp. 595–596.   26. Alexander, "Appomattox," 377–379 and "Lee at Appomattox," 925–926. Alexander's
fear of prison derived from the fact that Grant had stopped general exchanges of
prisoners for nearly a year.   27. John B. Gordon, *Reminiscences of the Civil War*
(New York, 1904), pp. 437–38; Alexander, *Memoirs,* p. 603. The Junction mentioned by Lee referred to the separate roads taken by the opposing armies. The road
joined at Appomattox Court House and the Federals, having the shorter route,
reached that point first, thus blocking Lee's line of retreat. Later Lee would give his
map to Venable to be burned. Alexander cut off a square with Lee's signature to pre-
serve as a souvenir, and it can be found in the Alexander papers, Library of Congress.
28. The entire scene with Lee is drawn from Alexander, *Memoirs,* pp. 604–606 and
"Lee at Appomattox," 926–927.   29. Alexander, *Memoirs,* pp. 608–609; Grant,
Memoirs, 2:484–485; Alexander, "Appomattox," 387–389. That same night Alexander watched souvenir hunters rip away pieces of the apple tree. Within two days
it had completely disappeared.

    30. *SHSP,* 38:12; Alexander, *Memoirs,* p. 612 and "Appomattox," 390–391.
31. Alexander, *Memoirs,* p. 613; the original parole slip, dated April 10, can be
found in the Alexander papers, Library of Congress.   32. Alexander, "Recollections," 1:119–120.   33. Alexander, "Appomattox," 400–401; *Official Records,*
46(1):1279.

Chapter XI

    1. Alexander, "Appomattox," 406–421; Alexander, *Memoirs,* pp. 615–616.
2. Eliza F. Andrews, *The War-Time Journal of a Georgia Girl, 1864–1865* (Macon, 1960), pp. 367–368.   3. G. T. Beauregard to Porter Alexander, August
27, 1865, and Josiah Gorgas to Porter Alexander, September 18, 1865, in Alexander
papers.   4. Adam Alexander to Marion Alexander, September 11 and October 1,
1865, in Alexander-Hillhouse papers. Alexander Lawton to John P. King, September
5, 1865, in Alexander papers.   5. W. N. Pendleton to Porter Alexander, October
9, 1865, and Francis H. Smith to Porter Alexander, October 10, 1865, in Alexander papers.   6. Porter Alexander to his wife, October 20 and October 22, 1865,
and Bettie Alexander to her husband, October 22, 1865, in Alexander papers.
7. Bettie Alexander to her husband, November 3, 1865, in possession of Mrs. Elizabeth Hilton.   8. Edwin L. Green, *A History of the University of South Carolina*
(Columbia, 1916), p. 86; *Columbia State,* April 29, 1910; Alexander Haskell to
Porter Alexander, January 9, 1866, in Alexander papers.   9. Custis Lee to
Porter Alxeander, February 4, 1866, in Alexander papers.

    10. *Columbia State,* April 29, 1910; Green, *South Carolina,* p. 87.   11.
Green, *South Carolina,* pp. 86–89; *Columbia State,* April 29, 1910; Joseph LeConte,

Autobiography (New York, 1903), pp. 235–239.   12. Longstreet to Porter Alexander, February 26, 1866, in Alexander papers; Green, *South Carolina,* p. 90; Adam Alexander to Marion Alexander, January 22, 1867, in Alexander-Hillhouse papers; H. Hull Jr. to Porter Alexander, September 21, 1866, in Alexander papers.   13. Report of the Secretary of War, *Executive Documents,* 40th Congress, 3rd Session, No. 1, Pt. 1, serial 1367, pp. 520–521; John H. Franklin, *Reconstruction After the Civil War* (Chicago, 1961), pp. 74, 102; Francis B. Simkins and R. H. Woody, *South Carolina During Reconstruction* (Chapel Hill, 1932), pp. 48–121. There is no clue as to the color of the remaining member.   14. Franklin, *Reconstruction,* p. 112; Green, *South Carolina,* pp. 92–94; Porter Alexander to Adam Alexander, January 5, 1869, in Adam Alexander papers.   15. Porter Alexander to Adam Alexander, January 5, January 22, and January 27, 1869, in Adam Alexander papers; Porter Alexander to Frederic Bancroft, October 25, 1908, in Bancroft papers; Porter Alexander to "Brother," January 9, 1869, in Alexander papers.   16. William D. Shue, "The Cotton Oil Industry," in *Publications of the Mississippi Historical Society* (Oxford, 1904), 8:264–273; Porter Alexander to Adam Alexander, April 27, 1869, in Adam Alexander papers.   17. Porter Alexander to Adam Alexander, May 27, 1869, in Adam Alexander papers.   18. Quoted in Simkins and Woody, *S. C. Reconstruction,* p. 295, which erroneously gives the year as 1870. See Porter Alexander to M. P. Hillhouse, March 6, 1880, in Alexander-Hillhouse papers, and Helen K. Hennig, ed., *Columbia 1786–1936,* (Columbia, 1936), p. 336.

Chapter XII

1. United States Bureau of the Census, *Historical Statistics of the United States, Colonial Times to 1957* (Washington, 1960), p. 276, series K, 298–306, p. 302; *Manufacturer's Record,* June 6, 1907.   2. Shue, "The Cotton Oil Industry," 272–273; Hennig, *Columbia 1786–1936,* p. 337.   3. C. P. Stone to Porter Alexander, March 5, 1870, in Alexander papers.   4. T. Harry Williams, *P. G. T. Beauregard: Napoleon in Gray* (Baton Rouge, 1954), pp. 264–265; G. T. Beauregard to Porter Alexander, June 17, 1870, and Stone to Porter Alexander, February 7, 1871, in Alexander papers.   5. Stone to Porter Alexander, May 22, 1871, and Porter Alexander to Mary Alexander, September? 6, 1904, in Alexander papers.   6. This brief synopsis is drawn from Theodore Voorhees, "The Freight-Car Service," in B. B. Adams, Jr. *et al., The American Railway* (New York, 1897), pp. 274–275.   7. This sketch of the various aspects of a superintendent's duties comes from an able article on railroad management written by Alexander himself. Doubtless he has drawn upon his own experiences in writing the piece. See Edward Porter Alexander, "Railway Management" in Adams, *The American Railway,* pp. 154–172. This book is composed of articles originally published in *Scribners Magazine;* Alexander's contribution may be found in slightly altered form in the 1889 edition, 5:27–48.   8. *Railroad Gazette* (Chicago), 4:436, hereinafter cited as *Gazette.*   9. Walter L. Fleming, *Civil War and Reconstruction in Alabama* (Cleveland, 1911), pp. 589–590, 604, hereinafter cited as *Alabama;* James F. Doster, *Railroads in Alabama Politics 1875–1914* (Tuscaloosa, 1956), 20; John F. Stover, *Railroads of the South 1865–1900* (Chapel Hill, 1955), pp. 88–89.

10. *Gazette,* 4:30, 341; *Commercial and Financial Chronicle* (New York), 14:124 and 15:219, hereinafter cited as *Chronicle;* Henry V. Poor, *Manual of the Railroads of the United States for 1873–74* (New York, 1874), p. 529, hereinafter cited, with appropriate year, as *Manual;* Fleming, *Alabama,* pp. 600, 604–605.   11. *Gazette,* 4:448 and 5:346; Poor, *Manual 1873–74,* p. 529.   12. *Chronicle,* 19:364, 366; Fleming, *Alabama,* p. 590: *Gazette,* 5:55, 116, 238, 349, 418, 437–438, 449. The original endorsed bonds at $16,000 per mile covered only the forty

mile stretch between Opelika and Sturdevant, or a total endorsement of $640,000. Thus, the $80,000 received here comprises a fresh subsidy beyond the original bond authorization.   13. Poor, *Manual 1874–75*, pp. 143–144; William H. Joubert, *Southern Freight Rates in Transition* (Gainesville, 1949), chap. 2.   14. *Thirty-Eighth Report of the President and Directors of the Central Railroad and Banking Company* (Savannah, 1874), p. 9, hereinafter cited, with appropriate number and year, as *Central Report*; *Gazette*, 5:515 and 6:145–146; *Chronicle*, 18:456; Adam Alexander to Porter Alexander, May 11 and November 6, 1874, in Alexander papers.   15. *Gazette*, 7:57, 210, 225, 231, 236, 245, 360, 378, 388; Alexander Lawton to Porter Alexander, April 10, 1875, in Alexander papers; *Fortieth Central Report 1875*, pp. 8–9; Poor, *Manual 1874–75*, p. 746, *Manual 1876–77*, p. 359 and *Manual 1877–78*, pp. 218–220; *Chronicle*, 20:501; Mary Cumming, *Georgia Railroad and Banking Company 1833–1945* (Augusta, 1945), pp. 84–85; Henry W. Thomas, *Digest of the Railroad Laws of Georgia*, Atlanta, 1895), pp. 229–230.   16. *Thirty-Eighth Central Report 1874*, p. 7 and *Thirty-Ninth Central Report 1874*, p. 6; *Chronicle*, 17:854, 19:639, and 20:130; Adam Alexander to Porter Alexander, November 6, 1874; Poor, *Manual 1876–77*, p. 30.   17. *Gazette*, 6:507. For background detail on the Southern Railway and Steamship Association see Joubert, *Southern Rates*, pp. 40–68; Henry Hudson, "The Southern Railway and Steamship Association," in William Z. Ripley, ed., *Railway Problems* (Boston, 1907), pp. 98–122; Charles F. Adams, Jr., *Railroads: Their Origins and Problems* (New York, 1878), pp. 170–173.   18. *Fortieth Central Report 1875*, p. 6; *Forty-First Central Report 1876*, p. 5; Poor, *Manual 1877–78*, pp. 218–220, 224–226; *Chronicle*, 25:456; *Gazette*, 9:503–504.   19. *Forty-Second Central Report 1877*, p. 8; *Gazette*, 9:221.

20. *Forty-Third Central Report 1878*, p. 8; *Chronicle*, 26:440.   21. *Dictionary of American Biography*, 9:395; Cumming, *Georgia Railroad*, p. 52ff.; Poor, *Manual 1876–77*, pp. 29–30; *Gazette*, 7:311; *Chronicle*, 22:xix (January 29, 1876). 22. *Gazette*, 8:188, 260 and 9:262; *Chronicle*, 22:469 and 24:466.   23. *Chronicle*, 22:586; *Gazette*, 9:32, 115; Thomas, *Digest*, p. 230.   24. *Gazette*, 9:226, 239; *Chronicle*, 24:495; Cumming, *Georgia Railroad*, pp. 85–87.   25. *Gazette*, 10:166, 278; *Chronicle*, 26:468.   26. *Gazette*, 10:247–248. See also *Augusta Chronicle and Constitutionalist*, May 7, 1880.

Chapter XIII

1. *Chronicle*, 28:xx (January 25, 1879); Poor, *Manual 1875–76*, p. 418 and *Manual 1877–78*, p. 224.   2. Cumming, *Georgia Railroad*, p. 88; Stover, *Southern Railroads*, pp. 149–50.   3. See U. B. Phillips, *The Life of Robert Toombs* (New York, 1913), pp. 270–272.   4. Walter McElreath, *A Treatise on the Constitution of Georgia* (Atlanta, 1912), 537–543; Ethel K. Ware, *A Constitutional History of Georgia* (New York, 1947), pp. 159–173; *Gazette*, 9:388, 405.   5. *Chronicle*, 26:113 and 28:16; *Gazette*, 8:137 and 10:312, 350, 407.   6. *Chronicle*, 28:501–502.   7. Ibid., 28:449, 501–502 and 26:285; *Gazette*, 11:203, 304. For details on the pool see Joubert, *Southern Rates*, pp. 48–51.   8. *Chronicle*, 29:63, 116, 456 and 30:41, 88.   9. See *Atlanta Constitution*, July 17, 1879, and *Gazette*, 11:570; Maxwell Ferguson, *State Regulation of Railroads in the South* (New York, 1916), p. 96.

10. Ferguson, *State Regulation*, p. 96. For a copy of these provisions see Edward Porter Alexander, *On Various Railway Questions* (Louisville, 1881), pp. 2–22.   11. Adams, *Railroads*, p. 81.   12. The following account is derived from Alexander, *Railway Questions*, pp. 2–22. His attitude toward the railroad question here and in his book written in 1887 (see chapter 15) bears a close resemblance to that of Arthur T. Hadley, *Railroad Transportation* (New York, 1885).

Both men in turn embody several concepts expressed by Albert Fink in his writings. 13. "Acts and Resolutions of the General Assembly of Georgia," No. 269, Part 1, Title 12, 1878–1879. A copy of the law can be found in *Gazette,* 11:566.   14. *Atlanta Constitution,* October 16, 1879. See also *Gazette,* 11:570.   15. *Gazette,* 11:610; *Chronicle,* 30:192; *Atlanta Constitution,* February 11, 1880.   16. Avery, *Georgia,* p. 636; Stover, *Southern Railroads,* pp. 227, 240; Raymond B. Nixon, *Henry W. Grady: Spokesman of the New South* (New York, 1943), p. 166; *Chronicle,* 30:168, 408; *Gazette,* 12:106, 175, 201, 551; *Forty-Fifth Central Report 1880,* p. 8.   17. *Gazette,* 12:12, 146, 296; *Chronicle,* 30:248, 448, 542–543.

Chapter XIV

1. *Augusta Chronicle and Constitutionalist,* May 7, 1880; C. H. Phinizy to Porter Alexander, April 25, 1880, in Alexander papers.   2. *Augusta Chronicle and Constitutionalist,* May 7, 1880; *Gazette,* 13:314.   3. Stover, *Southern Railroads,* chap. 10; Thomas D. Clark, *The Beginning of the L & N* (Louisville, 1933); Poor, *Manual 1881,* pp. 468–475; Nixon, *Grady,* p. 167; *New York Times,* January 21, 1880.   4. *Chronicle,* 29:358, 381 and 30:384; Nixon, *Grady,* p. 168; *Gazette,* 11:371, 528, 543.   5. For this episode see *Chronicle,* 30:519, 650 and 31:45, 191, 217, 403; *Gazette,* 12:263, 363, 551. The account in Stover, *Southern Railroads,* pp. 222–223, is somewhat misleading.   6. Avery, *Georgia,* p. 637.   7. Porter Alexander to his wife, October 3, 1880, and Bettie Alexander to her husband, September 13, 1880, in Alexander papers.   8. Nixon, *Grady,* p. 168; *Chronicle,* 30:222, 248 and 31:95, 306, 380; *Gazette,* 12:417.   9. Copies of the annual report, from which this account is drawn, can be found in *Chronicle,* 31:403–404 and *Gazette,* 12:550–552, the first being a more abridged version.

10. *Gazette,* 12:533; *Chronicle,* 31:382, 403. Alexander, of course, also served as a director.   11. *Chronicle,* 31:551, and 32:16, 33; *Gazette,* 12:648.   12. *Chronicle,* 32:70; *Gazette,* 13:129, 132, 575.   13. *Chronicle,* 32:334, 420, 551; *Gazette,* 13:129, 575; Cumming, *Georgia Railroad,* pp. 89–90.   14. *Chronicle,* 33:47; *Gazette,* 13:393, 562, 568. The L & N annexed this road into its system on November 1.   15. *Gazette,* 13:393, 544, 568; *Chronicle,* 33:41, 201, 544, 568. 16. *Gazette,* 13:559, 568, 593, 640.   17. Louisa Gilmer to Bettie Alexander, August 24, 1881, in Alexander papers.   18. *Forty-Sixth Central Report 1881,* p. 91. For details see chapter 15.   19. Porter Alexander to Bessie and Lula Alexander, December 19, 1881, in Alexander papers; *Gazette,* 13:719. The man named to this post, Milton H. Smith, became first vice-president when Alexander resigned in 1882 and later helped rescue the road from scandal in 1884. He ruled the company with an iron hand as president from 1891 until his death in 1921.

20. *Forty-Seventh Central Report 1882,* p. 18; *Chronicle,* 34:216, 264, and 35:88; *Gazette,* 14:95, 156, 278.   21. Albert Fink to Porter Alexander, March 24, 1882, in Alexander papers; Porter Alexander to M. P. Hillhouse, April 29, 1882, in Alexander-Hillhouse papers.   22. *Gazette,* 14:335; Porter Alexander to his wife, June 3, 1882, in Alexander papers. For the Fink boom see *Gazette,* 14:306, 333, 349, 351. An autobiographical sketch of Fink can be found in the Albert Fink papers, Library of Congress.   23. *Chronicle,* 36:11, 20; *Gazette,* 14:450, 622; Jeremy Gilmer to Porter Alexander, July 2, 1882, in Alexander papers.

Chapter XV

1. See T. B. Catherwood, ed., *The Life and Labors of William M. Wadley* (Savannah, 1885).   2. Thomas, *Digest,* p. 180; Poor, *Manual 1892,* p. 537; *Chronicle,* 18:374 and 23:430; *Thirty-Seventh Central Report 1872,* p. 7.

3. *Thirty-Eighth Central Report 1874*, p. 11 and *Thirty-Ninth Central Report 1874*, p. 7; *Chronicle*, 18:459; Catherwood, ed., *Wadley*, p. 11.   4. *Chronicle*, 14: 422, 20:130, 22:304, 33:611; *Gazette*, 10:278; *Forty-Third Central Report 1878*, p. 7, *Forty-Fourth Central Report 1879*, pp. 7–8, and *Forty-Fifth Central Report 1880*, p. 7; Poor, *Manual 1881*, p. 402, and *Manual 1892*, p. 537. 5. *Forty-Seventh Central Report 1882*, pp. 17, 21; Poor, *Manual 1881*, pp. 401, 413. 6. *Forty-Sixth Central Report 1881*, pp. 8–9.   7. The dividend fight can best be followed in the newspaper clippings in the William G. Raoul Scrapbooks (Emory University, Atlanta), and in the *Savannah Morning News*, 1880–1882. For Alexander's position see his detailed letter in *Savannah Morning News*, December 21, 1886.   8. *Gazette*, 13:734; *Chronicle*, 33:715. Detailed discussion of the Ocean controversy can also be found in the clippings in Raoul Scrapbooks.   9. Jeremy Gilmer to Porter Alexander, July 2, 1882; *Forty-Seventh Central Report 1881*, pp. 91–105; *Chronicle*, 33:526, 659; *Gazette*, 13:747. See also the *Savannah Morning News*, January–February, 1882, passim.

10. For the L & N infiltration see the Raoul Scrapbooks, W. W. Gordon Scrapbook (Southern Historical Collection), VI, and E. C. Anderson to W. W. Gordon, July 9, 1881, in W. W. Gordon papers, Southern Historical Collection. 11. *Gazette*, 14:13, 29, 559; *Savannah Morning News*, January 3, 1882. Later Alexander and Gilmer were also elected to the Ocean board.   12. *Gazette*, 14:16, 89–90, 93, 103, 107, 156; *Savannah Morning News*, February 16, 1882; Raoul Scrapbook, 2:63.   13. *Savannah Morning News*, February 16, 1882; *Macon Telegraph and Messenger*, February 18, 1882.   14. *Forty-Sixth Central Report 1881*, p. 74, and *Forty-Seventh Central Report 1882*, pp. 96, 120; *Gazette*, 14:364, 382; *Macon Telegraph and Messenger*, February 18, 1882; Raoul Scrapbook, 2:54, 67; John Gresham to W. W. Gordon, April 15, 1882, in Gordon papers.   15. Gilmer to Porter Alexander, July 2, 1882; Raoul Scrapbook, 3:9.   16. *Forty-Sixth Central Report 1881*, pp. 91–102, and *Forty-Seventh Central Report 1882*, pp. 115–130; *Gazette*, 14:399, 416, 433.   17. *Gazette*, 14:510, 512–513, 559; Catherwood, ed., *Wadley*, pp. 8–9; William Raoul to W. B. Johns(t)on, August 24, 1882, in William Raoul Letterbooks, Emory University.   18. *Forty-Seventh Central Report 1882*, pp. 16–18; *Gazette*, 14:661.   19. *Gazette*, 14:759. For the story of the certificates by an Alexander supporter see the circular by E. M. Green in Gordon Scrapbook, VI.

20. Raoul Scrapbook, 3:21–22.   21. Albert Fink to Alexander Lawton, December 13, 1882, in Alexander papers.   22. Louisa Gilmer to James Alexander, November 22, 1882, in Adam Alexander papers; *Atlanta Constitution*, January 2, 1883. That Alexander attributed his defeat to Hetty Green has been confirmed in an interview with his granddaughter, Mrs. Elizabeth Hilton, March 20, 1962. In contemporary accounts the stock was often referred to as the Cisco stock because it was held by the firm of J. J. Cisco & Company.   23. Harriett Cumming to James Alexander, January 23, 1883, in Adam Alexander papers.   24. Porter Alexander to his wife, March 13, 1884, and January 28, 1885, in Alexander papers.   25. Ibid.; Porter Alexander to Alexander Lawton, April 1, 1885, in Alexander Lawton papers, Southern Historical Collection.   26. Porter Alexander to his wife, January 3, August 30, August 31, and September 3, 1886, in Alexander papers; *Gazette*, 18:289.   27. Porter Alexander to his wife, January 29, 1885, in Alexander papers; Poor, *Manual 1885*, p. 762. Alexander, *Railroad Questions*, is a convenient collection of Alexander's earlier writings on railroad matters.   28. T. Harry Williams in Alexander, *Memoirs*, p. xxxiv. This account is drawn from Edward Porter Alexander, *Railway Practice* (New York, 1887). For the development of his ideas see the articles in Alexander, *Railroad Questions*.   29. Porter Alexander to Louisa Minis, April 12, 1900, in Minis family papers, Southern Historical Collection.

30. Albert Fink to Porter Alexander, February 24, 1885, in Alexander papers.
31. Ben F. Proctor, *Not Without Honor: The Life of John H. Reagan* (Austin, 1962), p. 244 and chaps. 17–18.

Chapter XVI

1. See the clippings from *Savannah Daily Times*, January ?, 1887, in Alexander papers, and clipping in Raoul Scrapbook, 3:45.   2. For background on the Richmond Terminal see Maury Klein, *The Great Richmond Terminal* (Charlottesville, Va., 1970).   3. *Chronicle*, 43:159, 395, 543, 711; *Gazette*, 18:732, 784, 801; *Savannah Morning News*, November 27, 1886. A copy of the circular can be found in the Alexander papers. For the "wrecker" rumors see *New York Times*, January 4, 1887.   4. *Chronicle*, 43:622. Raoul had declared only a 2 percent dividend in July, and his action aroused the natural suspicion that it was a political move. For the controversy see *Savannah Morning News*, December 2, 1886, and *Augusta Evening News*, December 2, 1886.   5. For this battle see *Gazette*, 18:879, and the relevant clippings in the Alexander papers.   6. *New York Times*, January 5, 1887; *Chronicle*, 43:607; *Gazette*, 18:803, 824; *Savannah Morning News*, December 4, 1886; undated *Atlanta Constitution* clipping in Raoul Scrapbook, 3:37. 7. *Savannah Morning News*, January 4, 1887; *Gazette*, 18:824, 896 and 19:8; *Chronicle*, 44:59; *New York Times*, January 4, 1887. Raoul later claimed that at the last moment Alexander's backers offered to switch sides if Raoul would let them name seven of the company's thirteen directors. Raoul declined and the New Yorkers voted for Alexander. Rumors to this effect appeared in several newspapers prior to the election and lend credence to Raoul's assertion. See William Raoul to C. W. Brewster, June 2, 1890, in Raoul Letterbook.   8. *New York Times*, January 4, 1887; *Gazette*, 19:240.   9. *Chronicle*, 44:381 and 45:744–746; *Gazette*, 19:240.

10. Porter Alexander to Alexander Lawton, March 22, 1888, in Lawton papers; *Chronicle*, 44:653 and 45:746.   11. *Chronicle*, 45:210, 792; *Gazette*, 19:490; David Schenck Diary (Southern Historical Collection), May 31 and June 12, 1887. 12. *New York Times*, March 12, 1888. See also the maps in Poor, *Manual 1891*, pp. 93, 105.   13. Porter Alexander to Lawton, March 22, 1888.   14. *New York Times*, March 12 and April 6, 1888; *Richmond Dispatch*, April 4 and April 6, 1888; *Gazette*, 20:244. For a copy of the pamphlet see *Chronicle*, 46:579–581. 15. *New York Times*, April 14, April 18, May 13 and May 24, 1888; *Richmond Dispatch*, April 13, April 22 and June 1, 1888; *Gazette*, 20:262; *Chronicle*, 46:511. 16. *Chronicle*, 47:50, 226, 274–275, 285–286; *Gazette*, 20:229, 245, 343, 465, 481, 564, 613. The projects can be more easily understood by referring to the map in Poor, *Manual 1891*, p. 93.   17. Poor, *Manual 1888*, p. 567; *Chronicle*, 47:19, 167, 274, 283, 286–287, 408, 561, 705; *Gazette*, 20:442–443, 774, 804.   18. *Chronicle*, 47:486–487, 499 and 55:938, 1078–1079; *Gazette*, 20:704–705; E. G. Campbell, *The Reorganization of the American Railroad System 1893–1900* (New York, 1938), pp. 100–102. For the later investigation of the Georgia Company sale see *Chronicle*, 55:895, 938, 1078–1079 and *Gazette*, 24:636.   19. W. W. Gordon to W. S. Chisholm, December 21, 1889, in Gordon papers.

20. *Chronicle*, 47:410, 664, 48:547, 728 and 49:527, 541; *Gazette*, 21:301, 660.   21. *Gazette*, 20:644; *Chronicle*, 49:18, 171, 267, 500, 541–542, 576, 715 and 50:102, 203.   22. *Chronicle*, 51:720.   23. Ibid., 50:800 and 51:89, 571–572, 720; *Gazette*, 21:812.   24. *Chronicle*, 51:877–878; *New York Times*, December 19, 1890; Julius Grodinsky, *Jay Gould* (Philadelphia, 1957), p. 578. 25. *Chronicle*, 52:462, 862; *Gazette*, 23:205, 296, 420. After the Terminal pur-

chased the Georgia Company, Inman had appeased the Central's minority holders by asking three of them, Hugh Comer, W. W. Gordon and Jacob Rauers, to remain as directors. But he ignored them in decision making, and nothing Alexander did could ease their resentment. "The kindest possible relations exist between Gen Alexander, the other Directors & ourselves," Gordon wrote Inman, "and Gen A. has appeared specially anxious to make everything specially pleasant to us. But in reality you allow him very limited authority." When Inman failed to change his methods, the trio refused to stand for reelection in 1890. W. W. Gordon to John Inman, December 21, 1889, and January 2, 1890, in Gordon papers.   26. Porter Alexander to "Chicken Pie," June 5, 1891, in possession of Mrs. Elizabeth Hilton.   27. *New York Herald*, August 8, 1891; *Chronicle*, 53:224, 408.   28. *Chronicle*, 52:922, 969, 53:256, 881, 922 and 54:34; *Gazette*, 23:890.   29. *Savannah Morning News*, December 30 and December 31, 1891, and January 3, 1892.

30. Ibid., January 1 and January 3, 1892; *Chronicle*, 54:32, 78; *Gazette*, 24:31–33.   31. See the *Savannah Morning News*, January 4, 1892.   32. *Chronicle*, 54:443. Copies of the suit and the decision can be found in the Emory University Library, Atlanta, and at the Bureau of Railroad Economics, Washington. 33. *Chronicle*, 54:525, 560, 844; *Gazette*, 24:258; *Savannah Evening Press*, April 28, 1910.   34. Alexander, "Recollections," 1:40.

Chapter XVII

1. Porter Alexander to Mary Alexander, May 11, 1902, in Alexander papers; W. W. Mackall, *A Son's Recollection of his Father* (New York, 1930), pp. 158–159. 2. Grover Cleveland to Porter Alexander, February 12, 1897, in possession of Mrs. Elizabeth Hilton. The account of this dispute, unless otherwise indicated, is drawn from John Bassett Moore, *History and Digest of the International Arbitrations to Which the United States Has Been a Party* (Washington, 1898), vol. 2, 1945– 1968.   3. The award can be found in Moore, *History and Digest*, 2:1964–1967. 4. Cleveland to Porter Alexander, February 12, 1897, in possession of Mrs. Elizabeth Hilton; Moore, *International Arbitrations*, 2:1967–1968.   5. Cleveland to Alexander, February 12, 1897; *New York Herald*, September 16, 1899.   6. For example see Porter Alexander to his wife, November 6, 1897, in Alexander papers. 7. Ibid., May 1 and May 2, 1897, in Alexander papers. The remainder of this chapter, unless otherwise indicated, is based upon the letters from Porter Alexander to his wife in the Alexander papers.   8. A copy of the award in its original pamphlet form can be found in the Alexander papers. A printed version can be found in Moore, *International Arbitrations*, 5:5074–5078. Discussion of the award can be best followed by using the map in Moore, 5:5079.   9. Edward Porter Alexander, "Sea Island Log" (microfilm copy in Southern Historical Collection), 131.

10. *New York Herald*, September 16, 1899.   11. Boggs, ed., *Alexander Letters*, p. 378; *Augusta Chronicle*, November 21, 1899.   12. Mary C. Hull to Mary Alexander, November 13, 1902, in Alexander papers; *Augusta Chronicle*, November 21, 1899.   13. *Augusta Chronicle*, April 29, 1900; Porter Alexander to Louisa Minis, May 2 and May 21, 1900, in Minis papers; Harriett Cumming to Porter Alexander, May 1, 1900, Bessie Ficklen to Will Craig, May 10, 1900, Porter Alexander to Will Craig, May 13, 1900, and Bessie Ficklen to Porter Alexander, July 1, 1900, in Alexander papers.   14. Porter Alexander to "Sister," February 23 and February 24, 1900, in Alexander papers; Alexander, "Sea Island Log," 141. 15. Boggs, ed., *Alexander Letters*, pp. 366–370. For Alexander's trip see his "Nicaraguan Journals," in the Alexander papers.

Chapter XVIII

1. Porter Alexander to Will Craig, September 26, 1900, and Porter Alexander to Hal ?, August 20, 1901, in Alexander papers. 2. Porter Alexander to Bessie Ficklen, May 16, 1898, in John R. Ficklen papers, Southern Historical Collection; Porter Alexander to Sarah Lawton, June 8, 1881, in Lawton papers; Franklin Mac-Veagh to Porter Alexander, January 20, 1887, in Alexander papers. For examples of his editorial contacts see Porter Alexander to his wife, August 30, 1886, and September 3, 1886, in Alexander papers. 3. For exact locations and dates of these articles see the bibliography. 4. Charles F. Adams, *Lee at Appomattox and other Papers* (Boston, 1902), p. 9. Bancroft makes the same sort of observation; see his "Southern Notebook," 2:121–122. 5. Mackall, *Recollections*, p. 159; *Chicago Interocean*, May 14, 1893; ? *Weekly-News*, May 13, 1893, clipping in Alexander papers; Porter Alexander to H. R. Duval, March 20, 1899, in possession of Mrs. Elizabeth Hilton. 6. Porter Alexander to Louisa P. Minis, July 2 and October 2, 1899, in Minis papers. 7. Ibid.; Porter Alexander to Frederic Bancroft, September 21, 1902, in Bancroft papers; Porter Alexander to Hal ?, August 20, 1901. 8. For the exchange of letters see *SHSP*, 5:47–53, 201–203; W. N. Pendleton to Porter Alexander, February 5, 1878, in Alexander papers. See also the letters from Huger, Sorrel, Cabell, Owen and Colston. 9. Alexander, "Recollections," 1:60–61. The undated article can be found in Alexander papers.

10. Alexander, *Memoirs*, pp. vii–viii. Isolated fragments of Alexander's thoughts on the political background to the war are scattered through his letters in the Bancroft papers. 11. Alexander, "Recollections," 1:61–65. 12. Mary Mason to Mrs. A. S. Mason, July 17, 1900, Porter Alexander to Hal ?, August 11, 1901 and ? to Mrs. A. S. Mason, August 7, 1901, in Alexander papers; Bancroft, "Southern Notebook," 2:121–122. Bancroft estimated Mary's age to be 28–30. 13. Mary Alexander to Alex Mason, January 5 and February 4, 1902, and Porter Alexander to Mary Alexander, May 1 and May 12, 1902, in Alexander papers; Porter Alexander to Louisa Minis, April 29, 1902, in Minis papers. 14. Porter Alexander to Mary Alexander, May 25, 1902, in Alexander papers; Bancroft, "Southern Notebook," 2:123. 15. Mary Alexander to Mrs. A. S. Mason, June 16, 1902, in Alexander papers; Mary Alexander to Bessie Ficklen, June 18, 1902, in Ficklen papers. For accounts of the celebration see *Centennial of the Military Academy*, 58 Cong., 2d Sess., House Doc. 789, serial 4750, 1:1–130 and *New York Tribune*, June 10, 1902. Alexander's speech can be most conveniently found in *Centennial*, 1:77–86. 16. T. Harry Williams, in his introduction to the new edition of the *Memoirs*, xxxiv, expresses the wish that Porter "had written two books—a general history and a personal narrative." In effect he did just that, for the original Grey-town recollections in their fading ledger books comprise a personal narrative. For the letters to Colston see the Bancroft papers. 17. Bancroft, "Southern Notebook," 2:120–123 and Porter Alexander to Frederic Bancroft, March 23, April 17 and August 8, 1902, in Bancroft papers. The account of Alexander and his relationship to Bancroft given in Jacob Cooke, *Frederic Bancroft, Historian* (Norman, 1957), pp. 88–92, is misleading and must be used with caution. 18. Alexander, "Sea Island Log," 206; Porter Alexander to Will Craig, February 20, 1903, and to Leopold Alexander, April 5, 1903, in Alexander papers; Porter Alexander to Frederic Bancroft, March 20 and April 12, 1903, in Bancroft papers. 19. Frederic Bancroft to Porter Alexander, February 22 and April 18, 1903, and Porter Alexander to Mary Alexander, May 21, 1903, in Alexander papers; Porter Alexander to Frederic Bancroft, May 8, 1903, in Bancroft papers; Bancroft, "Southern Notebook," 4:301, 319–325, 350.

20. Porter Alexander to Mary Alexander, January 1, January 7 and May 31, 1904, Porter Alexander to Mrs. A. S. Mason, January 26, 1904, and to Bessie

Ficklen?, May 15, 1904, in Alexander papers; *Confederate Veteran*, 16:336; Porter Alexander to Frederic Bancroft, January 26, 1904, in Bancroft papers.   21. See Alexander, *Memoirs*, pp. 363–446.   22. Porter Alexander to H. B. McClellan, August 12, 1885 and to H. R. Duval, March 20, 1899, in possession of Mrs. Elizabeth Hilton; *Battles and Leaders*, 3:365; *Confederate Veteran*, 12:7; SHSP, 4:97–111; Porter Alexander to Frederick Colston, January 30, 1905, in Bancroft papers.   23. Alexander, *Memoirs*, p. 417.   24. Ibid., pp. 392–393. Alexander's earlier views on these points can be found in the Alexander papers.   25. Porter Alexander to Louisa Minis, April 2, 1905, in Minis papers; Mary Alexander to Mrs. A. S. Mason, May 8, 1905, in Alexander papers; Porter Alexander to Louise ?, September 6, 1905, in possession of Mrs. Elizabeth Hilton; Porter Alexander to Frederic Bancroft, August 11 and September 13, 1904, and February 9, 1905, in Bancroft papers.   26. Mary Alexander to Mrs. A. S. Mason, October 23, 1905, Porter Alexander to Will Craig, December 27, 1905, and to George Baldwin, March 6, 1906, in Alexander papers; Bancroft, "Southern Notebook," 4:357–363; Porter Alexander to Frederic Bancroft, August 22, 1905, and to Frederick Colston, September 26, 1905, in Bancroft papers.   27. Porter Alexander to Leonard Mackall, April 3, 1906, and May 24, 1906, in possession of Mrs. Elizabeth Hilton; Porter Alexander to Louisa Minis, October 1, 1906, in Minis papers.   28. See for example the two evaluations of Jackson during the Seven Days campaign in Alexander, *Memoirs*, pp. 134–149 and "Recollections," 2:90–91.   29. An excellent example of his attitude towards his old army can be found in the manuscript article, "The Fighting of Raw Troops," in the Alexander papers. In it he wrote, "We can see Napoleon himself offering enormous odds that Richmond would fall within twelve months —but hedging immediately after the Battle of Bull Run. . . . The morale built up by the Army of Northern Virginia upon this foundation of Bull Run was something marvellous and well worth a whole chapter to itself."

30. See for example, *Confederate Veteran*, 15:244; *American Historical Review*, 13:163–166.   31. T. M. R. Talcott to Porter Alexander, May 2, 1907, Frederick Colston to Porter Alexander, May 16, 1907, and O. O. Howard to Porter Alexander, July 10, 1907, in Alexander papers. There are several other letters of praise from former comrades.   32. William A. Dunning to Frederic Bancroft, May 31, 1907, Charles F. Adams to Porter Alexander, July 11, 1907, and James K. Hosmer to Porter Alexander, May 13, 1907, in Alexander papers. For the review see *Nation*, 74:(1907), 542–544.   33. Theodore Roosevelt to Porter Alexander, July 16, 1907, in Alexander papers.   34. Porter Alexander to Bessie Ficklen, January 25, 1908, in Ficklen papers; Porter Alexander to Louisa Minis, September 20, 1908, in Minis papers.   35. Porter Alexander to Will Craig, March 5, 1908 and to Mary Alexander, May 28, 1908, in Alexander papers; Porter Alexander to Louisa Minis, September 20, 1908, in Minis papers; Porter Alexander to Bessie Ficklen, November 2, 1908, in Ficklen papers; Alexander, "Sea Island Log," 307. 36. Bancroft, "Southern Notebook," 4:361–369; Porter Alexander to Frederic Bancroft, November 8, 1908, in Bancroft papers. For the paper see *Annual Report of the American Historical Association*, 1 (1908), 225–234, hereinafter cited as *AHA Report*. Livermore and Swift were on the program with Alexander; Boyd was chief clerk at the Library of Congress.   37. Account of the meeting is drawn from Mary Alexander to Bessie Ficklen, January 7, 1909, in Ficklen papers, and *AHA Report*, 1:23–30.   38. Alexander, "Sea Island Log," 308–311.   39. Ibid.; Mary Alexander to Mrs. A. S. Mason, February 22, 1909, in Alexander papers.

40. Bancroft, "Southern Notebook," 4:368–369, 373–379.   41. Alexander, "Sea Island Log," 311; Walter Adams to Mary Alexander, June 24, 1910, in Alexander papers.   42. Alexander, "Sea Island Log," 311. For obituaries see *Savannah Evening Press*, April 28, 1910, *Augusta Chronicle*, April 30, 1910, and *New Orleans Picayune*, April 29, 1910. The verse is from a seventeenth-century Latin hymn entitled "Alleluia! The Strife O'er." See Hymn 181, *Pilgrim Hymnal* (Boston, 1958).

Bibliographical Essay

This survey does not attempt to be comprehensive or exclusive. It can be supplemented at any given point by manuscripts, general histories, monographs and biographies dealing with the people, events and circumstances involved in Alexander's life. I have tried to indicate such specific works in the footnotes.

Manuscript Collections

Any serious study of Alexander's life must begin with the extensive manuscript holdings in the Southern Historical Collection, University of North Carolina. The following collections all contain relevant materials:

Edward Porter Alexander papers
Alexander-Hillhouse papers
Alexander R. Lawton papers
Jeremy F. Gilmer papers
John R. Ficklen papers
Louisa Porter Minis papers

The first collection mentioned above consists of nine large boxes of materials of all kinds. Alexander was a meticulous preserver of his letters, papers and personal writings and mementos. As a result the papers enable one to reconstruct not only much of his life, but most of his personal habits, tastes and attitudes. For the biographer Alexander is an ideal subject. He was articulate, precise and comprehensive in virtually all of his writings whether formal or informal. His letters and other manuscripts remain a treasure of information on many subjects. The Alexander-Hillhouse papers comprise an invaluable supplement to Alexander's own papers. These four large boxes include not only Alexander's own letters to his father and other kinfolk, but also the large and well-preserved correspondence of his family dating back to the eighteenth century. From these papers the biographer can recreate ante bellum plantation life in Georgia in considerable detail.

The other collections mentioned are those of various members of the Alexander family. Letters from Alexander can be found in each of them, as well as pertinent background information on specific topics. The

Alexander folder in the Confederate Records, National Archives, Washington, D. C., has several important items pertaining to his war career, including letters, official reports and orders, and statistical materials. The Adam Alexander papers at Duke University, numbering 361 items, contain several valuable letters, and there are a few letters written by Alexander in other collections at the same library. The scant Alexander MSS. in the Library of Congress contains only souvenir items from his scrapbook.

A small but valuable collection of Alexander's papers remains in the possession of his granddaughter, Mrs. Elizabeth Hilton of Savannah. Two other collections are helpful in more limited areas. The Alfred J. Myer papers, Signal Corps Museum, Fort Monmouth, New Jersey, provide information on Alexander's signal experience. More important, the Frederic Bancroft papers, Columbia University, contain 204 letters and cards written by Alexander. Most of the information pertains to the Civil War and the ante bellum South, though there is much about Alexander's activities during his later years when the letters were written. Bancroft's "Southern Notebook" contains a detailed description of his first visit to South Island along with several other relevant items. Unfortunately the notebooks are written in Bancroft's cramped shorthand and require a patient exercise in translation.

Newspapers and Periodicals

There are a few points in Alexander's life at which newspapers and periodicals become extremely important. This is especially true of his railroad career. Correspondence for the period 1873–1892 is quite scant and sheds little light upon his activities and attitudes; thus the basic structure of his career must be gleaned from other sources. Fortunately there is an abundance of such material, and the persistent student can often find Alexander quoted on specific subjects in various newspapers.

Two periodicals are indispensable for piecing together Alexander's business career and obtaining background on the companies in which he was involved: the *Commercial and Financial Chronicle* (New York, 1865–1892) and the *Railroad Gazette* (Chicago, 1872–1892). The former was a weekly financial journal dealing primarily with the financial aspects of railroads, but it maintained a special column for happenings within specific companies and it frequently evaluated the internal situation of individual roads. Rumors of all sorts were faithfully reported and elaborated in the *Chronicle*, but a patient reading over several months' issues enables the student to separate fact from fiction. The *Gazette* was more a professional trade journal, devoting much of its space to technical railroad affairs. It, too, kept a column for company affairs and personnel changes, and in general it provides a sounder picture of physical growth and expansion than does the *Chronicle*. Both periodicals made it a habit to print at least the gist of company annual reports, with the *Chronicle* usually publishing more reports and the *Gazette* including longer excerpts of the reports it did print.

There is no satisfactorily systematic way to list the newspapers consulted. The rule of thumb used was to resort to newspapers of a place and date relevant to some crucial juncture of Alexander's career. Thus, the *Savannah Daily Times* provides excellent information on the critical Central Railroad elections of 1883 and 1887, while a perusal of Richmond and New York papers for the first half of 1888 is essential to understanding Alexander's "campaign" for the Terminal presidency. Similarly, the crisis evoked by the Danville's reneging on the Central lease can hardly be got at except through newspapers. For the war years I have relied upon various newspapers from Richmond, Augusta and Savannah, though the process here was necessarily more random and intuitive. In general the newspapers most frequently consulted were the *New York Times, New York Herald, New York Tribune, Richmond Enquirer, Richmond Dispatch, Augusta Chronicle, Augusta Daily Constitutionalist, Savannah Daily Times, Savannah Morning News* and *Savannah Evening Press*. Alexander himself was a diligent preserver of newspaper articles, and many helpful but unidentified clippings can be found in his papers and in his scrapbook.

Several other periodicals provide important information upon specific portions of Alexander's career. The *Southern Historical Society Papers* (Richmond, 1876–1959), 52 volumes, and the *Confederate Veteran* (Nashville, 1893–1932), 40 volumes, both contain articles and letters contributed by Alexander as well as materials referring to him. Needless to say, they also include a wealth of information on the various campaigns.

Alexander's Own Works

Together with his letters and other informal papers, Alexander's collected writings comprise the most important source for this biography. These are numerous and extensive; they cover virtually every phase of Alexander's life and reflect all of his manifold interests. Although he naturally did not publish everything he wrote, many of the manuscripts can be found among his papers. No attempt can be made here to list all of his published works; such a project would require a close survey of many periodicals for a period of four decades and is complicated by the fact that Alexander occasionally used a pseudonym. For example, he wrote several articles for *Forest and Stream* magazine under the name Jack Hidalgo. His output was prolific and his range of interests incredibly broad. Following are his most important published works:

Military Memoirs of a Confederate. New York, 1907.
Railway Practice. New York, 1887.
On Various Railroad Questions. Louisville, 1881.
Catteral Ratteral Doggeral. New York, 1890.
"Grant's Conduct of the Wilderness Campaign," *Annual Report of the American Historical Association,* 1 (1908), 226–234.
"Lee at Appomattox," *Century Magazine,* 63 (1902), 921–931.
"The Battle of Bull Run," *Scribners Magazine,* 41 (1907), 80–94.
"Confederate Artillery Service," *Southern Historical Society Papers,* 11 (1883), 98–113.
"The Great Charge and Artillery Fight at Gettysburg," *Battles and Leaders,* 3:357–368.
"Longstreet at Knoxville," *Battles and Leaders,* 3:745–751.
"The Seven Days Battle," *Southern Historical Society Papers,* 1:61–76.
"Sketch of Longstreet's Division," *Southern Historical Society Papers,* 9:512–518 and 10:32–45.
"The Battle of Fredericksburg," *Southern Historical Society Papers,* 10:382–392 and 445–464.
"Causes of Lee's Defeat at Gettysburg," *Southern Historical Society Papers,* 4:97–111.

Alexander's writings on the Civil War require special attention. In addition to his *Memoirs* he wrote two unpublished accounts of his experiences: the "Recollections" written in Greytown, and individual chapters on each campaign of the war—revision of which became the published *Memoirs.* Both versions can be found in Alexander's papers. Together the three accounts provide a vivid description of both the war and Alexander's role in it, but they must be carefully read and collated. In general the unpublished manuscripts furnish much more valuable information on Alexander himself. The essential difference between the published and unpublished memoirs is the deletion from the former of the rich stock of anecdotes and personal experiences that permeate the latter.

In writing his informal memoirs as a legacy for his family, Alexander told his own story in a charming, intimate and captivating style. Character sketches of his comrades and lucid explanations of his activities abound, as do superb insights into the campaigns themselves. For his published *Memoirs* Alexander naturally sacrificed this appealing warmth and intimacy for the more objective and rigidly analytical approach of the scholar, and rarely does he intrude upon his own narrative except where circumstances force him to the center of the stage, as on the third day at Gettysburg. Moreover, he was forced to cut his manuscript extensively in order to publish it in one volume, which meant that he had to omit a considerable amount of detail. The *Memoirs* are truly a classic of military history, but the unpublished manuscripts constitute the real story of Alexander the man in wartime.

Miscellaneous Published Works

Although no attempt is made to present a comprehensive bibliography here, certain works are instrumental for understanding Alexander's life and deserve special mention. Two indispensable volumes for tracing Alexander's family background are Marion Boggs, ed., *The Alexander Letters 1789–1900* (Savannah, 1910) and Margaret P. Hillhouse, comp., *Historical and Genealogical Collections Relating to the Descendants of Rev. James Hillhouse* (New York, 1924). The first contains a selection of family letters. The originals can all be found in the Alexander-Hillhouse and Edward Porter Alexander papers, but the volume also includes some reminiscences by family members, genealogical charts and valuable pictures. The second book is a genealogical compilation of the Hillhouse family and its related branches, including the Alexanders. Most of the materials gathered by the author in preparing the book can be found in the Alexander-Hillhouse papers.

Two short volumes, Eliza Bowen, *The Story of Wilkes County, Georgia* (Marietta, 1950) and WPA Writers Program, *The Story of Washington-Wilkes* (Athens, 1941), help reconstruct ante bellum life in Wilkes County. Basic to an understanding of West Point is *Centennial of the Military Academy*, 58th Congress, 2d session, House Document 789, serial 4750 (Washington, 1904), two volumes. It should be supplemented by a careful reading of the annual reports of the secretary of war for the period 1845–1857, which describe conditions at the Academy in some detail. G. W. Cullum, *Biographical Register of the Officers and Graduates of the U. S. Military Academy* (Boston, 1891), seven volumes, is very useful in checking facts and background material on Alexander's classmates and other personnel. An invaluable source for the signals system and its development is J. Willard Brown, *Signal Corps, U. S. A. in the War of the Rebellion* (Boston, 1896).

Every investigation of the war years must begin with United States

War Department, comp., *The War of the Rebellion: A Compilation of the Official Records of the Union and Confederate Armies* (Washington, 1880–1901), 70 volumes in 128 parts. Alexander's own writings are of course paramount for this study; they may be supplemented by the memoirs and accounts of numerous other participants, of which the following proved most useful:

R. W. Figg, *Where Men Only Dare to Go.* Richmond, 1885.

U. S. Grant, *Personal Memoirs.* 2 vols. New York, 1885.

J. E. Johnston, *Narrative of Military Operations During the Late War Between the States.* New York, 1874.

S. P. Lee, ed., *Memoirs of William Nelson Pendleton, D.D.* Philadelphia, 1893.

James Longstreet, *From Manassas to Appomattox.* Philadelphia, 1896.

W. M. Owen, *In Camp and Battle with the Washington Artillery.* Boston, 1885.

Equally important are the personal accounts in R. U. Johnson and C. C. Buell, eds., *Battles and Leaders of the Civil War.* 4 vols. New York, 1887–1888. Studies of individual campaigns abound and are too extensive to be mentioned here. Essential to an understanding of the Army of Northern Virginia and its personalities are Douglas S. Freeman, *Lee's Lieutenants* (New York, 1942), 3 volumes, and the same author's *Robert E. Lee* (New York, 1934–35), 4 volumes.

Two works dealing specifically with artillery deserve special mention. Jennings C. Wise, *The Long Arm of Lee* (New York, 1960) constitutes the only existing history of Lee's artillery. The book, drawn primarily from the *Official Records,* is honest and exhaustive. It is marred by minor errors of fact and, more important, by a polemical tone that attempts to defend Pendleton from many of the charges levied against him during and after the war. Since some of these charges were raised by Alexander, and since the latter's *Memoirs* sharply criticized Pendleton, Wise takes great pains to refute the allegations. He does not succeed. Nevertheless, Wise is fair to Alexander the officer if not to Alexander the critic, and any study of the Confederate long arm must commence with his book. An important supplementary volume, L. Van Loan Naisawald, *Grape and Canister* (New York, 1960), treats the development of artillery in the Army of the Potomac.

Alexander's postwar career must be approached more from the outside than any other phase of his life, since his surviving papers for this period are very scant. Helpful background material for his stay at the University of South Carolina is provided by E. L. Green, *A History of the University of South Carolina* (Columbia, 1916). A basic introduction to railroad finance can be found in Frederick Cleveland and Fred Powell, *Railroad Finance* (New York, 1912). There is no adequate history of the Louisville & Nashville Railroad. Mary G. Cumming, *Georgia Railroad and Banking Company 1833–1945* (Augusta, 1945), is skimpy and inadequate but the only available source on that company. For a history of the Richmond Terminal see Maury Klein, *The Great Richmond Terminal* (Charlottesville, 1970), and Fairfax Harrison, *A History of the Legal Development of the Southern Railway Company* (Washington, 1901). The problem of competition among southern railroads and the attempt to restrain it is illuminated by William Joubert, *Southern Freight Rates in Transition* (Gainesville, 1949). A basic reference work for any study of nineteenth century American railroads is Henry V. Poor, *Manual of Railroads* (New York, 1872–1892).

The most helpful book treating the development of southern railroads is John F. Stover, *Railroads of the South 1865–1900* (Chapel Hill, 1955). Describing the evolution of each important southern system individually, Stover develops the theme that northern interests gradually came to dominate every major southern line by 1900. His is a pioneer work of great benefit, but it tends to be superficial, poorly organized, and at times inaccurate. This volume, together with Stuart Daggett, *Railroad Reorganization* (Cambridge, 1924) and E. G. Campbell, *The Reorganization of the American Railroad System* (New York, 1938), comprise the standard accounts of the Richmond Terminal and especially its relationship with the Georgia Company. For a more recent interpretation see Klein, *The Great Richmond Terminal*. Stover's volume must be used with great care, for his research into the *Chronicle* especially was not sufficiently extensive to prevent him from being misled on several points. The annual reports of the Central of Georgia Railroad shed much light on Alexander's career with that company. A bound collection of these reports for the period 1853–1886 in five volumes can be found in the Emory University library.

Index